KU-389-060

HEBRIDEAN FOLKSONGS
II

Moses Griffiths del.

DUNVEGAN CASTLE

'Air Dùn Bheagain leag e chòrsa' (l.1147)

Reproduced by permission of the National Library of Wales

HEBRIDEAN FOLKSONGS

II

Waulking Songs from Barra, South Uist, Eriskay and Benbecula

Edited and translated by

J. L. CAMPBELL

Tunes transcribed from recordings and annotated by

FRANCIS COLLINSON

OXFORD
AT THE CLARENDON PRESS
1977

Oxford University Press, Walton Street, Oxford OX2 6DP

OXFORD LONDON GLASGOW
NEW YORK TORONTO MELBOURNE WELLINGTON
IBADAN NAIROBI DAR ES SALAAM LUSAKA CAPE TOWN
KUALA LUMPUR SINGAPORE JAKARTA HONG KONG TOKYO
DELHI BOMBAY CALCUTTA MADRAS KARACHI

© *Oxford University Press 1977*

All rights reserved. No part of this publication may be reproduced, stored in a retrieval system, or transmitted, in any form or by any means, electronic, mechanical, photocopying, recording, or otherwise, without the prior permission of Oxford University Press

British Library Cataloguing in Publication Data

Hebridean folksongs.
2 : Waulking songs from Barra, South Uist, Eriskay and Benbecula.
Index.
ISBN 0–19–815214–0
1. Campbell, John Lorne 2. Collinson, Francis
784.6′8′6773125 M1977.L3
Work-songs
Folk-songs, Gaelic

Printed in Great Britain
at the University Press, Oxford
by Vivian Ridler
Printer to the University

SEANN-ÒRAIN INNSE GALL

II

Òrain Luadhaidh bho Bharraidh
Uibhist a Deas, Éirisgeidh
agus Beinn na bhFadhla

Air an cruinneachadh 's air an deasachadh le
IAIN L. CAIMBEUL

Na fuinn air an sgrìobhadh le
FRANCIS COLLINSON

ATHA-NAN-DAMH
CLÒ-PHREAS CHLARENDON
1977

COPYRIGHT

The transcriptions of the tunes of the songs printed in this book are copyright, and the permission of both the collector and the transcriber must be obtained before they are reproduced, or sung, or broadcast professionally, with or without any added accompaniment.

MAR CHUIMHNEACHAN

AIR

ANNA AGUS CALUM AONGHAIS CHALUIM

RUAIRI IAIN BHAIN, MÓR BEAN NÌLL

AGUS SEINNEADAIREAN EILE BHARRAIDH

AGUS UIBHIST

NACH MAIREANN

IN MEMORY

OF

ANNIE AND CALUM JOHNSTON

RODERICK MACKINNON AND MRS NEIL CAMPBELL

AND THE OTHER SINGERS OF BARRA

AND UIST

WHO HAVE PASSED AWAY

CONTENTS

BELFAST PUBLIC LIBRARIES

INTRODUCTION

THIS book, the second volume of *Hebridean Folksongs*, contains a further forty-eight waulking songs recorded on the islands of Barra, Vatersay, South Uist, and Benbecula, between 1937 and 1965, the majority being from the Island of Barra. In a particular way it is a memorial to the late Miss Annie Johnston, Castlebay, Barra, and her brother Calum, and to the late Mrs. Neil Campbell, Frobost, South Uist, who have contributed so much of the material printed here, in Miss Johnston's case indirectly as well as directly, by bringing other very interesting singers to the microphone.

The waulking or milling songs preserved in the tradition of Gaelic Scotland and Cape Breton (chiefly in the Outer Hebrides) are one of the most interesting folk survivals of western Europe. They were sung to accompany and to give rhythm to the labour of the fulling of home-spun cloth by hand. As they have been preserved, they undoubtedly include songs that were originally sung to accompany the labour of rowing and of reaping in the Highlands in former times.

The process of the waulking, and the literary history of waulking songs, have already been described at length in the first volume of this series,[1] and it is not necessary to repeat these descriptions here. The labour of waulking was performed entirely by women, of whom a band of eight or ten would sit round a table, detached door, or a wicker hurdle, thumping and pounding the cloth, which had been soaked in urine (which acted as a mordant) and passing it in a sun-wise direction to the accompaniment of a series of songs such as are printed in these two volumes, and a third which is projected.

Most of the songs, except a few that seem to have been originally composed to different airs and later sung as waulking songs to waulking song airs, were clearly composed by women, often by

[1] J. L. Campbell and F. Collinson, *Hebridean Folksongs: A Collection of Waulking Songs by Donald MacCormick in Kilphedir in South Uist in the year 1893*, Oxford, 1969.

extemporization; as a whole, they give a vivid picture of life in the Highlands and Islands in the late sixteenth and the seventeenth centuries from the women's point of view. They are unsophisticated and completely spontaneous. At the same time, it is clear that the women who composed or extemporized the words of these songs had at their command a large store of formulaic passages and expressions which could be used freely—and sometimes quite inconsequentially—in improvising such poetry.[1] Passages such as those describing the 'skillful steersman' (e.g. lines 1284–7 here, the 'successful hunter' (1336–9), the 'tocherless lass' (1647–52), 'I was reared in greater comfort' (709–11), 'tell my lover I've got through the winter' (458–66)), occur repeatedly in different and otherwise unrelated waulking songs. When personal or place-names occur in the older waulking songs, they are usually powerfully evocative of traditional memories and associations recalling personally coloured feelings and sentiments.

We hope to list the most important of these motifs in our third volume. Their real origin is quite unknown.

The writer and his collaborator Mr. Francis Collinson had the privilege of attending and recording a genuine waulking at Gerinish, South Uist, on 29 March 1951. Twenty-five songs in all were sung by four different soloists, and three rolls of cloth were waulked, there being nine women in all at the waulking board. Today, genuine traditional waulkings are a thing of the past. According to information kindly given us by Mr. Fred MacAulay, Senior Gaelic Producer of the B.B.C., the last genuine waulking in Lewis took place at Shawbost in 1952; in Skye, at Kilmuir, about 1945; and in Harris, at about the same time. In Barra, it is doubtful whether any genuine waulkings had taken place since World War I, but the love of the Barra people for their traditional songs had kept them alive at the fireside, and at local concerts where they were performed in an imitation of the waulking style, or as solos. Those recorded between 1949 and 1951 at Castlebay in the chapel house through the kindness of the Rt. Revd. Monsignor Canon Ewen MacInnes were sung by a

[1] See Stith Thompson, 'The Challenge of Folklore', *P.M.L.A.*, September 1964; and *Hebridean Folksongs*, i. 22.

It is likely that the heat, excitement, and rhythm of the waulking would at times produce a state of semi-trance among improvisers of the songs, which would favour such formulaic passages coming into consciousness and being uttered. This results in some of the older waulking songs resembling dreams.

band of good traditional singers, brought together by Miss Annie Johnston, in the real traditional style.

In the first volume of *Hebridean Folksongs* the songs written down by Donald MacCormick in 1893 were printed in the order in which they occurred in his manuscript. In the present and in the forthcoming third volumes the songs are classified according to metre and refrain structure, thus bringing songs of the same type together and facilitating the study of the very archaic and interesting airs of these songs.

The present volume contains (1) songs sung as waulking songs but almost certainly not originally sung as such, including the interesting ballad *Am Bròn Binn* 'The Sweet Sorrow', which was recorded sung both as a ballad and as a waulking song to quite different types of airs; (2) songs in which the 'verse' (*ceathramh*) is a line of eight syllables, in every case but one with penultimate rhyme, a metre known in Gaelic as *caoine* and popular in the seventeenth century—the one exception, No. LVIII, has ultimate rhyme (8^1), a very rare metrical form; (3) songs in which the 8^2 line is divided into two halves of four syllables each, each followed by the same refrain or by different phrases of the refrain. Although a popular type of refrain is that of three phrases of which the first and third are musically identical or almost so, there is in fact a great variety in the refrain structure of these songs, which works strongly to prevent their singing from becoming monotonous. The question of the meaningless refrain syllables was discussed in the first volume.

Our third volume will contain songs in which the 'verses' are lines of six or of seven syllables, or couplets of the type AB, BC, CD, etc., or couplets with internal rhyme and rhyming of the last stressed syllables in even lines. The last type became popular in the eighteenth century and gives the impression of increasing sophistication and self-conscious composition. It is very doubtful if any waulking songs of single-line verse type were composed later than about 1700.

The texts in this book have two main sources. One is the transcription of the words on the actual recordings, and the other is from versions of the words found in earlier unpublished manuscript collections such as those of the Revd. Fr. Allan McDonald, Donald MacLachlan, the Very Revd. Canon Duncan MacLean, Mr. Donald MacIntyre ('Domhnall Ruadh', the well-known

Gaelic poet), Miss Annie Johnston, and my own Cape Breton collection made in 1937. It has thus often been possible to print alternative versions of the text of the same song, and avoid any appearance of establishing any particular version as the authoritative printed one. In the case of the ballad version of *Am Bròn Binn*, I am greatly indebted to the present Duke of Argyll, 'Mac Cailein Mór', and the Trustees of the eleventh Duke, for permission to print a most interesting version, hitherto unpublished, from the Dewar MSS.

The layout of this book is the same as that of our first volume, which itself resembles the layout of Bela Bartók and Albert B. Lord's *Serbo-Croatian Folk Songs* published by the Columbia University Press in 1951. We are aware that some readers would prefer the style of printing the tunes along with the texts; but the disadvantage of this is that it would make a *vis-à-vis* printing of the translations impossible, separate the musicological notes from the tunes, and require much more paper, if the tune in every case was to head the left-hand page. There is no doubt that, for purposes of musicological study, it is much better to have the tunes printed together.

There is a very slight change in the style of presenting the texts, in that the oral or manuscript source is stated at the head of each song; MacCormick's word *Atharraich* 'Change' between the different sections of the same song, is omitted; refrains are printed in italics, and given as recorded between the different sections, when there was a chorus as well as the soloist singing them.

The translations in this volume being more literal than those in the first one, the Glossarial Index is restricted for the most part to words not to be found in the glossary to Volume I, which itself was made exceptionally large owing to the free nature of those translations.

With this book we shall now have printed authentic versions of eighty-eight of the most interesting and beautiful waulking songs of South Uist and Barra; it is interesting that only thirty of these are represented in any way (sometimes only by bald versions of the tunes in the introductory pages) in the publications of Mrs. Kennedy-Fraser.

I have to express our deeply felt gratitude to all the persons who have at one time or another aided this work in any way, and particularly to the late Miss Annie Johnston and the singers themselves;

it is a matter of great regret to me that so much time has elapsed between collection and publication, though this has been offset to some extent by increasing knowledge and understanding, and access to alternative versions in the manuscript collections of waulking song texts referred to.

In addition, I must express my thanks to the Revd. William Matheson, M.A., Lecturer in Celtic at Edinburgh University, and to Dr. A. MacLean, Lochboisdale, South Uist, for their help over certain textual difficulties, and to Dr. Alan Bruford of the School of Scottish Studies for communicating to me a catalogue of the waulking songs in the Morison MSS. from the collection of the late C. R. Morison, Isle of Mull, now lodged in the School of Scottish Studies by his granddaughter Mrs. Mary Ford, Banff, and for permission to quote in the Notes from a very interesting version of No. LXI here in that collection. I am also greatly indebted to the Trustees of the tenth Duke of Argyll, and to the present Duke of Argyll, for permission to reproduce the entire text of the ballad *Am Bròn Binn* contained in the Dewar MSS. in Inveraray Castle. Mr. Collinson and I must also thank the FitzWilliam Museum, Cambridge, and the Library of Trinity College, Dublin, for permission to print transcriptions of the versions of the tune of 'Calen o custure me' in the FitzWilliam Virginal Book and the Ballet Lute Book, respectively, and the Revd. John MacLean, originally from Barra, for valuable help in correcting the proofs of this book; and the McCaig Trust for a grant of £500 towards the cost of its production.

J. L. CAMPBELL
Isle of Canna
30/9/75

THE SINGERS

BARRA

MY work of recording traditional Gaelic songs began on the Isle of Barra in January 1937, encouraged by Miss Annie Johnston, John MacPherson 'the Coddy', my wife, Compton MacKenzie, and other friends. This was with a clockwork ediphone machine, and was continued later in Cape Breton in the autumn of the same year, when some very interesting recordings of waulking and other songs were made from the late Mrs. Neil McInnis, Mrs. David Patterson, Mr. A. J. MacKenzie (all of Barra descent), and from Angus 'Ridge' MacDonald, of Lochaber descent, in Antigonish county.

In the winter of 1937/8 a Presto disc electrical recorder was obtained in America and brought back to Barra. With this some extremely interesting recordings were made of Miss Annie Johnston, Mrs. MacDougall ('Anna Raghnaill Eachainn'), Mrs. Mary Morrison ('Bean Phluim'), and Roderick MacKinnon ('Ruairi Iain Bhàin'), a few of which were reproduced in the set of 12-inch discs entitled *Gaelic Folksongs from the Isle of Barra* published by the Linguaphone Institute for the Folklore Institute of Scotland in 1950 with a booklet of words and translations.

These Presto recordings, made in March 1938, are the first electrical recordings of traditional Gaelic songs made in the field in Scotland, and are the earliest used for transcription purposes in this book. All have been copied on tapes.

In the winter of 1948/9 Mr. Calum Johnston made disc recordings of thirteen songs for me in a private studio in Edinburgh, where he was then living. In the summer of the same year I took the ediphone to Vatersay and made some recordings of Miss Elizabeth Sinclair ('Ealasaid Iain Dhunnchaidh'). In the same year I obtained a research grant from the Leverhulme Foundation, which is gratefully acknowledged, and a Webster wire recorder in America, which I was eventually able to use in the southern Outer Hebrides and at various places on the mainland where there were living traditional singers from the islands, after the machine had been held up for six months by the British customs. The Leverhulme grant covered two years during which about 1,200 wire recordings of traditional Gaelic songs and 350 of stories and anecdotes were made in the area described. Wire recordings are often denigrated, but the Webster was a very good machine, and provided that the wire was really new and not previously used and demagnetized (as was liable to be the case with wire purchased in Britain) the recordings were of good quality, and not liable to overprint, as is the case with tape.

The Ediphone, Presto, and Webster machines are all extinct today, but fortunately most recordings made on the first two were made again on the third, and nearly all were copied on tape, with which I began to work in 1956, and still do occasionally, though little has been possible since a Government indifferent to inter-island social life cut off direct communications between Canna and the Outer Hebrides in 1964.

In making this collection of recordings, I have been greatly helped by the following, who at times collaborated, using my apparatus: the Barra Folklore Committee (a body composed mostly of clergy and school teachers and other local notables); the Revd. Fr. John MacLean while parish priest of Bornish, South Uist; and the Revd. Fr. John MacCormick while parish priest of Eriskay, then Benbecula; Gordon Marsh, and John MacLean, M.A.

I list below the traditional singers represented in the present book. I must make it clear that the songs they sang were not special items learnt for performance at ceilidhs or concerts; they were part of the singers' everyday lives, something from the Gaelic oral culture which had surrounded them from their earliest childhood. The Gaelic-speaking parts of Scotland and Ireland were and still are strongholds of traditional oral culture, something which is very rare in western Europe today. Though no singer is represented by more than ten tunes in this book, nearly all of them would have been able to sing at least thirty or forty songs (including different versions of the same song), and would have known the refrains and airs and a few of the words of many others. Both this and the first volume of *Hebridean Folksongs* often give examples of different versions of the same air as sung by different singers, which is the reason why in the following list the same number of a song in the book sometimes appears against the names of different singers.

THE SINGERS

BARRA

Miss Annie Johnston ('Anna Aonghais Chaluim'): recorded in 1938, LXXIII, LXXXI, LXXXII.

—— with her brother Calum: XLVI, LI, LIV, LXVII, LXVIII, all recorded in 1950.

Calum Johnston ('Calum Aonghais Chaluim'): in 1948, LXXII; in 1949, XLIV, LII, LXXXVII.

The following singers were brought to the microphone to record by Miss Johnston in 1938:

Mrs. MacDougall ('Anna Raghnaill Eachainn'), a niece of Peigi Eachainn (MacKinnon) of whom Annie Johnston wrote that she had 'the finest store of folk-songs that any person living at the moment (1933) has ever heard':[1] XLI, XLVII, LXXII, LXXVIII, LXXIX. Miss Johnston's voice can be heard joining in the refrains of these songs on the recordings.

Mrs. Mary Morrison ('Bean Phluim'): XLVII (recorded in 1938 and again in 1950); XLVIII (recorded in 1950: in 1937 I had recorded a version from Mrs. David Patterson in Cape Breton).

In 1950 and 1951 Miss Johnston brought the following singers to the microphone at recording sessions in the chapel-house at Castlebay, Barra:

Mrs. John Galbraith ('Mór Iain Dhòmhnaill Phàdraig'), LXI.

Miss Mary Gillies ('Màiri Mhìcheil Nìll'), LV, LXXI.

Mrs. James MacNeil ('Anna Mhìcheil Nìll'), sister of Mary Gillies, LIII.

Mrs. Mary Johnston ('Màiri Iain Choinnich'), maiden name MacNeil, born on the now uninhabited island of Mingulay, south of Barra, LIX, LXIII, LXX.

Mrs. Mary MacNeil, Crìochan ('Màiri Ruarachain'), XLV, LXXX. Previously Mrs. Mary MacNeil, introduced by Miss Johnston, had recorded on my ediphone in 1937.

Miss Mary Morrison, Earsary ('Màiri Eóghainn Mhóir') a remarkable singer, LXXVI, LXXIX, LXXXIV, LXXXVI.

[1] See *Béal-oideas*, iv. 50. Peigi Eachainn and her sister Ealasaid spent most of their younger days on the now uninhabited island of Sandray.

All these ladies and their songs were announced by Miss Johnston on the recordings, and whoever was singing the solo parts of the songs, the others took up the refrains in the natural waulking style.

At the north end of Barra I was introduced to a different but equally interesting tradition by my friend the late John MacPherson 'the Coddy'.[1] This was that of the family represented by the late Roderick MacKinnon ('Ruairi Iain Bhàin') and his sister Mrs. Samuel MacKinnon ('Bean Shomhairle Bhig'), who were certainly traditional Gaelic singers of equal calibre with Miss Johnston's neighbours Peigi and Ealasaid Eachainn. In her book *A Life of Song* Mrs. Kennedy-Fraser describes how, guided by Miss Annie Johnston, she met Bean Shomhairle Bhig in 1923.[2] Unfortunately Bean Shomhairle Bhig[3] was no longer living by the time I first acquired recording apparatus in 1937, but her daughters were, as was her brother Roderick MacKinnon, his son Captain D. J. MacKinnon, and his daughter Mrs. Buchanan ('Ceit Ruairi Iain Bhàin'), and I found that a great deal of the family tradition was still maintained.

In this book, this family is represented as follows:

Roderick MacKinnon ('Ruairi Iain Bhàin'), LXXV, recorded in 1938. His daughter,

Mrs. Buchanan ('Ceit Ruairi Iain Bhàin'), L, LXXXV.

Bean Shomhairle Bhig's daughters,

Mrs. A. MacPhee ('Maighread Shomhairle Bhig'), living at Staonaibrig, South Uist, XLII.

Miss Janet MacKinnon ('Seònaid Shomhairle Bhig'), XLIV, LII, LXXIV.

Mrs. MacCormick ('Ciorstaidh Shomhairle Bhig') joined in the refrains of XLIV, LII, and LXXIV with her sister Janet MacKinnon. Her name was wrongly entered as 'Mrs. Maclean' in Vol. I above the music of nos. I, XIII, and XXXV, in which she also joined in the refrains of songs sung by her sister.

[1] See the Introduction to *Tales from Barra, Told by the Coddy*, first published in 1959.

[2] p. 188.

[3] Her Gaelic appellation means 'the wife of little Samuel'. In Mrs. Kennedy-Fraser's later volumes she is referred to as 'Mrs MacKinnon, Northbay'.

VATERSAY

The island of Vatersay was worked as a single farm until a land raid took place in 1908, when it was broken up into more than fifty holdings and settled from the now uninhabited island of Mingulary and the Castlebay district of Barra. The very strong influence of the isolated communities that formerly lived on the islands south of Barra, particularly Mingulay, in keeping some of the finest songs of the Gaelic oral tradition alive, should be noted. The following recordings made there are printed in this book:

Nan MacKinnon ('Nan Eachainn Fhionnlaigh'), the epilogue to LXVII. Nan MacKinnon is herself a very remarkable traditional singer, who has recorded over 400 songs for the School of Scottish Studies. Her style of singing waulking songs is highly individual and peculiarly slow.

Elizabeth Sinclair ('Ealasaid Iain Dhunnchaidh'), LXIV. This was recorded on the ediphone in 1949, and is the only such recording used here. Also a version of LXII.

SOUTH UIST

Apart from a few ediphone recordings made at South Lochboisdale in February 1937, recording in South Uist did not begin until the winter of 1949/50, though previously I had taken down in abbreviated script a number of stories, and the words of some songs from the late Seonaidh Caimbeul, 'Seonaidh mac Dhòmhnaill, 'ic Iain Bhàin', who was himself a bard.[1]

In the winter of 1948/9 I met, through the Revd. A. MacKellaig, then parish priest of Bornish, the late Angus MacLellan, later M.B.E., whose sister, the late Mrs. Neil Campbell ('Mór Aonghais 'ic Eachainn, Bean Nìll') it was eventually possible to record at length. Both Angus MacLellan ('Aonghas Beag') and his sister knew an enormous amount of traditional oral Gaelic song and story, and preserved a vivid memory of it into extreme old age. Angus MacLellan being 97 when he died in 1966, and Mrs. Campbell 102 when she died in 1970.[2]

[4] See *Sia Sgialachdan, Six Gaelic Stories from South Uist and Barra*, Edinburgh, 1939.

[5] See J. L. Campbell, *Angus MacLellan M.B.E.* (*'Aonghus Beag'*) *1869–1966*, *Scottish Studies*, x. 193–7.

Mrs. Neil Campbell, then living at Frobost, South Uist, knew a large number of waulking songs, many of them uncommon ones, which she sung with great conscientiousness, repeating lines and often singing the complete refrains (fireside singers often lighten their efforts by omitting the chorus refrains of such songs on most occasions). She was first recorded for me by the Revd. John MacLean in 1957 and the winter of 1958/9, latterly by myself, and is the singer of numbers XLIII, XLIX, LVI, LXIV, LXV, LXVIII, LXIX, LXXVII, LXXXIII, and LXXXVIII in this book.

One of the greatest, if not the greatest of, exponents of the Gaelic oral tradition living in South Uist in 1950 was the late *Duncan MacDonald*, 'Dunnchadh mac Dhòmhnaill 'ic Dhunnchaidh', Peninerine (1883–1954).[1] Duncan MacDonald had an immense fund of songs as well as of heroic tales, folk anecdotes, and local history, but unfortunately no voice. In this book one version of the tune of LVIII is transcribed from the singing of his daughter Kate.

In South Uist we both had the good fortune to be present at a genuine waulking at Gerinish on 29 March 1951, in which nine singers, including four different soloists took part. Twenty-five songs were recorded. Songs from this waulking printed here are LI in which *Miss Penny Morrison*, and LXXIV in which *Mrs. D. J. MacLellan* 'Màiri Mhìcheil' were the soloists.

Other South Uist singers represented in this book are *Miss Annie MacDonald* ('Anna Raghnaill'), from Lochboisdale but recorded on Canna, LXVII; *Mrs. Catriana Campbell* ('Catriana Seònaid'), Loch Carnan, LXVI, recorded at a ceilidh arranged by Mr. John MacInnes, M.B.E.; *Mrs. Archie Munro* ('Màiri a' Ghobha'), Lochboisdale, LXXIV.

There are no transcriptions of recordings made on Eriskay in the present volume, though there are some versions of texts collected there by Fr. Allan McDonald.

BENBECULA

The traditional singers of Benbecula were equally outstanding. Three of them were most kindly introduced by the late Dr. Calum

[1] See K. C. Craig, *Sgialachdan Dhunnchaidh*, Glasgow, 1944; Dr. Calum MacLean, 'Aonghus agus Donnchadh', *Gairm*, iii. 170; J. L. Campbell, 'Duncan of the Stories', *Scots Magazine*, September 1954, p. 473.

MacLean, whose voice can be heard on the wire, at a ceilidh arranged by him at what is now the airport, in 1949.

Mrs. Kate MacCormick ('Catriana nighean Ghill' Easbuig Ghriomasaidh'), Hacklett, whose husband Patrick MacCormick was a well-known storyteller, recorded XLI*a*, XLVII, LXXIV.

Mrs. Angus John MacLellan ('Penny Aonghuis 'ic Raghnaill, bean Aonghuis Iain'), Hacklett, originally from Iochdar in South Uist, LVII. Her husband was also a storyteller.

Miss Kate MacMillan ('Ceit Ruairi'), Torlum, LVIII.

In 1953 the Revd. John MacCormick, then parish priest of Benbecula, made for me some very interesting recordings from *Mrs. Fanny MacIsaac* ('Fanny nic Dhunnchaidh Ruaidh'), Muir of Aird, and *Mrs. Effie Monk* ('Bean Iain Aonghais 'ic Iain Bhig'), Gramsdale. Mrs. MacIsaac, whom I had previously recorded in October 1950, recorded in 1953 number LXII here; Mrs. Effie Monk recorded LX and the preceding story.

Most of the singers whose songs are transcribed here are represented in Volume I, and many of them will later be found in Volume III, which is in preparation.

CAPE BRETON

The text of No. LXVI here, and versions of L and LXXXVIII, are transcribed from ediphone recordings made by the late Mrs. Neil McInnis ('Anna nighean Nill 'ic Iain Ruaidh'), Glace Bay, a lady of mixed South Uist and Barra descent, who had excellent versions of many old waulking songs, in October 1937.

LIST OF FIRST LINES

THE enumeration of the songs continues that of Volume I, starting with XLI. The first lines of different versions, and in a few cases general titles, are included in the Index.

LIST OF FIRST LINES

WAULKING SONGS FROM BARRA, SOUTH UIST ERISKAY, AND BENBECULA

TEXTS WITH TRANSLATIONS

I. Songs probably not originally composed as waulking songs

WAULKING songs of which the 'verses' are single lines or half-lines are in the metre called *Caoine* in Gaelic. This can vary from a line of five syllables with ultimate syllables rhyming (5^{1}), e.g. vol. i, XIX, to a line of twelve syllables with penultimate rhyme, e.g. vol. i, XXXVII, lines 1322–30, but whatever the length of the line, it carries metrically four stresses, and is expressed musically in two bars in 2/4 or 6/8 time. (The intrusive or svarabhakti vowel which is so common in Scottish Gaelic is not counted metrically;[1] words containing it can only rhyme with similar words, and the singer has to adapt the tune to allow for it.) In waulking songs internal assonance is uncommon, and the type of line that occurs most frequently is that of eight syllables with penultimate vowel rhyme (8^{2}), the rhyming vowels being the same throughout the same section of any particular song.

Songs which were probably or certainly not originally waulking songs though now sung as such with one-line 'verses' are revealed by the circumstances that: (1) They are known to exist as ballads sung to traditional ballad airs—this is the case with No. XLI here. (2) Songs with internal rhyme, and usually only the even-numbered lines rhyming externally, some of which may have been originally reaping or rowing songs sung in couplets; an example of this is vol. i, XVII. (3) Songs of which the words and metre do not seem to fit the tune very well; a conspicuous example here is No. LXV. It may be said that in waulking songs of the ordinary type, passages of verse with internal and even-line rhyme can occur, e.g. vol. i, XXX, lines 1070–91, XXXIV, lines 1193–216, XXXV, lines 1226–9.

It will be noticed that there is a great variety in the structure and arrangement of the meaningless refrains of these songs, which

[1] See T. F. O'Rahilly, *Irish Dialects Past and Present, with chapters on Scottish and Manx*, p. 201.

carry the main part of the melodies; this prevents their singing from becoming monotonous. The most frequent type of refrain, however, is that of which the last phrase is identical or nearly identical with the first, expressed by the formula *a, b, a*; this is no doubt the easiest to sing, and probably also satisfies the liking of the human ear for the repetition of musical phrases.

METRICAL TYPES

1. 7^1+7^1 $^{(2+4)}$, with internal rhyme, refrains *a, b,* alternating. As a ballad the sung verse form is ABCD, CDEF, EFGH, etc., and there is no refrain. The rhyming is somewhat irregular.
2. 7^2+7^2 $^{(2+4)}$, with internal rhyme, refrain *a, b, a*; XLIV; in vol. i, XII.
3. 7^2+7^2 $^{(2+4)}$, with internal rhyme, refrain *a, bcd* alternating (the second part of *d* resembles *a*); XLII, XLIII.
4. 6^1 $(5^1)+6^2$ (5^2) $^{(2+4)}$, with internal rhyme, refrain *a, b, a*; XLV. (The metre shows that some lines of this song are sung out of order, and that others have been forgotten.)

In vol. i:

5. 6^2 $(7^2)+6^1$ (5^1) $^{(2+4)}$, with internal rhyme, refrain *a, b, c*: XVII.
6. 6^2 $(7^2)+6^2$ $^{(2+4)}$, with internal rhyme, refrain *a, b, a*; XXX, lines 1070–91 (concluding lines 7^2+7^2).
7. 7^2+7^2 $^{(2+4)}$, internal rhyme, refrain *a, bcd* alternating: XXXIV, lines 1193–1216.

XLI

Am Bròn Binn

(*a*) *LS. Mhic an Deòir, ii. 376–9*

Do réir beul-aithris, ann an linn Rìgh Artair bhith ann an Dùn Éideann, bha triath urramach Éireannach [ann] a chuir taigh-dìdein air a' chreig ris an abairte Ealasaid a' Chuain; agus ghoid e 'na braighde[an] ribhinn uasal, agus thug e i do'n dùn a thog e air Ealasaid a' Chuain, 's bha e 'ga gléidheadh an sin 'na braighde[an].

Bha Rìgh Artair latha anns a' bheinn a' sealg; laigh e a leigeadh a sgìos dheth. Chaidil e, agus bhruadair e air an ribhinn a bha ann am braighdeanas; agus ghabh e toil a cur saor, ach cha robh fios aige c'àite an robh i. Ghabh Sir Bhalbha os làimh dol ga h-iarraidh, nam faigheadh e long o'n Rìgh. Thug an Rìgh long dha, agus sheòl Sir Bhalbha gus an d'fhuair e air thuiteamas i; agus thug e dh'ionnsaigh Rìgh Artair i, agus b'ann do'n chùis chaidh an t-òran a leanas a dheanamh:

Turas a chaidh Rìgh Artair 's a shluagh
Gu tulach nam buadh a shealg,
Gun duine mar-ris an Rìgh,
Ach Sir Bhalbha, fo a lìon arm.
Gun duine, *etc.*

Chunnaic Rìgh Bhreatainn 's e 'na shuain
An aon bhean a b'àillidh snuadh fo'n ghréin;
'S b'fheàrr leis na na bh'aige a dh'òr,
An òigbhean a bhith aige fhéin.
'S b'fheàrr leis, *etc.*

Ach b'fheàrr leis tuiteam, ann an sin,
Le còmhrag fir, mar bha e fhéin,
Na dol a dh'iarraidh na mnà,
'S gun fhios aige cia 'n t-àite fo'n ghréin.
Na dol, *etc.*

Thubhairt Sir Bhalbha suairce ciùin
' 'S e mo rùn dol a dh'iarraidh na mnà,
Théid mi fhìn, mo ghille, 's mo chù,
'Nar triùir 'ga sireadh gun dàil.'
Théid mi fhìn, *etc.*

XLI

The Sweet Sorrow

(*a*) *Version from the Dewar MSS., ii. 376–9*

According to tradition, at the time when King Arthur was in Edinburgh, there was a distinguished Irish chief who built a strong keep on a rock called Ailsa Craig; and he took captive a noble maiden, and brought her to the fort which he had made on Ailsa Craig, and was keeping her a prisoner there.

One day, when King Arthur was hunting on the hill, he lay down to rest. He fell asleep, and he dreamt of the maiden who was in captivity, and wished to set her free, but he did not know where she was. Sir Gawain undertook to seek her, if he would get a ship from the King. The King gave him a ship, and Sir Gawain sailed until he chanced to find her; and he brought her to King Arthur, and it was about this matter that the following song was made:

One day King Arthur and his host
Went to the excellent hill to hunt,
With no one together with the King
But Sir Gawain, fully armed.
With no one, *etc.*

The King of Britain saw in his sleep
The most beautiful woman beneath the sun;
Sooner than all the gold he possessed,
Would he have the girl himself.
Sooner than, *etc.*

But he preferred to fall right there
In manly combat, with his peer,
Than to go in search of the maid,
Not knowing where beneath the sun.
Than to go, *etc.*

Sir Gawain, quiet and courtly, spoke:
'To seek the girl I am disposed
Myself, my servant, and my dog,
We three will go to search for her now.'
Myself, *etc.*

Seachd seachdainnean le strì
  Bha sinn sgìth a' siubhal cuain,
Gun chala, gun talamh, gun fhonn,
  Gun ionad anns an gabhadh an long tàmh.
Gun chala, *etc.*

Chunnacas an iomall a' chuain ghairbh
  Caisteal mór mìn-gheal gorm,
Uinneagan glaine air a stuagh,
  'S bu lìonmhor ann cuaich is còirn.
Uinneagan glaine, *etc.*

Air dhuinn bhith seòladh staigh ri bhun,
  Chaidh slabhraidh a chur a nuas,
'S roimh'n t-slabhraidh cha do ghabhar crith,
  Ach chaidhear oirre 'nam ruith suas.
'S roimh'n t-slabhraidh, *etc.*

Chunnacas an nighean, éiteag òg,
  An cathair òir 'na suidhe a steach,
Sgàthan glaine air a glùn,
  'S beannaicheam do a gnùis ghil.
Sgàthan glaine, *etc.*

ISE:

'Fhir a thàinig oirnn o'n chuan,
  'S truagh brìgh do bheannachadh ann,
[Thig fear na cathrach seo fhéin,
  Nach do dh'fhidir treun no truas.']
Thig fear, *etc.*

ESAN:

'Ged thigeadh am Fear Mór 'nam dhàil,
  Gun iochd gun bhàigh le a chlaidheamh cruaidh,
Air do chubhais-sa, a bhean bhlàth,
  'S coingeis liom a ghràdh seach fhuath!'
Air do chubhais-sa, *etc.*

ISE:

'Arm cha deargadh air an fhear,
  Ach a chlaidheamh rinn-gheal fhéin;
Agus is fheàrr dhut dol fo chleith
  Do àite air leath tearuinnt' o'n eug.'
Agus is fheàrr, *etc.*

With exertion for seven weeks
  We were tired sailing the seas,
Without harbour, land, or ground,
  Or place where the ship could rest.
Without harbour, *etc.*

At the edge of the rough sea
  We saw a great castle, white and blue,
Its gable end with windows of glass,
  And many a cup and goblet within.
Its gable end, *etc.*

When we had sailed in at its foot,
  A chain descended from above;
Trembling not before the chain
  I went upon it scrambling up.
Trembling not, *etc.*

I saw the maiden, fair and young,
  Inside, upon a throne of gold,
A mirror of glass upon her knee,
  I greeted her radiant face.
A mirror, *etc.*

SHE:

'O man who has come to us from the sea,
  Pitiful is your blessing's worth,
The owner of this throne will come,
  Who considers neither strong nor weak.'
The owner, *etc.*

HE:

'Though I encounter the Big Man,
  Merciless, with his sword of steel,
By your conscience,[1] o kindly maid,
  His love or his hate are the same to me.'
By your conscience, *etc.*

SHE:

'There's no weapon can do him harm,
  But his own white-pointed sword,
Better you should go to hide
  To a place apart, safe from death.'
Better you, *etc.*

[1] See note.

Chaidh Sir Bhalbha fo chleith,
  Agus a steach thàinig am Fear Mór:—
'Tha boladh an fharbhalaich a steach,
  Oirnn air teachd o thuinn na tràigh!'
Tha boladh, *etc.*

'Anmain, a sheircein, 's a rùin,
  Is mór an gaol a thug mi dhuit,
Cuir thusa do cheann air mo ghlùin,
  Agus seinnidh mi ciùin dhuit a' chruit.'
Cuir thusa, *etc.*

Chuir e a cheann air uchd na h-ighinn' ùir'
  Bu ghuirme sùil, 's bu ghile deud,
'S ge bu bhinn a sheinneadh i chruit,
  Bu bhinne an guth bha teachd o beul.
'S ge bu bhinn, *etc.*

Air dha bhith cuairteachadh nan cuan
  Chaidil e 'n suain 'na shiorram fann,
'S thug iad an claidheamh as a chrios,
  'S ghearr iad gun fhios deth an ceann.
'S thug, iad, *etc.*

Ghoid iad a' bhraighdeanach-s' gu léir,
  'S bha a bhean fhéin fo chumha thruim—
Siod agaibh aithris mo sgeul,
  'S mar a leugh iad am Bòrd Cruinn.
Siod agaibh, *etc.*

Latha do Rìgh Artair 's a shluagh
  Bhith air tulach nam buadh a' sealg,
Gun duine mar-ris an Rìgh,
  Ach Sir Bhalbha fo a lìon arm.

(*b*) *Mar Òran Luadhaidh. Anna Raghnaill Eachainn a' seinn*

Chunnaic Rìgh Bhreatainn 'na shuain
  Iolair' ó, ò ro hó,

An òig-bhean 's àille snuadh fo'n ghréin,
  Iolairean is hò ro hì,

Sir Gawain went and hid,
And in came the Big Man,
'There is the smell of a stranger inside
Come to us from the shore's waves!'
There is, *etc.*

'My soul, my darling, and my love,
Great the love I have given to thee;
Put thy head upon my knee,
Softly the harp I'll play for thee.'
Put thy head, *etc.*

He put his head on the young girl's breast,
She of bluest eye and whitest teeth,
Though sweetly she played the harp,
Sweeter the voice that came from her lips.
Though sweetly, *etc.*

After travelling o'er the seas
He fell into enchanted sleep;
From his belt they took the sword,
And stealthily cut off his head.
From his belt, *etc.*

Quickly they stole the captive away,
The Big Man's wife lamenting sore—
There you have the telling of my tale,
And how the Round Table was proclaimed.
There you have, *etc.*

One day King Arthur and his host
Went to the excellent hill to hunt,
With no one together with the King,
But Sir Gawain, fully armed.

(*b*) *As sung by Mrs. MacDougall, Barra, as a waulking song*

(*For tune, see p.* 272)

The King of Britain saw in his sleep

The fairest maid beneath the sun,

An òig-bhean 's àille snuadh fo'n ghréin,
Iolair' ó, ò ro hó,

'S gum b'fheàrr leis tuiteam dha cion
Iolairean is hò ro hì,

'S gum b'fheàrr leis tuiteam dha cion
Iolair' ó, etc.

Na còmhradh fir mar bha e fhéin.
Iolairean is ho, etc.

Na còmhradh, *etc.*
Labhair Sir Falach gu fìor
'Théid mi fhìn dha h-iarraidh dhut,
Mi fhìn, mo ghille, 's mo long,
'Nar triùir a shireadh na mnài.'

Bha mi sgìth a' siubhal cuain,
Fad seachd seachdainnean is dà mhìos;
Cha n-fhacas fearann no fonn
Air an deanadh mo long tàmh.

Steach o iomall a' chuain ghairbh
Chunnacas caisteal ìseal gorm,
'S uinneagan glaine ri stuaigh,
'S bu lìonmhor ann cuach is còrn.

An amm bhith teàrnadh r'a bhun,
Thànaig slabhraidh dhubh a nuas;
Cha do ghabh mi eagal no fiamh,
Ghabh mi oirre 'nam ruith suas.

Chunnacas ainnir bréidgheal òg
Anns a' chathair òir a staigh
Stròl dha'n t-sìoda fo a dà bhonn
'S gun bheannaich mi dh'a gnùis ghil.

'A fhleasgaich a thànaig o'n chuan,
Is duatharra do bheannachadh dhomh;
Teann nall do cheann air mo ghlùin,
'S gun seinneam dhut ceòl is cruit.'

The fairest maid beneath the sun,

For her love, he preferred to die,

For her love, he preferred to die,

Than to hold speech with one like himself.

Than to hold, *etc.*
Truly did Sir Gawain speak:
'To seek her for you I will go,
Myself, my servant, and my ship,
The three of us, to seek the maid.'

I was tired travelling the seas
For seven weeks and two months,
No land at all was to be seen
Where my ship could come to rest.

In from the verge of the rough sea
A low, dark-grey castle we saw,
Glass windows at its gable end,
Within many a quaich and drinking-horn.

When we approached its foot,
A black pot-chain came down,
I was not afraid at all
I went on it, hurrying aloft.

I saw a young white-kertched girl
Inside, on a throne of gold,
A roll of silk beneath her two feet,
And I blessed her fair face.

'Young man who has come from the sea,
Your blessing is gloomy for me;
Come and put your head on my knee,
So I may play harp music to you.'

Cruit air uchd na mìnghil ùir'
As guirme sùil 's as gile deud;
Thuit esan 'na shiorram shuain
An déidh bhith cuairteachadh a' chuain ghairbh.

Thug i claidheamh geur o a crios,
'S gheàrr i dheth gun fhios an ceann;
Sin agaibh deireadh mo sgeòil,
'S mar a sheinneadh am Bròn Binn.

XLII

Ach a Mhurchaidh òig ghaolaich

Maighread Shomhairle Bhig a' seinn

Ach a Mhurchaidh òig ghaolaich,
Hó hi ò,
Hao ri 's na hì ri rì,
Hoireann ó.

Bidh tu daonnan air m'aire,
Hó ho hì, hoireann ó,

Bidh tu daonnan air m'aire,
Hó hi ò,
Hao ri 's na hì ri rì,
Hoireann ó.

Nàile! chunna mi nìos thu,
Hó ho hì, hoireann ó.

Nàile! chunna mi nìos thu,
Hó hi ò,
Hao ri 's na, etc.

'S tu an dìollaid le seang-each
Hó ho hì, etc.

Do ghille or 'o chùlaibh,
'S e toirt ùmhladh do'n ealaidh;

A harp at the breast of the fair maid
Of bluest eye and whitest tooth;
He fell into a charmed sleep
After travelling the rough sea.

She took a sharp sword from her belt,
And stealthily cut off his head—
There you have the end of my tale,
And of how the Sweet Sorrow played.

XLII

But, beloved young Murdo

Mrs. Archie MacPhee singing

(*For tune, see p.* 274)

But, beloved young Murdo,

On my mind you'll be always,

On my mind you'll be always,

Yes, I saw you towards me,

Yes, I saw you towards me,

In a saddle on a fine horse,

With your servant behind you
Respecting your skill;

Bu tu sealgair a' gheòidh ghlais,
  Làmh a leònadh na h-eala,
'S a' choilich dhuibh air bàrr géige
  'S moch a dh'éibheas 'sa mhadainn,
'S na circeige riabhaich,
  Dha'm bu bhiadh am fraoch meangach,
Nàile! 's iomadh eun uaigneach,
  Bhios o d' luaidhe gun deathach!
'S tu gum fàgadh a' mhaoiseach
  Air a taobh 's i call fala,
Is damh a' chinn chròcaich
  Air a' mhòintich gun deathach!
Ach, a Mhurchaidh òig ghaolaich,
  Tha thu daonnan air m'aire,
'S truagh nach fhaicinn do bhàta
  Siùil àrda ri crannaibh,
Sgiobadh innt' a dhaoin-uaisle
  Chuireadh cluain ri muir ghreannaich,
Tighinn a steach ro' na caolais
  Far bheil gaol do dhà sheanar,
Steach gu Uibhist an eòrna,
  Far an òlte fìon ceannaich';
Gum biodh maighdeanan Chòrnaig
  Làn bòsd agus barraich,
'S iad a' tighinn air an òigfhear,
  'S nach eil dòigh aca shloinneadh;
'S ann is càirdeach dà uair thu
  Do dh'uaislean Shìol Ailein,
Do Mhac Nìll bho na Tùraibh,
  Do dh'Iain Mùideartach allail,
Do Mhac Fhionghuin bho'n Chréithich,
  Leis an éireadh fir gheala.
Ach, a Mhurchaidh òig ghaolaich,
  Tha thu daonnan air m'aire,
Ach nam faighinn air m'òrdan
  Bu leat móran do dh'fhearann,
Bu leat Eige agus Ìle,
  Cinn-tìre agus Arainn,
Agus Sléibhte bheag riabhach
  Le sliabh do chrodh ballach.

You were the hunter of the grey goose,
  Whose hand would wound the swan,
And the blackcock on branch-top
  That early calls in the morning,
And the little speckled moorhen
  That feeds on the heather,
Yes, many a rare bird
  Your lead will leave lifeless!
You would leave the roe deer
  On its side, bleeding,
And the red deer with its antlers
  On the moor lifeless!
But, beloved young Murdo,
  On my mind you'll be always,
Alas that I see not your ship
  With her sails mast-high hoisted,
A crew in her of nobles,
  Who would calm a rough ocean,
Coming in through the narrows
  Where your two grandsires' love is,
In to Uist of the barley,
  Where they drink wine imported.
The maidens of Cornaig
  Would be masterfully boasting,
Coming on the young man
  Whose ancestry they cannot relate;
You are connected twice over
  To the nobles of the race of Allan,
To MacNeil from the towers,
  To John Moydartach the valiant,
To MacKinnon from Creitheach
  With his followers, brave fellows,
But, beloved young Murdo,
  You are always on my mind,
If I had things my way,
  You'd have plenty of country,
You'd have Eigg and Islay,
  Kintyre, and Arran,
And little furrowed Sleat
  With its hillside covered with speckled kine.

XLIII

'S mi dol timcheall na dòirlinn

Bean Nìll a' seinn

'S mi dol timcheall na dòirlinn
Bheir mi hó ho ró hò
Rinn mi m'òrdag a ghearradh,
Hi rì ri rì ó
Ho hì hó ho ró hò.
Rinn mi m'òrdag a ghearradh,
Bheir mo hó, etc.
H-uile fear thig dh'a fiachainn
Hi rì ri, etc.

'S iad ag iarraidh a gearradh;
'S duilich dhomhsa sin éisdeachd,
'S gun na féithean am falach;
'S mi gun charaid fo'n ghréinghil
[Ris an déid mi 'gam ghearain.]
Tha m'athair 's mo mhàthair
As an àraich fo'n talamh,
Mar sin 's mo thriùir bhràithrean
Air a' bhàta dhubh dharaich.
Tha cloinn-nighean an gruaim rium
Bho nach d'fhuair mi dhaibh leannan,
Ach nam bithinn 'nam fhleasgach,
'S 'nam chleasaiche ròmhath,
Chuirinn cóigear no sianar
'Nan seasamh ri balla
As an léineagan fuara,
Chuid as suaraiche an anairt,
'S bhiodh Mór bhàn air an tùbh-s' ann
Té gun smùr air a malaidh,
Bhean a shiubhail a' Chrìosdachd,
Té gun chiall oirr' gun aithnte.

XLIII

As I went round the isthmus

Mrs. Neil Campbell singing

(*For tune, see p.* 275)

As I went round the isthmus
  I did cut my thumb,

  I did cut my thumb,
Everyone who comes to look at it

  Is wanting to cut it;
It is difficult for me to hear that
  With the sinews unconcealed;
And I without a friend under the fair sun
  To whom I can go to complain.
My father and my mother
  Are buried on the plain,
Likewise my three brothers
  On the black oaken galley.
Girls are annoyed with me
  Because I did not get them lovers;
But if I were a young man
  Very good at tricks,
I would set five or six
  To stand against a wall
In their cold linen garments
  Of the meanest cloth,
Fair Marion would be beside them,
  A girl of unblemished brow,
The woman who wandered over Christendom,
  A girl without sense or knowledge.

XLIV

Ged is grianach an latha

Calum Aonghais Chaluim a' seinn

Hò hao ri rì hó,
Hó hiù ra bhó ro hó hó,
Hao ri rì hó.

Ged is grianach an latha,
Gur beag m'aighear r'a bhòidhchead,
'S mi ri feitheamh a' chaolais,
'S gun mo ghaol-sa 'ga sheòladh;
Ach nam faicinn thu tighinn,
'S mi gun ruitheadh 'nad chòmhdhail,
'S mi gu rachadh 'nad choinneamh,
Air mo bhonnaibh gun bhrògan.
'S a cheart aindeoin luchd mì-rùin
'S mi gun dùraigeadh pòg dhuit,
Ged a chuirte mi 'm sheasamh
Air an t-Seisein Di-Dòmhnaich
Ann am fianais na cléire,
'S gun ach léine 'gam chòmhdach.
Tha mo chion air an fhleasgach
Dhonn, leadanach, bhòidheach;
'S ged nach eil thu de m'fhine,
Liom a b'inich do phòsadh,
Tha thu 'n fhine nach strìochdadh,
Do dh'fhìor-fhuil Chlann Dòmhnaill!

XLIV

Sunny though the day may be

Calum Johnston singing

(*For tune, see p.* 277)

Sunny though the day may be,
  Little joy its beauty gives me,
As I wait beside the narrows
  While my loved one sails not over;
If I only saw you coming,
  I would rush to the encounter,
I would go to meet you
  On my bare feet, shoeless;
In defiance of ill-wishers
  I would dare to kiss you,
Even though I were made to stand
  At kirk session on the Sunday
In the presence of the clergy,
  Wearing only a linen garment.
I love the handsome young man
  With hair brown and curling,
Though you're not of my clansfolk,
  I would eagerly wed you;
You're of the race unyielding,
  The true blood of Clan Donald!

XLV

Tha an oidhche nochd fuar

Mairi Ruarachain a' seinn

O hó hì, hiu à hó,
O hò ro ghealladh,
O ho hì, hiu à hó.

Tha an oidhche nochd fuar,
O ho hì, etc.
Tha i cruaidh le frasan,
Cha laigh mi nochd 'n suain,
'S cha n-e cruas mo leapa,
Ach a' caoi na dh'fhalbh bhuainn
Air Di-Luain de'n t-seachdain,
. . . .
Taobh a tuath Ceann Ratharsair.
A Mhic 'ill' Eóghanain 'ic Nill,
'S bochd, a Rìgh! mar thachair,
Chaidh a' mhin ort a dhith,
'S mar sin 's sìol na braiche.

Gura mise tha bochd truagh
. . . .
Mu'n nighinn chruinn duinn,
. . . .
Beul miuchair gun sgòd,
Deud bòidheach cailce;
Té nach laigheadh an smùr,
'S nach lig sùil 'na plaididh,
'S nach lig aoinfhear tha beò
Fo sgòd a breacain,
Gus am faigh i fear còir
Le deòin a' chlachain,
'S fear a chùnntadh dhi nì
Nuair bhiodh prìs air martaibh;

XLV

The night tonight is cold

Mrs. Mary MacNeil singing

(*For tune, see p.* 279)

The night tonight is cold,
  The squalls are severe,
I cannot sleep tonight
  Not from my bed's hardness,
But lamenting those who left
  Us, this week on Monday.
. . . .
  North of the point of Raasay.
Son of Gilleonan MacNeil,
  It is sad, alas, what has happened!
You have lost your meal,
  And likewise the grain for malting.

I am sick and sad
  . . . .
About the neat brown-haired lass,
  . . . .
Soft mouth without fault,
  Teeth chalk-white and pretty;
A girl who'd not lie in the dust
  Or allow a glance in her blanket,
Who won't let any man
  Under the corner of her blanket,
Till she gets a right one
  With the church's assent;
One who'd endow her with goods,
  When cows were of value,

Aig am biodh na h-eich ghorm,
   Chluinnte foirm na marcrachd.
'S math thig sìod' air mo rùn,
   Gùn ùr a' pasgadh,
Currac dubh os a chionn,
   Mach a bùth nam fasan.

One who'd own dark grey horses,
  Which could be heard ridden.
Well does silk suit my love,
  A new gown folding,
A black kertch above
  From the shop of the fashions.

2. Songs of single-line 'verses' of the metrical form 8^2 or 8^1

1. Line 8^2, refrain *a*, *b*, alternating: XLVI–XLIX. In vol. i, V, XXXII.
2. Line 8^2, refrain *a*, *bc*, alternating: L. In vol. i, VII, XXIII, XXV.
3. Line 8^2, refrain *a*, *bcd*, alternating: LI, LII. In vol. i, XV.
4. Line 8^2, refrain *a*: LIII. In vol. i, XXXV.
5. Line 8^2, refrain *abc*. LIV–LVII. In vol. i, XXXVII. (The last nine lines of this are 12^2, with the interior stressed vowels in each respective line the same, in *amhran* style, a rare thing in Scottish Gaelic.)
6. Line 8^1, refrain *aba*. LVIII. An unusual metre.
7. Line 8^2, refrain *aba*. LIX–LXVI. In vol. i, IV, VIII, XXXI, XXXVI.

XLVI

Seathan mac Rìgh Éirinn

Anna agus Calum Aonghais Chaluim a' seinn

B'annsa Seathan a' falbh sléibhe,
Hù rù o nà hi ò ro,
Mise lag is esan treubhach,
Nà hi ò ro hó hug ò ro,
Mise lag is esan treubhach;
Hù rù, etc.
Cha ghiùlaininn ach beag éididh,
Nà hi ò ro, etc.

Cha ghiùlaininn ach beag éididh,
Hù rù, etc.
Còta ruadh mu leath mo shléisne,
'S criosan caol-dubh air mo léinidh,
'S mi falbh le Seathan mar eudail.
Nà hi ò ro hó hug ò ro.

'S iomadh beinn is gleann a shiubhail sinn,
Bha mi an Ìle, bha mi am Muile leat, (Uibhist
Bha mi an Éirinn an Cóig' Mumha leat,
'S dh'éisd mi 'n Aifhreann 'sa Choill' Bhuidhe leat.
Hù rù o nà hi ò ro.

'S minig a chuala, 's nach do dh'innis e,
Gu robh mo leannan am Mighinis;
Nam biodh e 'n sin, 's fhad' o thigeadh e;
Chuireadh e bàta dha m' shireadh-sa,
'S chuirinn-sa long mhór 'ga shireadh-san,
Sgiobadh cliùiteach, ùrail, iriseal.
Nà hi ò ro hó hug ò ro,
Nà hi ò ro hó hug ò ro,
Nà hi ò ro hó hug ò ro.

Nam faighte Seathan ri fhuasgladh,
Dh'fhàsadh an t-òr fo na bruachaibh,

XLVI

Seathan son of the King of Ireland

Annie and Calum Johnston singing

(*For tune, see p.* 280)

Dear was Seathan going on the hillside,

I was weak, and he was valiant,

I was weak, and he was valiant,

I'd not wear but light apparel,

I'd not wear but light apparel,

Russet coat down half my thigh's side,
Around my shift a thin black girdle,
Going with Seathan as his darling.

Many a hill and glen we wandered,
I was in Islay, I was in Mull with you,
I was in Ireland in the province of Munster with you,
I heard Mass in the Yellow Wood with you.

Pity him who heard, and did not tell it,
That my lover was in Minginish;
If he'd been there, he'd have come long ago,
He'd have sent a boat to seek for me,
I'd have sent a ship to seek for him,
A crew famous, youthful, obedient.

If Seathan could be set free again,
Gold would be found beneath the river-banks,

Cha bhiodh gobhair an creig ghruamaich,
'S cha bhiodh lìon gun iasg an cuantan.
Nà hi ò ro hó hug ò ro,
Nà hi ò ro ho hug ò ro,
Nà hi ò ro ho hug ò ro.

B'annsa Seathan air cùl tobhtadh,
Na bhith le mac rìgh air lobhtaidh,
Ged bhiodh aige leaba shocair,
'S stròl dha'n t-sìoda bhith fo chasan,
'S cluasag dha'n òr dhearg a' lasradh.
Nà hi ò ro hó hug ò ro.

Tha Seathan an nochd 'na mharbhan, (bhalbhan
Sgeul as ait le luchd a shealga,
['S le mac caillich nan trì dealga,]
Sgeul as olc le fearaibh Alba.
[A Sheathain! a Sheathain m'anma!
Dhealbh-mhic mo rìgh o thìr Chonbhaigh!]
Hù rù o nà hi ò ro.

'S minig thuirt rium gum bu bhean shubhach mi,
Bean bhochd chianail chràiteach dhubhach mi,
Bean bhochd a thug spéis d'a bhuidhinn mi;
Nuair shaoil mi thu bhith 'san tòrachd,
'S ann a bha thu marbh 'nam chòmhdhail,
'S tu air ghuaillean nam fear òga.
Nà hi ò ro hó hug ò ro.

'S nuair a shaoil mi thu bhith 'sa ghailleann,
'S ann a bha thu marbh gun anam,
'S tu 'gad ghiùlain aig na fearaibh
Gu leitir nan corrbheann corrach.
Nà hi ò ro hó hug ò ro.

'S an oidhche sin a rinn iad banais dhut,
Ochóin, a Rìgh! cha b'ann ach t'fhalairidh!
Nach do chuir iad léin' dha'n anart ort?
Nach do lig iad ùir is talamh ort?
Nà hi ò ro hó hug ò ro,
Nà hi ò ro hó hug ò ro,
Nà hi ò ro hó hug ò ro.

There'd be no goats on gloomy precipice,
There'd be no net without fish in the oceans.

Better to be with Seathan behind a ruin,
Than with a prince in an upper story,
Though he had a bed most comfortable,
A roll of silk beneath his feet,
A pillow of red gold shining.

Seathan tonight is dead and lifeless
A tale of joy for his pursuers,
And for the hag of three thorns' son,
An evil tale for the men of Scotland;
Seathan! Seathan of my soul!
Son of my king from the land of Conway!

Pity him who told me I was a happy one,
A poor, sad, sore, mournful woman am I,
A poor woman who loved her company;
When I thought you were in the pursuit,
You were coming in death to meet me,
On the shoulders of young men carried.

When I thought you were in the snowstorm,
You were dead, your soul departed,
You were by the men being carried
To the country of steep mountains.

That night, that they made your wedding-feast
Alas, my God! 'twas but your burial,
Did they not put a linen shroud on you?
Did they not put soil and earth on you?

M'eudail an làmh sin, 's ged 's fuar i,
Bu tric agam, b'annamh bhuam i,
Le tiodhlaig dha'n t-sìoda bhuaidheach,
Gur tric a fhuair mi le duais i.
Hù rù o nà hi ò ro.

Cha dugainn a lagh no rìgh thu,
Cha ghibhtinn air Moire Mhìn thu,
'S cha tiodhlaiginn 'sa Chrò Naoimh thu,
Eagal 's nach fhaighinn a rithist thu!
Nà hi ò ro hó hug ò ro,
Nà hi ò ro hó hug ò ro,
Nà hi ò ro hó hug ò ro.

XLVII

Chailin òig as stiùramaiche

(*a*) *Bean Phluim a' seinn*

Chailin òig as stiùramaiche,
Cailin mise, buachaill' thusa,
Chailin òig, a hù ra bhó hó,
Cailin mise, buachaill' thusa,
Chailin òig as stiùramaiche,
B'fheàirrde banchaig buachaill' aice,
Chailin òig, a hù, etc.
B'fheàirrde banchaig buachaill' aice,
Chailin òig as, etc.
Ged nach dèan e ach falbh reimpe;
Théid e mach 'san oidhche fhrasaich,
Chuireadh e na laoigh am fasgadh,
Ghabhadh e gu suanach aca.

Latha dhomh 's mi falbh an fhàsaich,
Thachair orms' an donnabhean dhàna,
Shuidh sinn air cnoc, rinn sinn bànran;
Dh'iarr a' chailin nì nach b'fheudar—
Muileann air gach struth an Éirinn,
Caisteal air gach cnocan gréineadh.

Cold though it be, that hand is dear to me,
Seldom it stayed from me, oft it came to me
With a gift of silk most beautiful,
Often it brought a gift to me.

For law or king I would not give you up,
For gentle Mary I would not give you up,
In the holy enclosure I'd not bury you
For fear that I would not recover you.

XLVII

'*Calen o custure me*'

(*a*) *Mrs. Mary Morrison singing*

(*For tune, see p.* 283)

I am a girl, you are a herdsman

I am a girl, you are a herdsman

A dairymaid should have a herdsman,

A dairymaid should have a herdsman,

Though he does nothing but go before her;
He'll go out in the showery night,
He will put the calves in shelter,
He would go about them quietly.

One day as I walked the meadow,
The bold brown-haired woman met me,
We sat on a mound and talked together;
She asked for things I could not give her,
A mill on every stream in Ireland,
A castle on each sunny hillock.

Chaidh mi dhachaigh, 's laigh mi 'n là sin,
'S thug mi bliadhna mhór is ràithe
Ann an teasach na plàghach;
Dh'éirich mi 'n ceann nan cóig ràithean,
Thànaig is', an donnabhean dhàna,
Dhìrich i 'n staighir a b'àirde,
Ghlac i ursann as gach làimh dhi,
Dh'fhoighneachd i gu dé mar bhà mi?

'Tha mi gu bochd truagh mar 's àbhaist,
Olc le m' charaid, 's math le m' nàmhaid!'
'Ghràdh thu, b'fheàrr liom agam slàn thu!'

Chaidh mi mach air feadh na stràideadh,
Ghlac mi 'n caman, chuir mi pàm leis,
Ma chuir mi h-aon, chuir mi dhà leis.

Ach, mur h-è gur bean mo mhàthair,
'S gur h-è mo mhuime rinn m'àrach,
Dh'innsinn sgeul bheag air na mnài dhuibh:
Tha iad sgeigeil, bleideil, bàrdail,
'S an aigne mar ghaoth a' Mhàrta,
Mar uan Chéitein anns a' mhèilich,
Mar laogh féidh an déidh a mhàthar,
Mar mhuir a' lìonadh 's a tràghadh,
Mar liaghan air leaca bàna,
Mar easgann an lodan làthchadh.

(*b*) *Catriana 'Ill' Easbuig a' seinn*

Cailin òg, gun stiùir thu mise,
Éisdibh beag a staigh ma's àill libh,
Cailin òg, a hù ra bho ho,
Éisdibh beag a staigh ma's àill libh,
Cailin òg, gun stiùir thu mise,
'S dh'innsinn sgeul bheag air na mnài dhuibh;
Cailin òg, a hù ra bho ho,
'S dh'innsinn sgeul bheag air na mnài dhuibh;
Cailin òg, gun stùir thu mise,
Tha cuid dhiu gun chiall gun nàire,

I went home, I fell ill that day,
I spent a long year and a quarter
Lying ill with a high fever;
After fifteen months I got up,
She came, the bold brown-haired woman,
The highest stair she ascended,
She grasped a door-post in each hand,
And inquired how I was faring?

'Sick and miserable as always,
Bad for my friend, good for my foeman!'
'My love, I'd sooner have you healthy!'

I went out throughout the street,
I took a shinty, I struck a goal with it,
If I struck one, I struck two with it.

But, were not my mother a woman,
And the fostermother who reared me,
I'd tell you a little tale of women;
They are mocking, teasing, scolding,
Their minds are like the March wind blowing,
Like a lamb in May a-bleating,
Like a fawn following its mother,
Like the tide ebbing and flowing,
Like the tangles on the white rocks,
Like an eel in a muddy puddle.

(*b*) *Mrs. Kate MacCormick singing*

(*For tune, see p.* 286)

Young girl, you will guide me,
Listen within, if it is your wish,
Young girl, a hu ra bhọ ho,
Listen within, if it is your wish,
Young girl, you will guide me,
And I'll tell you a little tale of women,
Young girl, a hú ra bho ho,
And I'll tell you a little tale of women,
Young girl, you will guide me,
Some are without sense and shameless,

'S tha cuid dhiu gu fearail dàna.

Cailin òg, gun stiùir thu mise,
Cailin òg, gun stiùir thu mise,

B'fheàirrde banchaig buachaill' aice,
Cailin òg, a hù ra bho ho,
B'fheàirrde banchaig buachaill' aice,
Cailin òg, gun stiùir thu mise,
Chuireadh e 'n crodh-laoigh air fasgadh,

Laigh mi 'san teasaich an là sin,
Thug mi bliadhna mhór is ràith innt',
Cha dànaig i idir dha m' shealltainn;
Thànaig i 'n ceann nan cóig ràithean;
'Fhir ud a staigh, gu dé mar thà thu?'
'Olc le m' charaid, 's math le m' nàmhaid'
'Olc liom fhìn, gum b'fheàrr liom slàn thu'.

Cailin òg, gun stiùir thu mise,
Cailin òg, gun stiùir thu mise,

'S chaidh mi 'nam aodach an là sin,
'S dhìrich mi an uinneag a b'àirde;
Chunnacas clann an rìgh air fàireadh,
Caman òir ac' is buill airgid,
Ghlac mi caman, 's chuir mi bàir air,
'S ma chuir mi h-aon, chuir mi dhà air.
Cailin òg, gun stiùir thu mise.

(*c*) *Mar a chaidh e ghabhail do Mhgr. Ailein Dòmhnallach*

Chailin òig as stiùireamaiche,
Chailin òig o hù o ro ho.

Latha dhomh 's mi falbh an fhàsaich,
Thachair orm an donnabhean dhàna;
Thug ise na mionnan àrda
Nach bu mhise ragha dàimh dhi.
Cha b'fhaide na sin a bhà mi,
Nuair laigh mi an teasach na plàighe.

And some of them are bold and manly.

Young girl, you will guide me,
Young girl, you will guide me,

A dairymaid should have a herdsman,
Young girl, a hù ra bho ho,
A dairymaid should have a herdsman,

He'll put the milk-cows into shelter.

That day I lay in a high fever,
I lay a long year and a quarter,
She didn't come at all to see me;
Until the end of the five quarters.
'Yon man within, how are you?'
'Ill for my friend, well for my foeman!'
'Ill for me too, I'd prefer you healthy!'

Young girl, you will guide me,
Young girl, you will guide me,

That day I put on my clothing,
And I climbed to the highest window,
I saw the King's children in the distance,
With a golden shinty and balls of silver;
I took a shinty and struck a goal,
If I struck one, I struck two against them.
Young girl, you will guide me.

(*c*) *Version taken down by Fr. Allan McDonald, probably on Eriskay*

One day as I walked the grassland,
The bold brown-haired woman met me,
She made great asseveration
That I was not her choice connection.
No longer than that was I
When I fell ill with the plague of fever;

Thug mi bhliadhna mhór is ràithe
'Nam laigh' an teasach na plàighe,
Latha cheann a' chóigeamh ràithe
Dhìrich ise staighr' a b'àirde.

Os ise: 'Fhir a staigh, gu dé mar thà thu?'
Os esan: 'Tha mise gu tinn 's gu cràiteach,
Olc le m' charaid, 's math le m' nàmhaid.'
Os ise: 'Bròn orm mur fheàrr leam slàn thu.'
Os esan: 'Mur bhiodh gur bean mo mhàthair,
'S gum b'i 'n deagh-bhean Moire Mhàthair,
Dh'innsinn sgeul beag dha na mnà dhut:
Tha cuid dhiu gu modhail nàrach,
Cuid eile gun mhodh gun nàire.'

Dh'éirich mise air là'r-na-mhàrach,
'S chaidh mi mach air feadh na stràide,
Ghlac mi 'n caman 's chuir mi bàir leis,
Ghlac mi e 's gun chuir mi dhà leis,
Chuir mi cluichd air triùir a' Bhàillidh.
Chailin òig as stiùireamaiche.

'S fheàirrde banchaig buachaill' aice,
Théid e mach 'san oidhche fhrasaich,
'S cuiridh e na laoigh gu fasgadh.

(*d*) *O'n LS aig an Urr. Canon Mac 'Ill' Sheathain*

Chailin òig, an stiùir thu mì?

Latha dhomh 's mi falbh an fhàsaich,
Thachair orm an cailin donn dàna;
Thug mi dha'n eaglais air làimh i,
'S thug i mionnan mór an là sin
Nach gabhadh i gin am àite.
Cha b'fhada mar sin a bhà sin,
Nuair a ghabh mi fiabhras gràineil,
Thug mi bliadhna mhór is ràith' ann;
Thànaig i 'n ceann nan cóig ràithean,
Dhìrich i an uinneag a b'àirde,

I spent a long year and a quarter
Lying ill with the plague of fever;
One day after the fifth quarter
She climbed the stair that was highest:

Said she: 'Yon man within, how are you?'
Said he: 'I am sick and painful,
Ill for my friend, well for my foeman.'
Said she: 'If I wish you not healed, may sorrow befall me.'
Said he: 'Were not my mother a woman,
And the Virgin Mary the good one,
I'd tell you a little tale about women:
Some of them are polite and modest,
Others are rude and shameless.'

I arose on the next morning,
And went out throughout the street,
I took a shinty and struck a goal,
I took it, and struck two goals with it,
I defeated the team of the bailiff.

For dairymaid 'tis best a herdsman,
At night he'll go out when it's showery,
He will put the calves to shelter.

(*d*) *From Canon MacLean's manuscript*

Young girl, will you guide me?

One day as I walked the pasture,
The bold brown-haired lassie met me,
By hand I took her to the church,
And she swore great oaths on that day
That in my place she'd take no other.
Things were not like that for long,
When I took a nasty fever,
In which I spent a long year and a quarter;
She came at the end of five quarters,
She climbed up to the highest window,

Ghlac i ursann anns gach làimh dhi:
'Fhir tha shìos, cia mar thà thu?'
'Olc le [m'] charaid 's math le [m'] nàmhaid!'
' 'S olc leam fhìn, 's math leam slàn thu!'

Chuala Dia na briathran gràineil, [gràidheil?
Neartaich E mise 'nam shlàinte,
Chaidh mi 'nam aodach an là sin,
Ghabh mi mach air feadh na sràide,
Chunnacas clann an rìgh air fàire,
Le m' buill òir 's camain airgid;
Ghlac mi caman 's chuir mi bàin air,
Chuir mi buaidh na cluichd air Mànus,
'S nam fanainn, chuirinn a dhà air.

Shuidh mi air a' chnoc a b'àirde,
Thànaig an caile donn dàna,
Cupa dha'n fhìon anns gach làimh aic';
Chrom i a ceann 's gun ghabh i nàire,
Chrom mise e, 's gun d'rinn mi gàire.

Mur bitheadh gur bean mo mhàthair,
'S gur bean eile dh'àr gu làr i,
Dh'innsinn uirsgeul na mnà dhuibh,
Tha cuid dhiu gu ciallach nàrach,
Cuid eile gun chiall gun nàire,
Gur luaith' an gaol na ghaoth Mhàrtuinn,
No searrach a' ruith gu mhàthair,
No uan Céitein a' leum gàraidh,
No muirtiachd air leaca bàna; [bàithte.
Is tusa an cailin, is mise a h-àireach.

'S fheàirrde banchaig buachaill' aice,
Théid e mach 'san oidhche shneachda,
Paisgidh e bhanchaig 'na bhreacan,
'S cuiridh e 'n crodh-laoigh gu fasgadh—
Is cailin thusa, is buachaill' mise,
Cailin Gùithneach is buachaill' Loinneach.

She grasped the doorpost in each hand,
'You man below, how are you?'
'Bad for my friend, well for me foeman!'
'And bad for me, I'd like you healthy!'

God heard the hateful words, [loving words (?)
In my health He made me stronger,
On that day I put my clothes on,
I went out through the street,
I saw the King's children in the distance,
With silver shinties and balls golden,
I took a shinty and struck a goal,
I won the victory over Magnus,
If I'd stayed, I would have struck two on him.

I sat upon the highest hillock,
There came the bold brown-haired lassie,
Holding a cup of wine in each hand,
She bent her head, and was ashamed;
I bent mine, and gave a laugh.

Were not my mother a woman,
And she who delivered her another,
I'd tell to you a tale of women:
Some of them are wise and modest,
Others without sense and shameless,
Their love is quicker than a Martinmas gale,
Or than a foal running to its mother,
Or a May lamb a stone wall jumping,
Or a jellyfish on smooth white rocks; [immersed
You are the lass, I am her herdsman. rocks

A dairymaid should have a herdsman,
At night he'll go out when it's snowing,
He'll fold his dairymaid in his plaid,
He'll put the milk-cows into shelter—
You are a lass, I am a herdsman,
A malicious lass, a handsome herdsman.[?]

XLVIII

Bha mis' a raoir air an àirigh

(*a*) *Bean Phluim a' seinn*

Hù hoireann ó, hù hoireann ó (solo)
Hù hoireann ó, hù hoireann ó (tutti)

Bha mis' a raoir air an àirigh,
Hì hó éileadh, ho hoireann ó,

Bha mis' a raoir air an àirigh,
Hù hoireann ó, hù hoireann ó,

Cha b'ann ri aighear a bhà mi
Hì hó éileadh, ho hoireann ó.

Cha b'ann ri aighear a bhà mi,
Hù hoireann ó, hù hoireann ó,

Ach ri smaointinn ort, a ghràidhein,
Hì hó éileadh, etc.

Ach ri smaointinn ort, a ghràidhein,
Hù hoireann, etc.

Shaoil mi nach cumadh muir làn thu,
'S nach cumadh lìonadh no tràghadh,
'S nach mùth' chumadh an té bhàn thu—
Dh'aithnghinn a cuid cruidh air àirigh,
No a cuid ghearran gu deanamh àitich.

Hù hoireann ó, hù hoireann ó, (tutti)
Hù hoireann ó, hù hoireann ó, (solo)
Hù hoireann ó, hù hoireann ó, (tutti)

Bha mi raoir air àirigh luachrach,
'S dh'fhairich me fear làimhe fuaireadh
Sgaoileadh a bhreacain mu'n cuairt dhiom,
Càradh nan arm an taobh shuas dhiom;
Bhuail mi sad air 's thilg mi bhuam e,
Dh'aithnich mi nach b'e mo luaidh e.

XLVIII

Last night I was at the sheiling

(*a*) *Mrs. Mary Morrison singing*

(*For tune, see p.* 289)

Last night I was at the sheiling,

Last night I was at the sheiling,

Happiness I was not feeling,

Happiness I was not feeling,

But thinking of you, beloved,

But thinking of you, beloved,

I thought the high tide would not keep you,
That flowing or ebbing would not keep you,
That neither would the fair girl keep you—
I'd know her cattle at a sheiling,
Or her geldings for cultivating.

Last night I was at a rushy sheiling,
And I felt some cold-handed person
Spreading his plaid about me,
Putting his weapons beside me;
I struck him a blow and threw him from me,
I recognized it was not my lover.

Fhleasgaich, ma théid thu 'n taigh-òsda,
Na bi 'd mhisgeir, na bi 'd phòiteir,
'S na bi ri ceannach an stòpa—
Na na botail bheaga bhrònach,
Gabh an togsaid mhór 's gu leòir innt'!

Hù hoireann ó, hù hoireann ó (tutti)
Hù hoireann ó, hù hoireann ó (solo)
Hù hoireann ó, hù hoireann ó (tutti)

Fhleasgaich a dhìreas Gleann Cuaiche
Bheir soiridh bhuamsa gu Ruairi,
'S innis dha gu bheil mo luaidh air,
'S innis dha gu bheil mi fallain,
'S gun do chuir mi 'n geamhradh farum,
'S gun do thiarainn mi o'n earrach,
'S samhradh grianach a' chruidh-bhainne,
Gu foghar nan sguab a ghearradh.

Nighean donn an riobain uaine,
Cha dug 's cha dobhair mi fuath riut,
Gus an càirear anns an uaimh mi,
'S sgaoilear an ùir mu'n cuairt dhiom.

Hù hoireann ó, hù hoireann ó, (tutti)
Hù hoireann ó, hù hoireann ó, (solo)
Hù hoireann ó, hù hoireann ó. (tutti)

(*b*) *Bho'n LS aig Dòmhnall Mac an t-Saoir*

Chaidil mi a raoir air an àirigh,
Hù hoireann ò, hù hoireann ó,

Cha b'ann ri aighear a bhà mi,
Hi ù éile, ò hoireann ó.

Cha b'ann ri aighear a bhà mi,
Hù hoireann, etc.

Ach 'gat ionndrainn fhéin, a ghràidhein,
Smaointinn nach cumadh muir làn thu,
Nach mùth' chumadh lìonadh no tràghadh,
Nach mùth' chumadh an té bhàn thu,
Fhad' 's a choiteachadh dà ràmh i.

Young man, if the inn you enter,
Don't be a drunkard, don't be a toper,
Don't be buying little measures,
Or the little miserable bottles,
Take the big barrel with plenty in it!

Young man who ascends Glen Quoich,
Taking greeting from me to Rory,
And tell him that I love him,
Tell him that I'm healthy,
That I've got over the winter,
And I have survived the springtime,
And sunny summer of milk-cattle,
To autumn, time of reaping.

Brown-haired lass of the green ribbon,
I never did nor shall I hate you,
Until I am placed in the grave,
And earth is scattered around me.

(*b*) *Version from the Donald MacIntyre MS.*

Last night I slept at the sheiling,

Happiness I was not feeling,

Happiness I was not feeling,

But missing you yourself, beloved,
Thinking that high tide would not keep you,
Neither would flowing nor ebbing keep you,
Neither would the fair girl keep you,
As long as two oars would row her.[1]

[1] i.e. your little boat.

Chaidil mi raoir air a' bhuailidh,
Dh'fhairich mi crith, 's cha chrith fuachd e
Dh'fhairich mi grìs, 's cha ghrìs ruaidhe,
Dh'fhairich mi fear làimhe fuaire,
'S gliogadaich nan crios 'gam fuasgladh,
'S bhith cur nan arm an taobh shuas dhiom;
Dh'aithnich mi nach b'e mo luaidh e,
Cha b'e dhùisgeadh as mo shuain e,
Sgaoileadh e a bhreacan air m'uachdar—
Bhuail mi breab is thilg mi bhuam e,
Fear beag na fiasaige ruaidhe,
Thug cùl a chinn lag 'san luaithre!
Thuirt e rium gu robh mi duathail,
Thuirt mi ris nach robh mi suarach.

Fhleasgaich a dhìreas am bealach,
Cha chuir mise trom air t'eallach,
Ach thu ghiùlain mo chiad beannachd
'S fios dha'n àit' am bheil mo leannan,
Innse dha gu bheil mi fallain,
Gun do chuir mi an geamhradh fairis,
Gun do thiarainn mi ro'n earrach,
Rànaig mi samhradh a' bhainne,
Gu foghar nan sguab a ghearradh.

XLIX

Chaidh mi 'na ghleannain as t-fhoghar

Bean Nìll a' seinn

Hoireann ó, hi rì, hò ró,
Hoireann ó, hi rì, hò ró.

Chaidh mi 'na ghleannain as t-fhoghar,
Hoireann ó, hi rì, ho ro ho,

Chaidh mi 'na ghleannain as t-fhoghar,
Hoireann ó, hi rì, hó ró,

Last night I slept at the cowfold,
I felt a tremor, and not from shivering,
I felt gooseflesh, but not from erysipelas,
I perceived a man with a cold hand,
And the noise of belts being loosened,
And of weapons being put beside me;
I realized it was not my lover,
He wouldn't wake me from my slumber,
He would spread his plaid above me—
I gave a kick and threw him from me,
A little red-bearded fellow,
The back of his head made a pit in the ashes!
He said to me that I was stubborn,
I said to him I wasn't disreputable.

Young man who ascends the pass,
I will not add to your burden,
But carry my hundred blessings,
And news, to the place where is my lover,
Telling him that I am healthy,
That I have got over the winter,
That I have got through the springtime,
And have reached the milky summer,
Into autumn, time of reaping.

XLIX

I went into the small glen in autumn

Mrs. Neil Campbell singing

(*For tune, see p.* 290)

I went into the small glen in autumn,

I went into the small glen in autumn,

Thilg mi na cruinn, rinn mi 'n taghadh,
Hoireann ó, hi rì, hò ro ho,

Thilg mi na cruinn, rinn mi 'n taghadh,
Hoireann ó, hi rì, hò ró,

Ghabh mi 'n t-òigeir seòlta seadhach,
Oganach gun tòir 'na dheoghaidh,
Nì thu cruach is meall as t-fhoghair,
Théid thu dha'n bheinn am bi 'm faghaid,
Le do ghearra-choin meanbh-choin laghach,
Leat am fiadh air thùs na greigheadh.

Hoireann ó, hi rì, hò ró,
Hoireann ó, hi rì, hò ró.

Siod mo leannan, 's fhada bhuat e,
Cha b'e lurga bhreac o'n luath i,
Geal o'n teine, dearg o'n fhuachd thu.

Hoireann ó, hi rì, hò ró,
Hoireann ó, hi rì, hò ró.

Siod mo leannan, 's bòidheach riut e,
Coisiche na h-oidhche flich' thu,
Coisiche na h-oidhche faid' thu,
'S ruigea tu 'n t-àit' am biodh mise,
Leaba bheag an cùl na ciste,
Siod an leaba am biodh na gifhtean,
Ge bè rannsaicheadh gun fhiosd i.

Hoireann ó, hi rì, hò ró,
Hoireann ó, hi rì, hò ró.

'S binne liom na fuaim na h-aibhne
Fuaim do ghunna, do ghada, 's do ghoidein
Fuaim do ghoidein far na droighnich.

Hoireann ó, hi rì, hò ró,
Hoireann ó, hi rì, hò ró.

I cast lots, I made a choice,

I cast lots, I made a choice,

I took the young man skilled and sensible,
A youth without pursuit after him;
You'll make cornstacks in the autumn,
You'll go to the hill to join the hunt
With your nice little terriers,
The deer at the head of the herd is yours.

That's my lover, he's far from you,
Not a speckled shank from the ashes,
White from the fire, red from the cold are you.

That's my lover, to you he's handsome,
Walker of the wet night are you,
Walker of the long night are you,
You'd reach the place where I would be,
A little bed behind the coffer,
That's the bed where the gifts were,
Whoever searched it secretly,

Sweeter to me than the sound of the river
The noise of your gun, your ramrod, and your withy,
The sound of your withy off the blackthorn.

L

Tha Caolas eadar mi is Iain

(*a*) *Ceit Ruairi Iain Bhàin a' seinn*

Tha caolas eadar mi is Iain,
Hao ri hiu ò, hao ri e hó,

Tha caolas eadar mi is Iain,
O hao ri rì, hì ho ró na,
Hì hoireann ó, hao ri e hó.

Cha chaol a th'ann, ach cuan domhain,
Hao ri hiu ò, etc.

Cha chaol a th'ann, ach cuan domhain,
O hao ri rì, etc.

Truagh nach tràghadh e fo latha,
Nach biodh ann ach loch no abhainn,
Fiach am faighinn a dhol tarsainn
Far a bheil mo leannan falaich;
Truagh nach mi 's an t-òg gasda
Am mullach beinne guirme caise
Gun duine beò bhith 'nar faisge,
Sinn air pòsadh aig an altair,
Gun an còrr a bhith fa-near dhuinn
Fhad 's a bhios sinn beò no air maireann.
Théid mi nis a choimhead m'athar
'S na bheil beò a shliochd mo sheanar,
'S innsidh mi dhaibh mar a thachair.
O hao ri rì, hì ho ró na,
Hì hoireann ó, hao ri e hó.

Thuirt Ruairi Iain Bhàin, athair Ceit, rium anns a' bhiadhna 1943, 'Bha ise as a dheoghaidh, ach cha robh esan air a son. 'S i rinn an t-òran; bha ise 'san eilein.'

L

A sound there is between me and Ian

(*a*) *Mrs. Buchanan singing*

(*For tune, see p.* 292)

A sound there is between me and Ian,

A sound there is between me and Ian,

No sound it is, but a deep ocean,

No sound it is, but a deep ocean,

Would that it ebbed before the day,
That it were only a lake or river,
For me to try to get across
Over to meet my secret lover;
Alas that I and the fine youth
Were not on the top of a steep blue mountain,
Without a living creature near us,
Having been married at the altar,
With nothing else upon our minds,
As long as we were amongst the living.
I'll go now to see my father,
And those living of my cousins,
And I'll tell to them what has happened.

Ruairi Iain Bhàin, the singer's father, told me in 1943, that the woman who made this song was in love with Iain, but he was not in love with her. She was in the island when she made the song.

(*b*) *Mar a bha e aig Anna Nìll Ruaidh, ann an Ceap Breatann*

Tha caolas eadar mi is Iain,
Hi hu a hao ri a hu,
Cha chaol a th'ann, ach cuan domhain,
O hao ri rì rì ho ro,
Ho hi hoireann ho, hao ri ho hù.
Cha chaol a th'ann, ach cuan domhain,
Hi hu a, etc.
'S truagh nach traghadh e gu latha,
'S bhithinn-sa 'n Gleann Dubh mo laithean; (?)
'S truagh nach robh mis' is tusa, fhleasgaich,
Aig bun nan craobh fo bhàrr nam preasan,
'S truagh nach robh mise 's an t-òg gasda
Am mullach beinne guirme caise,
Gun duine beò bhith 'nar n-aisge,
Ach dall is bodhar is bacach;
'S thigeamaid am màireach dhachaigh,
Mar 's gum pòsamaid o'n altair.

'S truagh nach mise 's tusa, ghràidhein,
'N eilein ciùin mara nach tràghadh,
Gun sgoth gun bhiaorlainn gun bhàta,
Gun saor a dheanadh an càradh,
Ach coite beag is dà ràmh air.

'S ged bu nighean do Mhac Cailein mi,
'S dha'n Iarla Aondrainn 's dha'n Diùc Arannach,
O! 's miosa na sin mar thachair dhomh,
Bothan beag is eòrlaig arain dhomh,
Na maoir a' togail a' ghearraidh dhiom.

(*b*) *Version taken down from Mrs. Neil MacInnis, Cape Breton*

A sound there is between me and Ian,

No sound it is, but the deep ocean,

No sound it is, but the deep ocean,

Pity it ebbs not until day
And I would be in the Black Glen for my days,
Alas, young man, that you and I were not
At the foot of the trees beneath the bushes,
Alas that I and the fine youth
Were not on top of a steep blue mountain,
Without a living creature near us,
Except for one blind, deaf, and crippled;
And we would come home tomorrow,
As if we were married at the altar.

Alas that you and I, love, were not
On a quiet sea island, isolated,
Without a skiff or boat or galley,
Without a carpenter to mend them,
But only a little two-oared rowboat.

Though I were Argyll's daughter,
Or the Earl of Antrim's, or the Duke of Arran's,—
O! worse than that has befallen me,
A little hut and a bannock,
And the bailiffs lifting the rent off me!

LI

Dh'éirich mi moch madainn Chéitein

(*a*) *Anna agus Calum Aonghais Chaluim a' seinn*

Dh'éirich mi moch madainn Chéitein,
Hill ir inn is hóg a bhó,
Thug mi gu siubhal an t-sléibhe,

Iù na hi rì ri a ho,
Ho hì o ho lebh ó, hi o,
Hóg a bhó.

Thug mi gu siubhal an t-sléibhe,
Hill ir inn is hóg a bhó,
Còta ruadh mu leath mo shléisne,
Iù na hi, etc.
Còta ruadh mu leath mo shléisne,
Hill ir inn, etc.

Criosan caol-dubh air mo léinidh,
Chunnaig mi bhuam baidean spréidhe
Air tulaich ghuirm, is iad gun éirigh,
'S an cailin donngheal 'nan déidh sin;
Ghreas mi chas 's gun chas mi 'n éibhe
'Dean fuireach 's gum faighinn sgeula!
Bheil fallaineachd aca 'n Sléibhte?
Aig Dòmhnall Gorm, laogh mo chéille?
Chuala mi gun d'rinn e réiteach
Ri nighean Iarla nan geurlann,
Ri ogha biatach na féille—
Nan cluinninn gum b'fhior an sgeula,
Dhòirtinn fuil is ghearrainn féithean
'S bheirinn sic a cinn o chéile,
'S ghabhainn an t-aiseag 'na dhéidh sin
Mach o Mhórair nan geugan,
A steach gu Uibhist a' réidhlein!'

LI

I rose early on a May morning

(*a*) *Annie and Calum Johnston singing*

(*For tune, see p.* 293)

I rose early on a May morning,

I took to walking the hillside,

I took to walking the hillside,

A russet coat halfway down my thigh,

A russet coat halfway down my thigh,

A slender black belt around my shirt,
I saw in the distance a herd of cattle,
Lying down on a green hillock,
With a light brown-haired lass looking after them.
I hastened my footsteps and raised the cry
'Wait, so I can get the story,
Are they well in Sleat?
Is Donald Gorm, my love, well?
I heard that he had been betrothed to
The daughter of the sharp-sworded Earl,
To the grandson of the hospitaller;
If I heard the tale confirmed
I would shed blood and sever sinews,
I would tear her scalp to pieces,
And after that I'd sail across
Out to Morar of the branches,
In to Uist of the plains.'

Réitich mo leannan is té eile,
Gu cuireadach, cuachach, coireach,
Thigeadh e nuair smalteadh choinneal,
Dh'fhalbhadh e mun goir an coileach;
'S gu dé mo ghnothach, a Cholla,
Coimhead air fear donn gun onoir,
A rinn mo leaba an cois an doruis,
Rinn e sin, is gnìomh bu dona,
Thug e mo bhràisde as mo bhrollach,
Thug e bhuam mo chrios 's mo sporan,
'S mar sin 's mo phaidirean corrach.

Gu dé mo ghnothach 'na choille,
A' buain chraobh no cnò no sheilich?
Shaorainn, shaorainn, shaorainn fhathast,
Shaorainn an oidhche gu latha,
Gu robh mi 'nam gruagaich fhathast,
Cìreadh mo ghruaigeadh 's 'ga ceangal
Air lic luim os cionn taigh m'athar.

(*b*) *An teacs aig Mgr. Ailein Dòmhnallach*

Hi li rinn is hó ga bho-o
Dh'éirich mi moch madainn Chéitein,
'N driùchd air an fhiar, ghrian ag éirigh,
Dhìrich mi guala an t-sléibhe,
Chunna mi bhuam baidean spréidhe,
A' bhanarach fhéin 'gam feurach,
Slatag 'na làimh as an déidh sin,
An còta ruadh mu leth nan sléisdean.
Ghrios mo chas 's gun chas mi 'n fhéithe,
Dh'fhiosraich mi dhi, an robh i 'n Éirinn?
No 'n robh fallaineachd an Sléibhte,
No 'n d'rinn Dòmhnall Gorm réiteach?
Rìgh ! ma rinn, nar mheala fhéin e,
Ged nach b'ann le m' ragha céile,
Nighean Fir Fionndruim Éirinn
'S nighean fir fialaidh nan ceudan.

My lover's betrothed to another woman,
Alluring, curling-haired, deceiving;
He used to come when the candle was smoored,
He used to leave when the cock crew.
What have I to do, o Colla,
With watching a brown-haired man without honour,
Who made my bed beneath the door,
He did that, and he did a worse deed,
He took my broach from off my bosom,
He took from me my belt and my purse,
And likewise my knotted rosary.

What have I to do in his wood,
Picking fruit or nuts or sallows?
I would be free, I would be free, I would still be free,
I would be free from the night till the day,
I would be still a maiden,
Combing and binding my tresses
On a bare stone above the house of my father.

(*b*) *Version collected* (? *on Eriskay*) *by Fr. Allan McDonald*

I rose early one May morning,
The dew on the grass, as it was dawning,
I climbed up on the hillside's shoulder,
I saw a cattle herd in the distance
Being pastured by the milkmaid,
With a little rod in her hand behind them,
The russet coat halfway down her thighs,
My foot hastened, I approached the quagmire,
I asked her, had she been in Ireland?
Or were the people in Sleat healthy,
Or had Domhnall Gorm made a betrothal?
My God! if he did, may he not enjoy it,
Though it were not my choice of spouse,
The Earl of Antrim's daughter from Ireland,
Daughter of one who entertained hundreds.

Dé mo ghnothach-sa, a Cholla,
Choimhead air té ghorm gun onoir,
Nach d'rinn ris na h-uaislean labhairt,
Leath-shùil oirre 's i ag amharc,
An t-sùil eile an impis gabhail!
Dé mo ghnothach-sa, a Cholla,
Choimhead air té ghorm gun onair,
Rinn i mo leab' aig an dorus,
Thug i bhuam mo chrios 's mo sporan,
M'iuchraichean 's mo fhrìne brollaich.

Shaorainn, shaorainn, shaorainn fhathast,
Shaorainn an oidhche gu latha,
Gu bheil mi 'nam ghruagaich fhathast,
Cìreadh mo chuailein 's 'ga cheangal,
Air lic luim os cionn taigh m'athar.

LII

Tha an t-uisg', tha 'n ceò, air na beannan

Calum Aonghais Chaluim a' seinn

Tha 'n t-uisg', tha 'n ceò air na beannan,
Hao rì 's na hao ri ho ró,
Tha sneachda mór ann le gaillinn,

Ho lebh o hao ri iù ò,
Ró ho hao ri ri u bhi,
Hó na hì ho ró bha hao, ri ho ro o.

Tha sneachda mór ann le gaillinn,
Hao rì 's na, etc.
'S fheudar dhomh brògan a cheannach
Ho lebh o hao, etc.
Cha b'éiginn leam, 's e bu mhath leam,
Fhir a dh'fhalbh Di-Luain, an air' ort!
Fhir ud thall an comhair a' bhealaich
Cha chuir mise trom air t'eallach,
Giùlain bhuamsa mo chiad bheannachd,

What business is it of mine, Colla,
To look upon a grey hag without honour,
Who has never to the gentry spoken,
With one of her eyes regarding,
The other on the point of kindling!
What business is it of mine, Colla,
To look upon a grey hag without honour?
She made my bed beside the door,
She took my belt and my purse from me,
My keys, and the pin on my bosom.

I would be free, I would be free,
I would be free, night and day,
I am still a maiden,
Combing and binding my tresses
On a bare rock above the house of my father.

LII

Rain and mist are on the mountains

Calum Johnston singing

(*For tune, see p.* 296)

Rain and mist are on the mountains,

Heavy snow is there with tempest,

Heavy snow is there with tempest,

Shoes must I purchase,

I need not, but I'd like to do it.
Monday's traveller, take care,
Yon man over at the pass,
On you I'll put no heavy burden,
Carry from me a hundred blessings,

Bheir soiridh bhuamsa gu m' leannan,
Innis dha gu bheil mi fallain,
'S gun do chuir mi an geamhradh farum,
Gun do thiarainn mi bho'n earrach
Gu samhradh bàn a' chruidh-bhainne,
Gu foghar nan sguab a ghearradh.

Ceathramhnan eile, a réir Màiri nighean Alasdair

A cheist leughadair nan duilleag,
Bheireadh sgeul a baile Lunnainn,
Le each cruidheach nan ceum cuimir,
Òganaich o thìr a' mhurain,
'S o Shléibhte riabhaich na duillich,
'S mise nach eil suarach umad—
Nam biodh, bhiodh mu'n chruinne. . . . . .

LIII

Craobhan ó hòireann o ho

(*a*) *Anna Mhìcheil Nìll a' seinn*

Craobhan ó, hòireann o ho, (solo)
Craobhan ó, hòireann o ho, (tutti)

Sneachda 'ga chur air na beannan,
Craobhan ó, hòireann o ho,
Ghaoth 'ga reothadh ris na crannan;
Truagh nach robh mi 'm uiseig fhiadhaich,
Mór mo dhùil gun dig dha m' iarraidh
Teachdaireachd o mhac an iarla,
Gille 's litir, each is dìollaid,
Tà, cha n-fhaigh e mi am bliadhna.

Ochóin, a chiall, bidh mi brònach,
Bidh m'athair air tì mo phòsaidh
Ri fear odhar bodhar breòiteach,

Take my greetings to my sweetheart,
Tell to him that I am healthy,
And that I've survived the winter,
And that I've got through the springtime,
To reach summer of milk cattle,
And the autumn, time for reaping harvest.

Concluding lines, according to Màiri nighean Alasdair
(Canon MacLean's MS.)

O love, reader of book pages,
Who'd bring from London town a story,
On a well-shod, neatly stepping palfrey,
O youth from the land of bent-grass,
And from Sleat, striped and leafy,
I indeed do not despise you,
If I did, I would the whole world.

LIII

Snow has fallen on the mountains

(*a*) *Mrs. James MacNeil singing*

(*For tune, see p.* 299)

Snow has fallen on the mountains,

To the trees by wind it's frozen—
I'm no wild lark, 'tis a pity,
Great my hope there will come to seek me
From the son of the earl a message,
A lad and a letter, a horse and a saddle,
Nevertheless, he'll not get me this year.

Alas, my dear, I shall be sorrowful,
My father will be set on marrying me
To a dun, deaf, broken-down fellow,

Ri fear dall nach léir dha a bhrògan;
Bheir mi dà shlait diag 'na chòta,
Seiche mairt a chur dha bhrógan.

Mhic Dhòmhnaill Duibh a Loch Abar,
Siod, a Rìgh! nach mi bha agad!
Eadar do dhà làimh gu madainn,
Chuirinn geall gu faighinn cadal,
Ge bè àit' am bheil do leaba,
Am bun nan craobh no 'm bàrr nam baideal.

(*b*) *An teacs aig Dòmhnall Mac an t-Saoir*

Falbhan ò, hoireann o ho

Eudail a Rìgh! bu mhi brònag,
'S mi dol 'na chlachain Di-Dòmhnaich,
Cha n-ann le m' raghainn a dh'òigeir,
Le fear odhar, bodhar, breòite,
Le luidealach dubh gun eòlas!
'S mutha do cheann na cruach mhònadh,
'S caoile do chasan na 'm feòrnain,
Théid seiche an tairbh mhóir 'nad brògan,
Théid am bolla 'nad bhonnach còmhla,
Cha dean dà shlait dhiag dhut còta!

Fhir ud thall an còir nam bearraidhean,
'M faca tu mo chéile falaich, *na*
Fear osain duibh 's nam bròg barrallach,
Stiùramaich' air luing nan crannag thu,
'S mi gun earbadh siod ri d' gheallaimh
Long mhór a stiùireadh ri gaillinn
Fhad 's a mhaireadh bior dh'a darach,
No buill chaola chruaidhe theanna.

Mhic Dhòmhnaill duibh a Lochabar,
'S truagh, a Rìgh! nach mi bha agad
Eadar do dhà làimh gu latha,
Ge bè àite am bheil do leaba,
Am bun a' chroinn no 'm bàrr a baidein,
No air morghan gorm an aigeil.

To a blind man who can't see his shoes,
It will take me twelve yards of cloth to make his coat,
And a cow's hide to make his footwear.

Cameron of Lochiel from Lochaber,
If only, my God, that you had me
Between your two arms till morning!
I would sleep, I wager,
Wherever your bed may be,
At the foot of a tree or on the top of towers.

(*b*) *Text communicated by Donald MacIntyre*

My dear God! I am so wretched,
Going to the church on Sunday
Not with the youth I would have chosen,
But with a dun, deaf, broken-down fellow,
With a dirty ignorant lounger—
Your head's bigger than a peat-stack,
Your legs are thinner than a grass-blade,
A big bull's hide goes to make your footwear,
A boll of meal into your bannock,
Twelve yards of cloth a coat won't make you!

O yonder man around the ridges,
Have you seen my secret lover?
With his black hose and shoes with latchets,
On the masted ship a steersman,
To your white hand I would be trusting
To steer a great ship in a tempest,
As long as a piece of her oak-wood lasted,
Or her hard tight ropes so slender.

Cameron of Lochiel from Lochaber,
Alas, my God! you didn't have me
Between your two arms till morning,
Where your bed was, was no matter,
Beneath a tree or on a tower top.
Or on the grey sand of the ocean.

Ged tha mi 'nam uiseig riabhaich,
'S mór mo dhùil gun dig dham' iarraidh
Teachdaireachd bho mhac an iarla,—
B'annsa liom Mac Gabhra riabhaich
Dha'm biodh na coin mhóra strìochdte,
'S gearrain gu treobhadh na h-iadhair'.

LIV

Dh'éirich mi 's cha robh mi sunndach

Anna agus Calum Aonghais Chaluim a' seinn

Hao i o challa, hùg éile
Hao rì rì a bhó
Hó hi rì ri iùrabh o ro.

Dh'éirich mi 's cha robh mi sunndach,
Ghabh mi sìos mu shrath na dùthchadh,
M'eudail a thànaig o m' chùlaibh,
Marcraich' na fàlaire crùidhich,
Chumadh strian is stiorap dlùth ris;
M'eudail an t-uachdaran cliùiteach,
Nach deanadh an tuath a spùilleadh,
A thilleadh an crodh o'n chùnntais,
A bheireadh air an caoirich cùmhnadh.
Tha mis' an seo air mo ghlùinean
Ag iarraidh achanaidh, nam b'fhiù mi,
Saoghal fad' thoirt dhut, is ùine,
Mun déid thu 'n làthair na cùnntais.

Ochóin, a chiall, mo chiad thruaighe,
Nach robh mise far bu dual dhomh
Eadar Ciorcabost is Ruadal;
Cha b'e mo bhiadh breacag shuarach,
Cha b'e mo dheoch bùrn an fhuarain,
Bainne crodh-laoigh, 's e gun truailleadh,
Fìon 'ga ligeadh, beòir a cuachan,
Uisge-beatha nan Gall gruamach.

Though I am a brownish skylark,
Much I hope there comes to seek me
A messenger from the earl's son—
I'd prefer the son of swarthy Gabhra,
To whom the great dogs are obedient,
And the ponies for ploughing the fallow.

LIV

I arose, I was not happy

Annie and Calum Johnston singing

(*For tune, see p.* 301)

I arose, I was not happy,
I went down the country valley;
My darling 'twas that came behind me
Rider of the well-shod palfrey,
Who'd hold rein and stirrup tightly;
The famous chieftain was my darling,
A man who'd not despoil his tenants,
Who'd turn their cattle from the accounting,
Who their sheep-stock would be sparing.
I am here upon my knees,
Supplicating, if I deserve it,
That to you long life be given
Before you go to your accounting.

Alas, my dear, 'tis my first sorrow
That I was not in my own district
Between Kirkabost and Rodel;
My food would not be a miserable pancake,
My drink would not be cold spring water—
But calving cows' milk, unpolluted,
Wine from casks, and beer from goblets,
Whisky of the gloomy strangers.

Ged tha mise 'n seo air t'àrainn,
'S e mo dhùthaich fhéin as àille,
O bhonn a lagain gu a bràighe,
Gu Cille Moire nan àrmunn.

Hao o challa, hùg éile
Hao rì ri a bhó
Hó hi rì ri iurabh o ro
Hao rì ri a bhó
Hó hi rì ri iurabh o ro.

LV

Hùgan nan gù, théid mi dhachaigh

(*a*) *Màiri Mhìcheil Nìll a' seinn*

Hòireann ò, ho hù ro hò,
Hòireann éileadh, ho hi rì,
Hi rì ho ru bhì, hò ro hò.

Hùgan nan gù, théid mi dhachaigh,
Gu baile bòidheach a' chlachain,
Far an d'fhuair mi m'òg-altrum
Air bainne cìoch 's air fìon frasach,
Lasgairean a loisgeas fùdair,
Bheireadh air an ianlaith spùilleadh;
M'eudail mhór 's a luaidh an domhain,
Taobh a' chraobh cho blàth 's cho snodhach,
'S na taobh craobh nan caoran coimheach;
Gheall mi fhìn a bhith 'n siod romhad,
Buain an fhraoich 's a' sìor-bhuain chnothan;
Cha n-iarrainn bàta no barca,
Cha bhithinn-sa feitheamh ach do chasan.

Though I'm here around your precincts,
More beautiful is my own country,
From valley bottom to its uplands,
To Kilmuir of the stalwarts.

LV

Cheerfully I'll go homewards

(*a*) *Miss Mary Gillies singing*

(*For tune, see p.* 302)

Cheerfully I'll go homewards
To the pretty village with the church,
Where I was reared in my childhood
On breast milk and flowing wine;
There, are young men who'll fire gunpowder,
Who'll despoil the bird flock.
My darling, my love of all the world,
Approach the tree so tender and sappy,
Approach not the tree with strange berries,
I promised to be there before you
Gathering nuts and cutting heather;
I would not ask for a boat or a barque,
I would only be awaiting your footsteps.

(*b*) *Air dòigh eile, a Uibhist*

Hòireann ó ho hóro hó a,
Hóireann éile, hó hi rì,
Hì iù ra bhi, ó hó a.

Cha n-fhan mi 'm Mórair na's fhaide,
Hùgan nan gù, théid mi dhachaigh
Gu baile bòidheach nan clachan,
Cha n-iarr mi long mhór gu m'aiseag,
Bàta no biaorlainn na barca,
Gearraidh mi bheinn air a tarsainn,
Sgoiltidh mi mhòinteach fo m' chasan,
Ruigidh mi Rubh' Àird an aisig,
Far an d'fhuair mi gu h-òg m'altrum,
M'àrach cha bu shàile phartan,
Ach bainne cìoch nam ban basgheal.

LVI

Stoirm nan gobhar ri taobh na h-abhann

Bean Nìll a' seinn

Stoirm nan gobhar ri taobh na h-abhann,
'S e mheaghail a dhùisg mi.

Cha n-e uiseag a dhùisg mise,

Air fa ra lail hò ró,
Stoirm nan gobhar ri taobh na h-abhann,
'S e mheaghail a dhùisg mi.

Ach còmhl' an taigh mhóir 'ga bristeadh
Air fa ra, etc.
Còmhl' an taigh mhóir 's còmhla a' chitsinn
Còmhla nan ochd glas air fichead;

(b) A Uist version, from Donald MacIntyre's MS.

I will not stay in Morar longer,
Cheerfully I will go homewards
To the pretty village with the churches;
I will not ask for a ship to ferry me,
A boat or galley or barque,
I will cut across the hillside,
I will rend the moor beneath my feet,
I will reach Rubha Aird-an-aisig,
Where I was reared in my childhood
Not on the bree of green crabs,
But on the breast milk of white-palmed women.

LVI

The noise of the goats beside the river

Mrs. Neil Campbell singing

(*For tune, see p.* 303)

Refrain: The noise of the goats beside the river,
The bleating has awakened me.

It was not a lark that woke me

But the door of the big house being broken,

The door of the big house and of the kitchen,
The door of twenty eight locks;

Dh'fhiadhaich m'athair mi dha'n chùltaigh
'S cha b'ann gus mo thochradh chùnntais,
Ach 'gam chartadh as an dùthaich;
Chum mi Iain donn a dhìth air,
Iain bhig, a chiall 's a nàire
Cha n-ionntach mi fhìn 'gad thàladh
'S mac dhomh fhìn thu, 's mac dha m' bhràthair,
'S ogha beag dà uair dha m' mhàthair.
'S truagh nach mise bh'ann an Éirinn
Fo chlacha troma nach éirinn,
'S mi 'm màireach a' dol dha'n t-seisein
'S gura gann tha luchd mo leithsgeil.

LVII

Tha 'n crodh an diu dol air imprig

Penny Aonghais 'ic Raghnaill a' seinn

Ho ro laithill ó
Ho ri ho ro ho ill ir inn is hó gù
Ill ir inn is hó gù.

Tha 'n crodh an diu dol air imprig,
Ho ro, etc.
Dol a dh'iche fiar na cilleadh;
Ho ro, etc.
Thug sibh bhuam na bha agam,
Ho ro, etc.
Ràna mi taigh mór a' ghlinne,
Teine mór is ùrlar sguabte,
Seuraichean seachad mu'n cuairt ann . . .

My father invited me to the back room,
Not to count me out my dowry,
But to expel me from the district.
I kept brown-haired Iain from him,
Little Iain, my love, my darling,
No wonder that I sing your lullaby,
You are my son, you are my brother's,
Grandchild twice unto my mother;
Pity 'tis I was not in Ireland
Under heavy stones a-lying—
Tomorrow I go to the kirk session,
Few there'll be there to defend me.

LVII

The cattle today are being shifted

Sung by Mrs. A. J. MacLellan

(*For tune, see p.* 304)

The cattle today are being shifted,

Going to eat the grass of the churchyard,

You've taken my possession from me;

I reached the big house of the glen,
A big fire and a swept floor,
With chairs all around there . . .

LVIII

Mo shùil silteach, mo chridhe trom

Ceit Dhunnchaidh a' seinn

Hao ri rì 's na hi hoireann ó,
Ro ho hì o hì o hu ò.

Mo shùil silteach, mo chridhe trom,

O ho hì o hì o hu ò,
Hao ri rì 's na hi hoireann ó,
Ro ho hì hì o hu ò.

Sac air m'anail, cha tog mi fonn,
O ho hì, etc.
Cha tog fonn, cha n-éirich e liom,
Mu'n òg bhuidhe chamlagach dhonn
Dh'fhalbh an dé air bharraibh nan tonn,
Cha b'e 'n coite corrach do mhiann,
Long nan crannag daingeann fo dìon.

Sheòl am bàta fairis a null,
Sgiobadh oirre dh'fhearaibh mo rùin,
Fear nam mìogshuil meallach air stiùir,
'S cairt 'na làimh 's e dianamh a h-iùil;
Sealgair féidh thu 'm beannan a' chùirn,
Laoigh bhric bhallaich, choilich nan craobh,
'N eala bhàin as binne gu ciùil
'S an ròin mhaoil o aodann an tiùrr.

Sheòl am bàta fairis o thìr,
Bha luchd oirre a nìcheannan daor
Do dh'òr dearg, 's do dh'airgead an rìgh.

Tha mo leannan 'sa bhail' ud thall,
Rìgh ma thà, nach digeadh e nall?
O, 's ann riut a laighinn gu teann,
O, 's ann bhuat a dh'éirinn gun mheang,
Leabaidh rìomhach, cluasag fo'r ceann.

LVIII

My eye is tearful, heavy my heart

Kate MacDonald singing

(*For tune, see p.* 306)

My eye is tearful, heavy my heart,

My breath is caught, I'll not sing a song,

I will not succeed, I'll not sing a song
About the fair brown curling-haired youth,
Who yesterday left on the tops of the waves,
Your wish was not an unsteady boat,
But a ship with masts, watertight and strong.

The ship has sailed yonder across,
A crew on her of men I love,
He of the smiling eyes at her helm,
A compass in his hand as he lays the course;
Hunter of deer in the hill of cairns,
Of the blackcock and the speckled fawn,
Of the white swan which sweetest sings,
Of the smooth seal from the foreshore.

The ship has sailed across from the land,
With a cargo of precious things,
Of the king's silver, and red gold.

My love is in yonder town,
My God, if he is, would he not come o'er here?
Closely with thee would I lie,
Unharmed from thee would I rise,
From a fine bed, with a pillow beneath our heads.

LIX

Chì mi ghrian 's i falbh gu siùbhlach

(*a*) *Màiri Iain Choinnich a' seinn*

É ho hi o ho, hi iù ra bhó,
Ho ró ho hi, o hó hì,
Na hao ri ri o hò, hì iù ra bhó.

Chì mi ghrian 's i falbh gu siùbhlach,
É ho hi o ho, etc.
O, 's i dol timcheall Rubh' an Dùine;
Rìgh! ma thà, gu dé siod dhùinne?
Bidh mo bhràithrean fhéin air thùs ann
'S paidhir thaigh ri bial Loch Tùineart
Rìgh! ma thà, 's ma laigh 'sa chùirt e (?)
'S mo thriùir bhràithrean air a chùlaibh.

(*b*) *An teacs aig a' Chanonach Dunnchadh Mac 'Ill' Sheathain*

Hi leo hi o ho iù ra bhó,
Hi ho ro hi 's na bho hì,
Na hao ri ri o ho, hi iù ra bhó.

'S mi 'm aonar air buail' a' lochain,
Coimhead nam fear a' dol seachad,
Cha dug mi mo raghainn asda—
Nan dugadh, bu liom an gaisgeach
Fear mór nan calpannan cailceach,
'S na boineide guirm 's a' bhreacain,
'S dh 'fhàgadh tu 'n damh donn gun astar,
Fhuil a' drùdhadh feadh nan glacag.

Chì mi ghrian a' falbh gu siùbhlach,
'S a' ghealach air beannaibh Ùige,
'S am breac a' leum air an iùbhraich,
'S na féidh air leacach a' bhùiridh—

LIX

I see the sun setting swiftly

(*a*) *Mrs. Mary Johnston singing*

(*For tune, see p.* 308)

I see the sun setting swiftly

Around the point of Rubh' an Dùine,
My God! if it is, what is that to us?
My own brothers will be there first,
And a pair of houses at the mouth of Loch Tunord
My God! if they are, if he lay in the court
With my three brothers at his back . . .

(*b*) *Text communicated by Canon Duncan MacLean*

I am alone at the lochside cowfold,
Watching the men going past me,
I've not taken my choice amongst them,
Were I to choose, I'd choose the hero,
The big man whose calves are chalk-white,
Of blue bonnet and plaid of tartan;
You'd leave the red deer without motion,
His blood amongst the hollows flowing.

I see the sun setting swiftly,
And the moon upon Uig's mountains;
I see the trout on the boat leaping,
And the deer bellowing on the hillside;

Faodaidh iad sin, 's a bhith sunndach,
Tha mo shealgair donn gun dùil ris,
'S e 'na shìneadh as a' Chriùbhraich,
'S a ghunna sneap air a chùlaibh,
'S an daga 's an adhraic fhùdair.

Chì mi na féidh air an leacaich,
Faodaidh iad sin 's a bhith fallain,
Chaidh na sealgairean gu baile;
'S ann tha mo shealgair donn fo'n talamh,
Sealgair ròin thu, geòidh is eala,
Choilich dhuibh far a' bhearraich,
Dòbhrain duinn, 's an laoigh bhric bhallaich.

LX

'S trom an dìreadh

Oighrig bean Iain Aonghais 'ic Iain Bhig

Rinneadh an t-òran seo o chionn móran móran bhliadhnachan, nuair a bha MacLeòid anns an Eilein Sgitheanach. 'S ann a chuir Mac Leòid a dh'iarraidh nighean Fir Eige, agus a mhac a' dol dh'a pòsadh. Agus 's ann a bha tàmailt air na Dòmhnallaich bha ann an Eige, agus 's ann a rug iad air na gillean a bha a' sheo, a thànaig a dh'iarraidh na h-ighinn agus cheangail iad iad, agus lig iad air falbh leis a' ghaoith iad. Agus gu fortanach bha a' ghaoth leò agus *land* iad anns an Eilein Sgitheanach.

Agus bha a leithid a thàmailt air Mac Leòid, agus 's ann a chuir e daoine air falbh fiach am faigheadh e an fheadhainn a rinn an cron. Agus nuair a chunnaic na Dòmhnallaich am bàt' a' tighinn, thuig iad glé mhath dé bha dol, agus 's ann a chruinnich a h-uile h-aonan riamh aca, agus chaidh iad 'gam falach as an uaimh mhóir a th'ann an Eige.

Agus an fheadhainn a thànaig leis a bhàta, theann iad air an iarraidh, agus cha d'fhuair iad duine, agus thog iad air falbh, agus gu mì-fhortanach, nuair a bha iad pìos air falbh, thànaig cuideigin a mach as an uaimh, fiach am faiceadh iad 'n a dh'fhalbh iad as, agus chunnaic an fheadhainn a bh'as a' bhàt' iad, agus thill iad an uair sin, agus thànaig iad gu dorus na h-uamhadh agus dh'iarr iad air Mac Dhòmhnaill—[thuirt iad] nach biodh iad ag iarraidh duine ach an fheadhainn a rinn an cron a bha 'n seo; agus cha chuireadh iad duine a mach riù.

They can do that, they can be happy,
My brown-haired hunter's not expected,
He's lying stretched out in the Criùbhrach,
His triggered gun is behind him,
And his powder horn and pistol.

I see the deer on the hillside,
They can be there and be healthy,
For the hunters have gone homewards,
And my brown-haired hunter's buried,
Hunter of seal, of goose and swan,
Of blackcock from off the hillcrest,
Of speckled, spotted fawn and otter.

LX

Sad is the climbing

Mrs. Effie Monk

(*For tune, see p.* 310)

This song was made many, many years ago, when MacLeod [of Dunvegan] was in the Isle of Skye. It happened that MacLeod sent for the daughter of the tacksman of the Isle of Eigg, whom his son was going to marry. The MacDonalds in Eigg felt insulted, and they caught hold of the young men who had come to ask for the girl, and they bound them and let them go [in their boat] with the wind. Fortunately the wind was in their favour, and they landed in the Isle of Skye.

MacLeod was so affronted that he sent men to see if they could get the people who committed the misdeed. And when the MacDonalds saw the boat coming, they understood very well what was happening, and they all collected together and went to hide themselves in the big cave which is in Eigg.

The people who had come with the boat began to look for them, and didn't find anyone, and prepared to go away, and unfortunately, when they were a bit away, someone came out of the cave to see if they had gone away, and the men in the boat saw them, and returned then, and came to the entrance of the cave, and asked MacDonald—they said that they were only asking for the persons who had done the misdeed; but the MacDonalds would not send anyone out to them.

Agus nuair a chunnaic iad sin, chruinnich iad a h-uile fraoch agus tughadh taighe agus sian a ghabhadh fhaighinn a chruinneachadh, agus lìon iad suas dorus na h-uamhadh, agus chuir iad teine ris, agus thachd iad agus mharbh iad a h-uile duine bh'ann an Eige.

Agus 's air son seo a rinneadh an t-òran a bha a' sheothachd as a dheoghaidh sin, agus an duine cho duilich mar a thachair, gun duine ri fhaicinn ann an Eige.

E hó a hó, 's trom an dìreadh,
Hì hoireann ó, 's trom an dìreadh,
E hó a hó, 's trom an dìreadh,
'S trom an dìreadh.

'S fhad' an sealladh bhuam a chì mi, *é hó a hó,*
'S trom an dìreadh, hì hoireann ó,
'S trom an dìreadh, é hó a hó,
'S trom an dìreadh.

Chì mi Rùm is Eig' is Ìle, *é hó a hó,*
'S trom an dìreadh, hì hoireann ó,
'S trom an dìreadh, é hó a hó,
'S trom an dìreadh.

Far na rinn MacLeòid an dìobhail, *é hó a hó,*
'S trom an dìreadh, hì hoireann ó,
'S trom an dìreadh, é hó a hó,
'S trom an dìreadh.

Dhòirt e fuil 's gun chaisg e ìotadh, *é hó a hó,*
'S trom an dìreadh, hì hoireann ó,
'S trom an dìreadh, é hó a hó,
'S trom an dìreadh.

Chì mi Barraidh, an tìr ìseal, *é hó a hó,*
'S trom an dìreadh, hì hoireann ó,
'S trom an dìreadh, é hó a hó,
'S trom an dìreadh.

Chì mi Uibhist nam fear fialaidh, *é hó a hó,*
'S trom an dìreadh, hì hoireann ó,
'S trom an dìreadh, é hó a hó,
'S trom an dìreadh.

When they [the MacLeods] saw that, they collected all the heather and thatch and anything they could find, and they filled up the entrance of the cave, and set fire to it, and suffocated and killed everyone on Eigg.

It was for this that this song was made afterwards; the man who made it was so grieved at what had happened, when there was no one to be seen on Eigg.

E hó a hó, sad is the climbing,
Hì hoireann ó, sad is the climbing,
E hó a hó, sad is the climbing,
Sad is the climbing.

Distant the view that I can see, *e hó a hó,*
Sad is the climbing, hì hoireann ó,
Sad is the climbing, e hó a hó,
Sad is the climbing.

I see Rum and Eigg and Islay,
Sad is the climbing, hì hoireann ó,
Sad is the climbing, e hó a hó,
Sad is the climbing.

Where MacLeod has wrought destruction,
Sad is the climbing, hì hoireann ó,
Sad is the climbing, e hó a hó,
Sad is the climbing.

He has slaked his thirst with bloodshed,
Sad is the climbing, hì hoireann ó,
Sad is the climbing, e hó a hó,
Sad is the climbing.

I seele Barra, land low-lying,
Sad is the climbing, hì hoireann ó,
Sad is the climbing, e hó a hó,
Sad is the climbing.

I see Uist, isle of bountiful people,
Sad is the climbing, hì hoireann ó,
Sad is the climbing, e hó a hó,
Sad is the climbing.

Far an dianar an Fhéill Mìcheil, *é hó a hó,*
'S trom an dìreadh, hì hoireann ó,
'S trom an dìreadh, é hó a hó,
'S trom an dìreadh.

Hì hoireann ó, có nì sùgradh? *é hó a hó,*
'S trom an dìreadh, hì hoireann ó,
'S trom an dìreadh, é hó a hó,
Có nì sùgradh?

Có nì 'n gunna caol a ghiùlain? *é hó a hó*
'S trom an dìreadh, hì hoireann ó,
'S trom an dìreadh, é hó a hó,
'S trom an dìreadh.

LXI

Cha déid mi do Chille Moire

Mór Iain Dhòmhnaill Phàdraig a' seinn

Hoireann ó, ho hao ri ho ro, (solo)
Hoireann ó, ho hao ri ho ro. (tutti)

Cha déid mi do Chille Moire,

Hoireann ó, ho hao ri ho ro, (tutti)
Hùg is hùg is hùg is hoireann (solo)
Hoireann ó, ho hao ri ho ro. (tutti)

Ri Murchadh cha dean mi coinneamh,
Hoireann ó, etc.
Ri Murchadh cha dean mi coinneamh,
Cha n-eil ann ach òigeir foinneil;
Mhurchaidh bhig nan gormshuil greannmhor,
Shiùbhlainn leat ro na trì gleanntan,
Gleanntanan samhraidh is geamhraidh.
Ri Murchadh cha dean mi coinneamh,

Where they keep the Feast of St Michael,
Sad is the climbing, hì hoireann ó,
Sad is the climbing, e hó a hó,
Sad is the climbing.

Hì hoireann ó, who will be mirthful?
Sad is the climbing, hì hoireann ó,
Sad is the climbing, e hó a hó,
Sad is the climbing.

Who the slender gun will carry?
Sad is the climbing, hì hoireann ó,
Sad is the climbing, e hó a hó,
Sad is the climbing.

LXI

To Kilmuir I will not travel

Mrs. John Galbraith singing

(*For tune, see p.* 311)

To Kilmuir I will not travel,

I will not meet with Murdo,

I will not meet with Murdo,
He is only a foolish youth.
Little Murdo of the pleasant blue eyes,
I'd go with you through the three glens,
In the summer or the winter.
I will not meet with Murdo,

Cha n-eil ann ach òigeir foinneil,
Ruigea tu mu smàl do choinneal,
Dh'fhalbhadh tu mun goir an coileach.

Hoireann ó, ho hao ri ho ro, (tutti)
Hoireann ó, ho hao ri ho ro, (solo)
Hoireann ó, ho hao ri ho ro. (tutti)

LXII

Chaidh mis' a dh'Eubhal imprig

(*a*) *Fanny nic Dhunnchaidh Ruaidh a' seinn*

Hem bó, ho luì leó,
Ro challa leó éileadh,
Hem bó, ho luì leó.

Chaidh mis' a dh'Eubhal imprig,
Hem bó, etc.
'S thog mi gàrradh, lìon mi iothlann,
Cha n-ann dha'n eòrna ghlan thioram
Ach a dh'òigridh ceist mo chinnidh;
'S ghabh mi mo chead ris na beannan
A dh'Eubhal mhór 's Bheinn na h-Aire,
Caolas Rònaigh nan seòl geala
Gu Eilein nam Mucan mara.

'S ann agam fhìn bha na bràithrean,
Uisdean, Lachlann, Eachann, Teàrlach,
Iain is Raghnall is Ràghall,
'S Alasdair na gruaige fàinnich.

Mìle marbhaisg ort, a dhuine,
'S aotrom do cheum, 's trom do bhuille,
Ach mo mhollachd aig do mhuime
Nach do leag i ort glùn no uileann
Mun mharbh thu na fir oirnn uilig.

He is only a foolish youth,
You would come when the candle's put out,
You would leave before the cock crows.

LXII

I went to Eaval on a flitting

(*a*) *Mrs. Fanny McIsaac singing*

(*For tune, see p.* 313)

I went to Eaval on a flitting,

I built a wall, I filled a stackyard,
Not with clean dry barley,
But with youths beloved of my people;
I said farewell to the mountains,
To Eaval Mór and to Beinn na h-Aire,
To Rona Sound with white sails covered,
To the Island of the Whales.

'Twas I who had the brothers,
Uisdean, Lachlann, Hector, Charlie,
John and Ronald and Ranald,
And curly haired Alexander.

A thousand curses on you, fellow,
Heavy your blows, though light your footsteps;
My curses on your foster-mother,
For not laying on you her knee or elbow,
Before you killed all our people.

Uisdein 'ic 'Ill' Easbuig Chléirich
Far na laigh thu slàn nar éirich!
Sgeula do bhàis gu mnathan Shléibhte,
'S ugamsa mo dhearbh-chuid fhéin dhi.

(*b*) *Ceathramhnan air Huisdein mac 'Ill' Easbuig Chlèirich aig Ealasaid Iain Dhunnchaidh.*

Uisdein mhic 'Ill' Easbuig Chléirich,
Far an laigh thu slàn nar éirich!
O'n is mise chunnaic t'eugcoir
Mnathan 'nan ruith, crodh a' geumraich,
Sluagh nan creach 'ga chur o chéile!

Uisdein mhic 'Ill' Easbuig Chaluim,
'S minig a thachradh riut air bealach,
Fraochan feirge or 'o mhalaidh;
Dh'fheumadh e bhith làidir fearail,
Dh'fheumadh e 'n sin ciste 's anart,
Sluasaid gu cur ùir air fairis,
'S a bhith 'g iarraidh sìth dh'a anam!

'Fhuair iad greim air (Uisdean), 's cha doireadh iad sgath dha ach biadh saillte. Stairbh iad e leis a' phathadh' arsa Ealasaid.

LXIII

Chatriana a dh'fhalbhas gu banail

(*An teacs aig Mgr. Ailein Dòmhnallach*)

Eo rà le o bhì,
Hi rì bhó ì o ao,
Eo rà le o bhì.

Chatriana a dh'fhalbhas gu banail,
Tha do mheòirean air an gearradh
Le togail gàraidh mu'n *mhainnir*,
Le gléidheadh fiarach a' bhainne.

Uisdean Mac 'ill' easbuig Chléirich
Where you lie down whole, may you not arise!
May the women of Sleat get news of your death,
May I myself get my own share of it.

(b) Lines on Hugh son of Archibald the Clerk from Miss Elizabeth Sinclair's version.

Hugh son of Archibald the Clerk,
Where you lie down whole, may you not arise!
Since I have seen your wrongdoing,
Women running, cattle lowing,
The reivers parting the spoil!

Hugh, son of Archibald, son of Calum,
I pity him who contested your passage
When your eye was lit with anger,
He had needs be strong and manly,
He would need then shroud and coffin,
A shovel to put earth above him,
And peace for his soul to be prayed for!

'They got ahold of him (Hugh), and they would give him nothing but salt food. They starved him with thirst', said Elizabeth.

LXIII

Catriana, who goes so chastely

From Fr. Allan McDonald's MS.

(*For tune, see p.* 314)

Catriana, who goes so chastely,
Your fingers have been injured
Building a wall around the paddock,
Guarding the grazing of the cattle.

A fhleasgaich a dhìreas am bealach,
Giùlain bhuam-sa mo chiad beannachd
Dh'fhios a' bhuill am beil mo leannan,
Innis dha gu bheil mi fallain,
Gun do thiarainn mi bho'n earrach,
Gun do chuir mi 'n geamhradh seachad,
Rànaig mi samhradh a' bhainne,
Is foghar nan sguab a ghearradh.

Fhleasgaich, ma théid thu Ghleann Cuaiche,
Bheir mo bheannachd-sa gu Ruairi,
Is innis dha gu bheil mo luaidh air,
Ged a dh'fhàs e umam suarach.

'S aithne dhomh far bheil thu fantail,
Cha n-eil e 'n Ìle no 'm Manainn,
Cha n-eil e 'm Mùideart no 'n Cnòideart,
Cha n-eil e 'm Muile nam mórbheann,
Ach sìos is suas mu abhainn Lòchaidh,
'S muinntearas bliadhna aig Mac Leòid ort;
Tut! a ghiullain, tha thu gòrach,
'S mór gum b'fheàrr dhut mise phòsadh,
Na té eile 's buaile bhó leath',
Chùnntainn dusan dha'n chrodh mhór dhut,
No crodh druimfhionn, bhiorach, bhòidheach,
'S dhianainn plaide chaol is clò dhut,
'S anartan caola fo m' mheòirean.

LXIV

O, 's e mo ghaol an Anna

(*a*) *Ealasaid Iain Dhunnchaidh a' seinn*

O, 's e mo ghaol an Anna,
O hù, 's e mo ghaol an Anna,
O, 's e mo ghaol an Anna.

Young man who ascends the pass,
Bear from me my hundred blessings
To the spot where is my lover,
And tell him that I am healthy,
That I have survived the springtime,
That I have put past the winter,
And have reached the milky summer,
And the autumn, time of reaping.

Young man, if Glen Quoich you visit,
Take my blessing to Rory,
Tell him that I still esteem him,
Though to me he's grown indifferent.

I know where you are staying,
Not in the Isle of Man or Islay,
Not in Moydart or in Knoydart,
Not in Mull of the high mountains,
But up and down by the river of Lochy,
Hired by MacLeod for a year's engagement,
Tut! young fellow, you are foolish,
To marry me 'twould be much better
Than another girl with a fold of cattle,
I'd bring you a dozen cows as dowry,
White-backed, sharp-horned, beautiful cattle,
Fine plaid and cloth I would make you you,
And fine linen, with my fingers.

LXIV

O, my love is the Anna

(*a*) *Miss Elizabeth Sinclair singing*

(*For tune, see p.* 315)

O, my love is the Anna,
O hù, my love is the Anna,
O, my love is the Anna.

'S e mo ghaol, mo ghràdh an ainnir
O, 's e mo ghaol an Anna, etc.

Dà cheann caol is faobhar thana,
Dianamh an sgilb or 'o mhala;
'S duilich nach dànaig do leannan
Nach robh do bhuill chaol' 'gan tarraing,
'S do chuid chuplaichean 'gan teannadh
C'àit' am faigh mi 's tìr dhut leannan?
Cha ghabh thu mac fir a' bhaile,
Cha n-fhaigh thu Mac Nìll a Barraidh
Mac Fir Bheàrnaraidh na Hearadh
Gun dig an gùn ort o'n cheannaich',
Aparan as caoil' an anairt,
Neapaigin dha'n t-sìoda bhallach.

O, 's e mo chion 's mo ghràdh thu,
O hù, 's e mo chion 's mo ghràdh thu,
O, 's e mo chion 's mo ghrádh thu.

M' eudail air beannachd na màthar
'S duilich mar rinn iad do bhàthadh
Ro'n mhuir mhór nach d'rinn thu teàrnadh;
Chìreadh tu do leadan àrbhuidh'
Le cìr ìbhri 's le cìr chnàmha
Cìr dha'n airgead masa 's fheàrr leat
Thig an deis' ort air deagh-chàradh
Fasan ùr o làimh an tàilleir
Còta Lunnainneach o'n t-snàthaid
Bròg bhileach dhubh nan sàil àrda.

O, 's e mo ghaol a nist thu,
O hù, 's e mo ghaol a nist thu,
O, 's e mo ghaol a nist thu.

'S e mo ghaol, mo ghràdh, a nist thu;
Dh'fhalbh mo ghaol a dh'Eilear-Nis,
Cha bhi mi slàn mura dig thu
Urram mo chìrean 's mo chriosan,
Mo sgeanan beaga 's mo shiosar,
'S mo sporanan donna niosach.

('S i sgoth a bh'ann an Anna)

My love, my darling, is the maiden,[1]

Slim at each end and finely cutting,
Eyebrow moulded by the chisel;
Sad your sweetheart did not come,
That your fine ropes were not hauled,
That your shrouds were not tightened.
Where in the land shall I get you a lover?
You'll not take the son of the tacksman,
You'll not get MacNeil of Barra,
The son of the laird of Bernera-Harris;
The gown from the shopkeeper becomes you,
An apron of the finest linen,
And a spotted silken kerchief.

O, you are my love, my darling,
O hù, you're my love, my darling,
O, you are my love, my darling.

My treasure with a mother's blessing,
Sad it is how they drowned you,
Before the great sea you did not escape from;
You would comb your golden tresses
With a comb of bone and a comb of ivory,
A comb of silver if you prefer it,
The well-made dress becomes you,
A new fashion from the hand of the tailor,
A hand-sewn coat from London,
Black welted shoe with high heels.

O, you are my love now,
O hù, you are my love now,
O, you are my love now.

You are now my love, my darling,
My love has gone to Inverness,
I'll not be well unless you come,
Worthy of my combs, my girdles,
My little knives and my scissors,
And my brown stoat-skin purses.

[1] A boat.

(*b*) *Bean Nìll a' seinn*

Hó, 's e mo ghaol an Anna,
Ho hì, 's e mo ghaol an Anna,
Hó, 's e mo ghaol an Anna.

Bean a' chuailein chuachaich chlannaich,
Hó, 's e mo ghaol an Anna, etc.
Bean a' chuailein chuachaich chlannaich,
C'àit' am faigh mi 's tìr dhut leannan?
C'àit' am faigh mi 's tìr dhut leannan?
Mur gabh thu Mac Nìll a Barraidh,
No 'n gabh thu Mac Leòid na Hearadh,
No 'n gabh thu gin anns na fearainn,
No mac Ni Raghnaill 'ic Ailein,
Le chruachan 's le thaighean geala,
Luingeas luath air a' chuan Chanach.

Hó, 's e mo ghaol an Anna,
Ho hì, 's e mo ghaol an Anna,
Hó, 's e mo ghaol an Anna.

Ho hì, 's e mo ghaol a nisd thu,
Hó, 's e mo ghaol a nisd thu,
Ho hì, 's e mo ghaol a nisd thu,
Hó, 's e mo ghaol a nisd thu.

Dh'fhalbh mo ghaol a dh'Eilear-Nis bhuam

Hó, 's e mo ghaol a nisd thu,
Ho hì, 's e mo ghaol a nisd thu,
Ho, 's e mo e ghaol a nisd thu.

Cha bhi mi slàn gus an dig thu,
Hó, 's e mo ghaol a nisd thu, etc.
Ceannaicheadair mo chìr', mo chrios thu,
Sporan iallach nan iall nisneach,

(*b*) *Mrs. Neil Campbell singing*

(*For tune, see p.* 317)

Hó, my love is the Anna,
Ho hì, my love is the Anna,
Hó, my love is the Anna.

Woman of curling spreading tresses,

Woman of curling spreading tresses,
Where in the land shall I get you a lover?
Where in the land shall I get you a lover?
Unless you'll take MacNeil of Barra,
Or you'll take MacLeod of Harris,
Or someone in the lands,
Or the son of Ranald mac Allan's daughter,
With his white houses and his cornstacks,
And his swift fleet in the seas round Canna.

Hó, my love is the Anna,
Ho hì, my love is the Anna,
Hó, my love is the Anna.

Ho hì, now you are my love,
Hó, you are now my love,
Ho hì, you are now my love,
Hó, you are now my love.

My love has left me for Inverness,

Hó, you are now my love,
Ho hì, you are now my love,
Hó, you are now my love.

I'll not be well till you return,

You bought for me my comb, my belt,
My purse made of strips of ermine.

Hó, 's e mo ghaol a nisd thu,
Ho hì, 's e mo ghaol a nisd thu,
Hó, 's e mo ghaol a nisd thu.

O hao, 's e mo chion 's mo ghràdh thu,
O 's e mo chion 's mo ghràdh thu

'S deas air each thu, 's deas air làir thu,

Ó, 's e mo chion 's mo ghràdh thu,
O hìo, 's e mo chion 's mo ghràdh thu,
Ó, 's e mo chion 's mo ghràdh thu.

'S grinn thu tighinn air an fhàlair',
Ó, 's e mo chion, etc.
Stiorapan fo d' bhrògan àrda,
'S ann do Chlann Dòmhnaill a thà thu.

Ó, 's e mo chion 's mo ghràdh thu,
O hì, 's e mo chion 's mo ghràdh thu,
Ó, 's e mo chion 's mo ghràdh thu.

O hao, 's e mo luaidh 's mo raghainn thu,
Ó, 's e mo luaidh 's mo raghainn thu,
O hao, 's e mo luaidh 's mo raghainn thu,
Ó, 's e mo luaidh 's mo raghainn thu.

Théid thu 'na bheinn am bi an fhaghaid,

Ó, 's e mo luaidh 's mo raghainn thu,
O hì, 's e mo luaidh 's mo raghainn thu,
Ó, 's e mo luaidh 's mo raghainn thu.

Le d' ghille 's le d' chù 'nad dheaghaidh ann,
Ó, 's e mo luaidh, etc.
Le gunna caol a' bheòil laghaich,
Leagar fiadh bho thùs na greigheadh leat,
Earba bheag nan gearra-chas laghach.

Ó, 's e mo luaidh 's mo raghainn thu,
O hì, 's e mo luaidh 's mo raghainn thu,
Ó, 's mo luaidh 's mo raghainn thu.

Hó, you are now my love,
Ho hì, you are now my love,
Hó, you are now my love.

O hao, you're my love, my darling,
O, you're my love, my darling.

You are an expert horseman,

O, you're my love, my darling,
O hao, you're my love, my darling,
O, you're my love, my darling.

Handsome coming on a palfrey.

Your high boots in the stirrups,
'Tis Clan Donald you belong to.

O, you're my love, my darling,
O hao, you're my love, my darling,
O, you're my love, my darling.

O hao, you're my choice, my dearest,
O, you're my choice, my dearest,
O hao, you're my choice, my dearest,
O, you're my choice, my dearest.

You'll go to hunt upon the mountain,

O, you're my choice, my darling,
O hao, you're my choice, my darling,
O, you're my choice, my darling.

Your servant and your dog behind you,

With your slender gun of well-shaped muzzle
You'll shoot the leader of the deer-herd,
And the little roe-deer neatly footed.

O, you're my choice, my dearest,
O hao, you're my choice, my dearest,
O, you're my choice, my dearest.

Hó, 's e mo ghaol an Anna,
Ho hì, 's e mo ghaol an Anna,
Hó, 's e mo ghaol an Anna.

Fhleasgaich sin thall ris a' bhalla,
Hó, 's e mo ghaol, etc.
Tha mi saor, ge b'oil le t'amhaich,
Faodaidh mi mo ghruag a cheangal,
Faodaidh mi mo leum a ghearradh
Air lic luim os cionn taigh m'athar,
Faodaidh mi mo chrios a theannadh,
Dìridh mi Bheinn Mhór gun anail,
'S neo-ar-thaing do bhun do mhaladh.

Hó, 's e mo ghaol an Anna,
Ho hì, 's e mo ghaol an Anna,
Hó, 's e mo ghaol an Anna.

LXV

'S moch an diu a rinn mi éirigh

(*a*) *Bean Nìll a' seinn*

Hi rì rì, hill iù hill ò ro,
E hoireann ó, ho ro éileadh,
Hi rì rì, hill iù hill ò ro.

'S moch an diu a rinn mi éirigh,
'S moch an diu e, 's moch an dé e;
Dhìrich mi suas gual' an t-sléibhe,
Fhuair mi ghruagach dhonn gun éirigh
'G iomain a' chruidh-laoigh 's 'gam feurach
'Gan togail ri strath an t-sléibhe.

Hi ri rì, hill iù hill ò ró,
E hoireann ó, ho ro éileadh,
Hi ri rì, hill iù hill ò ró,
E hoireann ó, ho ro éileadh,
Hi ri rì, hill iù hill ò ró.

Hó, my love is the Anna,
Ho hì, my love is the Anna,
Hó, my love is the Anna.

Young man yonder at the wall

I am free, although you hate it,
I can bind my tresses,
I can cut a leap upon
The bare stone above my father's dwelling,
My belt I can tighten,
Climb Ben More without taking breath,
And no thanks to your attention.

Hó, my love is the Anna,
Ho hì, my love is the Anna,
Hó, my love is the Anna.

LXV

Early I arose today

(*a*) *Mrs. Neil Campbell singing*

(*For tune, see p.* 319)

Early I arose today,
Early today, early yesterday,
I climbed up the hillside's shoulder,
I found the brown-haired maiden lying,
Driving the cattle to their grazing,
Taking them up to the mountain valley.

'S ann ormsa tha aire na buaileadh,
Slàn dha'n fhear a chumadh bhuam i!
Slàn dha m' leannan, 's tamull bhuam e,
Làmh riofadh nam ball, 'ga fhuasgladh,
Làmh air an stiùir nuair bu chruaidh' i,
Cha b'fhear cearraig bheireadh bhuat i,
No fear làimhe deis' is fuachd air.

Ghabh mi sìos air strath na h-abhann,
Chuala mi torghan a's t-sobhal,
Mar gum biodh cléith-luadhaidh fo mhnathan,
No fir òg' ri iomradh ramhan;
Bheannaich mi gu ciùin air m'athair,
Có fhreagair ach fear an taighe:
'Dean-sa suidhe, 's e do bheatha,
'S gheobh thu deoch, ma tha ort pathadh,
A dh'fhìon, a bheòir, no uisge-beatha,
[No lionn làidir thig o'n dabhaich.']

(*b*) *Mar a tha e aig Mgr. Ailein Dòmhnallach*

Hì rì ri-il liù i leò-ro,
Eo hò ri no ho ro eileadh,
Hì rì ri-il liù i leò-ro.

Fliuch an oidhche nochd 's gur fuar i,
Ormsa bha aire na buaileadh,
Slàn do'n fhear a chumadh bhuam i,
Cha n-e Iain 's cha n-e Ruairi!
Siod mo leannan, 's tamull bhuam thu,
Làmh air an stiùir nuair bu chruaidh' i
Cha n-fhear cearraig' bheireadh bhuam thu,
No fear làimhe deise 's fuachd air,
No fear bàn an leadain dualaich!
Thug am bàta bàn an cuan oirr',
Guma slàn dha'n t-saor a dh'fhuaigh i!
Dh'fhàg e dìonach làidir luath i,
'S aigeannach gu siubhal cuan i.

Dh'éirich mi ro' bhial an latha,
Ghabh mi suas struth na h-abhann
Choimhead an eòrna a bh'aig m'athair,

'Twas I who had the care of the fold,
A health to the one who'd take it from me!
A health to my lover, absent from me,
He'd reef the ropes, and untie them,
His hand's on the helm when it was roughest,
No left-handed man would take it from you,
Nor a right-handed man, with the cold upon him.

I went down the river valley,
In the barn I heard a humming,
Like a band of waulking women,
Or young men with oars a-rowing;
I quietly addressed my father;
Who answered but the host:
'Sit down, you are welcome,
You'll get a drink, if you are thirsty,
Of wine, of beer, or of whisky,
Or of strong ale from the vat.'

(*b*) *Version taken down by Fr. Allan McDonald*

Wet the night is tonight, and cold,
I had the care of the cattlefold,
A health to him who'd take it from me,
It's not Ian, it is not Rory!
That's my lover, a while absent,
A hand on the helm when weather was hardest,
No left-handed one would take you from me,
Nor a right-handed one, benumbed,
Nor the fair curling-haired fellow!
The white boat took to the ocean,
A health to the carpenter who built her!
He left her strong and sound and speedy,
High spirited to sail the ocean.

I arose before the dawn,
I went up the strath of the river
To watch the barley of my father;

Chunnaic mi dròbh mór do dh'aighean,
Dithis mu'n cùl, triùir 'gan gabhail
Fear a b'òige a Chlann 'Ill' Sheathain.
Chuala mi bualadh 'san t-sabhal,
Mar gum biodh cliath-luadhaidh aig mnathan,
'S na fir òga 'g iomradh ramhan;
' 'S òl do dheoch ma tha ort pathadh,
A dh'fhìon no bheòir no dh'uisge-beatha,
No stuth làidir thig o'n dabhaich!'

LXVI

Tha sneachd air na beannaibh Diùrach

Na faclan aig Anna nic Nìll 'ic Iain, Ceap Breatann

O hi iù ra bhi hó,
O hi a bhó, ho ro éileadh,
O hi iù ra bhi hó.

Tha sneachd air na beannaibh Diùrach,
O hi iù, etc.
Cha doir uisge no ceò dhiù e;
A Rìgh! ma thà, gu dé sin dhuinne?
Cha truimid iad fhéin a ghiùlain!
Tha féidh air leacraich an dùine,
'S truagh nach mise bh'air an cùlaibh
Le m' ghunna 's le m'adhraic fhùdair,
Dh'fhàgainn an damh ruadh 'na chrùban,
Com na fala sileadh siùbhlach,
An eala bhàn as binne tùchan—

Tha port aig gillean Mhic Eachainn,
'S cha phort a th'aca, ach cion aisig;
'S truagh nach robh mo dhùrachd aca,
Bhiodh port orra gu cionn seachdain,
Togsaid branndaidh 's rogha thombaca,
Togsaidean fhìon air an cearcladh.

I saw a big drove of heifers,
With two behind them, three taking them,
The youngest of Clan MacLean;
I heard a beating in the barn,
As if the women were having a-waulking,
And the young men with oars were rowing;
'Drink your drink if you are thirsty,
Of wine or beer or of whisky,
Or of strong drink from the vat!'

LXVI

Snow lies on the hills of Jura

Words sung by Mrs. Neil McInnis, Cape Breton

(*For tune, see p.* 320)

Snow lies on the hills of Jura,

Rain nor mist will not remove it,
If it does, what does it matter?
The hills themselves feel it no burden!
Deer are on the stony hillside,
Alas that I was not behind them
With my powder horn and musket,
I'd leave the red stag lying wounded,
His bloodstained body bleeding freely,
And the white swan that sweetly warbles.

MacEachan's lads have got a tune,
No tune they have, but lack of ferry;
Pity they have not got my wishes,
A tune they'd have until the week's end,
A barrel of brandy, and choice tobacco,
Hogsheads of wine with hoops encircled.

Nighean chruinn donn, na bi 'n gruaim rium,
Cha n-iarrainn bó dhubh no ruadh leat,
No bó bhreac an iomall buaile,
Tha do thochradh leam 'nad ghruaidhean.

LXVII

Cha déid mór a Bharraidh bhrònaich

Anna agus Calum Aonghais Chaluim

Trod nan Cailleach

Bha bana-bhàrd aig Mac Nìll Bharraidh uair air an robh Nic Iain Fhinn mar ainm, agus bha i 'na bana-bhàrd ainmeil 'na latha fhéin. Aig an amm ud 's e nighean Mhic Leòid na Hearadh a bha pòsda aig Mac Nìll, agus bha piuthar dhi pòsda aig Mac 'ic Ailein, agus iad a' fuireach ann an Caisteal Ormaclait. Bha Mac 'ic Ailein 'na dhuine saibhir, cumhachdach; ach ged nach robh aig Mac Nìll ach an sgeireag bheag, bha e pròiseil uaibhreach, agus uaill mhór aige as a chuid dha'n t-saoghal. Bha eud mór aig an dà bhaintighearna r'a chéile.

Bha bana-bhàrd aig Mac 'ic Ailein cuideachd, dha'm b'ainm Nic a' Mhanaich; agus is iomadh uair a thilg Mac Nìll air Mac 'ic Ailein nach digeadh i an uisge na stiùrach do Nic Iain Fhinn air bàrdachd. Bha seo a' leamhachadh Mhic 'ic Ailein, aig an robh toiseach air Mac Nìll anns gach cothrom saoghalta, gum biodh e ri ràdha gun doireadh a' bhana-bhàrd Bharrach urram na bàrdachd o Nic a' Mhanaich, agus is e thachair gun do chuir na fir geall r'a chéile gum b'e a' bhana-bhàrd aige fhéin a b'fheàrr; agus shuidhich iad gun deante luadhadh ann an Caisteal Ormaclait, agus gun rachadh Nic Iain Fhinn chon an luadhaidh, agus gum biodh Nic a' Mhanaich 'na seise aice, agus gum faigheadh an dithist aca cothrom air i fhéin a dhearbhadh.

Seo mar a bh'ann. Dh'fhalbh sgoth is sgiobadh a Eòiligearraidh le Nic Iain Fhinn a dh'Uibhist. Bha struth is gaoth 'nan aghaidh, agus bha iad car anmoch mun do rànaig Nic Iain Fhinn a ceann-uidhe. Ach ghabh i suas chon a' Chaisteil, far am faca i còmhlan bhoireannach cruinn. Nuair a thànaig i faisg orra, 's ann a chual' i té dhiu 'ga càineadh fhéin; 's e 'm facal a bha 'na bial:

Nic Iain Fhinn, ban-eileineach,
Cailin spàgach, uinneineach!
Blad-chraois leathan, dealanach,
Stròn ghorm, ghoirid, mheallanach,
Bus is spor is spreillean ort,
Taobh dearg a seicheadh am muigh!

Neat brown maid, be not cross with me,
Nor black nor red cow I'd ask with you,
Nor speckled cow from verge of paddock,
In your cheeks I have your dowry.

LXVII

Mor will not go to miserable Barra

Told and sung by Annie and Calum Johnston

The Old Wives' Flyting

Once upon a time MacNeil of Barra had a bardess called Nic Iain Fhinn, 'the daughter of fair-haired John', who was a famous poetess in her day. MacNeil was then married to a daughter of MacLeod of Harris, and her sister was married to Clanranald, and they were living at Ormaclate Castle. Clanranald was a wealthy, powerful man. But although MacNeil only owned a little rock, he was proud and arrogant and very vain of his worldly possessions. The two ladies were very jealous of each other.

Clanranald too had a bardess, called Nic a' Mhanaich 'the Monk's daughter'. Many a time MacNeil was casting it up to Clanranald that she (Nic a' Mhanaich) could not come anywhere near to Nic Iain Fhinn in composing poetry. Clanranald, who was better off than MacNeil in every worldly respect, was vexed that it was being said that the Barra bardess would win poetic honours from Nic a' Mhanaich. Eventually they each made a wager that his bardess was the better, and they decided that there should be a waulking at Ormaclate Castle, and that Nic Iain Fhinn should go to the waulking, and that Nic a' Mhanaich should be in her party, and that they two of them should then have the chance to prove themselves.

So it fell out. A boat with a crew went from Eoligarry to Uist with Nic Iain Fhinn. Tide and wind were against them, and it was rather late before Nic Iain Fhinn reached her destination. But she went up to the castle, where she saw a band of women gathered together. When she came near to them, she heard one of them abusing her, in these words:

Nic Iain Fhinn, she-islander,
Club-footed, thick-ankled quean!
With broad greedy flashing mouth
And short lumpy blue nose;
Snout and claw and blubber-lips,
And the red side of her hide outside!

Cha do dh'éisd Nic Iain Fhinn ris a' chòrr, ach leum i a stigh am miosg nam ban Uibhisteach, agus ghlaodh i an àird a claginn 'Thig thusa a mach, 's lig mise a steach, gun dianainn an trod sunndach, sanntach, ris a' chaillich chutaich, chataich, ulpaich, alpaich, uinneinich!'

Agus shuidh i air a' chleith-luadhaidh mu choinneamh Nic a' Mhanaich.

Thòisich an té Uibhisteach, Nic a' Mhanaich, mar seo:

Cha déid Mór a Bharraidh bhrònaich,

Hó ró, hùgaibh ì,
Hùgaibh ise, 'n dùgaibh éileadh,
Hó ró, hùgaibh i.

Cha déid Catriana 'ga deòin ann,
Hó ró, etc.
No Anna bheag, ma's i as òige,
Far am bi na sgait air fleòdradh
Dallagan is sùilean rògach,
Giomaich 'gan tarruing a frògaibh,
Strùbain 'gan cladhach le'm meòirean,
Muirsgein 'gan tarruing a lònaibh—

Cha do lig Nic Iain Fhinn na b'fhaid' i; thòisich i mar seo:

'S fhada mi 'm chadal 's mi dòltram,
Tha lionn-dubh mo chinn air dòrtadh,
'G éisdeachd ri bleideig an Ròdha!
C'uim' nach do dh'fhoighneachd thu 'm bu bheò mi?
'S gheobhadh tu comain do chòmhraidh,
Nam fòghnadh éisginn mo bheòil dhut!
A chailin dubh 's a dhubh-bhrògach,
Cheangladh t'athair leis na ròpan,
Struth as a smuig feadh nan lònaibh!
Ogha rag-mheàrlaich an eòrna,
Nighean cailleach dhubh an fhòtais,
Bradag nan obag 's nan òisneag
Bheireadh air na luingeis seòladh
Air aodann na Beinn' Móir' Dì-Dòmhnaich,
A chuireadh na cuirp mharbh an còmhlan,
Cha b'e mo thìr an tìr bhrònach—
Tìr a' chorca, tìr an eòrna,

Nic Iain Fhinn did not listen to any more, but jumped in amongst the Uist women, yelling at the top of her voice 'You come out and let me in, so I can make the flyting with the stumpy, catty, lumpy, greedy, thick-ankled hussy.' And she sat down at the waulking board opposite Nic a' Mhanaich.

Nic a' Mhanaich, the Uist woman, began like this:

(*For tune, see p.* 321)

Mór will not go to miserable Barra,

Catriana won't willingly go there,

Nor little Anna, though she's the youngest;
Where the skates are marinated,
And the sunken-eyed dogfish,
Lobsters pulled from hiding-places,
Where they dig cockles with their fingers,
Where razor-fish are pulled from puddles!

Nic Iain Fhinn did not let her go any further: she began like this:

Long am I asleep in doldrums,
Melancholy has overwhelmed me
Listening to the she-bletherer from the Ròdha;
Why did you not ask if I were living,
You'd get what your discourse merits
If satire from my mouth suffices.
Brazen hussy, and black-footed,
Bound with ropes was your father
A stream from his snout among the puddles!
Grandchild of the thief of barley,
Black witch of wickedness's daughter,
Thieflet of spells and incantations,
Who would set the fleets a-sailing
On the face of Ben More on Sunday,
Who would set dead men in combat—
My land is not a miserable country,
A land of oats, a land of barley,

Tìr uisge-bheatha agus bheòire,
Tìr ichinnich is òil i;
Dh'fhàsadh peasair, dh'fhàsadh pònair,
Dh'fhàsadh biolair air a lòintean,
Fàsaidh lìon air chnocain chòmhnard.
Gheobhadh Éireannaich an leòr innt',
Nam fòghnadh muc, im, is feòil dhaibh,
Sitheann mu seach agus ròsda,
'S mairtfheoil 'ga bruich, muc 'ga stòbhadh,
Tubhailtean geal' air na bòrdaibh,
'S gille frithealadh an còmhnaidh!
C'à na shuidh i ann a seòmbar,
Ged bhiodh an sìoda 'ga còmhdach,
'S ged a bhiodh i air a h-òradh
O mhullach a cinn gus a brògan,
Nighean Tighearna no Tòisich,
Nach b'airidh Gill' Eóghanain Òg oirr'?
'S ann a bha e shliochd nam fear móra,
Thogadh creach 's a thilleadh tòrachd!

Thionndaidh Nic Iain Fhinn an uair sin ris a' Chasadh:

O hùg o, chailleach chrùbach, *o hùg o*, lùgach, iollagach!
O hùg o, bhradach, bhriagach, *o hùg o*, bhialach, ionasdach!
O hùg o, bhreugach, sgeulach, *o hùg o*, éisgeach, inisgeil!

O hùg o, tha do theanga *o hùg o*, leathan, còmhnard,
O hùg o, tha trì roinn oirr', *o hùg o*, 's faobhar leòit' oirr',
O hùg o, chaidh i ri cloich *o hùg o*, air a bhòn-dé!

O hùg o, ... *o hùg o*, mi thighinn dhachaigh
O hùg o, b'fheàrr dhomh bhith muigh, *o hùg o*, 'na mo bhreacan
O hùg o, [na] 'g éisdeachd ris na *o hùg o*, chluinn mi ana-cainnt,
O hùg o, sìor-chur sìos, *na* *o hùg o*, air Niall a' Chaisteil.
O hùg o, cha b'e do dhìol *o hùg o*, dh'aodach leap' e—
O hùg o, cluasagan òir *o hùg o* deirg a' lasradh,
O hùg o, 's na h-eich chruidh-each *o hùg o*, shrianach ghlasach,
O hùg o, chàireadh e flùr *o hùg o*, air an dealt dhaibh!

A land of beer and of whisky,
A land of drink and provisions;
Peas and beans would grow in it,
Water-cress upon its ponds;
Flax upon its flat-topped knolls;
Irishmen would get their fill there
If pork, butter, and meat sufficed them,
Venison in turn, and roasted.
Beef being boiled and pork being stewed,
With white cloths upon the tables
And serving lads there always waiting;
Where did ever sit in chamber,
Even if her dress was silken,
Even if she had been gilded
From the top of her head to her shoes,
A daughter of laird or thane
Of whom young Gilleonan was unworthy?
He was of the race of great men
Who'd lift the spoils, turn back pursuers!

Nic Iain Fhinn then turned to the second part of the air:

O, you crippled, sneaking, giddy, thieving,
lying, gossiping, ... truthless,
tattling, scurrilous, slanderous harridan!

Broad and level is your tongue,
Three points it has, and a cutting edge,
It went to the whetstone the day before yesterday!

. . . . I coming home,
I'd be better outside in my plaid,

Than listening to the slander I've heard,

Always abusing Neil of the Castle,
It was not your due of bed-clothing
Golden pillows red and shining,
Well-shod horses bitted, bridled,

He would put flour on the dew for them!

O hùg o, bu tu a' bhradag *o hùg o*, dh'fheann na caoirich,
O hùg o, dh'icheadh tu na *o hùg o*, caoirich mhaola,
O hùg o, 's tu 'gan draghadh *o hùg o*, as na fraochaibh!
O hùg o, shluigeadh tu, *na* *o hùg o*, muc le gaoiseid,
O hùg o, shluigeadh tu na *o hùg o*, searraich mhaola,
O hùg o, chrochadh t'athair *o hùg o*, leis na taodan,
O hùg o, dh'fhalbh do mhàth-air *o hùg o*, air an t-sluagh aotrom!

O hùg o, gun déid an clò *o hùg o*, gun im gun fheòil!

Thionndaidh Nic Iain Fhinn ris a' chiad fhonn a rithist:

'S truagh nach fhaighinn siod air m'òrdan,
Slaodadh ris an Tùr air ròpa,
Taod mu d' chlaban, calp mu d' dhòrn dheth,
Dà shac dhiag gu teine mòna,
Bradag bhith 'na miosg 'ga ròsladh,
'S na coin mhór bhith 'gad shròiceadh,
'S na mucan ag iche t'fheòla!

Agus lean Nic Iain Fhinn oirre mar sin, agus gu dé thachair ach nuair a sguir i dhe a càineadh, thuit an té Uibhisteach 'na plod air a' chleith m'a coinneamh. 'Togaibh a' chailleach a mach as an taigh is cuiribh té eile 'na h-àite' arsa Nic Iain Fhinn, ''s gun mhi leathach.' Dh'fhalbh na h-Uibhistich an uair sin gu greim a dheanamh oirre, agus rinn ise an uair sin falbh còmhla ris an sgiobadh Bharrach. Nuair a rànaig iad an sgoth aca, leum iad innte, gheàrr iad an ròpa, thug iad a mach agus rànaig iad Barraidh. Bhuinnig Nic Iain Fhinn an geall!

Thuirt Nan Nic Fhionghuin, ann an Bhatarsaidh, rium 'Sin agad Nic Iain Fhinn, 's i thuirt an rud mu dheireadh!

Nic Iain Fhinn ban-eileineach,
Cailin spògach uinneineach,
'S iomadh cudaig le ceann a dh'ich i,
Gun an luath ruadh a chrathadh aiste!

'Siod an rud a bhiodh iad ag ràdh rithe as na h-eileinean. 'S ann o na sìdhichean a fhuair i a bàrdachd. Bha leannan-sìdh aice, aig Nic Iain Fhinn, agus 's e muime bh'aice, bha a h-athair pòsda a rithist; agus ged is a muime fhéin a bh'ann, bha i cho math dhi. Bha fhios aice gu robh i falbh leis a' leannan-shìdh a bha 'n seo, 's cha robh i air son gum

You were the thief who flayed the sheep,
The hornless sheep you used to eat,
Dragging them from the heaths,
A pig with its bristles you'd devour,
The bare foals you would devour;
Your father was hung with hempen ropes,
Your mother went off with the fairy host,

The cloth will go without butter or meat!

Nic Iain Fhinn turned to the first air again:

Pity you weren't at my disposal
Being dragged on a rope to the Tower (Kismul)
A thong round your skull, a turn round your fist,
With twelve bags of peat for a fire,
The she-thief roasted on a spit,
While big dogs were tearing you
And pigs were eating your flesh!

And Nic Iain Fhinn went on like that. And what happened but when she stopped satirizing her, the Uist woman fell dead on the waulking-board opposite her. 'Take that old hag out of the house and put another one in her place' said Nic Iain Fhinn 'I'm not half finished'. Then the Uist people went to catch hold of her, and she made off with the Barra crew. When they reached their boat, they jumped aboard, cut the rope, sailed off, and reached Barra. Nic Iain Fhinn had won the wager!

Nan MacKinnon in Vatersay told me 'There you have Nic Iain Fhinn, she had the last word.

Nic Iain Fhinn, she-islander,
The club-footed thick-ankled quean,
She ate many a cuddy with its head
Without shaking the red [peat] ashes off it!

'That's what they used to say about her in the islands. It was from the fairies that she got her talent for making poetry. She had a fairy lover, did Nic Iain Fhinn. She had a stepmother, her father had married a second time. Though she was her stepmother, she was very good to her. Her stepmother knew she was going with a fairy lover, and she

biodh i falbh leis idir. Agus cha n-fhaigheadh i nist dha'n t-sìdhein nan icheadh i rud 'sa bith mu falbhadh i; na's lugha na dh'fhalbhadh i 'na trosgadh, cha n-fhaigheadh i dha'n t-sìdhein idir.

'Ga brith cho fàilidh 's a dh'éireadh ise, chluinneadh a muime i, agus bhiodh i toirt oirre rudeigin a ghabhail,—iche, mu falbhadh i. Ach an latha bha 'n seo, co dhiù, chual' i—bha i dìreach gu dùnadh an dorus nuair a dhùisg a muime, 's i falbh a choinneachadh a leannan-shìdh. Cha robh fhios aice gu dé dheanadh i oirre; rug i air a' chuman 's chaith i as a deoghaidh e. Bhuail stradagan dha na bha as a' chuman oirre, agus nuair a rànaig i, thuirt a leannan-sìdh rithe:

' "O, cha n-eil e gu feum dhut a bhith fiachainn ri tighinn, cha n-fhaigh thu gu tighinn idir" ars e fhéin. 'Chuir iad an siantan fhéin an diu asad. Ach bheir mi dhut buaidh na bàrdachd, o'n a tha sinn a' dealachadh. Ma chuireas tu do theangaidh 'nam bhial, cuiridh tu fonn orra.'

' "Well, cha ligeadh an t-eagal dhi a teanga a chur 'na bhial, air eagal gu robh e dol a thoirt aiste an teanga. 'S fhuair i buaidh na bàrdachd gu dìcheannach,[1] ach cha chuireadh i fonn riamh orra. 'S an aoir sin a chuala sibh, 's e 'n té Uibhisteach a chuir am fonn air, 's e fonn na té Uibhistich a bha i leantail. Cha chuireadh i fonn riamh air na h-òrain, ach gun deanadh i iad. Sin mar a chuala mise." '

[1] *Sic*.

didn't want her to be going with him at all. Nic Iain Fhinn would not get into the fairy mound if she were to eat anything before she went out; unless she went fasting, she wouldn't get into the fairy mound at all.

'No matter how quietly she got up, her stepmother would hear her, and would make her eat something, before she left. But this day, anyway, Nic Iain Finn was just about to close the door, going to meet her fairy lover, when her stepmother awoke. She didn't know what she should do about her; she picked up the cogie and threw it after her. A drop of what was in the cogie struck her. When she arrived, her fairy lover said to her:

' "Oh, it's no use for you to try to come, you'll not get to come at all, they have taken the enchantments off you today. But since we're parting, I'll give you the power of composing poetry. If you put your tongue in my mouth, you'll compose airs for them [as well].

' "Well, she was afraid to put her tongue in his mouth, for fear he was going to bite it off. She got the power of composing poetry excellently, but she could never make airs for her poems. That satire you heard, it was the Uist woman who made the air for it, it was the Uist woman's tune that Nic Iain Fhinn was following. She could never make airs for the songs, but she could make the words. That's what I heard." '

3. Songs of single-line 'verses' of four syllables each (8^2 divided)

THE 'verse' here consists of an eight-syllable line rhyming on the penultimate syllable divided into two halves of four syllables each.[1] When each half-line is sung to the same tune and is followed by a refrain of the *a*, *b*, *a* type, the whole melody can be expressed in four bars of music, e.g. LXXXI here. But more intricate structures with alternating refrains are frequent, and when such songs are sung at the fireside, it is sometimes difficult to decide where they really end. In many cases, however, it is clear that when sung at a waulking, the first and last half-lines of the song are only sung once, and that the song therefore ends with the refrain first sung after an even-numbered half-line.

Even when the odd- and even-numbered half lines are sung to the same tune, they are not quite on the same footing, as it is the penultimate syllables of the even-numbered half-lines which carry the rhyme, and the vowels of these must be consistently either long or short throughout the same section of the song, whereas the penultimate syllables of the odd-numbered half-lines are not under any such restriction.

There is an archaic feeling about this style of singing and the melodies connected with it. We do not know of any other language where verse in 8^2 metre is divided for singing in this way.

Types

(*a*) *Alternating Refrains*

1. A*a*, B *bcd*, B *a*, B *bcd*: LXVIII (Mrs. Neil Campbell).
2. A*a*, B *bcda*, B *a*, C *bcda*: LXVIII (Miss Annie Johnston); LXXV.

[1] One song to be printed in our third volume consists of a 7^1 line divided into halves of 4^2 and 3^1. This is *Phiuthar chridhe chomain chléibh* as sung by Mrs. Neil Campbell. Cp. K. C. Craig, *Òrain Luaidh Màiri nighean Alasdair*, p. 93.

3. A *a*, B *bcb*, B *a*, C *bcb*: LXX.
4. A *a*, B *a*, C *a*, D *b*; C *a*, D *a*, E *a*, F *b* (*b* is complex): LXXI.
5. A *a*, B *a*, C *b*, D *a*; C *a*, D *a*, E *b*, F *a*: LXXII, LXXIII.
6. A *a*, B *b*, C *a*, D *c*; C *a*, D *b*, E *a*, F *c*: LXXIV.
7. A *aba*, B *aba*, B *cba*, C *aba*; B *aba*, C *aba*, D *cba*, E *aba*: LXXVIII.
8. A *abc*, A *dbc*, B *abc*, B *dbc*: LXXXV, LXXXVI, LXXXVII.
9. A *aba*, B *aba*: LXXVI,[1] LXXVII, LXXIX, LXXX, LXXXI, LXXXII, LXXXIII, LXXXIV. In vol. i, VI.

(*b*) *Not Alternating.*

10. A *abcdabc*, B *abcdabc*: LXXXVIII.

Other forms in vol. i:

11. A *abc*, B *abc*: III.
12. A *ab*, B *ab*: X, XXIX.
13. A *a*, B *a*, C *b*, D *c*; C *a*, D *a*, E *b*, F *c*: XXVII.[2]
14. A *aba*:[3] XXVII.

[1] The syllables of *b* change after the first section of the song.

[2] As sung by Mrs. Duncan MacDonald. A particular refrain is sung between the different sections of this song.

[3] Apparently from the text. The tune has not been recovered.

LXVIII

An Spaidearachd Bharrach

(*a*) *LS. an Òbain*

A' BHAN-UIBHISTEACH:

Fa liù o ho,
A Dhia! 's gaolach
O hao ri ho ho,
Rì ho ho, ri ho ho,
Fal iù o ho.

A Dhia! 's gaolach — lium an gille,
O hi a hao, — *O hao ri ho ho,*
Ri ho ho, ri ho ho,
Fal iù o ho.

lium an gille,
O hi o hao,

Dh'am bheil deirge, — 's gile 's duinnead,
O hao ri ho ho, etc. — *O hi o hao,*

Dalta nam bàrd, — thùs nam filidh,
Ogha an fhir o'n — Chaisteal Thioram thu,
Bheireadh air an — togsaid sileadh,
Cha n-ann le bùrn — gorm na linge,
Le fìon dathte — 's e air mire,
Le fìon théidear — cian 'ga shireadh.

A' BHANA-BHARRACH:

Ach eudail mhór — 's a Dhia fheartaich!
C'àit an d'fhàg thu — Ruairi an Tartair,

LXVIII

The Barra Boasting

(*a*) *South Uist Version from the Oban MS.*

(*For tune, see p.* 322)

THE UIST WOMAN:

My God! the lad

My God! the lad is loved by me,

is loved by me,

Who is red and white and brown,[1]

Fosterling of bards leader of poets,
Grandson of the laird of Castle Tioram,
Who would make the hogshead pour,
Not with blue-green pond water,
But with red wine and it playing,
With wine they go afar seeking.

THE BARRA WOMAN:

My dearest dear— oh God of power!
Where did you leave Rory the Noisy?

[1] Referring to his complexion and the colour of his hair. The Uist woman alludes to the Clanranalds; the Barra woman to the MacNeils of Barra.

No Niall Glùndubh, no Niall Frasach,
Gill' Eóghanain mór an gaisgeach?
Chrathadh am flùr fo na martaibh,
Dhòirteadh am fìon fo na h-eachaibh,
Air ghaol bùrn nan lòn a sheachnadh,
Bheireadh cruithneachd dhaibh 'san fhrasaich,
Chuireadh strian an airgid ghlais riu.
Chuireadh cruidhean òir fo'n casan!

A' BHAN-UIBHISTEACH:

A bhradag dhubh bheag a bhrist na glasan,
Fàgaidh mi ort an dubh-chapull,
Cha d'fhuaradh riamh staoileadh agaibh,
Ach Barraidh dhubh bheag chrìon-dubh, chlachach,
Oighreachd fhuair sibh bhuainn an asgaidh,
Nuair a chunnaic Dia 'nur n-airc sibh,
Eilean fiadhaich am bi na fachaich,
E gun rùm 's gun fhiar 's gun fhasgadh,
'S e air fleòdradh leis na sgaitibh!

Sgrìobh Mgr. Ailein Dòmhnallach (LS. Orain Luadhaidh, fol. 115): ' 'S ann an Cill Donain a bha iad a' luadhadh. Sgàin a' bhan-Uibhisteach leis an tàmailt. B'fheudar falbh 'san oidhche leis a' bhana-Bharrach mum marbhte i.'

(b) *Anna agus Calum Aonghais Chaluim a' seinn*

A' BHANA-BHARRACH:

A bhradag dhubh bhrist na glasan
O hi o hù,
O hao ri ò,
E o ho hu ò,
Fa liù o hó, o hì o hao.

bhrist na glasan
O hì o hù

A Mhuilgheartach, *na,*
O hao ri o,
E o ho hù o,
Fa liù o ho, o hì o hao.

Or Neil Black-knee or Neil of the Showers
Or Gilleonan the great hero?
Who'd shake out flour before his cattle,
Who'd pour out wine before his horses,
So they'd drink not stagnant water,
Who'd give them wheat in their mangers,
Who'd bridle them with silver bridles,
Who'd shoe their hooves with golden horseshoes!

THE UIST WOMAN:

Little black thief who broke the fetters,
On you I'll leave the 'black mare'[1]
You never yet got any title,
But little black Barra withered and stony,
Lands you got from us for nothing,
When God saw that you were starving,
A wild island haunt of sea birds,
Without extent or grass or shelter,
Washed around by rays and skates!

Fr. Allan McDonald wrote in his MS. collection of waulking songs, fol. 115: 'It was at Cill Donain that the waulking was. The Uist woman fainted at the insult. They had to go away by night with the Barra woman, or she would have been killed.'

(*b*) *Annie and Calum Johnston singing*

(*For tune, see p.* 323)

THE BARRA WOMAN:

Little black thief who broke the fetters,

who broke the fetters,

You sea hag,

[1] A penalty for defeat in a bardic contest. See note.

A Mhuilgheartach, *na*, nan cochull craicinn,
O hì o hù *O hao ri o*, etc.

Cuiridh mi ort an dubh-chapull
C'àit an d'fhàg thu Ruairi an Tartair?
'S a mhac cliùiteach Niall a' Chaisteil?
Is Niall Glùndubh, is Niall Frasach?
Mo cheòl-ghàire Ruairi an Tartair!
Bheireadh am fìon d'a chuid eachaibh,
Chuireadh crùidhean òir fo'n casan,
'S chuireadh am flùr air an dealt dhaibh?
'S iomadh claidheamh glégheal lasrach,
'S iomadh targaid fuilteach, stracach,
Chunnaig mo shùil anns a' chaisteal—
'S a chuid dhaoine mar na farspaich
'S gach ian eile thà 'san ealtainn;
Chìteadh 'nad thalla mùirn is macnas,
Mairtfheoil 'ga bruich, crodh 'gam feannadh
Gachdan air òl, sùrd air dannsa,
Pìob is fiodhall dol 'nan deannruith,
'S cruit nan teudan cur ris an annsgair.

O hao ri o,
E o ho hù o,
Fa lìù o ho, o hì o hao.

LXIX

Tàladh Dhòmhnaill Ghuirm

Bean Nìll a' seinn

'S nàil ì, ro ho ì,
'S nàil ì, ro ho ì,

[Ar liom gur h-i] ghrian 's i 'g éirigh,
Ho nàil i bhó hò,

ghrian 's i 'g éirigh,
Ho nàil ì, ro ho ì,

You sea hag   of the skin coverings,

I'll put on you   the 'black mare';
Where did you leave   Rory the Noisy?
And his famed son   Neil of the Castle?
And Neil Black-knee,   and Neil of the Showers?
My music, my laughter   Rory the Noisy,
Who'd give wine   to his horses,
Who would shod them   with gold horseshoes,
Who'd put flour   on the dew for them?
Many a sword   bright and shining,
Many a targe   rent and bloody
My eye has seen   in the castle,
With its men   like the blackbacks,
And every other   bird in the bird-flock.
In your hall would be seen   mirth and merriment,
Beef being cooked,   cattle being flayed,
Strong drink drunk and   lively dancing,
Pipes and fiddles   quickly playing,
And stringed harps   adding to the uproar!

LXIX

Donald Gorm's lullaby

Mrs. Neil Campbell singing

(*For tune, see p.* 325)

Methinks it is   the sun arising,

the sun arising,

'S i gun smal oirr',
Ho nàil i bhó hò,

'S i gun smal oirr', no air na reultan;
Ho nàil ì, ro ho ì, *Ho nàil i bhó hò,*

no air na reultan;
Ho nàil ì, ro ho ì.

Nuair théid mac mo rìgh-sa fo làn-éideadh,
Gu robh neart na cruinne leis agus neart na gréineadh,

Neart an tairbh dhuibh 's àirde leumas.

Nàil liom 's gura, nàil liom 's gura,
Nàil i bhó hò, nàil ì, ro ho ì.

Dh'fhoighneachd a' bhean thall ud dha'n mhnaoi eile,
'No có 'n long ud a staigh fo'n eirthire?'
'Gu robh don' t'fhoighneachd ort, [c'uim an ceilinn?]
Tha long Dhòmhnaill [long mo leinibh,]
[Long mo rìgh-sa long nan Eilean,]
Gu bheil stiùir òir oirr', tha trì chruinn sheilich innt',
Gu bheil tobar fìon' innt' shìos 'na deireadh,
Agus tobar fìor-uisge ['sa cheann eile,]
Ho nàil i bhó hò,
['sa cheann eile,]
Ho nàil ì, ro ho ì.

Nàil liom 's gura, nàil i bhó hò.

No dimness on her,

No dimness on her, or on the stars,

or on the stars;

When my king's son is arrayed in armour,
May he have the earth's strength and the strength of the sun,

The strength of the black bull that jumps the highest.

Nàil liom 's gura, nàil liom 's gura,
Nàil i bhó hò, nàil ì, ro ho ì.

Yonder woman asked of the other woman

'What is that ship in under the shore?'
'Ill asking on thee! why should I hide it?

It is Donald's ship the ship of my fosterling,
The ship of my ruler, the ship of the Isles!
She has a helm of gold and three masts of willow,
There's a well of wine in her down in her stern,
And a well of fresh water in her bow!'

LXX

Chuala mi 'n dé sgeul nach b'ait liom

Mairi Iain Choinnich a' seinn

Hù ra bho ho,

Chuala mi 'n dé
  Fail ill o ho,
  Ro hoireann o ho,
  Fail ill o ho.

Chuala mi 'n dé
  Hù ra bho ho,
sgeul nach b'ait liom,
  Fail ill o ho,
  Ro hoireann o ho,
  Fail ill o ho.

sgeul nach b'ait liom,
  Hù ra bho ho,

Gu robh t'àrdrach gun àr fhasgaidh,
  Fail ill, etc.

['S i gun chroinn 's gun siùil gun slataibh.]
Bhrist i 'n càbla, dhragh i 'n t-acair',
Bhrist i gach ball b'fheàrr a bh'aice,
'S tu fhéin ag òl air a haitse.

  Hù ra bho ho, (tutti)
  Hù ra bho ho, (solo)
  Hù ra bho ho. (tutti)

Chuala mi 'n dé sgeula neònach—
M'òg-leannan donn dol a sheòladh,

Cha n-ann dha'n Fhraing no dha'n Òlaind,
Air Dùn Bheagain leag e chòrsa [i còrsa
'S air Dùn Tuilm nam bratach bòidheach.

LXX

Yesterday I heard a tale unjoyful

Mrs. Mary Johnston singing

(*For tune, see p.* 326)

Yesterday I heard,

Yesterday I heard a tale unjoyful,

a tale unjoyful,

That your galley was without shelter,

Without masts or sails or rigging,
Her cable broken, her anchor dragging,
Every best rope on her was broken,
While you were on her hatch a-drinking.

Yesterday I heard a strange story—
That my young brown-haired lover was going a-sailing,
Not to France nor to Holland,
For Dunvegan his course was making,
For Duntuilm of beautiful banners.

Pòsar nighean   òg an rìgh leat,
Nuair thig thu mach   seinnear pìob leat,
Nuair théid thu steach   seinnear fìodhall,
Seinnear clàrsach   nan teud binn leat;
Thig an gartan   's am bi sgàrlaid
Air calpannan   geal mo ghràidh-sa.

Fhleasgaich a chaidh   seachad sìos orm,
Fois or 'o cheum,   till a nìos rium,
Cha b'ann mar sin   liginn dhìom thu,
Le corruiche   no le mìothlainn,
Le mnaoi phùsda   no mnaoi dhìolain,
Leis a' mhnaoi òig   rinn am mìostadh,
Lig mo leannan   sìnte sìos rithe,
'S mi fhìn gu h-òg   fallain fìorghlan.

Shiùbhlainn, shiùbhlainn,   shiùbhlainn fhéin leat,
Shiùbhlainn Alba   leat is Éirinn,
Shiùbhlainn machaire   fada réidh leat,
Shiùbhlainn ro' choill'   mhór nan geug leat
Ged bhiodh do bhean   òg an eud rium—
Raghainn air sin   's a bhith réidh rium. [riut

LXXI

Alasdair mhic Cholla gasda

Màiri Mhicheil Nìll a' seinn

Alasdair mhic, *hó hò*,   Cholla gasda, *hó hò*,
As do làimh-sa, *hó hò*,   dh'earbainn tapachd, *trom éile.*

Chall éileadh i, (solo)
Chall o ho ró, (tutti)
Chall éileadh ì, (solo)
Chall o ho ró, (tutti)
Challa na hao ri ri, (solo)
Chall o ho ro ó, (tutti)
Haghaidh o ho ó, trom éileadh.

You will marry the king's young daughter
When you come out they'll play pipes for you,
When you go in they'll play fiddles,
They'll play the sweet stringed harp for you.
Well becomes the scarlet garter
On the white calves of my lover.

Young man who went on down past me,
Halt your step, come up back to me;
It is not like that that I'll let you leave me
With wrathfulness or with displeasure,
With a married woman or a mistress,
With a young woman who had lured you,
Who let my lover lie down beside her,
While I am young and pure and healthy.

I'd go, I'd go, I would go with you,
I'd go through Scotland and Ireland with you,
I'd walk the long smooth sandhills with you,
I'd go through the great leafy wood with you,
Though your young wife were jealous of me;
Her choice is that or to be at peace with me.

LXXI

Splendid Alasdair, son of Colla

Mary Gillies singing

(*For tune, see p.* 327)

Splendid Alasdair, son of Colla,
From your arm I'd expect valour,

Chall éileadh ì, etc.

As do làimh-sa, *hó hò*, dh'earbainn tapachd, *hó hò*,
Mharbhadh Tighearn', *hó hò*, Ach' nam Breac leat, *trom éile*.
Chall éileadh ì, etc.

Mharbhadh Tighearn', *hó hò*, Ach' nam Breac leat, *hó hò*,
Thiolaigeadh e, *hó hò*, an oir an lochain, *trom éile*.
Thiolaigeadh e, etc.

Ged 's beag mi fhìn chuir mi ploc air,
'S chuir siod gruaim air Niall a' Chaisteil,
'S dh'fhàg e lionndubh air a mhac-sa,
'S bha Ni Lachlainn fhéin 'ga bhasadh,
'S bha Nic Dhòmhnaill 'n déidh a creachadh;
Cha b'iaonadh sin, b'fhiach a mac e
Dronncair, pòiteir, seòlt' air marcraichd,
Ceanndard an airm an tùs a' bhatail,
Sheinneadh pìob leat mhór air chnocan,
Dh'òladh fìon leat dearg am portaibh.
Chuala mi 'n dé sgeul nach b'ait liom,
Glaschu bheag bhith 'na lasair,
'S Obair-eadhain an déidh a chreachadh, *trom éile*.

Chall éileadh ì, (solo)
Chall o ho ró, (tutti)
Chall éileadh ì, (solo)
Chall o ho ró, (tutti)
Challa ha hao ri ri, (solo)
Chall o ho ró, (tutti)
Haghaidh o ho, trom éileadh.

LXXII

A phiuthrag 's a phiuthar

(*a*) *Calum Aonghais Chaluim a' seinn*

A phiuthrag 's a phiuthar, *hù rù*, ghaoil a phiuthar, *hù rù*,
Nach truagh leat fhéin, *ho hol ill eó*, nochd mo chumha, *hù rù*.

From your arm I'd expect valour,
Auchinbreck's laird was killed by you,

Auchinbreck's laird was killed by you,
And was buried at the lochside,
And was buried, etc.

Though small I be, I cast a sod on him,
Which made Neil of the Castle gloomy,
And left his son melancholy,
Lachlann's daughter herself was lamenting,
And Donald's daughter her hands was wringing;
'Tis no wonder, her son was worth it,
Copious drinker, clever horseman,
Army leader foremost in battle,
You'd play the great pipes on a hillock,
You would drink red wine in houses,
I heard today a tale amazing,
That little Glasgow is a-blazing,
And Aberdeen has been plundered.

Chall éileadh ì, etc.

LXXII

Little sister, beloved sister

(*a*) *Calum Johnston singing*

(*For tune, see p.* 331)

Little sister, beloved sister,

Do you not pity my grief tonight?

Nach truagh leat fhéin nochd mo chumha,
hù rù, *hù rù,*
'S mi 'm bothan beag, ìseal cumhag,
ho hol ill eó, *hù rù.*
'S mi 'm bothan beag, *etc.*
Gun lùb sìomain, gun ghad tughaidh,
'S uisge nam beann sìos 'na shruth leis,
'S mise bhean bhochd, chianail, dhuilich,
Thug mi 'n tochradh dhut an uiridh,
Fhuair mi fhìn i 'm bliadhna buileach,
'S mi 'gan aiseag ro' Chaol Muile.
'S ro' Chaol Ìle 'm bi na luingeas.

Dhìrich mi suas Beinn an Sgrìobain,
'S Laigheabhal Mhór nan each grìsfhionn,
Cha d'fhuair mi ann na bha dhìth orm,
Té bhuidhe, 's a falt mar dhìthein;
Dh'iarr mi, dh'iarr mi, dh'iarr mi 'n innis,
Dh'iarr mi gach ball 'm biodh tu mire,
Dh'iarr mi 'n duilleag 'm biodh tu leughadh.

Cha chualas riamh glaodh bu truaighe
Na glaodh leinibh 'n déis a bhualadh,
'N déis a mhàthair fhéin thoirt uaidhe;
Cha chualas riamh glaodh bu bhinne,
Na iomradh ràmh, is iorram ghillean,
Ged a bhristeadh ràmh, cha tilleadh,
Ach fear eile chur 'na ionad;
Bheireadh sibh i chaladh tioram,
Do dh'acairseid Chaluim Chille.

(*b*) *Bho LS. an Òbain*

Phiuthrag 's a phiuthar, ghaoil a phiuthar,
ho ho, *ho ho,*
Gur minig a bha, mi 's tu 'm bruthach,
och o dail ò, *ho gù ho ro.*
Gur minig a bha, *ho ho,* mi 's tu 'm bruthach, *ho ho,*

Do you not pity my grief tonight?

In a little hut I am, low and narrow,

In a little hut I am, low and narrow,
Without a roof-rope or a wisp of thatching,
With the rain of the hills streaming into it,
I am a poor woman sad and miserable,
I gave the dowry to you last year,
I got it myself this year entirely,
Ferrying them[1] through the Sound of Mull,
And the Sound of Islay where the fleets are.

Ben Sgrioban I ascended,
And Laigheabhal Mhór with its spotted horses,
I found not there what I was wanting,
A girl with hair like the golden daisy,
I sought, I sought, I sought the meadow,
I sought each spot where you used to be playing,
I sought the book you used to be reading.

Never was heard a sadder crying
Than the cry of a child that's been beaten,
Or after his mother's been taken from him.
Never was heard a sweeter crying
Than the rowing of oars with lads singing,
Though an oar broke, there's no returning,
But another oar would replace it;
You'd bring her to a sheltered haven,
To the anchorage of St. Columba.

(*b*) *Version from the Oban MS.*

Little sister, beloved sister,

Often were you and I on a hillside,

Often were you and I on a hillside,

[1] i.e. the cattle which made up the dowry.

Am bothan beag, ìseal cumhang,
och o dail ò, ho gù ho ro
Am bothan beag, *etc.*
Gun lùb sìomain, gun strad tughaidh,
'N dìle mu'r ceann, 's bhiomaid subhach.

'Phiuthrag 's a phiuthar 'm faod thu éirigh?'
'Cha n-fhaod, a ghaoil 'm faod thu fhéin e?
Tha 'm bainne mar dh'fhàg thu 'n dé e,
Tha 'n crodh 's na laoigh feadh a chéile,
Bhó dhruimfhionn donn 's a laogh fhéin ann.'

Cha chualas riamh geum bu chruaidhe
Na geum Duibhein, is geum Ruaidhein,
Ach do gheum-sa, Dhubhach ghuailfhionn;
M'eudail an làmh 'm biodh a' bhuarach,
M'eudail a' chas bhiodh 'ga h-uallach,
Sìos is suas air feadh na buaile,
'S cha dug thu riamh breab do'n bhuaraich,
Cha mhuth' thug thu bearn air buailidh.

Shiubhail mi 'm fàsach dh'iarr mi 'n innis,
Dh'iarr mi bun is braigh' a' ghlinne,
Dh'iarr mi gach àit' 'm biodh tu mire,
Dhìrich mi suas Beinn an Sgrìobain,
Theirinn mi nuas a' Bheinn Ìseal,
Bheinn Chreagach ruadh bha 'n taobh shìos dhi,
Eubhala mhór nan each grìsfhionn.

Fhleasgaich a' ghunna, dean fuireach ri m' sgeula,
'S mis' théid an urras air 'n fhuil a bhith 'd léinidh;
Cha n-fhuil fithich cha n-fhuil féidh i,
Fuil na banchaig mharbh thu fhéin i,
Cheangail thu a falt ris na geugan,
Dh'fhag thu ghruagach dhonn gun éirigh,
Phiuthrag 's a phiuthar, ghaoil a phiuthar.

In a little hut   low and narrow,

Without a roof-rope   or a wisp of thatching,
With the flood above us,   and we'd be happy.

'Little sister,   can you arise?'
'I cannot, my dear,   can you yourself?
The milk is as   you left it yesterday,
The cows and calves   are all mixed up,
The brown white-backed cow   and her calf there.'

Never was heard   a louder bellow
Than that of Duibhean   and that of Ruadhan,
Except your bellow,   white-shouldered Dubhach;[1]
Beloved the hand   that held the fetter,
Beloved the foot   that was held in it,
Up and down   throughout the cowfold,
You never gave   a kick to the fetter,
You never made   a gap in the enclosure.

I walked the pasture,   I sought the meadow,
I sought the foot   and the head of the glen,
I sought each place   you used to be playing,
I climbed up   on Sgrioban's ben;
I descended   the low mountain,
And the red rocky   one below it,
And great Eaval   of piebald horses.

Young man with the gun,   await my story,
I'll pledge my word   your shirt is bloody,
Not with raven's   blood or deer's blood,
But the dairymaid's blood   you yourself killed her,
You bound her hair   to the branches,
You left the brown girl   lying lifeless.
Little sister,   beloved sister.

[1] Duibhean, Ruadhan, Dubhach: names of cows.

LXXIII

'S muladach mi o chionn seachdain

Anna Aonghais Chaluim a' seinn

'S muladach mi, o chionn seachdain
o hi a bho, O hi a bho,
Aig fhad a bha mi gun t'fhaicinn,
hao ri ho ro o hi a hao.
Aig fhad a bha mi gun t'fhaicinn,
o hi a bho o hi a bho,
Alasdair ùir a' chùil chleachdaich,
hao ri o ho o hi o hao,
Alasdair ùir, a' chùil chleachdaich,
o hi, etc. *o hi*, etc.
Sealgair geòidh thu, ròin is eala,
Bric a nì leum, 'n fhéidh nì langan;
Cha bu nì liom buaile mhart dhut,
Airgiod air bhòrd, òr air bhasaibh;
Nan cluinninn thu thighinn dha'n chlachan,
Ghearrainn an tràigh, dhianainn astar.
O hi a bho, o hi a bho.

Soiridh bhuam-sa null gu Muile,
Soiridh eile le tìr Gheàrrloch,
Far am faighte na fir dhàicheil,
Chuireadh a' chluichd air an tàileasg,
'S air na dìsnean geala cnàmha,
'S air na cairtean breaca bàna;
'S tha 'n t-amm againn bhith dhol dhachaigh,
Am bealach ud thall a chur seachad.

LXXIII

Sorrowful am I since a week

Annie Johnston singing

(*For tune, see p.* 332)

Sorrowful am I   since a week

At how long   I have not seen you,

At how long   I have not seen you,

Young Alasdair   of the curling locks.

Young Alasdair   of the curling locks,

Hunter of wild goose   of seal and swan,
Of leaping trout,   of bellowing deer;
For you I'd not grudge   a fold of cattle,
Silver on a table,   gold on hand-palms,
If I heard of you   coming to the village,
I would cut across the strand,   I would hurry.

Farewell from me   across to Mull,
Another farewell   to the land of Gairloch,
Where were found   the handsome fellows,
Who used to play   at backgammon,
At the dice   of white bone,
And at the cards,   white and spotted;
It's time for us   to be going homewards,
To put behind us   yonder pass.

LXXIV

Coisich, a rùin

(*a*) *O'n LS. aig Dòmhnall Mac an t-Saoir*

Coisich, a rùin, lùb nan geal-làmh,
hù ill o ro, ho i ibh ó,

Ceud soiridh bhuam, dha na Hearadh,
hù ill o ro, och hoireann eó.

Ceud soiridh bhuam, dha na Hearadh,
hù ill o ro, ho i ibh ó,

Gu Iain Caimbeul donn mo leannan,
hù ill o ro, och hoireann eó.

Gu Iain Caimbeul donn mo leannan,
hù ill o ro, ho i ibh ó,

Innis dha-san gu bheil mi fallain,
hù ill o ro, och hoireann eó.

Gun do chuir mi 'n geamhradh fairis;
Bu tric a laigh mi fo t'earradh,
Ma laigh, cha b'ann aig a' bhaile,
'N lagan uaigneach, 'n cluain a' bharraich,
Gum b'iad na h-eòin ar luchd faire,
'S gaoth nan àrdbheann draghadh fairis,
'S uisge fìorghlan fuarghlan fallain
Mar fhìon uaibhreach dol an glaine,
Sinn beul ri beul breug cha chanainn,
Do bheul cùbhraidh sùghadh m'anail,
'S mi fo chirb do bhreacain bhallaich.
Fo bhile na luinge fada,
Fo theanga 'n fhéidh a nì langan.

'S fliuch an oidhche nochd 's gur fuar i,
Gun dug Cloinn Nìll druim a' chuain orr';
Ma's fhìor dhomh fhìn, chì mi bhuam iad,
Le'n longanan loma luatha,
Le'm brataichean gorm is uaine,

LXXIV

Walk, my beloved

(*a*) *Version in Donald MacIntyre's MS.*

(*For tune, see pp.* 333–7)

Walk, my beloved white-armed youth,

Remember me to the Isle of Harris,

Remember me to the Isle of Harris,

To John Campbell my brown-haired lover,

To John Campbell my brown-haired lover,

And say to him that I am healthy,

That I have put the winter past me.
Often I lay beneath your covering,
If I did so 'twas not at home,
In a secret valley, in a dell of birch-trees,
It was the birds who were our watchmen,
While the mountain wind was blowing over us,
With clear fresh water cold and healthy
Like proud wine being poured in glasses.
We mouth to mouth, I'd not be lying,
Your sweet lips my breath drinking,
With me beneath your plaid of tartan,
Beneath the gunwale of your galley,
Within earshot of deer a-calling.

Wet is the night tonight, and chilly,
Clan Neil have taken to the ocean,
If I am right, I can see them,
With their galleys bare and speedy,
With their banners blue and green,

Le'n ulagan cruinne cruaidhe,
Mo leannan fhìn air bhòrd fuaraidh,
Greim air an stiùir nuair bu chruaidh' i;
Cha b'fhear cearraig bheireadh bhuat i,
No fear làimhe deis' is fuachd air;
Their mi 'n fhìrinn 's cha n-i an t-sochair,
'S tu 'm fireannach liom bu docha
Shaltair air feur gorm no fochann,
Laigh air a thaobh deas no toisgeal,
No chuir cas am bròig no 'n osan.

Gura mise nach eil fallain
Bho'n chiad Mhart o thùs an earraich,
M'òg-fhleasgach donn ris a' bhalla
Cùl do chinn air deile daraich,
Freasdal léine chaoil dha'n anart;
Cha n-eil feum air léigh 'nad bhaile,
Ged nach eil, tha feum air anart,
Móran mór do choinnlean geala.
Gura mise th'air mo sgaradh,
Air mo ghualadh, air mo ghearradh,
Falbh am màireach leat o'n bhaile,
Ma tha, cha n-ann chon do bhanais—
Gus do chur 'san ùir am falach,
Dh'aindeoin na bheil beò 's na chailleadh.
Thug mi 'n oidhche a raoir air t'fhaire,
Bheir mi 'n oidhche nochd ann fhathast,
Cha laigh smal air coinnlean geala
Gun déid ùir air sùil mo leannain,
Ùir air sùil mo cheud-ghràidh falaich.

Réiteach an nochd 'sa bhail' uarach,
Ma dh'fhaodas mi nì mi buanachd,
Sùilean ghobhar 'n ceann nan gruagach;
Nan cluinninn té eile luaidh riut
Spìonainn bun is bàrr mo chuailein,
Gu falbhadh m'fheòil 'na ceò uaine.

Mo mhil, mo mhil, mo mhil fhìn thu,
Mo shiucar is mo cheòl fìdhle,
Mo cheòl clàrsaich 'n àird 's an ìseal,
Mo dhìtheinean eadar ghartaibh.

With their pulleys round and hard,
My love himself is on the weather side,
His grip's on the helm when it's hardest;
'Twas no left-hander who'd take it from you,
Nor a right-handed man who's shivering.
I'll tell the truth it is no comfort,
You are the man I most am liking,
Who trod on grass or on cornfield,
Who on his right or left side lay,
Or who put his foot in shoe or stocking

'Tis I indeed who am not healthy
From the Shrove Tuesday, beginning of spring tıme,
My brown-haired youth is against the wall,
The back of your head on a plank of oak,
With only a slender shroud of linen
Doctor's not needed in your homestead,
Though he's not, a shroud is needed,
Also many, many white candles.
'Tis I indeed who am shattered,
Tormented I and torn to pieces,
Going tomorrow with you from the village,
If I am, 'tis not to your wedding,
But to bury you in earth covered.
Despite who lives and who survives not,
I spent last night at your wake vigil,
I'll spend the night tonight there also,
There will be no smooring of white candles
Till earth is put on the eyes of my lover,
Earth on the eyes of my first secret sweetheart,

Betrothal tonight in the upper village,
If I can I'll take advantage,
Amorous eyes in the heads of maidens;
If I heard another girl name you
I'd tear my hair out by the roots,
My flesh would turn into green vapour.

You are my honey, my own honey,
My sugar and my violin music,
My harp music high and low,
My marigolds in the cornfields.

(*b*) *Mar a tha e 'san LS. aig Anna Nic Iain*

'S fliuch an oidhche, nochd 's gur fuar i,
Hù il o ro, O hi ibh o,

Ma thug Cloinn Nìll druim a' chuain orr'
Hù il o ro, Boch ho rinn ó.

Luchd nan seòl àrd 's nan long luatha,
'S nam brataichean gorm is uaine,
'S nan gunnachan caola, cruadhach;
'S iomadh sgeir dhubh anns na shuath i,
'S iomadh liaghan dearg a bhuain i,
Agus bàirneach ghlas a bhuain i.
Cha b'fhear cearraig feireadh bhuat i
No fear làimhe deis le tuaigh e;
Feir thu mach, *na* dhruim a' chuain i,
'S feir thu steach a dh'uisge Chluaidh i.

Thoir soiridh bhuam do na Hearadh,
Gu Sean Caimbeul donn mo leannan,
Sealgair geòidh thu, ròin is eala,
Bhric a nì leum 'n fhéidh ni 'n langan,
'S an dòbhrain duinn, 's an laoigh bhallaich,
'S na circeig' bhig' air nead falaich.
Moire! 's mise th'air mo sgaradh,
Mas i 'n fhairge ghlas thug bhuam thu,
Rocach nan ròn t'aodach uachdair,
'S a' ghaineamh bhàn nì dhut cluasag;
Nan cluinninn té eil' bhith luaidh ort,
Leumadh mo shròn àird na stuaidhe.

Gura mise th'air mo sgaradh,
Réiteach an nochd bhith 'nad bhaile,
Réiteach an nochd 'sa bhail' uachdrach,
'S cha léir dhomh fhìn gu dé 'm buannachd.

'S gur minig a laigh mi fo t'earradh,
Ma laigh, cha b'ann aig a' bhaile,
An lagan uaigneach cluain a' bharraich,
An lagan fàsaich, fad' o'n bhaile,

(*b*) *Miss Annie Johnston's MS. version*

Wet is the night tonight, and chilly,

If Clan Neil took to the open ocean,

Folk of high sails and swift galleys,
And of banners blue and green,
And of slender guns of steel.
Many a black rock she rubbed against,
Many a red tangle she reaped,
Many a grey limpet she plucked.
'Twas no left-hander who'd take her from you,
Nor right handed man with an axe;
You'd take her out to the open sea,
You'd bring her in to the water of Clyde.

Remember me to the Isle of Harris,
To John Campbell my brown-haired lover,
Hunter of the goose of seal and swan,
Of otter brown of spotted fawn,
Of leaping trout of bellowing deer,
Of little grouse in her hidden nest.
Mary! 'tis I who am shattered,
If the grey sea has taken you from me,
If seaweed is your outer clothing,
If the white sand is now your pillow!
Were I to hear another girl name you,
I would lose my temper utterly.

It is I who am shattered,
A betrothal tonight in your homestead,
A betrothal tonight in the upper township,
I cannot see what is the profit.

Often I lay beneath your cover,
If I did, it was not at home,
In a lonely valley a bower of birch-trees,
In an empty valley far from home,

Far na cluinnte storm na mara,
Deatach de'n cheò bhith 'gar dalladh,
'S duilleach nan craobh bhith 'gar falach.

Mo bhuaile bhó mo chrodh-laoigh thu,
Mo sheisreach, *na*, dol an cruinn thu,
Mo dhìthein thu eadar ghartaibh,
Leus mo shùl thu, mo shròl air cnoc thu.

LXXV

A Mhic a' Mhaoir

O'n LS. aig a' Chanonach Dunnchadh Mac 'Ill' Sheathain, comhla ri corra-cheathramhnan o chaochladh dhaoine eile

Hiu na hao ri,
A Mhic a' Mhaoir, 's daor do shùgradh,
Hiu na hao ri, o hoireann o, ro ho éile,
o ho éile.
Hiu na hao ri,
's daor do shùgradh,
Hiu na hao ri,
'S daor a cheannaich mi bho thùs thu,
o hoireann o, etc. *Hiu na hao ri,*
mi bho thùs ri,
o hoireann o, etc.
Mharbh thu ghruagach dhualach dhùbhdhonn,
Gur h-ann 'sa choill' rinn thu 'n diùbhail,
Piostal do thaoibh rinn mo chiùrradh,
Chuir thu fùdar gorm 'nam shiùlean,
Chuir thu luaidhe ghlas 'nam ghlùinean!
A bhràithribh ghaoil, bithibh ciùin ris,
Cha do thog e miar no sùil rium;
Chaidil thu raoir air mo chùlaibh,
Rìgh, ma chaidil, cha b'ann brùideil,
Cha bu bhruaillein liom do dhùsgadh.
'S a Mhic a' Mhaoir a ghaoil 's a rùin,

Where unheard was the noise of the sea-storm,
The swirling mist kept us blinded,
The leaves of the trees kept us hidden.

You are my cattlefold and my cattle,
My team of horses for the ploughing,
My marigold among the cornfields,
The light of my eye, on knoll my banner.

LXXV

O son of the Steward

Canon MacLean's text, with some lines from various other reciters

(*For tune, see p.* 338)

O son of the Steward! costly your wooing!

costly your wooing!

Dearly I've paid for you from the start,

Dearly I've paid for you from the start,

You've killed the dark-brown curling-haired maiden,
It was in the wood you did the mischief,
By your side pistol I was wounded
You put gunpowder in my eyes,
You put grey lead in my knees!
Beloved brothers be kind to him,
Neither finger nor eye he lifted to me;
Last night you slept behind me,
My God, if you slept it was not brutally,
To me your wakening was no vexation.
O son of the Steward, my love, my dear,

Cha phàigh an 'Donn' dhut an t-ùnnlagh,
No 'Dubhbheag' no 'Chiar' no 'n 't-Siùbhlach'!

Ghaoil, ma théid thu as an dùthaich
Na taobh Diùraidh, na taobh Lùngaidh,
No Colbhasaigh nan struth siùbhlach,
Bidh mo chàirdean ort an diùmbadh,
Bidh mo bhràithrean as an cionn dhut,
Gun dig m'athair 'n seo thoirt cùis dhiot,
Bheir iad mise leò air ghiùlan,
Air each gorm nan strian dùbailt.

'S a Mhic a' Mhaoir, gur tu as docha
Shiubhail sliabha, fiar no fochann,
No chuir bròg air stròn a choiseadh.

'S truagh nach cluinninn siod, 's nach fhaicinn
Farum do shluaigh, fuaim do bhrataich,
Glaodh do phìoba bhith dol seachad,
Air luing 's air bàt' no air barca,
Ged nach beò mi gus siod fhaicinn.
Gum bu mhath liom sin a thachairt.

LXXVI

Mo rùn Ailein

Màiri Eóghainn Mhóir a' seinn

Dh'éirich mi moch, *hó hò,* madainn earraich, *hó hò,*
Mo rùn Ailein, hó hò, mo rùn Ailein, hó hò,

Dhìrich mi suas gual' a' bhealaich,
Shuidh mi air cnoc, lig mi m'anail,
Dh'amhairc mi bhuam fad mo sheallaidh,
Chunnacas do long mhór 'san t-seanail,
Có bh'air an stiùir ach mo leannan?
'S e bheireadh i slàn gu caladh,
Fhad 's a mhaireadh stagh no tarraig.

The 'Brown' will not pay the fine for you,
Nor 'Little Black' nor the 'Dun', nor the 'Speedy'[1]

My love, if you go out of the district,
Don't go near Jura, don't go near Lunga,
Nor Colonsay of the tidal currents,
My relations will hate you,
Above them my brothers will be against you,
My father will come here to accuse you,
They will take me with them for my funeral
On a grey horse with reins doubled.

O son of the Steward, you I preferred
Of any who trod hillside, grass or braird,
Or who put shoe on the point of his foot.

Alas I'd hear not that, nor see it,
The tumult of your host, the sound of your banner,
The noise of your pipes when they're passing,
On galley or ship or on a barque.
Though I am not alive to see that,
It is what I would like to happen.

LXXVI

My love Allan

Miss Mary Morrison singing

(*For tune, see p.* 341)

Early I rose one spring morning,
My love Allan, hó hò,

I climbed up the pass's shoulder,
I sat on a mound to get my breath,
I looked around as far as I'd see;
I saw your galley in the channel,
Who was at the helm but my lover?
He would take her unharmed into harbour,
As long as stay or halyard lasted.

[1] Names of cows.

Hala ho éile, hó hò,
Hala ho éile, hó hò,
Hala ho éile, hó hò.

Cha déid mise, *hó hò*, chaoidh cha déid mi, *hó hò*,
Hala ho éile, hó hò, *hala ho éile, hó hò*,

Cha déid mise 'n cois na cléitheadh,
'S diamhain dhomh siod, ann cha déid mi,
Cha n-eil m'àite an dràsd fhéin ann,
Aig gruagaichean . . . . . .
Aig mnathan Uibhist, aig mnathan Shléibhte,
Aig gruagaichean luadhadh le chéile.

Hala ho éile, hó hò,
Hala ho éile, hó hò,
Hala ho éile, hó hò.

Mile marbhaisg! luchd nam breugan,
Thog iad ormsa, mo chuid fhéin dhiu,
Gu robh mo chrios 'n àird ag éirigh,
Dé ma thà, 's gun . . . . . .
Cha n-ann o bhruinnein no o bhréinein,
Ach o Sgoilear donn na Beurla,
Théid a Shasunn 's a Dhùn Éideann,
Nì e 'n duilleag bhàn a leughadh,
'M fianais an Rìgh, 's ann a théid e.

Hala ho éile, hó hò,
Hala ho éile, hó hò,
Hala ho éile, hó hò.

LXXVII

Latha dhomh 's mi an Caolas Rònaidh

(*a*) *Bean Nìll a' seinn*

Laill leathag, ó hó
Laill leathag, ó hó.

Latha dhòmh 's mi, *ó hó*, [an Caolas Rònaidh,] *ó hó*,
laill leathag ó hó, *laill leathag, ó hó*,

I'll not go, I'll never go,

I'll not go near the waulking-board,
That's useless for me, there I'll go not,
My place is not there at this moment,
With maidens . . . . .
With Uist women, with Sleat women
With maidens waulking together.

A thousand curses on the liars,
Who said of me, my share of them,
That I showed signs of being pregnant;
What if I am? . . . . .
'Tis by no churl nor by a deceiver,
But by the brown-hair'd scholar of English,
Who'll go to England and to Edinburgh,
Who can read the white page
In the King's presence, there he'll go.

LXXVII

One day when I was at the Sound of Rona

(a) Mrs. Neil Campbell singing

(*For tune, see p.* 343)

One day when I was at the Sound of Rona,

Thàna bleidein, *ó hó*, staigh fo chòrsa, *ó hó*
laill leathag, *ó hó*, *laill leathag*, *ó hó*,
Le mheilbheid, *ó hó* etc. 's busa sprògach, *ó hó* etc.
Dh'fharraid i dhiom [le càil còmhraidh]
Gu dé b'fhasan do Chloinn Leòdach?
'Sìol nan capull, bacaich, spògaich,
Nach tuig àsuig . . . . . .'
Struth as a bus feadh nan lònaibh!

laill leathag, *ó hó*,
laill leathag, *ó hó*

Latha dhomh 's mi [an Caolas Rònaidh]
Thàna bleidein staigh fo chòrsa
Le mheilbheid 's busa sprògach
Dh'fharraid i dhiom [le càil còmhraidh]
Gu dé b'fhasan do Chloinn Dòmhnaill?
'Fìon 'ga ligeadh, deòir 'ga dòrtadh,
'S an treas-tarraing chur 'sna stòpan!'

(b) an teacs bho Chomh-chruinneachadh Gheusdo

A' BHEAN LEÒDACH;

Mhairghread chridhe, nighean an *Tòisich*,
Falt buidhe air dath an òir ort,
'S cian am bliadhna liom o'n phòs thu,
['S ann gu d' bhaile thriall am mórshluagh,
Thriall Mac Coinnich is MacLeòid ann,
'S MacFhionghuin bho Shrath nam bó ann.]

A' BHEAN DÒMHNALLACH:

'S mi 'nam shuidh' air Caolas Rònaidh,
M'aghaidh air Hiort nan eun móra,
Thànaig bleidein, bleideil, bòsdail,
Le mheilbheid 's le spuir 's le bòtainn,
'S dh'fhoigheachd e dhiom le càil còmhraidh
Gu dé b'fhasan do Chlann Dòmhnaill?
Dhomhsa b'aithne beus bu chòir dhaibh,

There came a blether   in under the shore,

Wearing velvet,   with thick lips;
She asked of me   in a kind of converse
What was the fashion   of the MacLeods?
'Race of horses   lame, splay-footed,
Who understand not a boat, ...'
A stream from her mouth   Amongst the puddles.

One day when I   was at the Sound of Rona,
There came a blether   in under the shore,
Wearing velvet,   with thick lips,
She asked of me   in a kind of converse
What was the fashion   of Clan Donald?
'Wine being broached   beer being poured,
Thrice-distilled whisky   being put in stoups!'

(*b*) *The text from the Gesto Collection*

THE MACLEOD WOMAN:

Margaret, my dear,   *Macintosh's*[1] daughter,
With yellow hair   golden coloured,
'Tis long since the year   methinks, you married,
[To your village   a great host travelled,
MacKenzie travelled,   and MacLeod there,
And MacKinnon   from Strath of the cattle.]

THE MACDONALD WOMAN:

As I sat at   the Sound of Rona,
Facing St. Kilda   of the great auks,
There came a pleading   boastful blether,
Wearing velvet,   spurred and booted,
Who asked of me   in a kind of converse
What was the fashion   of Clan Donald?
Well I know   their usual habit,

[1] See note.

Fìon 'ga ligeadh, beòir 'ga h-òl ac',
An treas tarraing 'ga chur an stòpaibh;
Cha b'ionnan dhaibh sìol nan Leòdach,
Sìol a' chapuill bhacaich, spògaich,
Bheathachadh air mol is fòghlach,
Air dùdan dubh 's air gulm eòrna,
Air uisge bog a' phuill-mhòna,
Cha ghoirear riu ach 'pruis-òidhidh',
Taod mu'n claigeann, 's goid mu'n dòrnaibh!
Thug thu teicheadh, phrasgain ghealltaich,
No 'n cuimhne libh là Ghleann Shealltainn?
Sheas sibh 'san fhraoch mar na cearcan,
Chaidh sibh 'san loch mar na lachain,
Chaidh sibh 'sa chuan mar na farspaich!

A' BHEAN LEÒDACH:

Có i 'n long taobh staigh an eilein?

A' BHEAN DÒMHNALLACH:

Don-bhuaidh ort! [c'uim' an ceilinn?]
Tha long Dhòmhnaill Ghuirm nan eilein;
Dh'fhàg i 'n rubh' ud 's an rubh' eile,
Chuir i bòrd far long Mhic Coinnich,
'S dh'fhàg i long Mhic Leòid air deireadh!

A' BHEAN LEÒDACH:

Mur bhitheadh mo chridh' a' dìobradh,
'S mo ghuth lag air beagan spìdidh,
'S mi gun seinneadh an tuireadh cinnteach
Dha na fearaibh tha'n taobh shìos dhiom
An Dùn Bheagain nan long lìonmhor;
'S ann aig Ruairi tha 'n long fhada,
Théid i dh'Ìle, théid i dh'Arainn,
Fir òg ag òl air a sarcuinn.

Wine being broached,   beer drunk by them,
In stoups pouring   thrice distilled whisky;
The race of the MacLeods   is not like them
Race of the limping   broad-hoofed palfrey,
Who were fed on   chaff and rank grass,
On black mill-dust   and awns of barley,
On stagnant water   of the peat-hags,
Who are called only   by 'prush-oiey!'
A rope round their heads,   a withe round their fetlocks!
You ran away,   you cowardly rabble,
Do you recall   Glen Haultin's battle?
You stayed in the heath   like grouse sitting,
You went in the loch   like the mallards,
You went in the sea   like the black-backs!

THE MACLEOD WOMAN:

What ship is that   inside the island?

THE MACDONALD WOMAN:

Bad luck to you!   [why should I hide it?]
'Tis Donald Gorm   of the Isles his galley;
She left yon point   and the other behind her,
She has out-tacked   MacKenzie's galley,
She left MacLeod's   ship behind her!

THE MACLEOD WOMAN:

If my heart   were not failing,
And my weak voice   of little vigour,
I would surely   be reciting
About the men   who are below me
In Dunvegan   of many galleys;
It is Rory   who has the galley
That goes to Islay   and to Arran,
With young men drinking   on her sarking.

LXXVIII

Gu dé nì mi nochd ri m' nàire?

Anna Raghnaill Eachainn a' seinn

Fire, fàire, hó ro ho
Gu dé nì mi, *o ro ho,*   nochd ri m' nàire, *o ro ho,*
fire, fàire, hó ro ho,   *fire, fàire, ó ro ho.*
    nochd ri m' nàire, *ho hì o ho,*
    fire, fàire, o ro ho,

Dheoghail an crodh, *hó ro ho,*
fire, fàire, hó ro ho,
Dheoghail an crodh, *ho hì o ho,*   -laoigh 'san fhàsaich, *hó ro ho,*
fire, fàire, hó ro ho,   *fire, fàire, o ro ho.*
Dheoghail Buidheag   dheoghail Blàrag,
'S dheoghail gach aon   mar a b'àbhaist.
Guma slàn, 's gun   a bhiodh an t-àrmunn
Dh'fhalbh o sheachdain   gus am màireach,
Cha n-eil aoinfhear   rinn sibh àireamh
Gu Ciadaine   tùs na ràithe.

LXXIX

'N robh thu 'sa bheinn?

Anna Raghnaill Eachainn a' seinn

Éileadh le hó ro, ho hu a
''N robh thu 'sa bheinn?,   'n d'fhuair thu na féidh?'
ó ho hù a   *ó ho hù a*
éileadh le hó ro, ho hu a,   *éileadh le hó ro, ho hu a,*
'Cha d'fhuair, no 'n leath,'   'Có bha bhuat dhiu?'
'Nighean Buidheig,   ogha Ruadhain,
Nighean na bà   's fheàrr 'sa bhuailidh.'

LXXVIII

What shall I do tonight to my darling?

Mrs. MacDougall singing

(*For tune, see p.* 344)

What shall I do   tonight to my darling?

   tonight to my darling?

The cows have suckled,

The cows have suckled   in the pasture,

Buidheag has suckled,   so has Blàrag,
Each one has suckled   as is their habit.
Farewell, farewell,   to the warrior,
Who left a week   ago tomorrow,
It is not one man   that you numbered
Until Wednesday   beginning of the quarter.

LXXIX

Were you on the hill?

Mrs. MacDougall singing

(*For tune, see p.* 345)

'Were you on the hill,   or did you find the cows?'

'No, nor half of them.'   'Which did you miss?'
'The daughter of Buidheag,   the grand-daughter of Ruadhan,
The daughter of the best   cow in the cattlefold.'

LXXX

Gura h-e mo ghaol an t-Iain

Màiri Ruarachain a' seinn

Hì a bhó, o hì o hó, hì a bhó (solo)
O hi o hó, hì a bhó. (tutti)

Gura h-e mo, *hi a bhó*,   ghaol an t-Iain, *hì a bhó*,
O hi a hó, hì a bhó,   *O hi o hó, hì a bhó*,

Dha'n dug mi   mo chiad ghaol falaich,
Fear osain ghuirm   's nam bròg barriall,
'S dh'aithnghinn fhéin e   cheud a dh'fhearaibh,
Ged bhiodh sneachd   ann, is gailleann
Sìobadh fionn, 's gun,   gàbhadh mara.

Ho hi a bhó, hì a bhó, (tutti)
Ho hi a bhó, hì a bhó, (solo)
Ho hi a bhó, hì a bhó. (tutti)

LXXXI

'S mise bhean bhochd

(*a*) *Anna Aonghais Chaluim a' seinn*

'S mise bhean bhochd, *hó hi o hù*,   chianail dhuilich, *na, ho hì o hù*,
ho ro ho éileadh, hó hì o hù,   *ho ro ho éileadh, hó hì o hù*,

Air mo chreachadh, *na, hó hì o hù*   . . . . .
ho ro ho, etc.

'S fhuair mi 'n naidheachd, *na*,   air tighinn dhachaigh,
Armailt an rìgh   innealt, asanta,
Marcraich nan each   strianach, eangach,

LXXX

My beloved is the Ian

Mrs. Mary MacNeil singing

(*For tune, see p.* 347)

My beloved   is the Ian,

To whom I first gave   my secret love,
He of the blue hose   and the latcheted shoes,
I would recognise him   out of a hundred,
Though it were snowing,   and there was a storm,
With spindrift   and peril at sea.

LXXXI

I am a poor woman

(*a*) *Annie Johnston singing*

(*For tune, see p.* 348)

I am a poor woman,   sad and sorrowful,

I have been plundered   . . . . .

I got the news   on coming home,
The Royalist army   well-equipped, ordered,
The rider of horses   well-shod and bridled,

Ge b'oil liom sin, sin na thachair, *na*
Mharbh thu 'n coirneil, 's leòin thu 'n caiptein, *na*
'S dh'fhàg thu na Goill marbh gun anam, *na*
'S thug thu do shluagh slàn as dhachaigh, *na*
Murchadh an Éirinn, ...
Nan gabht' éirig as mo leanabh, *na*
Cha bhiodh crodh-laoigh anns na gleannain, *na*
Cha bhiodh caoirich bhàn' 'sna beannan, *na*

(*b*) *Air dòigh eile a Barraidh; ma dh'fhaoidte Ruairi Iain Bhàin*

O hi ho hu o, horo ho éileadh

Murchadh an Éirinn, 's mise bhean bhochd,
Chràiteach, dhuilich, cha n-e m'iothlann,
No mo chruachan, no mo thaigh mór,
No mo chitsinn dhol 'na lasair,
No m'aona nighean dh'fhalbh dh'a h-asaid bhuam,
Ach mo chùirtear 'n làimh an Glaschu,
'S iad a' maoidheadh a chur a Shasunn,
'S do Dhùn Éideann nan ceud fasan;
Nan gabht' éirig, éirig mo leinibh-sa,
Nan deanadh nì dhomhsa t'fhaighinn as,
Cha bhiodh airgiod glas am falach ort,
Cha bhiodh crodh-laoigh aig a' bhaile,
Cha bhiodh eich mhóra feamnadh fearainn ann,
Cha bhiodh gobhair an Creig Ruairi,
Bhuainte an t-òr ann mar an luachair!

LXXXII

'S muladach truagh, 's cianail thà mi

Anna Aonghais Chaluim a' seinn

'S muladach truagh,
Hao ri ibh o,
Hò ro hù o,
Hao ri ibh o.

's cianail thà mi
Hao ri ibh o,
Hò ro hù o,
Hao ri ibh o.

Though I dislike it, it is what happened,
You killed the colonel, you wounded the captain,
You left the Lowlanders lying lifeless,
You brought your host homeward safely.
Murdo in Ireland . . . . . .
If a ransom for my child were accepted,
There would be no cows in the valleys,
There would be no white sheep on the hillsides.

(b) Another Barra version, possibly Roderick MacKinnon

Murdo in Ireland, I am a poor woman,
Pained and sorrowful not for my stack-yard,
Nor for my oat stacks nor for my big house,
Nor for my kitchen set on fire,
Nor for my one daughter lost in childbirth
But for my courtier captive in Glasgow,
Whom they threaten to send to England,
And to Edinburgh of the hundred fashions.
If a ransom for my child were accepted,
Or if goods could get you out for me,
Grey silver would not be hid from you,
There would be no cows at the township,
There would be no great horses spreading manure there,
There would be no goats on Rory's crag,
Gold would be reaped there like the rushes!

LXXXII

Sorrowful, sad, miserable am I

Miss Annie Johnston singing

(*For tune, see p.* 349)

Sorrowful, sad, miserable am I,

O'n latha sin   dh'fhalbh am bàta
Hao ri, etc.   *Hao ri*, etc.

Dh'fhalbh crodh Eachainn   dh'fhalbh crodh Theàrlaich
Dh'fhalbh thu, leannain   dh'iomain na bàirich,
Bheir soiridh bhuam   . . . . . .
Dh'fhios an lagain   ìseil bhòidhich;
Ghairm a' chuthag,   's ghairm an smeòrach,
'S ghairm gach eun   'san ealtainn còmhl' ann
Bheir soiridh bhuam   . . . . . .
Dh'fhios an lagain   ìseil bhòidhich,
Fàsaidh peasair,   fàsaidh pònair,
Fàsaidh corca   's fàsaidh eòrn' ann
'S fàsaidh lìon ann   'na chuachan òrbhuidh',

Hao ri ibh o,
Ho ro hù o,
Hao ri ibh o,
Ho ro hù o,
Hao ri ibh o.

LXXXIII

Chuir iad mise an ceann na cléitheadh

Bean Nìll a' seinn

Chuir iad mise, *hì ill o ho*   (solo)
hù ill o ro, hì ill o ho   (tutti)
'n ceann na cléitheadh, *hì ill* etc.

'N dùil nach iomairinn   's an dùil nach éibhinn
'S 'n dùil nach dugainn   tulgag eutrom.

Gur cianail bochd   an nochd a thà mi
Bho'n chuir mi cùl   ri luchd ceàirde
Dhiùlt mi, dhiùlt mi   dhiùlt mi 'n tàilleir
Dh'fhuaigheadh gu grinn   leis an t-snàthaid
Dhiùlt mi 'n griasaich'   chuireadh sàil ann
'N dùil gun digeadh   saor an tàthaidh
Chuireadh an long   mhór air sàile
. . . . . .   guma slàn leis.

Since that day the ship departed,

Hector's cattle have gone, and Charlie's,
You've gone, my love, to play at shinty;
Give my farewell . . . . .
To the pretty low-lying valley,
Where the cuckoo called and the mavis,
Every bird in the flock sang there together.
Give my farewell . . . . .
To the pretty low-lying valley,
Peas grow there, beans grow there,
Oats and barley also grow there,
Flax grows there in golden bunches.

LXXXIII

They set me at the waulking board's head

Mrs. Neil Campbell singing

(*For tune, see p.* 351)

They set me at the waulking board's head,

Thinking I'd not push, that I'd not sing,
That I'd not give (the cloth) a light tossing.

Poor and sad am I tonight,
Since I turned my back on the craftsmen,
I refused, I refused, I refused the tailor,
Who sewed neatly with the needle;
I refused the cobbler who put a heel there,
Hoping that the joiner would come,
Who'd put the great ship on the sea,
. . . . . farewell to him.

LXXXIV

'S tìm dhomh bhith falbh

(*a*) *Màiri Eóghainn Mhóir a' seinn*

'S tìm dhomh bhith falbh,

Ho hì e bhó, (solo)
Hò ro nàilibh, ho hì e bhó. (tutti)

bhith cur umam,
Ho hì e bhó, etc.

Bhith dol a null air na grunnan,
Null a shealltainn air mo mhuime,
Bean na coiseadh caoile cruinneadh,
'S i nach dug riamh dhomh droch-urram,
Mo chur a bhleith no a dh'fhuine,
Ach a chìreadh cinn 's 'ga chumadh,
Sìor-chur gràinn' air léintean thuilinn,
'N seòmbar àrd a steach ro' uinneig.

Cha déid mise do Chinn Gheàrrloch,
No Loch Shubhairn nan craobh àrda,
Far am fàsadh meas air meanbh-lus,
Smiaran dubha, caora dearga,
Dearcagan air bhàrr na calltainn.

Ho hì e bhó, (solo)
Ho ro nàilibh, ho hì e bhó, (tutti)

Ho hì e bhó, (solo)
Ho ro nàilibh, ho hì e bhó, (solo)

Ho ro nàilibh, ho hì e bhó. (tutti)

LXXXIV

I must be going

(*a*) *Miss Mary Morrison singing*

(*For tune, see p.* 352)

I must be going,

getting ready,

To be going across the shallows,
Over to see my foster-mother,
Woman of foot neat and slender,
Who never gave me aught but respect,
Or set me to grind or to bake,
But to combing and fixing tresses,
Embroidering shirts of twilly,
In a high room beside a window.

I'll not go to Kingairloch,
Or Loch Hourn with its tall trees,
Where berries grow on little bushes,
Blackberries and red rowanberries,
Little nuts on the top of hazels.

(*b*) *Bho LS. an Òbain*

Ho hi a bhó,
Ho ro nàilibh,
Ho hi a bhó.

'S tìm dhomh bhith falbh, 's bhith cur umam,
Bhith dol a nunn air na grunnan,
Dol a shealltainn air mo mhuime,
Bean na coise gile cruinne,
'S nach dug riamh dhomh droch-urram,
Mo chur an tràigh no bhuain dhuileasg,
No bhuain bhàirneach ri cois tuinne,
Mo chur a bhleith, no a dh'fhuine;
'S ann a bhithinn staigh ri uinneig
Fuaghal shìoda, leughadh dhuilleag,
Sìor-chur gràinn' air léine cuileanach.

Ort a dh'fhàs a' mhaise mhullaiche,
Cha phiorraid i, ad na currac i,
Maise gruaige dualach duinne i.
Fleasgaich a chaidh seachad sìos orm,
Fois air do cheum, till a nìos rium,
Cha n-ann mar sin liginn dhiom thu
Le mnaoi phùsda, le mnaoi dhìolain,
Leis a' mhnaoi òig rinn am mìannas,
Lig mo leannan sìnte sìos rith',
'S mi fhìn gu seang foinnidh fìorghlan.

Cha déid mise 'na Bhail' Iarach,
No 'n Bhaile-bheag tha 'n taobh shìos deth,
Far am faighear am meas air a' mheanbh-lus,
Smiara dubha, caora dearga.

Chunnaic mi 'n dé seachad suas thu
Féileadh ort na phleatadh cuaiche,
Gunna bheòil bhig air do ghualainn;
Cha b'e do bhiadh breacag shuarach,
Cha b'e do dheoch uisg' an fhuarain,
Ach bainn' a' chruidh laoigh gun truailleadh,
Fìon is beòir air bhòrd duin' uasail,
'S gheibhinn cadal air do chluasaig.

(b) Version from the Oban MS.

I must be going, getting ready,
To be going across the shallows,
Over to see my foster-mother,
Woman of foot neat and white,
Who never gave me aught but respect,
Sent me to the shore or to pick dulse,
Or to get limpets at the wave's edge,
Or to grind, or to bake;
Indoors I'd be beside a window,
Sewing silks, reading pages,
Embroidering fine apparel.

Upon your head grew a thing of beauty,
Not a head-piece, not a head-dress,
But beautiful hair brown and curling,
Young man who went along past me,
Rest your step, come back to me,
'Tis not like that I'll let you leave me,
With a wife or with a mistress,
With a young girl who got her longing,
Who let my lover lie down with her,
While I was virginal, chaste and lively.

I'll not go to the lower township,
Nor to the little one that's north of it,
Where fruit is found on small bushes,
Blackberries and red rowan berries,

I saw you yesterday go past me.
Wearing a plaid in flowing pleats,
A small-bore gun on your shoulder,
Your food was not a contemptible scone,
Your drink was not cold spring water,
But dairy cows' milk unpolluted,
Wine and beer on gentry's table,
And I would sleep upon your pillow.

LXXXV

Dhìrich mi suas an Coire Riabhach

(*a*) *Ceit Ruairi Iain Bhàin a' seinn*

E ho hì ibh, hó ill a bhó,

Dhìrich mi suas, an Coire Riabhach
hó hoireann ó, ó hug ò ro,
E hó hì ibh, hó ill a bhó E hó hì ibh, hó ill a bhó.

Cha d'fhuair mi ann na bha mi 'g iarraidh
ho hoireann, etc. *o hug ò ro*, etc.

Banchaig a' chruidh dhruimfhinn chiardhuibh
Sùil 'ga sireadh cas 'ga h-iarraidh,
'Ga toirt as na beannan fiadhaich
Ris an lagan ìseal ghrianach,
o hug ò ro,

E ho hì ibh hó ill a bhó, (tutti)
E ho hì ibh hó ill a bhó, (solo)
E ho hì ibh hó ill a bhó. (tutti)

Gura h-e mo, rùn an t-uasal
ho hoireann ó o hug ò ro
E ho hì ibh hó ill a bhó, E ho hì ibh hó ill a bhó,

Chunnaic mi 'n dé seachad suas thu
ho hoireann, etc. *o hug ò ro*, etc.
Éileadh ort, *na*, breacain guailleadh
Le d' ghunna sneap or 'o ghualainn,
Claidheamh chinnghil or 'o chruachan,
Dol a shealg na h-éilde ruaidhe
'S an ròin léith o bheul na stuaigheadh,
'N eala cha dig slàn bho d' luaidhe.

E ho hì ibh hó ill a bhó, (tutti)
E ho hì ibh hó ill a bhó, (solo)
E ho hì ibh hó ill a bhó. (tutti)

LXXXV

I climbed up the Brindled Corrie

(*a*) *Mrs. Buchanan singing*

(*For tune, see p.* 353)

I climbed up   the Brindled Corrie,

I found not there   what I was seeking,

The milker of cattle   white-backed, dark grey,
My eye searching   my foot seeking her,
To take her from   the savage mountains
To the sunny   low-lying valley.

The nobleman   is my love,

I saw you passing   yesterday,

Wearing a kilt,   a shoulder plaid,
With your musket   on your shoulder,
A white-headed sword   at your haunches,
Going to hunt   the red hind,
And the grey seal   from the wave's edge,
The swan will not   escape your lead.

(*b*) *Bho LS. an Urramaich Dhunnchaidh Leathainich*

ESAN:

Dh'éirich mi moch, madainn ghrianach,
O hoireann ó, O hug ó ro,
'S dhìrich mi suas an Coire Riabhach;
Cha d'fhuair mi ann na bha mi 'g iarraidh,
Banchag a' chruidh dhruimfhionn chiara,
Bean dhonn 's a falt mar tha an dìthein,
Sùil chorrach ghorm as glan lìonadh,
'S gruaidh thana dhearg as glan sìoladh.

Shiubhail mi fàsach 's dh'iarr mi 'n innis,
Dh'iarr mi 'm bun is braigh' a' ghlinne,
Dh'iarr mi 's gach àit' am biodh tu mire—
Cha b'ann a' streup ris na gillean,
Fuaghal léintean 's leughadh dhuilleag.

C'àite 'n cualas geum bu chruaidhe
Na geum Dhuibhein is geum Ghruagain,
No do gheum-sa, Shubhach ghuaillfhionn?
Ag ionndrainn Iain dhonn na gruaige.

ISE:

'S toil liom, 's toil liom 's toil liom Ruairi
Chunnaic mi 'n dé seachad suas thu,
Do ghunna sneap or 'o ghualainn,
'S nan tachradh tu an còir na buaile,
Ghlacainn cuman 's lunndrainn buarach;
'S cha b'e do dheoch bùrn an fhuarain,
Deoch de bhainne blàth gun truailleadh;
Chàirinn leaba bhàrr na luachrach,
Laighinn fhìn leat taobh an fhuaraidh,
Eagal, a ghaoil, gum biodh am fuachd ort.

(*b*) *Text from Canon MacLean's MS.*

(*For tune, see p.* 353)

HE:

I arose early one sunny morning,

I ascended the Brindled Corrie,
I found not there what I was seeking,
The dairymaid of the dun white-backed cattle,
A brown girl, her hair like the marigold,
A rolling blue eye of clear fulness,
This red cheek of best breeding.

I walked the pasture, I sought in the meadow,
I sought in the foot and the head of the glen,
I sought in each place you used to be playing,
Not at horse-play with the young men,
But sewing shirts and reading pages.

Where was there heard a louder bellow
Than that of Duibhean and that of Gruagan,
Or your bellow, white-shouldered Subhach?
Missing Ian of the brown head of hair.

SHE:

I like, I like, I like Rory,
Yesterday I saw him passing,
Your triggered gun upon your shoulder,
Were we to meet around the cowfold,
I'd take a pail, I'd fix a fetter,
Your drink would not be of cold spring water,
But of warm milk unpolluted,
I'd make a bed out of the rushes,
I'd lie with you on the weather side,
For fear, my love that you'd be cold.

LXXXVI

Turadh am muigh

Màiri Eóghainn Mhóir a' seinn

E hó hì ibh, ó ho lebh ó (solo)
E hó hì ibh, ó ho lebh ó (tutti)

Turadh am muigh, *ó hoireann ó* (solo)
E hó hì ibh, ó ho lebh ó, (chorus)

Turadh am muigh, *hó hug ò ro,* (solo)
E hó hì ibh, ó ho lebh ó, (tutti)

's an là glasadh, *ó hoireann ó,*
E hó hì ibh, ó ho lebh ó,
's an là glasadh, *hó hug ò ro,*
E hó hì ibh, ó ho lebh ó.

Chì mi, chì mi dhrùidh an fhras orm,
Air mo bhreacan, air mo leacainn,
Mo ghunna caol tighinn an asgaidh,
hó hug ò ro,

E hó hì ibh, ó ho lebh ó, (tutti)
E hó hì ibh, ó ho lebh ó, (solo)
E hó hì ibh, ó ho lebh ó. (tutti)

Chì mi, chì mi . . . . .
Chì mi na féidh th'air an leacaidh,
Cha n-eil ann, *na,* neach 'gam bacail,
Loisgeas riutha smùid no deatach,
Fùdar gorm, luaidhe chnapach,
hó hug ò ro,

E hó hì ibh, ó ho lebh ó, (tutti)
E hó hì ibh, ó ho lebh ó, (solo)
E hó hì ibh, ó ho lebh ó. (tutti)

LXXXVI

It is dry outside, the day is dawning

Miss Mary Morrison singing

(*For tune, see p.* 354)

It is dry outside,

It is dry outside,

the day is dawning,
the day is dawning,

I see, I see, the shower has soaked me,
Has soaked my plaid, has soaked my cheek,
My slender gun, coming freely.

I see, I see . . . . .
I see the deer which are on the hillside,
There is no one to prevent them,
Who'll shoot at them with smoke of gunfire,
With blue powder and lumpy lead,

Ma tha mo shealgair donn an tasgaidh,
'N cistidh chinn chaoil, saoir 'ga bannadh
Is gus do chur sìos fo'n talamh,
Far nach cluinn mi thu 's nach fhaic mi.
Hó hug ò ro,

E hó hì ibh, ó ho lebh ó, (tutti)
E hó hi ibh, ó ho lebh ó, (solo)
E hó hì ibh, ó ho lebh ó. (tutti)

LXXXVII

Fhir a' chinn duibh

(*a*) *a réir Anna Aonghais Chaluim*

Raghainn e hó, rao o hó,
Fhir a' chinn duibh, *o hì i o,* 's a' chùil dualaich, *o a hò,*
Raghainn e hó, ro a hó, *raghainn e hó, ro a hó,*
Fhir a' chinn duibh, *o hó,* etc. 's a' mhuineil ghil, *o a hò,*
Raghainn, etc. *raghainn,* etc.
'S òg a cheangail mi mo ghruag dhut,
Cha b'ann le stìom ach 'na dualan,
Fhir a' chinn duibh, 's a' mhuineil ghil,
'S aithne dhomh fhìn dé chum bhuam thu,
Tainead mo chruidh- laoigh air bhuailtean,
Cha n-eil bó dhubh no bó ruadh ann,
No bó idir air 'n déid buarach;
Fhir a' chinn duibh 's a' mhuineil ghil,
'S aithne dhomh fhìn dé chum bhuam thu,
Muthad mo ghaoil ort, 's lughad m'fhuath ort.

(*b*) *Bho'n LS. aig Maighstir Ailein Dòmhnallach*

E o hì o,
Fhir a' chinn duibh, ...
O i ri o hug òireanan
'S aithne dhomh fhìn dé chum bhuam thu—
Meud mo ghaoil ort, lughad m'fhuath ort,

If my brown-haired hunter's buried,
In a tapering coffin secured by joiners,
To put you beneath the earth,
Where I'll neither hear or see you.

LXXXVII

O black-haired one

(*a*) *Annie Johnston's version*

(*For tune, see p.* 356)

O black-haired one of curling locks,

O black-haired one of whitest neck,

Very young I bound my hair for you,
Not with a snood but in plaits;
O black-haired one of whitest neck,
I know myself what kept you from me,
My few milk-cows in the cattlefolds,
There's neither black nor red cow there,
Nor any cow there to be shackled.
O black-haired one of whitest neck,
I know myself what kept you from me—
How much I loved, how little I hated you.

(*b*) *Version from Fr. Allan McDonald's MS.*

O black-haired one . . . . .

I know myself what kept you from me,
How much I loved how little I hated you,

Tainead mo chruidh air a' bhuailidh—
Thugainn, a bhó dhubh, thugainn, a bhó ruadh!
'S aithne dhomh fhìn dé chum bhuam thu—
Gun mo chaoirich [bhith 'sna bruachan,]
Gun mo mhàthair shuidh' 'n taobh shuas dhiom,
M'athair a bhith marbh 'san fhuarlic,
Gun mo bhràithrean bhith ri m' ghualainn;
'S nan digeadh tu 'n còir na buaileadh
Cha bu deoch liom dhut an t-uachdar,
Bainne chrodh-laoigh . . . .
Deoch dha'n fhìon dearg bhuam gun d'fhuaireadh,
Uisge beatha nan Gall gruamach.

'S nan digeadh tu 'n còir na buaileadh,
Chàirinn leaba, ghearrainn luachair,
Liginn plaide bhàn far cuaich dhut,
'S laighinn fhìn leat taobh an fhuaraidh,
Eagal 's gun ruig gaoth no fuachd thu,
Fhir mhuineil ghil 's a' chùil dualaich!

LXXXVIII

'S toil liom, 's toil liom

(*a*) *Bean Nìll a' seinn*

'S hu hoireann ó, hi ri o ho
Ro hoireann ó, ho hì o hó,
Hu hoireann ó, hi ri o ho.

'S toil liom, 's toil liom,

O hì o hó,
Hu hoireann ó, hi ri o ho,
Ro hoireann ó, ho hì o hó,
Hu hoireann ó, hi rì o hó.

'S toil liom aona-mhac donn mo pheathar
O hì, etc. *O hì*, etc.
'S toil liom Sgoilear donn na Beurla

My milk-cows' fewness at the cattlefold,
Come hither, black cow! come here, red cow!
I know myself what kept you from me,
My having no sheep [upon the braesides,]
My having no mother to sit beside me,
My father lying beneath the gravestone,
My having no brothers at my shoulder;
If you would come near the cowfold,
I would not think cream was a drink for you,
The milk of milk cows . . . .
A drink of red wine I would get you,
And whisky of the surly Lowlanders.

If you would come near the cowfold
I'd prepare a bed, I would cut rushes,
I would unfold a white plaid for you,
I'd lie with you on its weather side,
For fear that the wind or the cold would reach you,
O white-necked one of curling back hair!

LXXXVIII

I like, I like

(*a*) *Mrs. Neil Campbell singing*

(*For tune, see p.* 357)

I like, I like

I like the brown-haired only son of my sister,

I like the brown-haired scholar of English,

Théid thu Shasann 's do Dhùn Eideann
Bheir thu dhachaigh leabhar sgeula
Air each crùidheach nan ceum eutrom.

Nigh'n dubh, nigh'n dubh, banchaig a' chruidh,
Chaidil thu 'm muigh an innis a' chruidh;
'S gil' thu na 'n gruth, 's deirg' thu na 'n fhuil,
'S luaith' thu na 'n gunn', 's toil liom, 's toil liom.

(*b*) *bho'n LS. aig Dòmhnall Mac an t-Saoir*

Hù hoireann ò, hi rì o ho,
Rò hoireann ò, hi rì o ho,
Hù hoireann ò, hi rì o ho.

Nighean dubh, nighean donn 'm falbh thu liomsa?

Gheibh thu coinneal laist' ad lainnteir,
Gheibh thu fìona 's fheàrr am' luing-sa,
Gheibh thu fear as fheàrr dha m' mhuinntir,
Mas beag leat sin, bidh mi fhìn leat.

Nighean dubh, nighean dubh, 's gil' thu na 'n gruth,

'S deirg' thu na 'n fhuil, 's binn' thu na 'n guth,
'S luaith' thu na 'n luinn . . . .
Chaidil thu 'm muigh an innis a' chruidh

'S toil liom, 's toil liom, 's toil liom Seumas,
'S toil liom Sgoilear donn na Beurla,
Théid thu Shasuinn 's do Dhùn Eideann,
Air each cruidheach nan ceum eutrom,
Bheir thu dhachaigh leabhar sgeula.

(*c*) *Air dòigh eile, bho Anna nighean Nìll, Ceap Breatann*

Hù hoireann ó, hi rì o hó,
Ró hoireann ó, ho hì o hó,
Hù hoireann ó, ho rì o hó.

Latha bha mi 'n lic Dùn bheagain,
Bha mi crith le móran eagail.

You'll go to England   and to Edinburgh,
You'll bring home   a story book
Riding a well-shod horse   that steps lightly.

Brown-haired maiden   dairymaid of cattle,
You slept outside   in the cow meadow,
You are whiter than curds,   redder than blood,
Swifter than gunshot   I like, I like.

(b) Version from Donald MacIntyre's MS.

Black-haired girl, brown-haired girl,   will you go with me?
You'll get a candle   lit in your lantern,
You'll get the best   wine in my galley,
You'll get the best   man of my people,
If you don't like that   I myself will be yours.

Black-haired girl, brown-haired girl,   you are whiter than curds,
You are redder than blood,   you are sweeter than the voice,
You are swifter than. . . .   .
You slept outside   in the meadow where cows graze.

I like, I like,   I like Hamish,
I like the brown-haired   scholar of English,
You'll go to England   and to Edinburgh,
On a well-shod horse   stepping lightly,
You'll bring home   a book of stories.

(c) Another version, from Mrs. Neil McInnis, Cape Breton

One day as I was   on the door-step of Dunvegan,
I was shaking   with great terror.

Nighean dubh, nighean donn, nighean donn bhòidheach,

. . . . 'm falbh thu liomsa?
Gu baile nam faoileann fionngheal?
Gheibh thu fìon is beòir 'nam luing-sa,
Gheibh thu seisd is siucair *candy*,
Coinneal ri céir laist' an coinnleir,
Gheibh thu fear òg 's fheàrr dha m' mhuinntir,
Mur gabh thu sin, bidh mi fhìn leat,
Nuair théid thu steach òlar fìon leat,
[Nuair théid thu mach] seinnear pìob leat,
Seinnear fiodhull nan teud binn leat.

O, 's gòrach a' chlann 's òg le chéil' iad,
Dhiùlt thu 'n Sgoilear donn na Beurla,
Théid a Shasunn, a Dhùn Éideann,
Gu fianuis an Rìgh, mo ghaoil, ma théid thu,
Bheir thu as, *na* 'n leabhar sgeula,
'S nì thu 'n duilleag bhàn a leughadh.

Black-haired girl, brown-haired girl,   pretty brown-haired girl,
. . . .   will you go with me
To the village of   the white beaches?
You will get wine   and beer on my ship,
You'll get tunes   and sugar candy,
A wax candle lit   in a candlestick,
You'll get the best   young man of my folk,
You'll get me if   you won't take that.
When you go in   wine you will drink,
When you go out   pipes played for you,
The fiddle of sweet   strings played for you.

O, the children are foolish,   they are both young,
You refused the brown-   haired scholar of English,
Who goes to England   and to Edinburgh,
If you go, my love   before the King,
You'll take away   a book of stories,
The white page   you will be reading.

NOTES ON THE TEXT

LIST OF ABBREVIATIONS

(*For general bibliography, see Volume I, pp.* 345–9)

A. J. (1).	Small notebook containing the words of seven waulking songs written out by Miss Annie Johnston for Mrs. Kennedy-Fraser on her first visit to Barra in 1908, communicated by the Revd. Kenneth MacLeod.
A. J. (2).	Small notebook containing the words of 49 songs taken down by Miss Annie Johnston in Barra in 1931, and communicated by her to the writer. Many of the songs were taken down by Miss Johnston from her mother, others from her neighbour Ealasaid Eachainn (MacKinnon).
A. M. D.	Alexander MacDonald, *Ais-eiridh na Sean Chánoin Albannaich*, Edinburgh, 1751.
A. M. V.	Alexander MacDonald, *A Galick and English Vocabulary*, Edinburgh, 1741.
Barra MS.	Words of some waulking songs, apparently taken down from Mr. Roderick MacKinnon (Ruairi Iain Bhàin) around 1938, communicated to me.
B.Gh.	*Bàrdachd Ghàidhlig, Specimens of Gaelic poetry*, ed. by W. J. Watson, third edn., revised by Angus MacLeod, Stirling, 1959.
Canon MacLean.	MS. collection of the words of 44 songs, mostly waulking songs and a few in more than one version. These were taken down mostly from Mrs. Mary MacCuish (Màiri nighean Alasdair), a few from Mrs. Angus MacIntyre (mother of the late Donald MacIntyre, 'Dòmhnall Ruadh', the bard), Mrs. Donald Steele, and Mrs. Fanny MacIsaac. The collection was made while Canon MacLean was parish priest of Bornish, South Uist, in the 1930s, at the suggestion of the writer, and communicated to him on 10 May 1955.
C.C.	A. MacLean Sinclair, *Clàrsach na Coille*, edited by Hector MacDougall (Glasgow, 1928).

C.G. Alexander Carmichael, *Carmina Gadelica*, Six volumes, Edinburgh, 1928–71. The third and fourth volumes were edited by James Carmichael Watson, the fifth and sixth by Angus Matheson, the last completed by the Revd. William Matheson.

C.J. Small notebook containing words of songs taken down by Mr. Calum Johnston, brother of Miss Annie Johnston.

D. C. M. Small notebook containing manuscript songs transcribed in the field by D. C. MacPherson. Some of these later appeared in his *Duanaire*, published in Edinburgh in 1868.

Dieckhoff *A Pronouncing Dictionary of Scottish Gaelic, based on the Glengarry Dialect*, by Henry Cyril Dieckhoff, O.S.B. (Edinburgh, 1932).

Dinneen *Foclóir Gaedhilge agus Béarla. An Irish-English Dictionary* (Dublin, 1927).

D. McI. MS. collection of 59 songs, mostly waulking songs, made by Donald MacIntyre, South Uist, the 'Paisley Bard', and presented by him to the writer in 1950. I am informed by Mr. John MacMillan, Bornish, that Donald MacIntyre learnt his waulking songs from his own mother and from Finlay MacCormick the first cousin of Donald MacCormick, whose collection of waulking songs forms vol. i of *Hebridean Folksongs*.

Dwelly *The Illustrated Gaelic Dictionary, compiled by Edward Dwelly* (Fleet, 1930).

F.F.S.U. Margaret Fay Shaw, *Folksongs and Folklore of South Uist* (London, 1955). Includes 34 waulking songs. The introduction describes the life of the singers in the 1930s. Second edition in preparation (OU Press).

Fr. Allan MS. MS. collection of waulking songs made by Fr. Allan McDonald (1859–1905) on Eriskay in the 1890s, now in Edinburgh University Library. Includes some translations.

F. T. Frances Tolmie, '105 Songs of Occupation from the Western Isles of Scotland with Notes and Reminiscences', *Journal of the Folk-Song Society*, vol. iv (London, 1911).

Gesto Coll. Keith Norman MacDonald, *The Gesto Collection of Highland Music, including the second part or appendix of 67 pages* (Leipzig, 1895). Includes tunes contributed by Miss Frances Tolmie.

G.F.B. J. L. Campbell, Annie Johnston, and John MacLean, M.A., *Gaelic Folk Songs from the Isle of Barra*, five twelve-inch discs and book of words with translations. Linguaphone Co. (London, 1950). Includes 9 waulking songs.

G.S.N.S. — Helen Creighton and Calum MacLeod, *Gaelic Songs in Nova Scotia*, National Museum of Canada, Bulletin No. 198, Anthropological Series No. 66, Department of the Secretary of State, Canada. 1964.

G.W.S.U. — Fr. Allan McDonald, *Gaelic Words and Expressions from South Uist and Eriskay* (Dublin, 1958; Oxford, 1972). The first entries were of rare words from the MacCormick Collection of waulking songs.

H.F. — J. L. Campbell and Francis Collinson, *Hebridean Folksongs*: A collection of Waulking Songs made by Donald MacCormick (Oxford, 1969), vol. i.

J. L. C. — MS. collection of Gaelic songs, mostly waulking songs, recorded by the writer and his wife in Cape Breton and Antigonish County, Nova Scotia, in the autumn of 1937.

K. — The Killearnan MS. collection of Gaelic songs made by the Revd. Angus MacDonald between 1874 and 1895, in Edinburgh University Library. Closely connected with the *MacDonald Collection of Gaelic Poetry*, see below.

K. C. C. — K. C. Craig, *Órain Luaidh Màiri nighean Alasdair* (Glasgow, 1949). 150 waulking song texts taken down from Mrs. Mary MacCuish, Snaoiseabhal, South Uist, who was also Canon MacLean's informant.

L.F. — J. F. Campbell, *Leabhar na Féinne* (London, 1872).

McD. — The Revd. A. MacDonald, minister of Killearnan, and the Revd. A. MacDonald, minister of Kiltarlity, *The MacDonald Collection of Gaelic Poetry* (Inverness, 1911). Includes 56 waulking songs from the Outer Hebrides, 9 of them from Marion MacLennan, as is revealed in K.

McEachen — *Faclair Gailig us Beurla a chaidh a chur a mach le Eobhan Mac Eachainn* (Perth, 1862).

M.P.K.M. — *Miscellany Presented to Kuno Meyer* (Halle, 1912).

O. — Manuscript containing 17 waulking songs, and two or three other songs, taken down by the late Donald MacLachlan, Connel, in Oban in the 1890s, probably from Colin Campbell, piper, an old soldier who was a native of South Uist. The texts of the waulking songs are good, and clearly related to other South Uist versions. Donald MacLachlan, whose family came

	from Conaglen in Ardgour, died in 1921 aged about 76.
O.S.A.	*The (Old) Statistical Account of Scotland* (Edinburgh, 1791–9).
R.I.A. Contrib.	Royal Irish Academy, *Contributions to a Dictionary of the Irish Language* (Dublin, 1913–).
S.G.S.	*Scottish Gaelic Studies* (Aberdeen, 1926–).
T.G.S.I.	*Transactions of the Gaelic Society of Inverness* (1870–).
W.S.B.	*Waulking Songs from Barra*. Scottish Tradition 3, recorded and documented by the School of Scottish Studies, University of Edinburgh (London, 1972). LP disc containing seven waulking songs, and some piping, plus illustrated texts with translations.

The above manuscript sources naturally overlap. They contain in all approximately 220 different waulking songs, some in more than one version; some are only fragments. It is to be feared that the airs of about 12 or 15 per cent of them are now totally lost.

NOTES

XLI (*a*)

Am Bròn Binn

('The Sweet Sorrow')

Recorded as a waulking song from Mrs. MacDougall ('Anna Raghnaill Eachainn'), Castlebay, Isle of Barra, on disc in March 1938, with Miss Annie Johnston, who arranged the session, joining in the refrain. Recorded as a ballad from Mrs. Patrick MacCormick, Hacklett, Benbecula, on wire on 21/11/49 (wire recording no. 13), and on tape from Mrs. Morrison ('Bean Alasdair Mhòir'), at Milton, South Uist, on 26/4/61. The survival of the two entirely different styles of singing this song until quite recently is a matter of considerable interest; both types of air are printed in this book.

In the past the ballad has enjoyed wide popularity in the Highlands and Islands. Eight versions of it were collected by Dr. Alexander Carmichael, and two of them are printed, with translations and apparatus, in *C.G.* v. 85–105. Of these eight, the text of three had been printed in the *T.G.S.I.*, in a paper read by the Society's secretary, Mr. William MacKenzie, on 19/11/1879, to which they had been contributed by Carmichael, who had taken them down in North Uist in 1868, 1869, and 1870. Carmichael's other versions were from North Uist (2) South Uist (1, printed in *C.G.* v), Barra, 1, and unknown, 1.

Other versions have been printed, as follows: *Reliquiae Celticae*, i. 368, headed 'Bas Artuir', from the MacLagan MSS, taken down *c.* 1775, provenance not stated; *Leabhar na Féinne* (1872), p. 208, two versions, one collected at Lochalsh by D. C. MacPherson in January 1872, the other in Islay by Hector MacLean in 1860. D. C. MacPherson's version also exists in D. C. M. 157, as originally roughly written down from recitation; it reveals that a line has been omitted in printing, *Uinneagan gloine ri stuaidh*, which should precede *Bu lìonmhor innt'* (MS. *ann*) *cuach agus cup*. Oscar and Fionn appear in this version, which was sung as a waulking song. A version, presumably from Tiree, is printed in A. MacLean's *Clàrsach na Coille* (2nd ed., p. 195). A Skye version, with traditional (waulking song) air and translation, was published by Miss Frances Tolmie in her collection (F. T., no. 90, p. 251).

The ballad was made the subject of a particular study by George Henderson in his contribution to *M.P.K.M.* entitled 'Arthurian Motifs in Gadhelic Literature' (pp. 18–33). This includes a version from South Uist, recited as a ballad; Henderson also refers to the poem's being sung as a waulking song.

As an art song, *Am Bròn Binn* was presented by Mrs. Kennedy-Fraser in *Songs of the Hebrides*, iii. 175, under the title 'The Sea-Quest', with 'Melodies collected by Frances Tolmie, Skye, and Miss Annie Johnson (*sic*), Barra. Words collected and collated by Kenneth MacLeod'. (In fact, the first nine lines of the Gaelic were copied from F. T., no. 90, and the verse at 'The Lady Sings', p. 183, appears to be from Hector MacLean's version in *Leabhar na Féinne*.)

Besides these recorded and printed versions mentioned above, the following MS. versions have been available to us:

(1) That in vol. ii of the Dewar MSS. at Inveraray Castle, taken down from John MacNair, Glen Leahan (Lean) in Cowall, Argyllshire, probably in the 1860s (Dewar himself died in 1872, see MacKechnie, The Dewar MSS., Glasgow, 1964).

(2) A version taken down by the late Canon Duncan MacLean around 1936, probably from Mairi nighean Alasdair at Snaoiseabhal, South Uist, who gave to him and to K. C. Craig the texts of many waulking songs (Canon MacLean, IV, 9).

(3) A version in the Carmichael papers, taken down from Siusaidh Dhomhnallach (Mrs. MacDonald), Eilean Circeabost, North Uist, by Donald MacLean in 1865.

(4) Another version, fair copy in Carmichael's hand, no provenance mentioned.

(5) A version in the collection of ballads and stories made by George Henderson in South Uist in 1892, not the same as that he published in *M.P.K.M.* in 1912.

The variants from all these versions of *Am Bròn Binn* would fill far more space than is available here; only the most important are noted in this book. There are three main versions of the story contained in the ballad, as follows:

(1) The King of Britain goes out hunting, rests, falls asleep, and dreams

of the most beautiful girl he had ever seen. One of his courtiers, whose name is given in various forms as 'Sir Bhalbha', etc. equated by George Henderson with 'Sir Gawain' of Arthurian tradition, volunteers to search for her if the King will give him a ship.

After a long voyage Sir Bhalbha finds the girl a prisoner in a castle at the edge of the ocean. On his arrival a chain descends from the castle, which he immediately climbs, to find the girl seated on a throne in one of the rooms. He is warned by her that the lord of the castle, a giant or ogre called 'The Big Man', is shortly due to return and can be expected to show him no mercy. The 'Big Man' can only be killed with his own sword. The girl advises Sir Bhalbha to hide.

He does this. On his return the 'Big Man' suspects the presence of a stranger, but is persuaded to rest while the girl lulls him to sleep with harp music and song. When he falls asleep Sir Bhalbha emerges from hiding and the two of them take the 'Big Man's' sword from his belt, and cut off his head with it. Sir Bhalbha then sails off with the girl, leaving the 'Big Man's' widow lamenting.

(2) This is the same story as (1) except that the 'Big Man' does not come into it at all. It is Sir Gawain who is tired after his long sea journey, and is lulled to sleep by the music of the girl, who then removes his sword and kills him treacherously.

(3) This is a long, involved, and rather incoherent version of the ballad story, which goes on to tell of the hero rather inconsequentially being mixed up in a war against the children of the King of Greece (i.e. the Emperor of Byzantium).

No. 1 of these story-versions is best exemplified by the version of the ballad in the Dewar MSS., which is published here for the first time by the kind permission of the Trustees of the Tenth Duke of Argyll. It is also the story in the version of the ballad published by George Henderson in the *M.P.K.M.* It seems to us to be much the most coherent and probable version of the story.

No. 2 is the version of the story as given in the versions of the ballad recorded from all three of the reciters named at the beginning of these notes. It is also that contained in the version taken down by Carmichael from John MacLeod, Iochdar, South Uist, in January 1865, and printed in *C.G.* v. 100. The reciters with whom we have discussed the ballad expressed strong feelings about the treachery of the heroine; but it does seem that this version is simply that of (1) with a lacuna.

No. 3 seems to be associated with North Uist, and is exemplified by the three versions printed in *T.G.S.I.* ix, and also by the first version printed in *C.G.* v. 92, which also gives the impression of having been conflated. The Byzantine ending can hardly belong to the original ballad, the hero's name at the beginning of the whole being 'Sir Ghallabha' and in the latter part 'Bile Buadhach'.

The reciters of three versions asserted that the heroine was a witch (*C.G.* v. 100; *T.G.S.I.* ix. 69, and Canon MacLean, iv, 9). The reciter of the last said *Rinneadh a rann do Shiùsaidh nighean Righ Lochlainn aig an robh buidseach. Bha i dol chuca 'nan cadal 's togail an cuid, ma dh'fhaoidte 'gam marbhadh*. 'The poem was made to Susie daughter of the King of Norway, who was a witch. She used to appear to them while they were asleep, and take their property, and perhaps kill them.' John MacLeod, in *C.G.* v. 100, said that the maiden in the castle was a witch who lured Sir Falaich there to kill him for revenge.

Introduction to Dewar MS. version: *Dùn a thog e air Aill-séid-chuan*, i.e. *Ealasaid a' Chuain*, the Gaelic name for Ailsa Craig, in the Firth of Clyde. This is the only version where the scene of the ballad is localized.

an t-òran a leanas. The MS. has *leasas*.

3. *Gun duine*, etc. When the poem is sung as a ballad, the structure of the quatrains is ABCD, CDEF, EFGH, and so on, the last two lines of each verse being repeated as the first two lines of the following verse.

4. The name of the hero is variously given as *Shiphapan* (MacLagan MS., a copying mistake?), *Sir Bhoilidh*, *Sir Ghallmhai*, *Sir Gallo-aidh*, *Fionn Falaich*, *Fios Falaich*, but most often *Sir Falaich* (? cf. Irish *falaidhe*, 'grim').

10. *Còmhrag*, 'combat', is right in this context, as it is in the MacLagan MS. version (*Rev. Celt.* i. 368):

B'ìonnsa leis tuitim an shin
Ann comhrag an Fhir a b'fhear[r] dealbh
Na Bhean a Sh[e]inneadh an ceol
'S nach fhaicte i beo no marbh

'He would sooner fall there in combat with the man of best appearance, than that the woman who played the music should not be seen dead or alive.'

In most of the other versions, as in Anna Raghnaill Eachainn's here, the first two lines take the form:

Gum b'fheàrr leis tuiteam 'na cion, (or *'ga cion*, *dha cion*)
Na còmhradh fir mar bha e fhéin.

'He would sooner fall into her affection, than (have) the conversation of a man such as he was himself.'

In two of the versions (Henderson's, Mrs. Patrick MacCormick's) confusion has arisen, and *còmhrag* has been substituted for *còmhradh* in this latter passage, with detriment to the sense.

22. MS. *ghuirm*.

28. MS. *chaidhear urra*.

29. MS. *an ighean eididh òg*. Cf. *C.G.* vi. 118, *éiteag na h-oidhche*, 'fair one of the night' (under *riollag*). The usual word here is *b(h)réidgheal*, as in line 89.

35, 36. These lines are represented by a gap in the Dewar MS.; they are an essential part of this version of the ballad. Here given as they occur in the version printed by George Henderson.

39. *Air do ghuidhe-sa. L.F., Air do shuidhe-sa; M.P.K.M., Air bhur cumha-sa; C.C., Air mo chuirc-sa.* This last is not the original reading in John MacLean's MS., which is *Air do chuichsa.* A number of marginal suggestions in MacLean Sinclair's handwriting include the word *cubhais*, 'oath', which is almost certainly the original word in this context. Cf. Dinneen, '*Dar mo chubhais*, on my conscience'. *Cubhais*, 'oath, conscience', is in Dwelly, marked obsolete. Another example of the expression is in verse 2 of the ballad of Oisean and Patrick in *The Fians* of J. G. Campbell (1891), *Air a (Air do) chumha-sa, Mhic Fhinn.*

58. *'Na thruim seamh.* The usual expression here is *'na shiorran suain'*, 'in an enchanted sleep', but *T.G.S.I.* ix. 72, in a comparable passage, has *'na throm seimh*, similarly Mrs. Susie MacDonald's version *'na shuain seimh.* Cf. MacAlpine's Dictionary, *seamh*, 'an enchantment to make one's friends prosper'; Carmichael, *seamhas*, 'spell, charm, enchantment', *C.G.* vi. 123.

59. MS. *á chrios.*

61. MS. *a' bhraighdeach-s'.*

64. The only other version to mention the Round Table is that in the MacLagan MS., *Rel. Celt.* i. 369:

Cuiribh na Shuidhe m Bord Cruinn,
Cuiribh e le muirn 's le Ceol

'Set the Round Table, set it with rejoicing and with music.'

XLI*b*

This is the version, sung as a waulking song, recorded from Mrs. MacDougall ('Anna Raghnaill Eachainn'), Castlebay, Barra, in 1938. Lines 71 and 72 are not on the recording, but were known to the reciter.

The song was sung as a waulking song with single line verses, each line after the first being repeated with a different phrase of the refrain, which contains the word *iolairean* (eagles!).

There is remarkable consistency between this version and those of John MacLeod (*C.G.* v. 100), Mrs. Patrick MacCormick, and Mrs. A. Morrison, all from South Uist or Benbecula.

71. The unascribed version in the Carmichael papers has here *Gum b'fhearr leis tuiteam na tuar* (? *'na thuar*) that is, he would prefer to decline in his appearance. But *t[h]uar* here makes no internal rhyme with any word in the next line, so *cion* is the better reading.

XLII

Ach a Mhurchaidh òig ghaolaich

('But beloved young Murdo')

This fine song appears to be unpublished. It might well have been lost, for it seems to have been known only to the family of Mrs. Samuel MacKinnon ('Bean Shomhairle Bhig') of Bruernish, Barra, and the present generation had forgotten most of the words; but I found that the full text had been communicated to me by an unidentified Barra correspondent in 1938. The tune was first recorded from Miss Janet MacKinnon, who was visiting Canna, in 1954 (wire recording no. 1136). Miss MacKinnon recorded it again, on tape, at Northbay on 28/1/64, and her sister, Mrs. Archie MacPhee, who remembered a few more of the words, but only the first four lines, recorded it again at Staoinibrig in South Uist on 30/1/64.

108. The singer (Mrs. MacPhee) had *Bu tu 'n diollaid* which does not make sense; the MS. has *'S tu* 'and you' which must be right.

111. The order of the lines in the MS. is 111, 112, 116, 117, 113, 114, 115, and 116. This does not seem right following the 'hunter' in line 111, the natural order is the naming of the birds and animals hunted.

114. The MS. has *'S moch a dh'éigheas le langan. Langan,* however, means the bellowing of deer, not the call of a bird. The corresponding line 1085 of No. xxx in vol. i has *'S moich' a dh'éibheadh ro' latha.* D. McI. has *S moich a dh eubhadh s,am mhaduinn* and this reading I have adopted.

137. *sìol Ailein,* the MacDonalds of Clanranald.

140. MS. *challail,* glossed 'foremost in deeds'. The *-ch* of *Mùideartach* repeated by mistake.

XLIII

'S mi dol timcheall na dòirlinn

('As I went round the isthmus')

Recorded from Mrs. Neil Campbell ('Bean Nìll') at Frobost, South Uist, on tape on 1/2/64. The text is transcribed from the tape, except line 158, which the singer omitted, but which is necessary for the metre, and which is found in the version published in K. C. C. 20, the only other one known to us.

The story behind the song is forgotten.

XLIV

Ged is grianach an latha

('Sunny though the day may be')

Recorded from Mr. Calum Johnston ('Calum Aonghais Chaluim') in Edinburgh on 11/12/49, wire recording no. 71. Words transcribed from the recording.

Apparently unpublished. In D. C. M. there is a waulking song to a version of the same refrain beginning with lines similar to nos. 175, 176, 179, and 180 here. It is rather feebly ribald. The opening lines must have been something of a commonplace, for in an eloquent poem on the decline of the Clan MacLean after the Campbell takeover of Mull and Tiree, by the Revd. John MacLean, who succeeded the Revd. John Beaton as minister of Kilninian in Mull in 1702 and died in 1754, the first verse reads

Ged is grianach an latha
'S beag mo shunnd-sa ri aighear,
O'n la chuala mi naidheachd mo leoin.

'Though the day is sunny, I have little humour for joy, since the day I heard the news that wounded me' (MacLean Sinclair, *The Gaelic Bards from 1715 to 1765*, p. 61).

The Revd. John Beaton made an equally eloquent poem on the same subject, which is printed in *The Gaelic Bards from 1411 to 1715*, p. 144.

XLV

Tha an oidhche nochd fuar

('The night tonight is cold')

Recorded from Mrs. Mary MacNeil (Màiri Ruarachain') at Castlebay, Barra, on 29/12/49 on wire, no. 106. The same singer had previously recorded it for me on the ediphone in January 1937, one of my earliest recordings. Text transcribed from the wire recording.

The song is apparently unpublished. No song we have heard was more obviously not originally sung as a waulking song; the lines, often irregular in length, are mostly 6^1 and 6^2 alternatively, and the words at times have to be almost tortured to fit the melody. Moreover, the metre proves that some lines were being sung out of order, and others must have been forgotten. The latter are indicated by dots. The order of the lines as sung was 195, 196, 202, 205, 204, 206, 207, 209, and 211. Lines 197–201 here are from a version taken down in 1931 by Miss Annie Johnston, very probably from Mrs. Mary MacNeil, who was a neighbour. The other lines are identical.

203. Gill' Eóghanain used to be a favourite name of the MacNeils of Barra.

206. The second section of the song has little, if anything, to do with the first.

XLVI

Seathan mac Rìgh Eireann

(Seathan, son of the King of Ireland)

First recorded on disc (xxxiv) from Miss Annie Johnston at Northbay, Barra, in March 1938. Re-recorded by the Barra Folklore Committee at Castlebay on 7/8/50 from Miss Johnston and her brother Calum on wire (no. 433). The text is transcribed from the wire recording.

This song has been widely known in the Highlands and Islands in different versions, often localized. In view of its poetic merit and literary interest, it is surprising that it does not seem to have been printed until 1888, when it appeared in *T.G.S.I.*, in a paper on 'The Waulking Day' by Mrs. Mary MacKellar, read to the Society on 9 March 1887 by Mr. John Whyte. This version (pp. 204 to 208) has 53 lines, and a translation is given.

A version of 57 lines, taken down from Màiri·nighean Alasdair by K. C. Craig, is printed in K. C. C., pp. 118–20, text alone. Two versions, one from Skye with the air, opening words, and English translation of about 14 lines, the other from South Uist with text of 50 lines, were printed by Miss Frances Tolmie (no. 51, pp. 207–10 in F. T.). A variant of the air published by Miss Tolmie was printed in the *Journal of the English Folk Dance and Song Society*, by Miss Lucy Broadwood, i. 90, in 1933.

In 1954 a very long version of the song (192 lines) taken down by Alexander Carmichael from Janet MacLeod on Eigg in 1905, was printed in *C.G.* v. 67–81. Fragments of 18 lines taken down from Mary Henderson, Morvern, and 30 lines from Jessie Matheson, Kilmuir, Skye, are also printed there. Carmichael refers to seven other informants: Mór MacNeil and Mary Boyd in Barra; Mary MacDonald, and Mary Campbell on Mingulay; Mary MacRae, Letterfearn, Glenshiel; Mary Ferguson, Carinish, North Uist; and an old woman from Knoydart, living in Oban.

Janet MacLeod told Carmichael that 'when I first remember, *Seathan* by itself would be sufficient to complete the waulking, however tough the cloth' (*C.G.* v. 63). It certainly must have been exhausting to sing, if it really ran to 192 lines, each repeated twice with a different phrase of the refrain each time; but Carmichael may have done some conflation here, as was the case in some other instances.

The song appears in Mrs. Kennedy-Fraser's *Songs of the Hebrides*, ii. 73–9, under the title 'Death-Keening of a Hero' 'Air and words collected by Kenneth MacLeod, from Janet MacLeod, Skye and Eigg, and Mary

Henderson, Morven. Latter part of air from Mary MacDonald, Mingulay.' No mention of Carmichael. Mary MacDonald's version of the air is a variant of that printed by Miss Frances Tolmie and Miss Lucy Broadwood, referred to. The air used by Mrs. Kennedy-Fraser for the first part of the song is unknown to us and probably that of a different song originally.

In her book *Outer Isles* (London, 1902) Miss Ada Goodrich Freer gives an account, allegedly first hand, of the singing of this song on Eriskay by 'Maighread Mhór' who was one of Fr. Allan McDonald's informants; but the information seems to be entirely derived from Fr. Allan's notebooks (pp. 269–70).

The version of the air to which the song was sung by Annie and Calum Johnston is superior to those previously published.

MS. sources: Fr. Allan MS. fol. 95 (32 lines); folklore notebook V, item 194, from Mrs. Donald MacEachen, Eriskay, 22 lines; VI, 29, 18 lines and comments, apparently the version referred to by Miss Freer; Canon MacLean I, 7, from Màiri nighean Alasdair, 65 lines (8 more than in the version taken down drom her later by K. C. Craig, and variations in the order); D. McI., 102, 58 lines, generally similar to the version of Màiri nighean Alasdair.

The lines occurring in Canon MacLean but not in the version taken down by K. C. Craig may be noted:

After line 8 of K. C. C. 119:

Thigeadh na caoirich o'n chruaitich

After line 25 of K. C. C. 119:

Fhad 's a mhaireadh bùrn na linnidh dhomh,
'S thiormaichinn air bhàrr an iubhair i
'S bheirinn pàiste a làimh do ghille-se i

After third line from foot of K. C. C. 119:

'S seòmar dìonach làidir bhotaidh
Sheathain chridhe is ait leam fhéin thu
'S beag an t-àite an cuirinn fhéin thu

After sixth line from foot of K. C. C. 119:

Dh'òl mi deoch a tobar a Ruadha leat

The first five of these lines occur in the version in D. McI.

Though no two of the reciters agree about the order of the lines, the story behind the song is clear enough. It is a passionate lament by his mistress for Seathan, who has been on the run, but has been treacherously trapped and killed by his enemies. There are clear signs of Irish and Catholic influences in the poem, which contains some highly poetical passages.

227. *Seathan.* The metre proves that *Iain*, the modern Scottish Gaelic word for 'John', has been substituted for *Seathan* in some other songs, see lines 503, 719, and 1485.

229. *air beag éididh.* J. F. Campbell of Islay defined the Scottish Gaelic terms for clothing as follows: '*earradh*, a dress, costume; *Aodach* is any clothes good or bad; *trusgan* is a good dress; *éideadh* is a distinguishing dress or uniform; *earradh* is a dress rather distinguishing an individual from others. *Éideadh Gàidhealach* [Highland dress] we could never say *an t-earradh Gàidhealach*' (*Popular Tales of the West Highlands*, iii. 395).

236. *'sa Choill' Bhuidhe. T.G.S.I.* xiii. 205, *'s a' Chill-Chumhainn*; *C.G.* v. 70, *sa Chill Chumha*; *sa Chill Chumhann.* F. T., *sa Choill Chumhai-(n)g*, p. 208; Fr. Allan MS. waulking songs, fol. 96, *'sa Chaol chumhag*; V, 194, *sa Chaol Chumhag*; VI, 29, *sa Choill Bhuidhe*; Canon MacLean I, 8, *air a Chumhag*; K. C. C. 119, *an eaglais a' Chumhaig*; D. McI. 103, *an eaglais a chumhaig.*

Fr. Allan McDonald annotates the words in V, 194 as follows: 'The Caolas Cumhag between Vatersay and Bentangaval, Barra. There is a cave there called *Uamh Moire Céireadh*, and there is or was an altar in it.' He was told this by Mrs. Donald McEachen, Eriskay, in January 1897.

In VI, 29 he wrote about two months later, annotating lines from another version, presumably Maighread Mhór's, 'the *Coill Bhuidhe* (is) changed frequently into . . . *'sa Chaolas Chumhag* to localize the scene in . . . Barra'.

According to Hogan's *Onomasticon Goedilicum*, p. 187, there is a '*Cell Cumha*, Kilcoo parish in the barony of Iveagh, Co. Down, said locally to be C. Cuma in Irish.' He does not mention any Coill Bhuidhe.

237. *Minig* is used for *mairg* in Uist and Barra.

238. *Mighinis* is the district of Minginish in the Isle of Skye. Probably Old Norse *Miðjunes*, 'Middle Headland'.

243–6. This passage implies that were Seathan to be released, the prosperity that was supposed to attend the rule of a good chief or king would follow. But in other versions the idea is that no ransom would be too great to pay for him. For example, in the D. McI. version (spelling normalized):

Nam faighte Seathan ri fhuasgladh,
Thigeadh an crodh far na buaileadh,
Thigeadh na gearrain bho'n luachair,
Thigeadh na caoirich bho'n chruaitich,
Thigeadh na bric bho na bruachaibh,
Cha bhiodh bó dhubh no bó ruadh ann,
An ìochdar no 'n uachdar na buaileadh
Nach tigeadh, a ghaoil, 'gat fhuasgladh;
Bhiodh togail air crodh na tuathadh,
Bheireadh siod an aona bhó bhuamsa,
'S falt mo chinn nan gabhte bhuam e!

'If Seathan were to be released, the cattle would come from the cattlefold, the geldings would come from the rushes, the sheep would come from the rocky ground, the trout would come from the river-banks; there would not be a black or a red cow in the bottom or the top of the cattlefold, that would not come, my love, to release thee; there would be a round-up of the cattle of the tenantry, that would take my only cow from me, and the hair of my head if it were accepted from me.'

254. This line is not on the recording. It is, however, in a version of the song written out for me by Miss Annie Johnston some years previously. Janet MacLeod told Carmichael that the 'Hag of the Three Thorns' was a witch, a sister of the King of Ireland, who loathed Seathan, and who encompassed his death by treachery, hoping thereby that her own son would be the King's heir (*C.G.* v. 65).

256, 257. These lines are also not on the recording, but are in a copy of the song previously written out for me by Miss Annie Johnston.

Other versions have *a Tìr Chonaill* (from Donegal) for *o thìr Chonbhaigh*, e.g. *C.G.* v. 70, K. C. C. 118. D. McI. has *o linn Chonaill.* But *Chonbhaigh* certainly fits the rhyme better here. Cf. Hogan's *Onomasticon*, p. 288: *Conbaidh*; the chief Baile of the Hi Ingardeil in Caoille, Munster, now Conway Móre, the seat of Ennismore; must be Conva tl. in parish Ballyhooly, barony Fermoy, Co. Cork; 'Convamore, seat of Earl of Listowell, on the Blackwater, flings embellishments over the parish and reciprocates groupings of scenery with the hills and lands and woods and sinuous vale around it' (from the Parliamentary Gazeteer of Ireland).

258. Some versions have *bean shiubhail*, 'a wandering woman'.

267. It is interesting, in view of what is said about Conbhaigh above, that Hogan says there was a 'Baili of the Ui Ingarduil in Caoile, Munster' called Lettir (*Leitir*) (*Onomasticon*, p. 48).

268–9. There is an interesting note by Fr. Allan McDonald to the corresponding passage in the version of the song which he took down from Maighread Mhór on Eriskay in 1897:

'Fragments of *Seathain*, a fulling song. The first stanze are attributed to Flora McDonald. She came back to Uist on a visit from Skye. A *luadhadh* was going on. She went in and added these as her contribution to the singing. If the verses speak the truth her marriage cannot have been altogether happy:

Chuir m'athair mi dh'àite carraideach
An oidhche sin a rinn e bhainis dhomh;
Nach truagh, a Dhia! nach i 'n fhalairidh,
Nach d'rinn iad an giuthas a cheannach dhomh.
Lìonmhor bòrd am bi mi 'n tarruinn ann,
Nach d'rinn sgian am biadh a ghearradh dhomh.'

'My father sent me to a troublesome place, the night that he made the wedding-feast for me; what a pity, my God! that it was not the (my) wake, that they had not bought pine wood [i.e. a coffin] for me; (there is) many a table where I shall be brought, where knife did not cut food for me.'

Cf. *C.G.* v. 76; K. C. C. 120. Miss Freer implies that the whole song was composed by Flora MacDonald, and that the wanderings referred to were those of Prince Charles Edward, though 'we think it probable that some stanzas from a different song have crept in'. This is certainly wrong, and it is doubtful whether any part of the song was composed by Flora MacDonald; but the tradition related by Maighread Mhór to Fr. Allan McDonald is of interest as affording evidence that different sections of a waulking song might be improvised by different persons at the waulking board.

Note that the text here has *banais dhut*, and Fr. Allan McDonald wrote (*Gaelic Words from South Uist*, p. 35) that *Bainis* could mean 'any feast', so the translation could be 'That night that they made a feast for you.'

273, 274. *Annamh* and *buaidheach* are dialect forms of *ainneamh* and *bòidheach* respectively, cf. Fr. Allan, op. cit.

277. Fr. Allan McDonald, VI, 29 has here:

Cha tugainn a Mhoire mhìn thu,
Ged thigeadh i 's a làmh sìnte,
Nan tugadh, dh'iarrainn a rìst thu,
Cha tugainn a dh'Iosa Crìosd' thu.

'I would not give you to gentle Mary (the Virgin Mary), even if she came with outstretched hand; if I did, I would ask for you back again; I would not give you to Jesus Christ.'

Fr. Allan McDonald's informant added '*Cha n-eil fios gu dé 'n creutair a rinn e, ach bha i bleideil 's bha i aineolach*' 'I don't know what kind of creature made it (the song), but she was impertinent and she was ignorant'; the reciter was 'scandalized at the irreverent freedom of the last lines'.

XLVII

Chailin òig as stiùramaiche

('Calen o custure me')

Recorded from Mrs. MacDougall (Anna Raghnaill Eachainn) at Castlebay, Barra, in March 1938 (disc. no. XXIV); another Barra version from Mrs. Mary Morrison (Bean Phluim) at Castlebay the same month (disc no. XL), and from her again at Castlebay on 29/12/49, with chorus (wire no. 114); from Mrs. Kate MacCormick, Hacklett, Benbecula, on 21/11/49 (wire no. 21); from Miss Annie MacDonald, a native of the Lochboisdale district of South Uist, on Canna on 31/12/54 and again on 4/6/55 (wire nos. 1123 and 1130).

Other versions: Fr. Allan MS., fol. 101 (printed here; K. (1895), p. 206 (from Marion MacLennan) and another version on p. 208 (source not given: this last not printed in MacD., where Marion MacLennan's version is printed on p. 246); Canon MacLean I, 13 (from Màiri nighean Alasdair); Barra MS. (*c.* 1937).

Printed: *Òranaiche* (1879), p. 21 (no source given). *T.G.S.I.* xv. 158, in paper on 'The Sheiling, Its Tradition and Songs' read to the Society by Mary MacKellar on 8/2/1888; *An Deo-Ghréine*, I. 33 (November 1905) in an anonymous article giving the *Òranaiche* text and a version of the tune in sol-fa 'from the Mòd prize-winning compilation of unrecorded Gaelic melodies sent in this year by John Cameron of Paisley'. *Celtic Review*, iv. 314, attempted reconstruction of a full text (80 lines) from five different sources in Eigg, Skye, Uist, Lorne, and Morvern, plus the *Òranaiche* text, by Kenneth MacLeod (sources of individual lines not stated) (April 1908).

On 3/12/1908 Malcolm MacFarlane read a paper to the Gaelic Society of Inverness on 'Studies in Gaelic Music' in which the Irish origin of this song was discussed, including the possible identity of its refrain with the unintelligible words spoken by Pistol in Shakespeare's *Henry V*, 'Callen o custure me'. MacFarlane gave the *Òranaiche* version of the words accompanied by the Irish tune from A. P. Graves's *Irish Song Book* in sol-fa (*T.G.S.I.* xxvii. 60). MacFarlane had actually printed the *Òranaiche* version of this song with the Irish tune twice before, in the *Celtic Monthly* in 1896 and 1902 (vol. iv. 200; vol. x. 184). In his lecture to the Gaelic Society of Inverness he gave another version of the text, which he said had been sent to him by 'an old man, since deceased, named Donald Beaton, residing in Australia, where he had been for fifty-four years', containing 'words which help to correct apparently defective lines in both of the already recorded versions'. This is accompanied by another tune written in sol-fa, which MacFarlane said he had taken down from an unnamed Ballachulish man, and which in fact would fit the *Òranaiche* version of the refrain of the song. MacFarlane added that 'evidently there is another tune in Lochaber not recorded'. The Irish versions of the tune from the FitzWilliam Virginal Book and the Ballet MS., and the Ballachulish version, are printed in the musical section here.

Curiously enough the version of the words which MacFarlane said he had received from Donald Beaton is identical with that written on p. 208 of K., and the version of the tune which he said he had taken down from a Ballachulish man is identical with that contained in John Cameron's prize-winning compilation of unpublished Gaelic melodies that was printed in *An Deo-Ghréine* in November 1905. The Beaton-Killearnan version of the text is very similar to that of Mary MacKellar; possibly both are Skye versions. In his Inverness lecture MacFarlane made no reference to the collated version printed by Kenneth MacLeod in the *Celtic Review* eight months earlier.

Other printed versions: MacD. 246 (1911); K. C. C. 62 (1949), from the same source as Canon MacLean. Art version: Mrs. Kennedy-Fraser, *Songs of the Hebrides*, iii. 68–71, called 'The Courting of the King of Erin's daughter', with 6 lines of text, and refrain, and tune 'as learnt by Kenneth MacLeod from Ann Henderson, Morvern'. Ann Henderson was a famous reciter. This is preceded by a précis in English of the collated version of the text which Kenneth MacLeod had printed in the *Celtic Review* in 1908.

In 1973 the song, with others, was discussed by Dr. Alan Bruford in an article on 'The Sea-Divided Gaels' in *Irish Folk Music Studies*, and versions of the air recorded from Mary Morrison, Nan MacKinnon, Kate MacDonald, and Mrs. Kate MacCormick (all of whom figure in the present book) were compared with the Irish version from the Ballet MS.

Mary MacKellar said of the song in 1888 that it was 'said to have been composed by a young man who was travelling the mountainside, when he met a young woman of great beauty, who pretended to be a maid of the sheiling. She fascinated him with her charm of looks and manner, and when she asked him to become her herdsman, he followed her, to find she had deceived him, and her beauty was only seeming. She was one of the weird women of the fairy hills, and he regrets having met her.' (*T.G.S.I.* xv. 158.)

Kenneth MacLeod's account of the background is more elaborate.

> 'A young hero goes to woo the King of Erin's daughter, who, however, makes such impossible conditions that the suitor leaves in a temper. No sooner is he gone than the lady changes her mind, and, disguising herself as a milkmaid, meets him among the shielings, makes love unblushingly to him, and brings him to her feet.
>
> 'Soon after this encounter the hero takes ill, and lies on a fever-bed for five quarters—but never once in all that time comes his lady-love to inquire for him. When at last she does come, she merely flings a word at him, but even that is enough to pull him out of bed and send him to the shinty-strand to do great deeds. There, after he has relieved his feelings by cursing womankind for their sauciness and fickleness, he suddenly discovers that the King of Erin's daughter and the maid of the shieling are one and the same person—and there and then he carries her away to the church and marries her.'

Kenneth MacLeod's reconstruction of the ballad which must lie behind this waulking song may be the right one; at the same time it must be said that none of the reciters we have recorded, or of the MSS. that have been consulted, could give or have given an account of the story that lies behind it, and there is no general agreement about the order of the incidents that occur in it. The fullest modern version is that which Canon MacLean and K. C. Craig took down independently from Màiri nighean Alasdair of Snaoiseabhal, South Uist.

In this version the incidents occur in the following order:

A. The young man met a girl in the country, who swore to be faithful to him. (There is no mention of her requests in this version; in the *Òranaiche* and in Fr. Allan McDonald's versions she refuses him.)

B. The young man was taken ill with fever for 15 months, at the end of which the girl came to ask how he was, and he told her.

C. Presumably as a result of her visits, he recovered, and won a game of shinty. (A victory at shinty is a well-known motif in Gaelic folktales.)

D. The girl came to see him again, and (in Canon MacLean's version) says she is ashamed. The young man complains of the fickleness of women, comparing them to various unstable creatures and phenomena.

E. The young man ends by saying that a dairymaid (*banchaig*, the woman in charge of a dairy, an important person on old Highland farms) is the better of having a herdsman, who can do certain things for her (implying a reconciliation).

Taking the other versions of the song referred to or printed in this book, these incidents are found in the following orders:

	A (meeting requests)	B (illness)	C (shinty)	D (women's fickleness)	E (dairy-maid and herds-man)
Òranaiche	2	3	4	5	1
McD.	1	2	3	–	4
Fr. Allan McDonald	1	2	4	3	5
Barra MS.	1	4	5	3	2
Mrs. Mary Morrison	2	3	4	5	1
Mr. Kate MacCormick	–	2	3	1	–
Mary MacKellar	1	–	–	–	2
Donald Beaton	1	–	–	–	2
Mrs. MacDougall	1	2	(not completely recorded)		
Annie MacDonald	1	–	–	2	–
Kenneth MacLeod's reconstruction	1	3	4	5	2

In the case of Mrs. MacDougall's version, the Presto disc unfortunately ran out before the end of the song. Kenneth MacLeod's reconstruction had 8 additional lines at the end, source not stated, to the effect that the King of Ireland's daughter, mentioned only in the *Òranaiche* version of those known to us, was the same person as the dairymaid, and was reconciled with and married the young man. The other versions certainly imply that the dairymaid and the 'bold brown-haired woman' are one and the same person, but they do not tell of any full reconciliation and marriage. On the other hand, they have quite a number of lines not found in Kenneth MacLeod's reconstructed version, which itself has 80 lines, not counting the refrain.

Almost certainly this song is a ballad adapted to be sung as a waulking-song. The question is, what is its relationship to the Irish song *Calen o custure me,* which according to W. H. Grattan Flood's *A History of Irish Music* (1906) was a ballad entered on the books of the Stationers' Company in 1581–2 and of which the tune, or a version of it, was printed in Clement Robinson's *A Handfull of Pleasant Delites* in 1584. Gratton Flood quoted Chappell's *Popular Music,* saying that 'Chappell tells us that . . . in the same year (1537) the Annals of Ulster place the death of O'Keenan, a famous instrumentalist—namely, Bryan son of Cormac O'Keenan—who is said to have composed the charming melody, *Cailin og a stuir me*' (*sic*). In 1537 the Annals of Ulster record the death of Brian Ó Cianain, a famous player of stringed instruments, but nothing is said there of his having composed this song.

In an article in *Éigse,* i. 125 discussing the origin of Pistol's famous unintelligible remark to the defeated Frenchman in Shakespeare's play *Henry V*, and its identity with the refrain of an Irish song now only preserved in the Hebrides, the late Professor Gerard Murphy drew attention to the insight of Edward Malone, 'the great Irish eighteenth century editor of Shakespeare' who first saw that Pistol was quoting the, to him, meaningless refrain of an Irish song that had become popular in London in the second half of the sixteenth century. According to Professor Murphy, the first person to draw attention to the similarity between the refrain 'Calen o custure me' and the Scottish Gaelic refrain *Chailin òg nach stiùr thu mi?* was David Comyn in his *Irish Illustrations to Shakespeare* (1894, p. 13). Comyn reproduces the refrain line as printed in the *Òranaiche* in 1879, and which was probably his source. Comyn's book must have been seen by the Revd. A. MacDonald 'Killearnan' not long after publication, for the identification is discussed in the list of contents of his MS. collection of Gaelic songs, which was made between 1874 and 1895, and in which the two versions of this song come at the end, though no mention is made of Comyn's name. In his MS. Killearnan says that 'the version given above by Marion MacLennan could be extended in Benbecula'. In the list of contents in MacD., a collection which is based to a very considerable extent on K., attention is again drawn to the similarity to 'Calen o custure me', but with the usual reticence about sources shown in that volume, Marion MacLennan's name is not mentioned.

In the Scottish Gaelic versions of this song there is an unusual amount of variation in the line of the refrain from which the song takes its title, as well as some uncertainty whether the opening words are in the nominative or the vocative case, and if the second, of the gender of the word *Cailin.* In the versions of the song that are available to us, one finds *Cailin òg, Chailin òg,* or *Chailin òig,* i.e. (O) young lass,

a stiùradh mi	who would guide me
a(n) stiùir thu mi?	will you guide me?

nach stiùir thu mi?	won't you guide me?
gun stiùir thu mise	may you guide me
a' stiùramaiche	the guide (?)
as stiùramaiche	who is guidingest (?)

The word *stiùramaiche* or *stiùireamaiche* is not in the dictionaries, but Miss Annie Johnston wrote me once that in a version of the song *'S e mo leannan am fear ùr* known to her, the couplet,

'S e mo leannan Gille Calum,
Stiùramich an daraich thu

occurred, *stiùramaich* (*stiùramaich'*) meaning 'steersman'. She thought the refrain of the present song should be *Cailin òg a' stiùramaiche*. It may be added that the Lewis version of this song printed in *Eilean Fhraoich* has here '*Carpenter' an daraich thu*, and that the corresponding couplet does not occur at all in the version of the song printed in MacD. 217.

All this variation however, suggests that this line of the refrain is a corruption of something else. The first person to draw attention to the fact that the uncorrupted Irish form of the refrain had been preserved was Professor Gerard Murphy in the article in *Éigse* referred to. Professor Murphy pointed out that this was contained in a verse of a poem 'beginning on folio 26 of a late seventeenth century Fermanagh manuscript, now preserved in the British Museum, numbered Additional 40766, catalogued by Dr. Robin Flower on p. 165 of Volume II of the Catalogue of Irish MSS. in the British Museum. The poem has been edited, doubtless from this manuscript, by Professor T. F. O'Rahilly in his second edition of *Dánta Grádha*, pp. 97–99.' The eighth stanza seems to preserve the original Irish form of most of the title-words of the ballad which, we have been told, was 'tolerated' to John Allde in 1582 as *Callen o custure me*. The stanza is as follows:

Dom anródh nár fhoghlaim mé
seinm Chailín ó Chois tSiúire,
i dtráth suain le sreing n-umha,
nách beinn uaidh i n-aontumha.

'It may be translated: "I am unfortunate in never having learnt to play The Girl from Beside the Suir (*Cailin ó Chois tSiúire*) on a copper string when sleep-time came, so that as a result I might not be unmarried." ' (The poet is lamenting that with more musical skill he might have been able to find a wife.)

As Professor Murphy goes on to remark, none of the Scottish refrains recorded for this song seem entirely natural. 'It is easy to see how they could have been unintentionally altered from the Irish line by Scottish singers unaware of the existence of the River Suir in Munster. There can be little doubt, then, but that *Callen o custure me* is based on an Irish line *Cailin ó Chois tSiúire mé* . . . and not on one of the Scottish refrains' which presumably are also based on it.

In a subsequent number of *Éigse* (ii. 198) Colm Ó Lochlainn drew attention to an Irish translation of the Song of Songs contained in

British Museum MS. Egerton 167 written by Lucas Smyth in 1709–10 and quoted in Dr. Robin Flower's *Catalogue*. This translation is made into eight-syllable line rhyming verse, i.e. the same metre as the present song and of many other waulking songs, and likewise is provided with a refrain to be sung after every line that is very similar to this one:

Tuggach póg re póig a bhéil dhamh,
Callíon ó shruch Íordain mé.
As fearr do chíocha ná an fíon créurag,
Callíon ó shruch Íordain mé.

'I am a girl from the River Jordan'. The tunes recorded for *Chailin òig as stiùramaiche* would fit this.

Despite these remarkable resemblances, the loss of the Irish words of the ballad, and the marked difference between the Irish and the Scottish versions of the air, present certain difficulties. As the anonymous writer of the article in *An Deo-Ghréine* in November 1905 pointed out, the song appears to be an older ballad adapted as a waulking song. If this is the case, and it very probably is, the words preserved in Scotland may very well derive from the original text of the ballad; but the rather monotonous tune to which the song is now sung in the Outer Hebrides cannot be that which appealed to educated Londoners in the sixteenth century. It is certainly quite different from the Irish air as printed by Graves; though the version published in *An Deo-Ghréine* in 1905 and later in Malcolm MacFarlan's paper of the Gaelic Society of Inverness may do something to bridge the gap. The tunes themselves are to be found in the musical section of this book.

It may be added that the refrain of this song occurs in another made by Murdoch Mor MacKenzie of Achilty, who died about 1689, on the occasion of his contemplating a second marriage. This is printed in 'Further Gleanings from the Dornie Manuscripts' by the Revd. William Matheson (*T.G.S.I.* xlv. 178). The song begins:

Is garbh a nochd an oidhch' ri m' thaobh
a chailin òig, nach stiùir thu i

It may be noted that most of the lines are in the metre 7^1, whereas the metre of the song printed here is 8^2.

XLVII*a*

This version was recorded from Mrs. Mary Morrison ('Bean Phluim') twice, the first time in Miss Annie Johnston's house in March 1938 on disc XL, the second time at Castlebay on 29/12/49 on wire, recording no. 114.

In 1938 Mrs. Morrison sang the song alone, repeating each line twice with alternating refrain; in 1949 she sung it with a chorus, but sung each line once only, again with alternating refrain. She made slight differences in the wording. These are noted below, as well as some variations in two other Barra versions of the song, one recorded from Mrs. MacDougall ('Anna Raghnaill Eachainn') in 1938, the other communicated to me in MS., possibly by Mr. Calum Johnston.

284. In the Barra MS., the following line is *Chàireadh e fodhcha leapa shocair*, 'he would prepare a comfortable bed beneath her', then the following lines:

Cailinn òg na gruaige duinne mi,
Cailinn gu tobhar 's gu talamh mi,
Cailinn gu deanamh nam feannag mi,
Cailinn ri gaoith mhóir 's ri gailinn mi.

'I am a young brown-haired girl, I am a girl fit for fetching seaweed and working the land, I am a girl able to make lazy-beds, I am a girl able to stand high winds and gales.'

293. Cf. Dinneen, *bliadhain mhór*, a long year.

294. Cf. Fr. Allan, '*Teasach*, the worst of fevers'. Mrs. MacDougall here had *Ann an aiceid mhóir na blàthach*, 'In the great pain of fever'. *Blàthachd, blàthach*, for *plàighe* (gen. *plàgha* in Irish)? Cf. line 342.

296. After this line Mrs. MacDougall had *Sheall i staigh air uinneig clàiridh*, 'she looked in at the ground floor (?) window'.

298. This line was omitted in 1949.

299. *Dh'fheòraich i* in 1949.

301. After this line, the Barra MS. has:

Ghuidh mi gu cruaidh, cruaidh, ri m' Shlànair,
'S fhuair mi furtachd air mo shlàinte,
'S gun d'éirich mi 'n sin an là sin.

'I prayed hard, hard, to my Saviour, and I obtained relief in my health, and I got up then on that day'.

303, 304. In 1938 the singer placed these lines after 291, but this is obviously the right place for them. After 304 the Barra MS. has:

'S chuir mi chliuc air criù a' Bhàillidh.

'And I won the game over the factor's team'.

314. Miss Annie Johnston added the line *Mar liaghan air leaca bàna*, 'like sea-tangle on white flat rocks' (which is swayed back and forth by the waves).

XLVII*b*

Recorded on wire from Mrs. Patrick MacCormick, Hacklett, Benbecula, on 21/11/49 (no. 21).

331–4. A game of shinty played with a silver shinty stick and a golden ball (and often won by the hero against odds) is a recurring motif in

Gaelic folk-tales. Cf. for instance the story of the Herding of Cruachan (*Waifs and Strays of Celtic Tradition*, ii. 96–101), and the Barra version of the story of Conall Gulbann, *T.G.S.I.* xliv. 157. In the *Táin Bó Cuailnge* there is reference to the bronze shinty stick and silver ball of the young Cu Culainn (Stowe version, edited by Cecile O'Rahilly, p. 27). This makes it possible that this passage, which occurs in many of the versions of this song, may be an interpolation. The singer has *miche* for *mise* in the refrain throughout.

XLVII*c*

This is the version in Fr. Allan MS. It was probably taken down on Eriskay around 1897, but there is no reference to its provenance.

XLVII*d*

This is the version that was taken down from Màiri nighean Alasdair by Canon MacLean around 1936; it differs in some interesting respects from the version of the same song taken down from the same reciter by K. C. Craig about ten years later (K. C. C. 62).

362. *fàsach*, usually an empty place, desert, prairie, but also the word given to Edward Lhuyd for 'a pasture' by an Argyllshire speaker in 1700, and for 'a field' by an Invernessshire one a few years later.

Latha dhomh, etc. This is the first line in seven of the versions mentioned here, and also in that of Nan MacKinnon in the School of Scottish Studies archives. It is probably the right one. Many Irish Gaelic songs begin with such words ('One day as . . .')

363. K. C. C. *donn mèath orm.*

367. K. C. C. *Cha b'fhada fhuair mi mo shlàinte.*

369. In K. C. C. the next line is *Cha tàinig ise gam shealltainn*, 'she did not come to see me'. It obviously should be here.

373. K. C. C. *Fhir ud tha stoigh.*

374. Canon MacLean, *Olc le charaid 's math le namhaid.*

375. After this line K. C. C. has:

'S tha mi guidhe ris an Ardrigh
Nach lùb mi mo ghlùin ri làr dhut.

'And I pray to God that I shall not bend my knee to you' (? bear a child to you).

This would explain the word *gràineil* in the next line, which Canon MacLean questioned, writing *gràidheil* in the margin with a question-mark.

386. Canon MacLean has *an caile*, K. C. C. *an cailin*. Both words are given as feminine in Dwelly, but *cailin* is masc. in Irish, as it often is in these waulking songs, and *caile* can be masc. or fem. See Dinneen.

388. K. C. C. here has *Chrom i a ceann 's gun d'rinn i gàire*, 'she bent her head and laughed', which reverses the sense. This line is followed in K. C. C. by

'Tog do cheann 's na biodh ort nàire.
Teann a nall. Dian suidhe làimh rium.

'Lift your heard, don't be ashamed. Come over here. Sit down beside me.'

This is followed by line 390 here, and the inverted commas are not closed until the end of the poem.

The question is, who says what to whom. The poem makes better sense if Canon MacLean's transcription of line 388 is accepted, and the inverted commas are closed at the end of line 399, though perhaps lines 400 to 405 may be part of the hero's remarks and not a general statement.

395. Canon MacLean, *Gur luath an gaol*; K. C. C., *Luaithe an aigneadh*. The March wind of other versions seems more appropriate than the 'wind of Martinmas' here; cf. the well-known passage in Gaelic folk-tales about the speed of the hero's ship, e.g. in Connall Gulbann, *T.G.S.I.* xliv. 176, *tha i cho luath ris a' ghaoith luath Mhàirt tha reimpe* 'she is as fast as the swift wind of March that is before her', and the only thing that is said to be swifter is *aigne nam ban baoth*, the minds of foolish women.

398. K. C. C. *leacan bàthte.*

399. This line is not in K. C. C.

405. Canon MacLean has *Calein Gùithneach 's buachaill Loinneach* '*oi* like *oi* in *loinn*'. It is possible that clan or district names are involved, the first could be *Guibhneach* (*Duibhneach*, 'Campbell'), but I do not know what the second could be.

XLVIII

Bha mis' a raoir air an airigh

('Last night I was at the sheiling')

Recorded from Mrs. Mary Morrison ('Bean Phluim') at Castlebay, Barra, on 2/3/50 on wire no. 270 (by the Barra Folklore Committee). I also recorded a version of the words only from Mrs. Geoghegan ('Màiri Seasaidh na Caillich') at Bruernish, Barra, on ediphone on 28/6/48. In Nova Scotia, recorded from Mrs. David Patterson (*née* Katie MacNeil) at Benacadie, Cape Breton, on ediphone on 6/10/37.

MS. versions: D. MacI., p. 6, printed here; Calum Johnston, p. 10.

Printed: text alone, K. C. C. p. 24 (44 lines); text (only 6 lines), translated, with tune, *G.S.N.S.* 130; art version, Mrs. Kennedy-Fraser, *From the Hebrides*, p. 82, the tune is used for a song called 'The Ninth Wave', 'Words from Kenneth Macleod. Air from North Bay, Barra'.

This song is typical of many waulking songs; it was obviously composed by a woman (or women), and it contains several different sections, distinguished by different rhyming vowels, all but two of which are on unrelated subjects.

Taking these in the order in which they occur in K. C. C., the longest version, we have:

A. The girl telling how last night she was at the sheiling, wondering why her lover was not coming.
B. She hears, and is frightened by, the approach of a stranger, whom she repels.
C. Consists of advice given to a young man, how to behave in an inn.
D. A young man is advised not to woo the 'dairymaid of the glen' as she has no dowry.
E. A girl sends her message by a traveller to her lover to tell him she has got through the difficulties of winter and springtime and is well.

To these Mrs. Mary Morrison added another section, in which a young man swears eternal fidelity to his brown-haired girl (F).

It is interesting to compare the order in which these sections occur in the different versions:

Mrs. Mary Morrison:	A, B, C, E, F
Mrs. Geoghegan:	B, A, C, E
Calum Johnston:	A, B, D, E
Donald MacIntyre:	A, B, E
Mrs. Patterson:	A, B, D, C

The fact is that while sections A and B together tell a story (Donald MacIntyre having the best version of B), the other sections are floating themes, which occur in other waulking songs at random, e.g. for E, cf. lines 425–432, 598–606 and 844–51; and for F, cf. lines 512–15 in vol. i.

This, and the fact that the same breaks occur in Mrs. Patterson's version, from Cape Breton, where immigration from Barra and Uist ceased after around 1830, proves conclusively that the sudden changes in subject of waulking songs were not caused by the omission or oblivion of intervening lines, but are due to the habit of improvising or adding fresh sections to such songs for the purpose of making them long enough for the work in hand, the waulking of the cloth.

XLIX

Chaidh mi 'na ghleannain as t-fhoghar

('I went into the small glen in autumn')

Recorded on tape from Mrs. Campbell ('Bean Nìll') at Frobost, South Uist, on 22/3/65. Text transcribed from recording.

Printed versions: text, translation, and tune, F. T. No. 68, p. 227 (17 lines); *F.F.S.U.* 213 (5 lines only).

The opening section of this song has something in common with that of xv in vol. i.

486. Mr. John MacInnes, M.B.E., tells me that in South Uist *gada* 'is used locally here for a little withe, and for steel rods used by blacksmiths; and in reference to a gun it refers to a rod used in place of a pull-through'.

486. The *n* of *goidein* is not clear on the tape. The song must have been composed in a dialect where the stressed vowels of *aibhne/ghoidein/droighnich* all rhymed.

L

Tha caolas eadar mi is Iain

('A sound there is between me and Ian')

Recorded from Mrs. Buchanan ('Ceit Ruairi Iain Bhàin') at Castlebay, Barra, with chorus, on 5/4/51, on wire no. 715. Her father, Ruairi Iain Bhàin (Roderick MacKinnon) also used to sing this song, and I took down the words from him on 23/2/43 (15 lines).

So far as we know, this song has not been printed. But see K. C. C. 10, where ten lines apparently belonging to this song, end another.

Manuscript versions: Canon MacLean, I, 20, taken down from Màiri nighean Alasdair; it is not in K. C. C. 16 lines; Calum Johnston, p. 50, 14 lines.

In Nova Scotia, recorded on ediphone from Mrs. Neil MacInnis (Anna Nìll Ruaidh, *née* MacDonald) at Sydney, Cape Breton, on 20/10/37 (21 lines). Printed here.

Mr. Roderick MacKinnon, the father of Mrs. Buchanan, told me that '*Bha ise as a dheoghaidh, ach cha robh esan air a son. 'S i rinn an t-òran; bha ise as an eilein.* 'She was after him, but he didn't want her. It was she who made the song. She was in the island.' Which, he added, she couldn't leave. She got him in the end.

488. Metre and rhyme make it clear that 'Iain' must originally have been 'Seathan'.

496, 511. The version taken down by Canon MacLean has as the next line *Ach fraoch is ianach s an ghlaisein,* (sic) 'but heather and wild-fowl and the sparrow' (?). (K. C. C. 10 has *gasan* in this line, stems, branches).

513. Following this line, Canon MacLean's version ends with 6 lines:

Chuir iad mi a dh'fhaire an t-sobhail,
Rìgh! ma chuir, cha b'ann 'ga ghleidheadh,
Thill mi mo cheum 's mi thigh'nn dhachaigh;

Chuala mi farum 'san t-sobhal,
Mar gum biodh cliath-luadhaidh aig mnathan,
No gill' òg ag iarraidh mnatha.

Cf. K. C. C. 99, and this book, lines 940–4, and 969–71. The passage can hardly belong to this song originally.

521. There were earls (not dukes) of Arran from 1467. The earldom of Argyll was created ten years earlier, but that of Antrim only in 1620, for Sir Ranald Mac Sorley MacDonnell, so this song must have been made later than that date.

LI

Dh'éirich mi moch madainn Chéitein

('I rose early on a May morning')

Recorded from Annie and Calum Johnston by the Barra Folklore Committee on 3/8/50 (wire no. 432). Previously I had recorded this song from Mrs. MacDougall ('Anna Raghnaill Eachainn') on the ediphone on 24/4/37. Both recordings were made at Castlebay. Also recorded from Miss Penny Morrison at a genuine waulking at Iochdar, South Uist, on 29/3/51, wire no. 635 (16 lines).

The text of the song is that in A. J. (1), when the words were written out for Mrs. Kennedy-Fraser, possibly in 1908 at the time when Mrs. Kennedy-Fraser first called at Miss Johnston's parents' house in Barra (see *Gairm*, vi. 74). When Miss Johnston wrote out the words again in 1931 in A. J. (2), she had forgotten the last three lines.

Other MS. versions: Fr. Allan MS, fol. 93 (30 lines); D. MacI. 14 (24 lines). K. C. C. (30 lines). (The songs with the same first line printed in the *Oranaiche*, p. 475, the appendix to *Gesto Coll.*, 8, and in F. T. p. 225, are different).

Art version: Mrs. Kennedy-Fraser used the tune, as sung by Roderick MacKinnon ('Ruairi Iain Bhàin') for the song 'A MacLeod Bridal' in *More Songs of the Hebrides*, p. 8. The first two lines of the song here occur in the preceding song in the same book, set to a different tune.

In Nova Scotia I recorded the tune and 4 lines of the song from Mrs. David Patterson, Benacadie, Cape Breton, on ediphone on 6/10/37.

532, 570. D. MacI. has *èibhe*, and as the next line, *Choinnich mi 'bhean bhòidheach bhreidgheal*, 'I met the pretty white-kertched woman'.

536, 573. Following this line, D. MacI. has:

Ach ma rinn nach biodh i reidh ris
Mar a th ann ri rogha cèile

'But if he did, that she would not be reconciled to it, unless it was to her chosen husband.'

535, 573. This would probably be Domhnall Gorm Mór, who succeeded to the chiefship of the MacDonalds of Sleat in 1587, and died in 1616 or 1617. He is often mentioned in waulking songs, see allusions in vol. I. He did not marry a daughter of the Earl of Antrim.

552, 585. The D. MacI. version has, following this line:

Thog e orm go robh mi torrach

'He put it about that I was pregnant.'

559, 589. Following this line, D. MacI. has:

Shaorainn is ged rachainn na b'fhaide

'I would be free, though I were to go further.'

579. I take *gorm* to be derogatory here, so have translated *té ghorm* as 'grey hag'.

588. Fr. Allan McDonald seems to indicate that he thought these lines should be inserted after line 577; but they seem to belong to the end of the song.

LII

Tha 'n t-uisg, an ceò, air na beannan

('Rain and mist are on the mountains')

Recorded from Mr. Calum Johnston on wire on 11/12/49 at Edinburgh, wire recording no. 70. Also from Miss Janet MacKinnon at Northbay, Barra, on tape on 28/1/64.

Apparently unpublished. There is a version in Canon MacLean, loose-leaf no. 1, which adds lines 607–13 printed here.

594. Following this line, Canon MacLean has *Cha n-fhaigh mi triall chon a' bhaile*, 'I will not be able to get home'.

597–606. These lines are a cliché in waulking songs, compare lines 458–66, and 844–951.

613. This line is two syllables short; possibly the word *uile* has been omitted at the end ('The whole world').

LIII

Sneachda 'ga chur air na beannan

('Snow has fallen on the mountains')

Recorded from Mrs. Mary MacNeil ('Mairi Ruarachain') at Castlebay on 2/3/50, and from Mrs. James MacNeil ('Anna Mhìcheil Nìll') at Castlebay on 9/3/50, both by the Barra Folklore Committee (wire recordings nos. 280 and 308).

MS. sources, D. MacI. 15 (printed here); Canon MacLean, IV, 8; O. 45. In a letter dated 10 May 1955, Canon MacLean told me that he had got the words of this song from Mrs. Angus MacIntyre, mother-in-law of Duncan MacDonald the famous South Uist storyteller.

Printed, text alone, K. C. C. 42. The text of the song has a good deal in common with that of the version of the well-known waulking song *Héman dubh* that is printed in *T.G.S.I.* xli. 348–9 in 'Gleanings from the Dornie Manuscripts' by Professor Angus Matheson. The air, of course, is entirely different.

643. The version in O., which begins *A mhic a' bhodachain bhrònaich*, 'O son of the miserable little carle' consists of the section where the girl complains of the miserable marriage she is being forced to make, and one other, corresponding to lines 643–50 here:

Ghruagach ud a chòir a' bhealaich, a,
Am faca tu mo chéile falaich, a,
Cha n-fhaca mi, cha robh m'aithne air.
Dh'aithnichinn thu thar cheuda fearaibh
Dh'aithnichinn togail do shiùil gheala,
Fuaim an t-sìobain 'ga chur thairis,
Fuaim an t-sìde ris na crannaibh,
Fuaim an fhìon a' dol 'sa ghlaine.

'Yon maiden near the pass, have you seen my secret lover?' 'I haven't, I didn't know him.' 'I would recognize you out of hundreds of men, I would recognize the hoisting of your white sails, the sound of the spindrift passing over, the sound of the weather against the masts, the sound of wine being poured into the glass.'

Here where D. MacI. has *Fear ud thall*, Canon MacLean has *A mhoighdean òg* and K. C. C. has *Mhoighdeann òg*.

649. For *bior*, Canon MacLean and K. C. C. have *bìth*, 'pitch'.

660. Canon MacLean *mac Eora*; K. C. C. *mac Eabhra*; Mrs. Mary MacNeil has *Mac Amhraidh*; *T.G.S.I.* xli. 349, *Mac Annra.*

LIV

Dh'éirich mi 's cha robh mi sunndach

('I arose, I was not happy')

Recorded from Annie and Calum Johnston on 3/8/50 at Castlebay, by the Barra Folklore Committee, on wire no. 430.

Apparently unpublished. The only MS. version known to me, apart from the ones in the notebooks of Annie and Calum Johnston, is that taken down in South Uist by Canon MacLean, where the song is on looseleaf 2. In Canon MacLean's version, there is a difference of order; first comes the section corresponding to lines 663–71 here, then that corresponding to lines 676–83, then that to lines 684–7, then that to lines

672–5. Finally there is a section of 4 lines not corresponding to anything in the Barra version:

'S ann a raoir nach d'fhuair mi 'n cadal
Cha b'e adhaltranas mo leapa,
Cur an dòbhrain duinn o chaidreamh,
'S a' bhric o'n linnidh an aigeil

'Last night I got no sleep, not because of the adultery of my bed, putting the brown otter from his fellows, and the trout from the pool of the deeps.'

Lines corresponding to the first two of these occur in K. C. C. 96. There the expression is *dochartas mo leapadh*, 'the sickness of my bed'.

671. Canon MacLean *cùmhradh.*

678. Canon MacLean *Ruadhphort.* Miss Annie Johnston thought that Ruadal was Rodil in Harris (usually Ròghadail).

685. Following this line, Canon MacLean has:

'S i mo dhùthaich fhéin as àille,
Cheann Loch Braon gu taobh Loch Àlainn
Gu Cille Mhoire nan àrmunn,
Far an seinnte pìob is clàrsach,
Far 'm bi farum air bhròg[*an*] *àrda.*

'My own country is the most beautiful, from the head of Loch Broom to the side of Lochaline, to Kilmuir of the heroes, where pipes and harp are played, where there is the sound of high boots.'

LV

Hùgan nan gù, théid mi dhachaigh

('Cheerfully I'll go homewards')

Recorded from Miss Mary Gillies at Castlebay on 9/3/50 by the Barra Folklore Committee, wire recording no. 307.

MS. version D. MacI. 108, printed here.

What seems to be a version of the air, said to be from Barra, but without words or the singer's name, is printed on the top of p. xviii of Mrs. Kennedy-Fraser's *Songs of the Hebrides*, iii. Otherwise this song appears to be unpublished.

LVI

Cha n-e uiseag a dhùisg mise

('It was not a lark that woke me')

Recorded from Mrs. Neil Campbell ('Bean Nìll') at Frobost, South Uist, on tape, in April 1963.

Màiri nighean Alasdair's version of the text is printed in K. C. C. 25. I have seen no other version anywhere.

Refrain: *meaghail* (pronounced *meo'ail*) here must mean 'bleating', cf. Irish *meigel*, a bleat (*R.I.A. Contrib.*). This meaning is not recorded in Scottish Gaelic dictionaries, but cf. Dieckhoff, *meaghail*, 'the mewing of a cat, the barking of a young dog'. The word is not to be confused with *meadhail*, 'rejoicing', of identical pronunciation (vol. i, p. 536), which is a by-form of *meadhair*, cf. *B.Gh.* l. 6730.

The words *gobhar*, *abhann*, and *meoghail* (*meaghail*) in this peculiar refrain must originally have rhymed, which suggests strongly that the song was made in a different Gaelic dialect from that of South Uist. For *storm*... 'noise' see vol. i, l. 1268 and note. *Abhann* is the old genitive of *abha*, 'river'.

LVII

Tha 'n crodh an diu dol air imprig

('The cattle today are being shifted')

Recorded from Mrs. Angus John MacLellan, Hacklett, Benbecula, on a Wirek tape recorder in 1954. We have not found anyone else who knows this song.

MS. version, Fr. Allan MS., fol. 113 (3 lines only). Printed, text alone, K. C. C. 79; text and translation, *C.G.* i. 282, under the title of *Cronan Cuallaich*, 'A Herding Croon', taken down from Murdoch Maccuis, cattleherd, Grimnis, North Uist. *T.G.S.I.* xxvii. 396, from the MacNicol MS.; the first song on the page, beginning *'S mi 'm shuidh air leth chreig a bhile* appears to be connected.

Tune with 4 lines of text and translation, F. T., no. 66, p. 223; 3 lines of this and refrain had been printed in K. N. MacDonald's *Puirt-a-Beul*, p. 11, with tune in sol-fa, and the note 'It is a lament for a woman's departure. The cows are lowing after, and longing for her return.' Miss Tolmie's version was taken down from Mary Ross, Killmaluag, Skye, in 1901. A version of the tune taken down by Lucy Broadwood from Catriana MacLean in Arisaig in 1906 is printed in the *Journal of the Folk Song Society*, viii, 300. From what is said about the words of this version, it is clear that they differed very considerably from the version here. As Miss Broadwood points out, there is a resemblance to the Skye dance that is on p. 99 of *Albyn's Anthology*.

Art version: Mrs. Kennedy-Fraser, *Songs of the Hebrides*, iii. 36, 'Uist Cattle Croon. Cronan Cuallaich. Words sung by a cattle herd at Grimnis, by permission from Dr. Carmichael's "Carmina Gadelica". Air noted by Frances Tolmie from Mary Ross, Kilmaluag, Skye. Arr. for voice and piano (or harp), with translation, by M. Kennedy-Fraser.' Three lines of text are printed. In the first of these, Carmichael's *imirig* is changed to *imirich*; in the second, *feur na cille* is changed to *feur an fhirich*; Kenneth MacLeod's hand is evident here.

As printed in K. C. C., the song is on the following subjects:

(1) The poetess regrets that the cattle are going to be moved, with the herdsman driving them and the milkmaid following.

(2) On her going out without shoes, coat, or plaid, and reaching the big house of the glen, where there was a fire, plenty of chairs, and young men sitting drinking.

(3) On how Ailean Donn was in a sheiling with another man's sweetheart, and how he would get the girl he wanted, with her relations' consent, if he came back.

(4) How the poetess is sorrowful climbing and descending the mountain (two lines that occur elsewhere) in a state of pregnancy which she is keeping concealed from all her relations.

LVIII

Mo shùil silteach, mo chridhe trom

('My eye is tearful, heavy my heart')

Recorded from Miss Kate MacMillan, of Torlum, Benbecula, on 21/11/49 (wire recording no. 19), and from Miss Kate MacDonald at Peninerine, South Uist, on 10/1/50.

D. MacI. 46 (19 lines). Text alone, K. C. C. 76 (21 lines).

The text transcribed from Miss Kate MacDonald's recording is printed here. Miss Kate MacMillan only sang lines corresponding to nos. 741, 742, 738, and 737, 750–2, 754, and 755 here, in that order. The version in D. MacI. is very close to that of Miss Kate MacDonald, with some variation in the order of the lines. The song does not seem to be widely known. The metre, 8^1, is very unusual.

745. D. MacI. has *'m beannabh nan stùc.*

749. This line is not in the other versions mentioned here.

LIX

Chì mi ghrian 's i falbh gu siùbhlach

('I see the sun setting quickly')

Recorded from Mrs. Mary Johnston (Màiri Iain Choinnich) at Castlebay, Barra, on 5/4/51 (wire recording no. 721). After singing seven lines, the singer, who was in her eighties, said the song was too heavy for her to continue.

MS. version, Canon MacLean I, 6, presumably from Màiri nighean Alasdair, printed here.

Printed, text alone, K. C. C. 74 (27 lines); text, translation, and tune, *F.F.S.U.*, no. 92, p. 231, 5 lines only, beginning *Chì mi bhuam air bruaich an lochain*. There is also a version of the text in *T.G.S.I.* xv. 143 in a paper contributed by the Revd. John MacRury, Snizort, Skye entitled 'A Collection of Unpublished Gaelic Poetry' read to the Society on 27/2/1889, beginning *'S mi 'm aonar air airidh 'n leachduin* (22 lines).

There has been a good deal of confusion here. The lament for the deceased successful hunter whom the wild game will no longer need to fear is a recurrent theme or motif in waulking songs, cf. F. T., no. 75, which itself has a passage from VII of vol. i, beginning *Di-Sathuirne ghabh mi mulad* (the Gaelic text of F. T. no. 75 is printed in K. N. MacDonald's *Puirt-a-Beul*, p. 47). Four lines from LXVI here appear in the K.C.C. version of LIX.

758. *Rubh' an Dùine* is on the north-east coast of North Uist; *dùna* as gen. of *dùn* is found in Irish, and *Sgorr an Dùine* is a Canna place-name. One would suspect that this line referred to a ship weathering this headland, and that something had been omitted before.

761. K. C. C. has a place-name *Tunord* (short *u*) on p. 23, and *Puirt-a-Beul* has *Ceann-Loch-Luinnard* (*sic*), also short *u*.

774. *Iùbhraich* is presumably a place-name.

778. *A' Chriùbhrach* is presumably a place-name, but I have not been able to identify it. The preceding song in K. C. C. has the line *'S car' thu Mhac Iain o'n Chriùraich* on p. 73. *Mac Iain* was the patronymic of the MacDonalds of Glencoe.

LX

'S trom an dìreadh

('Sad is the climbing')

Recorded from Mrs. Effie Monk, Torlum, Benbecula, for me by the Revd. John MacCormick on Wirek tape recorder in 1953.

MS. version, D. MacI. 101.

Printed, text alone, K. C. C. 124.

The song is on the famous incident of the massacre of the MacDonalds on the Isle of Eigg, smothered by the MacLeods who lit a great fire at the mouth of the cave in which the entire population of the island, except two or three persons, had hidden on observing the approach of the MacLeod galleys. The incident is described in the MS. 'Description of the Isles of Scotland' printed by W. F. Skene as the third Appendix in the third volume of his *Celtic Scotland*. The anonymous author of the MS., which was written before 1595, stated specifically that the incident took place in March 1577, and that 395 persons—which must mean about eighty families—perished in it (p. 433).

This story is frequently repeated, but there are difficulties about accepting it as it stands. These may be summarized as follows:

There is no reference to the incident in contemporary state records; nor by Hugh MacDonald or the MacVurich historians of the MacDonalds.

Fr. Cornelius Ward the Irish Franciscan who visited Eigg in 1625 found over 200 people on the island and makes no reference to any massacre having previously taken place there.

Martin Martin makes no allusion to the incident in his book on the Western Islands of Scotland (1703) although he had visited Eigg himself.

Practical difficulties: it would have taken 395 persons a very considerable time to enter the cave one by one through its long narrow entrance; and in any case the tracks of so many would have led the raiders immediately to the cave, whereas the story is that the raiders found no one and left, and only returned when a scout unluckily showed himself, and found the cave by following his footsteps in the snow.

The story in fact did not surface until 1785, when it appeared in Boswell's *Journal of a Tour to the Hebrides*, having been told to Boswell and Dr. Johnson by young MacLean of Coll, who informed them that he had 'been in the cave, and seen great quantities of bones in it; and he said that one can still observe where families have died, as big bones and small, those of a man and wife and children, are found lying together'. Boswell adds tantalizingly 'this happened in——time' (Pottle and Bennett, Yale edition from the original MS., 1963, p. 247).

In his account of Eigg written for the Old Statistical Survey (1793) the Revd. Donald MacLean, minister of Eigg, said: 'About 40 skulls have been lately numbered here. It is probable a greater number was destroyed, if so, their neighbouring friends may have carried them off for burial in consecrated ground.' (*O.S.A.* xvii. 289). But it is difficult to see how this could have happened if the whole population of Eigg had perished. In any case it would have been more natural to have sealed up the cave.

After the story became known in the late eighteenth century, visitors to Eigg, including Sir Walter Scott, who landed there in 1814, started to remove bones from the cave. Around 1820 Scott's correspondent, John MacCulloch, visited the island and found no skulls in the cave at all. It is possible that after Scott had removed one with the disapproval of the Eigg people, the minister or the priest of the island made them bury the others.

The popular MacDonald story or the origin of the whole incident was that some MacLeods, on their way back to Skye from the mainland, landed on Eilean Chathasdail beside Eigg and raped some women tending cattle there, and were killed or ill treated by the MacDonalds, in consequence of which the MacLeods made their retaliatory expedition. The MacLeod story was that some MacLeods had so landed, had been refused food, and had slaughtered some of the MacDonalds' cows to sustain themselves, in consequence of which the MacDonalds ill treated them barbarously.

It is significant, however, that a rejected project for a marriage is mentioned as the first cause of the incident, not only by Effie Monk, but by D. MacQuarrie, Isle of Eigg, and Alexander MacLean, Raasay (notebooks of Dr. Calum I. MacLean in the archives of the School of Scottish Studies). This ties in with an unindexed reference to the Isle of Eigg in the History of the MacDonalds by Hugh MacDonald (Scottish History Society, *Highland Papers*, i. 68):

> 'Alexander MacLeod of Harris, having married the Laird of Muidort's [i.e. MacDonald of Clanranald, who owned Eigg] daughter sent her home some time thereafter, but the Laird of Muidort afterwards apprehending him in Egg hanged MacLeod's brother and kept himself prisoner for seven years at Castle Tirrim where he got his back broke which made him hunch backed all his lifetime.'

In consequence of which he was nicknamed 'Alasdair Crotach'. It is significant that the Bannatyne MS, quoted by Canon R. C. MacLeod in his book *The MacLeods of Dunvegan*, the Revd. Donald MacLean in the *O.S.A.*, and Hugh Miller in *The Cruise of the Betsey*, all mention the tradition connecting Alasdair Crotach with the massacre. This places the incident early in the sixteenth century; the story told by Hugh MacDonald provides an ample reason for it, and the earlier date is much more likely.

789. D. McIntyre has *Muile* for *Rùm*.

790, 791. These lines are not in either K. C. C. or D. McI., which versions closely resemble each other, although the order of the lines differs. D. McI. begins:

'S trom 's gur muladach leam fhìn e,
Ma gheibh mi am bruthach seo dhìreadh,
Chì mi (etc.)

'I feel it heavy and sad, if I manage to climb this hill-side.'

Lines 790 (with *Mac Colla* for *Mac Leòid*) and 791 are found in another song, beginning *Luchd tighe dheanadh mo fhreagairt*, Macdonald Collection, p. 32.

792. K. C. C. and D. McI., *Eilean nam Muc* for *Barraidh*.

795, 796. These lines are not in either K. C. C. or D. McI.

LXI

Cha déid mi do Chille Moire

('To Kilmore I will not go')

Recorded from Mrs. John Galbraith, Earsary, at Castlebay, Barra, on 3/1/50, wire recording no. 155. Sung with chorus.

There are only two other versions of this song known to us. One was printed in the book *Sgeulaiche nan Caol* (1902), by John MacFadyen, in an article about the waulking of the cloth. This contains only the refrain and lines 798, 799, and 800 here, with another not in Mrs. Galbraith's version:

Innis dhomhsa dé fàth t'anntlachd

'Tell me what is the cause of your displeasure'.

The other version is in the Morison MS. from Mull, recently acquired by the School of Scottish Studies. Through the courtesy of Dr. Allan Bruford, we have been allowed to have a copy of this version. It is a very interesting one, containing no fewer than 46 lines in seven sections, from the last of which it is clear that the song is of Isle of Mull provenance. Cille Moire is therefore Kilmore in Mull, not Kilmuir in Skye. The first section of the Morison MS. version is:

Cha teid mi do Chille-Mhoire
'S ri Murchadh cha dian mi coinneamh
Cha 'n eil ann ach oigear doini
Cha chu[i]r[e]adh e lamh na bhoineid
Ged thigeadh Iarla na choinneamh

'I will not go to Kilmore, I shall not meet with Murdo, he is only a poor young man, he would not put his hand to his bonnet, though an earl met him.'

This is equating *doini*, which is underlined in the MS., tentatively with *dòinidh*, 'miserable', *Songs of John MacCodrum*, l. 1020. It is certainly more apt than the *foinneil* 'handsome' of Mrs. Galbraith's version.

It is clear from the Morison MS. version that the girl who makes the song is married to someone else. Another unsatisfactory Murdo occurs in the song printed in K. C. C. 95, of which we hope to include a version in our third volume.

LXII

Chaidh mis' a dh'Eubhal imprig

('I went to Eaval on a flitting')

Recorded from Mrs. Fanny McIsaac, Torlum, Benbecula, by Fr. John MacCormick in 1953, on the Wirek tape recorder.

This song, and the similar version printed in K. C. C. 23 (26 lines), can be compared to the version of 50 lines, with tune in sol-fa notation and translation by Professor Derick Thomson, published for the first time by the Revd. A. J. MacVicar in his *Hebridean Heritage* (1966), pp. 7–11. The subject of the song is a lament for the MacVicar brothers in North Uist who were murdered by Hugh MacDonald, 'Hugh son of Archibald the Clerk', who coveted their lands there; the lament was made by a sister.

In Barra a waulking song on the subject of Uisdean mac 'Ill' Easbuig Chléirich, and other things, is sung to the refrain *Hó hó la ill eó*, *Ho hì ho ho nàilibh*, I recorded this from Mrs. MacDougall ('Anna Raghnaill Eachainn') in March 1938 (disc xxv) and I took down words of another version from Miss Elizabeth Sinclair on Vatersay in June 1949; the passages in this referring to Uisdean are printed here. Another version (only 7 lines) was recorded by the Barra Folklore Committee from Miss Mary Morrison, Earsary, on 2/3/50 at Castlebay, and there is another version in Miss Annie Johnston's second notebook (A. J. (2), p. 11) (17 lines). Transcriptions of the recordings of Mrs. MacDougall and Miss Mary Morrison's singing of their versions can be seen in vol. i, pp. 266 and 267.

In Uist, the waulking song beginning *Rinn mi mocheirigh gu éirigh* is sung to this tune and refrain (vol. i, No. VIII; K. C. C. 94; *F.F.S.U.* 250), and there has been further confusion with some lines also occurring in the waulking song beginning *'S mise bhean bhochd, chianail, thùrsach* (vol. i, No. II; K. C. C. 102; *F.F.S.U.* 246).

Mrs. Kennedy-Fraser noted a version of the air printed here, in Benbecula ('*Na him bo ha liù leo, Hua ho ro eile*'), *Songs of the Hebrides*, vol. ii, p. xii.

812. Eaval and Beinn an Fhaireachaidh are hills on the east side of North Uist; the Sound of Rona is the sound between Rona and Raasay; the 'Island of Whales' is probably the Isle of Muck.

815–18. Lines similar to these occur in vol. i, No. II, lines 61–5, and in the version of the same song in K. C. C. 94–5. They do not occur in the version of the present song in K. C. C. 23.

824. Hugh MacDonald, 'Uisdean mac 'Ill' Easbuig Chléirich' was hated. The story of how he met his death by being fed salt beef and refused water in prison, after his plot to deprive Donald Gorm Mor of Sleat of his property had been discovered, was told by the Revd. Alexander Macgregor in his account of the parish of Kilmuir, Skye, in the New Statistical Account. This is quoted by Alexander MacKenzie in his *History of the MacDonalds*, pp. 190–2.

828. Ealasaid Dhunnchaidh's version of the passage on Uisdean was preceded by lines similar to 278–305 of vol. i, and followed by a passage similar to lines 308–13.

829. Miss Mary Morrison has *gun éirich*, but this goes against the sense of the line.

836, 837. Miss Mary Morrison has *tu* 'thou' for *e* 'he'.

LXIII

Chatriana a dh'fhalbhas gu banail

('Catriana, who goes so chastely')

Recorded from Mrs. Mary Johnston ('Màiri Iain Choinnich') at Castlebay, Barra, on 5/4/51 (wire recording no. 736).

Unpublished. The only other text known to us is in Fr. Allan MS., fol. 84. His version of the text is printed here, as Mrs. Johnston's was shorter (only 17 lines), and there were difficulties about the transcription of certain words.

842. Both Fr. Allan MS. and the tape recording have *ainnir* here, but the word makes no sense in this context, which suggests that it is a corruption of *m(h)ainnir*, defined in Fr. Dieckhoff's dictionary as 'a fold used to keep the kids apart from the goats'.

See also *Dàin Iain Ghobha*, ii. 58, where it is glossed 'sheep-fold on the hill-side'.

843. The following line in Mrs. Johnston's version is *Bheiribh oirbh, togaibh leannan*, which can be translated 'Hurry up, get a lover'.

844–51. Here again we have the passage that occurs so often in these waulking songs, the message sent to the lover to tell him the girl is well after having got through winter, spring, and summer, cf. lines 458–66 and 599–606. Ruairi and Gleann Cuaiche (Glen Quoich) are sometimes mentioned in connection with this.

864. *Buaile bhó*, implies a fold of pedigree or well-bred cattle, a very valuable thing in the old Highlands.

LXIV

O, 's e mo ghaol an Anna

('O, my love is the Anna')

The Barra version was recorded from Miss Elizabeth Sinclair ('Ealasaid Iain Dhunnchaidh') on ediphone in June 1949 on Vatersay, and words and tune were transcribed by myself and Francis Collinson respectively, and printed in *Gairm*, iv, 368. The 'Anna' of this song is supposed to have been a boat. There is however some confusion with the similar song *O, 's fhada bhuainn Anna*, which will be included in our third volume. This was made to a girl who was said to be too haughty to accept ordinary suitors.

The Uist version, which differs considerably, was recorded from Mrs. Neil Campbell ('Bean Nìll'), Frobost, South Uist, on tape on 13/5/65. There is a closely related version in D.MacI. 98, and a more differing one in K. 3, where it is stated by the writer that 'The Following "Oran Luaidh" was sent to me by the Revd. Roderick Macdonald, Minister of South Uist. He took it down from the recitation of "Anna Peigidh", a daughter of "Peigidh Ruadh", a famous shebeener in South Uist.'

The Killearnan version, which apart from the refrain has 26 lines of text, is printed in McD. 227.

The version in D. MacI. (32 lines) is so close to that recorded from Mrs. Neil Campbell, that I have added the lines from it which are not found in her version. These are 901–2, 907–8, 913, 915–16, and 919–26. The last section, however, is not found in the other versions, and may not really belong to the song.

Nothing was said in Uist about the song's being addressed to a boat. The changing refrain words should be noted.

878. The 'son of the tacksman of Bernera' referred to here could well have been John, son of Sir Norman MacLeod of Bernera. Sir Norman, who had a distinguished career in the service of King Charles II, died in 1705 in his nineties. John was an advocate at the Scottish Bar and was guardian to Norman, nineteenth chief of MacLeod. The MacLeods of Bernera were descended from a younger son of Sir Rory Mor MacLeod. See J. C. W. 137–40.

897. K. has *A sporrain dhuinn nan iallan liosach*, D. MacI. (l. 909 here) *Sporan iallach nan iall nisneach.* A purse made of weasel skin was considered very lucky, never empty, see Revd. A. Stewart, *Twixt Ben Nevis and Glencoe*, p. 168.

903. *Mac Ni Raghnaill 'ic Ailein.* It is quite likely that this Raghnall mac Ailein was Ranald MacDonald of Benbecula, fourth son of Allan IX of Clanranald, who died on Canna in 1636. He was a well-known person in the Hebrides. If so, his only daughter, Flora, married John MacDonald of Griminish, and his grandson referred to here was Archibald who succeeded his father in Griminish around 1700 (*Clan Donald*). Cf. vol. i, ll. 572, 697, and 1069.

914–18. The successful hunter. Cf. lines 542–6 of vol. i, practically identical.

920–6. i.e. she is not pregnant. Cf. lines 558–62, 588–92.

LXV

'S moch an diu a rinn mi éirigh

('Early I arose today')

Recorded from Mrs. Neil Campbell ('Bean Nìll) at Frobost, South Uist, in the winter of 1958–9 by the Revd. John MacLean, Bornish, on tape on my machine.

MS. version: Fr. Allan MS., fol. 36 (rough) 88 (fair copy), printed here.

Printed versions: text alone, K. C. C. 45 (15 lines); MacD. 261 (17 lines); in K. from which the MacD. text comes, the song is stated to be 'from Marion MacLennan'. Text (but only 3 lines), translation, and tune, *F.F.S.U.* 212.

This song is a very good example of the indeterminate nature of some waulking songs. As sung by Mrs. Neil Campbell, the first section is one much more closely associated with the songs No. XXXI of vol. i and LI of the present volume, cf. *Eilean Fraoich*, p. 62. The second section, on the skilful steersman, is found in several other songs, cf. lines 367–73 of vol. i, and lines 1278–87 and 1322–33 here. Only the last section of the song appears to be original, and even then there is an echo of the first two lines of Fr. Allan McDonald's version in the version of *Hò mo leannan, hé mo leannan*, printed on p. 217 of MacD.

Dh'éirich mise 'm beul an latha,
Strath-na-h-amhuinn (*sic*) *ghabh mi null.*

'I arose at day-break, and crossed the strath of the river.'

940, 969. Mrs. Neil Campbell pronounced the word for 'barn' as *sobhal* here; Fr. Allan McDonald so wrote it in his rough copy, then changed it to *sabhal* in his fair copy in MS. The rhyme proves that the song must have been composed in a district where the word was pronounced *sabhal*.

941–2. Compare the first two lines of the song on p. 67 of *Eilean Fraoich*.

945. MacD. has *bean an tighe*.

949. This line is from the MacD. version.

LXVI

Tha sneachd air na beannaibh Diùrach

('Snow lies on the hills of Jura')

The air of this song was recorded on wire (no. 832) from Catriana Caimbeul at Loch Carnan on 10/4/51. She only remembered one or two lines of the song. The text printed here is that recorded on ediphone from Mrs. Neil McInnis, Glace Bay, Cape Breton, on 8/10/37.

Other version: text alone, but lacking the first line, *T.G.S.I.* xli. 350, from the Dornie MS. (paper by Professor Angus Matheson). Lines corresponding to the first four lines of the song here occur in K. C. C. 74, in the middle of the song beginning *Mi 'm aonar air buail' an lochain*, which is a version of LIX here, where they do not occur.

985–6. A pun is involved, a very rare thing in Gaelic verse. *Port*, (1) a port, harbour, (2) a tune, and the expression *a bhith ri port* means 'to be held up on port awaiting a ferry'.

989. My transcription, made in 1937, of the ediphone recording, which cannot be played now, as the machine is obsolete and broken down, was *Cuideachd branndaidh*; but the *T.G.S.I.* text shows the word must be *togsaid*.

990. The *T.G.S.I.* text concludes this section with the lines:

'S mi ri port aig bialaibh Phabaidh,
siaban a' cur dhiom mo bhreacain.

'And I am held up opposite Pabbay, sea-spray taking my plaid off me.'

Presumably Pabbay in the Sound of Harris is meant.

LXVII

Cha déid Mór a Bharraidh bhrònaich

('Marion won't go to miserable Barra')

This song, of which only a fragment has ever been printed, was widely known, in part at least, among traditional singers in Barra and Vatersay, and those of Barra descent in Cape Breton; it represented the triumph of their famous seventeenth-century bardess, Nic Iain Fhinn, in a flyting with Clanranald's bardess Nic a' Mhanaich, held at Ormacleit in South Uist. For this reason the song was forbidden to be sung at social gatherings or ceilidhs in Cape Breton, where the descendants or emigrants from Barra and South Uist live side by side around Christmas Island and Beaver Cove on the eastern shores of the Bras d'Or lake; the song could start a fight.

This song, and the next, have such strong individuality that I have felt justified in printing conflated texts. The basis of the text here is the version sung, recorded and communicated by Annie and Calum Johnston in Barra, who had the best and fullest version. The sources of the additional lines are indicated in the following notes. The recordings of the song have been as follows:

Ediphone, Miss Annie Johnston at Castlebay on 13/5/37; Mrs. Patterson, Benacadie, Cape Breton, on 30/9/37; Mrs. Neil McInnis, Glace Bay, Cape Breton, on 8/10/37.

Disc, Mrs. Mary Morrison ('Bean Phluim') at Castlebay, Barra, 19/3/38.

Wire, Annie and Calum Johnston together, by the Barra Folklore Committee at Castlebay on 3/8/50, no. 418.

Tape, Nan MacKinnon on Vatersay on 16/5/65.

In addition, versions of parts of the song were taken down from Mrs. J. R. Johnston, Beaver Cove, Cape Breton, on 1/10/37, and from Miss Sinclair ('Ealasaid Iain Dhunnchaidh') on Vatersay in June 1949.

MS. versions; Canon MacLean (from Màiri nighean Alasdair) I, 13, 25, and V, 18; and an interesting one communicated to me in 1948 by Mrs. Mary Morrison (daughter of Somhairle Beag, Northbay, Barra), when living in Oban.

Printed: text alone, K. C. C. 20; with tune and translation, F. T., no. 73, p. 233, and Tocher, 12, pp. 134–8, from Nan MacKinnon (but these are only fragments of the song, which Miss Tolmie admits is much longer. Her version was from Mrs. MacLean, Castlebay, Barra). A passage corresponding to lines 1009–14 here occurs in another song printed in MacD. on 249–50; K. C. C. 80; and Vol. i, lines 841–6; lines 1047–9 here also occur in this song, *'S muladach mi 's mi air m'aineoil*, represented in K. C. C. as a flyting between a Harris and an Uist woman. The passage also occurs in a short version in K, where it is said to have been taken down from Marion MacLennan.

Nic Iain Fhinn 'the daughter of Fair Ian' is the reputed authoress of *Là dhomh 's mi am Beinn a' Cheathaich* (No. XXXVII in vol. i), and of the Barra bardess's part of the next song in the present book, *A bhradag dhubh a bhrist na glasan*, as well as of the great part of *Cha déid Mór a Bharraidh bhrònaich* replying to the opening lines of the Uist poetess. All three poems praise the old MacNeils of Barra. The epithet *ban-eileineach* 'she-islander' in line 995 implies that she came from Mingulay or from one of the smaller islands south of Barra, formerly known as the 'Bishop's Isles'. Mr. Donald MacPhee, 'Dòmhnall Bàn Eileineach', born on Mingulay (which was evacuated in 1908) and living at Brevig, Barra, told me in a letter written in Gaelic on 13/3/39 that there was a tradition that she was born at Cliat in Barra, and had been a midwife and a nurse to the MacNeils of Barra while they were still living in Kismul Castle. Nan MacKinnon related in 1965 how Nic Iain Fhinn had got her power of poetic composition from the fairies.

995. There were three sources for this verse: Annie and Calum Johnston, Roderick MacKinnon ('Ruairi Iain Bhàin'), taken down on 23/2/43, and Canon MacLean. Annie and Calum Johnston had lines 995 and 996; Ruairi Iain Bhàin lines 995, 996, 999, and 1000; Canon MacLean has 995–8. According to Canon MacLean, I, 25, '*Bha Nic Iain Fhinn 'a cleachdadh dol a staigh gu tighearna air choireigin a h-uile madainn a dh'iarraidh a cuid. Air a' mhadainn àraid a bha 'n seo, dhiùlt e a thoirt dhi gus an deanadh i aoir dhi fhéin. Seo mar a thuirt i*:

'A Nic Iain Fhinn don'-eileineach,
A chailleach spàgach uinneineach,
Dà shùil ghorm meallanach,
'S blad chraos leathan gallanach.'

'Nic Iain Fhinn used to go into the house of some laird or other every morning to ask for her portion. On a certain morning, he refused to give it to her until she made a lampoon on herself. This is what she said:

'Daughter of Fair Ian, evil islander,
Club-footed thick-ankled hag,
With two protruding blue eyes,
And a gluttonous cavernous mouth.'

(taking *gallanach* to be a form of *goileanach*). In the other version of this quatrain in Canon MacLean the corresponding line is *Brat chruisg leithean dhealanach*.

1001. It is a remarkable testimony to the historicity of this poem, that there actually were three daughters of John of Moydart, chief of Clanranald, in the seventeenth century, named Mór, Catriana, and Anna, and that one of them, Catriana, did marry a MacNeil of Barra. This is proved by the entry in the Book of Clanranald, '*Anno Domini 1670 an bhliadhna do theasda Eoin Muideordach an éirisgáigh an uibhisd agus do cuiredh a chorp an Thogh mór ar fágbail aon mic.* i. *Domnall agus triur inghen, Mór bainntigerna Chola, Catriona bainntigerna Bharraigh, agus Anna bainntigerna Benni-mhaola*' 'Anno Domini 1670, the year in which John Moydartach died at Eriskay in Uist, and his body was interred in Howmore, leaving one son, i.e. Donald, and three daughters, Mór, Lady of Coll, Catriana, Lady of Barra, and Anna, Lady of Benbecula' (*Rel. Celt.* ii. 206).

The terms of Catriana's marriage contract are known. It was between 'Gallean (Gill' Eóghanain) Mcneill eldest lawfull sone & appeirand air to Neill Mcneill of Barray' and 'Katherine McRonald' 'lawfull dochter' of 'John McRonald of Moydart captane of the Clan Ronald'. The contract is dated 28 April 1653 (which means that this song must have been composed before that date). Catriana's dowry was to be 100 cows with their calves or stirks and 3,000 merks Scots money (£166. 13*s.* 4*d.* sterling) to be paid in three instalments by the 2 May 1654, with certain penalties for delays. In fact, the dowry was not paid by 31 January 1663, when the Lords of the Council at Edinburgh issued a decree ordering John of Moydart to make payment within ten days under the pain of being put to the horn as a rebel and distrained upon if he failed to do so (Clanranald Papers, Bonds, etc., no. 77). Settlement was not made until 18 May 1668, when 'Gallean' MacNeil gave a discharge to Donald, the son of John of Moydart (who was still living) who had given 'full & compleit payment and satisfactioune' (Clanranald Papers, Bonds, etc., no. 93). The document, in which there are a number of gaps, was witnessed by the Revd. Angus McQueen, minister of South Uist, John Kirk, and James McQueen, writer in the Isle of Skye. Probably John of Moydart, who had been heavily involved in the royalist side in the Civil War, was in financial difficulties in the 1650s.

Two other young women are mentioned in the versions of the song taken down by Frances Tolmie (Una and Seònaid), Canon MacLean (Sìne and Seònaid), and K. C. Craig (Sìle and Seònaid), in an additional line; but there is no mention of their names in the Clanranald genealogy in the *Clan Donald*.

Unless otherwise stated, the lines printed here are from Annie and Calum Johnston's version of the song.

1004. *Fleòdradh* means 'washing', cf. Fr. Allan. This line refers to the washing of skates in salt water prior to their curing. This is necessary to remove the urea, which is present in the flesh of all selachians (sharks, skates, and rays).

1006. This line occurs only in Canon MacLean.

1007. This line refers to the famous cockles of the Tràigh Mhór strand in Barra, of which Dean Munro wrote in 1545 that 'ther is na fairer and more profitable sands for cokills in all the world' (*Book of Barra*, p. 33). The line here is Elizabeth Sinclair's version; Annie and Calum Johnston have *Strùbain 'gan tarruing 'nan còta*, and Canon MacLean has *Gur e strùban is biadh beòil dhaibh.*

This whole passage illustrates the contempt that Highlanders had for fish as a diet in the old days; it was associated with extreme poverty. Cf. the couplets in the song beginning *Tha mulad, tha mulad/Tha lionn dubh orm fhéim* as sung by Mrs. Kate Nicholson, which we hope to print in our third volume:

'S ann a gheobhte 'n taigh t'athar
Cinn is cnamhan an éisg,
'S ann a gheobhte 'n taigh m'athar
Cinn is casan an fhéidh.

'In the house of your father would be found fish-heads and fish-bones; in the house of my father would be found the heads and feet of the deer.'

The only fish that might be exempted from this contempt were the salmon and the trout.

Cf. J. C. Watson, *Gaelic Songs of Mary MacLeod*, p. 33; and K. C. C. 118.

1009. Cf. line 507 of vol. i, *'S chuir siod dòltramachd air m'aire.* For *dòltram*, cf. Armstrong's Gaelic dictionary, *doltrum*, 'grief, anguish, vexation' (1825). If the word is a borrowing of the English *doldrum*, 'dumps, low spirits', the earliest instance of this recorded by the *O.E.D.* is only fourteen years earlier. Scots has *doldram, dulderdum*, adj., 'confused, stupid, silenced by argument' (*S.N.D.*, 1825) and *doldrum*, 'low spirits and ill-temper' (*Chambers's Scots Dictionary*). For *'s mi dòltram*, Mrs. Mary Morrison ('Bean Phluim') and Ealasaid Iain Dhunnchaidh have *'s mi m' ònar*. Mrs. MacLean (F. T., no. 73) has here the lines:

'S fhada mi 'm chadal 's mi dìomhair,
'S ma dhùisgear, gur garbh mo chìocras

'Long am I asleep and in solitude, if I am awakened, I shall be ravenous.'

This is apposite enough, but it does not preserve the rhyme.

1010. Ealasaid Iain Dhunnchaidh, *orm air dòrtadh.*

1011. The Ròdha is a place on South Uist, on the shore near Gearrabhailteas.

1014. Annie Johnston *éisginn*; Calum Johnston wrote *ascaoin.*

1015–18. These lines from Mrs. Mary Morrison ('Bean Phluim') only.

1020. This line only in F. T. and McD. The first has *Bradag nan obag, 's nan òisinneag*, translated 'The mischievous woman practising tricks of witchcraft'; the second has *A bhradag nan obag 's nan òthan* (p. 250). *C.G.* ii. 60 has *Fear agus bean, A dheanadh nan òisnean*; the word *òisnean* is not translated, nor explained in Carmichael's glossary. *Òthan* appears to be a word of obscure meaning, see *C.G.* vi. 113.

1022. Ben More, the highest hill in South Uist.

1023. This line only in Nan MacKinnon's version and that in McD. The latter has *a chòmhrag* 'to fight' for *an còmhlan*.

1027. Ealasaid Iain Dhunnchaidh had *Tìr an iche, tìr an òla*.

1028. This line only in the versions of Canon MacLean, and of Mrs. Neil McInnis, Cape Breton.

1029. This line only in Mrs. McInnis's version.

1030. This line only in Canon MacLean and in F. T.; in the latter it is *'S fàsaidh lion 'na chruachan òr-bhuidh*, 'Flax grows in golden yellow heaps'.

1031. This line is in all the versions. Ealasaid Iain Dhunnchaidh has *eilthirich*, 'strangers'. Canon MacLean has written *cliathanaich*, probably = 'workers at the waulking board', above *Éireannaich* in V, 19.

1034–5. These lines only in the versions of Mrs. Mary Morrison ('Bean Phluim'), and Mrs. Mary Morrison, Oban.

1035. This line only in the versions of Mrs. Mary Morrison ('Bean Phluim') and Canon MacLean; in the latter it is *Gillean* (*Fir* written above) *a' frithealadh mu bhòrdaibh*.

1041. This line only in the versions of Mrs. Mary Morrison ('Bean Phluim') and Mrs. Neil McInnis, Cape Breton.

1043–4. These lines only in the version of Mrs. Neil McInnis.

Having brusquely taken the word from Nic a' Mhanaich, first accusing her of being the daughter of criminals and a witch, then vindicating Barra from Nic a' Mhanaich's taunt of poverty, and declaring that Gilleonan, MacNeil of Barra's heir, is worthy of the noblest and richest of brides, Nic Iain Fhinn now turns to the second part of the song, called the *Casadh*, sung to a different tune in accelerated tempo, with each half-line preceded by a three-syllable refrain. (*Casadh* is defined in Dinneen as, amongst other things, 'the beginning of the second part of an air'.)

The *Casadh* consists mostly of personal abuse. The longest versions are from Annie and Calum Johnston, Mrs. Mary Morrison, Oban, and Mrs. J. R. Johnston, Beaver Cove, Cape Breton. Portions of it were also sung by Mrs. Mary Morrison ('Bean Phluim'), Castlebay, and Mrs. Neil

McInnis and Mrs. Patterson in Cape Breton. I had the distinct impression that none of the singers was willing to sing the *Casadh* in full; it was considered '*tuilleadh is mi-mhodhail*', too rude, and there are probably parts of it which have never been recorded.

1051–8. Except for line 1052, which is also in Mrs. Patterson's version, these lines were only in that of Mrs. Mary Morrison, Oban, which differs considerably from the others.

1054. Niall a' Chaisteil, 'Neil of the Castle' (Kismul) was the father of Gilleonan Òg, who is mentioned earlier in the poem. The appellation may have arisen from his seizure of Kismul Castle in 1613.

1058. Something in the texts of Mrs. Mary Morrison, Oban, and one of my Canadian informants follows here which is not very easy to understand. Before line 1059 Mrs. Morrison's communicated version has (as written)

Thug u 's thu u o hug o
Clann Illonain
Ged dhaibh [=*ghabh*] *iad sios*
Baile Biosdale
Ca dhe cur mi
Tidh no chethir
Calach dhu na
Ghein u chiora, etc.

The Cape Breton reciter, possibly Mrs. McInnis, had:

Theann an triùir ud *suas go Baghasdail*
Luidheach, luideagach, *Clann 'Ille Adhamhnain.*

Something about the expedition to South Uist seems to be involved.

1061. This implies that the sheep had died on the hill.

1065. This means that Nic a' Mhanaich's mother is accused of having gone with the fairy host. Cf. Reginald Scott, *A Discourse concerning the Nature and Substance of Devils and Spirits* (London, 1565), Book II, p. 51: 'Many such [i.e. country folk] have been taken away by the sayd Spirits, for a fortnight, or a month together, being carryed with them in Chariots through the Air, over Hills, and Dales, Rocks and Precipices, till at last they have been found lying in some Meddow or Mountain bereaved of their sences, and commonly of one of their Members to boot.' See also Campbell and Hall, *Strange Things*, p. 297.

1066. This line is only in Mrs. J. R. Johnston's version. It means that the women at the waulking board would not receive their usual entertainment, a great insult.

1067–73. Ealasaid Iain Dhunnchaidh had all seven of these lines, or versions of them. She did not sing the *Casadh*, but had these lines following line 1022. Annie and Calum Johnston had 1067, 1070, 1071, and for 1073, *'S na coin mhóra 'g iche t'fheòla.*

1067. Ealasaid Iain Dhunnchaidh had *Truagh nach robh thu seal air m'òrdan*, 'it is a pity you were not at my disposal for a while'.

1068. *An Tùr* is understood to mean Kismul Castle, the ancient stronghold of the MacNeils of Barra.

1071. Mrs. Mary Morrison ('Bean Phluim') had *Bradag air bior 's i 'ga ròsdadh*, 'the villainess being roasted on a spit'. Ealasaid Iain Dhunnchaidh has *Bleideag eatorra 'ga ròsladh*, 'The little bletherer being roasted between them'.

1072. Ealasaid Iain Dhunnchaidh had *'S coin 'gad dhraghadh le'n spògan*, 'dogs pulling at you with their paws'.

Epilogue. *Thuit an té Uibhisteach 'na plod.* A good instance of the powers of satire, famous in Gaelic tradition.

'Nic Iain Fhinn would not get into the fairy mound if she were to eat anything before she went out'. It is a remarkable coincidence that cooked food was also obnoxious to the fairies of Maori folklore, who in many ways resemble the fairies of Scottish Highland tradition, except that the colour associated with them was red and not green. See A. W. Reed, *Treasury of Maori Folklore*, p. 212 and *passim*.

LXVIII

An Spaidearachd Bharrach

('The Barra Boasting')

This song is obviously closely connected with the preceding, and in Barra tradition the protagonists are said to be the same persons. If the songs were really composed on the same occasion, the order should probably be reversed, as Nic Iain Fhinn, the Barra bardess, is credited with the last word and the victory over her South Uist opponent, Nic a' Mhanaich, who has the last word in the present song.

Recording from Annie and Calum Johnston by the Barra Folklore Committee at Castlebay, Barra, on 3/8/50; previously recorded from Miss Johnston on ediphone on 21/5/37 and on disc XXXV on March 1938; and in South Uist from Mrs. Neil Campbell ('Bean Nìll') at Frobost by the Revd. John MacLean on tape in November 1957.

Annie and Calum Johnston only sang the Barra bardess's part of the song; Bean Nìll sang the first two sections; the text of the complete song printed here is taken from O. 33.

Other versions: text alone, Fr. Allan MS. fol. 115 (eleven half-lines only); Canon MacLean, iv. 4 (21 lines); K. 5. (49 half lines); A. J. (2) 64 (18 lines).

Printed: text alone, McD. 230 (same text as K. 5; this is a version which resembles that of O.); K. C. C. 1.

Three lines of the song are quoted by the Revd. J. Gregorson Campbell in *Witchcraft and Second Sight in the Scottish Highlands*, p. 212 n. It must have been known on Tiree.

Art version: Mrs. Kennedy-Fraser, *Songs of the Hebrides*, i. xv (air only, from Mrs. Cameron and Mrs. MacLean, Barra); i. 4, where the song is titled 'The Ballad of MacNeil of Barra' 'Old Words and Air noted down by Mrs. Kennedy-Fraser from the singing of Ann Macneil, Barra' 'Words from John Macneill, Eriskay, Mrs. MacLean, Barra, and Isle of Eigg version'.

Only the Barra bardess's part of the song is given. The text of this is printed in full, with a *vis-à-vis* translation, presumably by Kenneth MacLeod; the text is practically identical with that in Miss Annie Johnston's 1931 notebook, but whether she copied it from *Songs of the Hebrides*, or whether in fact Mrs. Kennedy-Fraser actually got it from Miss Johnston (she could not have taken down the Gaelic words herself) is uncertain.

About the song, the Revd. A. MacDonald, minister of Killearnan, says in K. that it is 'from the Revd. Rodk. Macdonald. Note by the collector:— This *Oran Luaidh* was composed *impromptu* by a Barra woman and a Uist woman actually at the waulking board. The *luadh* gathering was frequently the scene of disputation when a parliament of women met and took an opportunity of discussing local and public questions in such a manner as the genuine talent of the country could display.' Fr. Allan McDonald has the note *'S ann an Cill Donain a bha iad a' luaghadh. Sgàin a' bhean Uibhisteach leis an tàmailt. B'fheudar falbh 'san oidhche leis a' bhana-Bharrach mu'm mairbhte i.* 'It was at Kildonan that the waulking was held. The Uist woman burst at the insult. They had to go away with the Barra woman by night, or she would have been killed.' This supports the Barra tradition about the bardic encounter.

We print a conflated South Uist version first, as in this the song is given in its correct form as an abusive dialogue between the Barra and South Uist bardesses. It is a flyting between these two, not a 'ballad of MacNeil of Barra' as it is called by Mrs. Kennedy-Fraser, and it is important that it should not be stereotyped in the latter incomplete and incorrectly titled form. The version printed here is based on the Oban MS. text, and lines added from other sources are indicated in the notes below.

The versions in O., in K., and MacD. are divided into two parts only, the first two sections of the song as printed here being attributed to the Barra bardess, and the last to the Uist woman. On the other hand, the version of Màiri nighean Alasdair as preserved by both Canon MacLean and K. C. Craig gives the first and last sections to the Uist bardess and only the middle one to Nic Iain Fhinn. As Nic Iain Fhinn would have been most unlikely to praise anyone connected with Castle Tioram, the Clanranald stronghold, in such a bardic contest, it seems to us that this method of dividing the dialogue is the right one, and it is followed here.

1078. The Oban MS. has *A dhiasg sgaolach*. K. and McD. have *Moire 's e mo ghràdhsa 'n gille*.

1079. Bean Nìll, *Dha'm bheil deirgead 's gile muineal*. Following this line, K. and McD. have *Théid thu 'n tigh mhór 's do 'n a' chitsin*, which seems hardly apposite here.

1080. K., McD., *Dalta nan dàn*. Canon MacLean, *Dalta nam bàrd Is mnatha gile thu*. K. C. C. *Dalta nam bàrd 's na mnatha gileadh thu*, 'You are a fosterling of bards, and of the fair woman.' Bean Nìll, *Dalta nam bàrd thùs na' fil' thu* (? *mil thu*).

1081. Identification of the person described seems to be impossible. It can hardly be John of Moydart's heir Donald, as he was born around 1615, and would have been about 35 in 1650, when this song and the preceding were probably composed. It cannot be his son, for his marriage to his cousin Mór MacLeod did not take place until 1656 (not 1666 as is stated in the *Book of Dunvegan*, I, 57, as the Revd. Archibald MacQueen was cross-examined by the Synod of Argyll in May 1658, about his having performed this marriage, Donald having been excommunicated by the Synod as a Catholic and a Royalist; see Argyll Synod Minutes, II, 169). It cannot be a younger brother of Donald, as according to *The Clan Donald* he had only the sisters who are mentioned in the preceding song.

1084–5. O.: *Le fion dachte? cian ga shireadh.*

McD.: *Le fion théidear cian ga shireadh*

Canon MacLean:	*Le fion uaibhreach*	*buan ga shileadh*
	Le fion shéisdir	*'s a air mhìre* (*sic*)
K.C.C.:	*Le fion uabhrach*	*buan ga shileadh*
	Le fìon na sheusdar	*'s e air mire.*

McD. had *iarraidh* for *shireadh* the first time, but the rhyme proves this cannot be right. I do not know what *shéisdir* or *na sheusdar* here could mean, but the *théidear* of McD. makes good sense. The lines are not in Bean Nìll's version.

1086. O.: *Ach fheudail mhor 's a dhia astaich*

Bean Nìll: *Mhuire 's a Rìgh! 's Fhir a' cheartais!*

Canon MacLean, K.C.C. *A Dhia fheartaich* only, throwing the half-lines out of order.

McD. only *Ciod a nì mis'*, a half-line missing also.

1087. Ruairi an Tartair, 'Noisy Rory' was the chief of the MacNeils of Barra who flourished at the end of the sixteenth century, and the beginning of the seventeenth. He appears to have had a legitimate family by Mór, sister to Donald MacDonald of Clanranald, and an illegitimate one by Mary MacLeod, only daughter of William MacLeod of Dunvegan and widow of Duncan Campbell of Auchinbreck. On 11 March 1613 the Register of the Scottish Privy Council recorded his complaint that he and his legitimate son Gillevuan Oig (Gill' Eóghanain Og) had been seized and imprisoned by his natural sons Neill Oig (Niall Og) and Gillevuan, whose mother was described as 'mother to Sir Dougall Campbell of Auchinbreck' (who was Mary MacLeod).

The usurpation was permanent. In February 1626 the Irish Franciscan Fr. Cornelius Ward visited Barra and performed the marriage ceremony for 'the lawful heir of the island'. 'His younger brother, however, having seized the castle (i.e. Kismul) by force and having apprehended his father and this elder brother, did not release the father until his death, nor his brother until he had made by oath renunciation of his inheritance' (Translation of Latin text made by Dom Denys Rutledge O.S.B.).

This 'Neill Oig' is the same person as Niall a' Chaisteil who is mentioned in the Book of Clanranald as chief of the MacNeils in 1639 (*Reliquiae Celticae*, ii. 175), and in line 1109 here. He had been reconciled to the Catholic Church by the Irish Franciscan Fr. Hegarty in 1632. His dispossessed elder brother is known as Niall Uibhisteach in Barra tradition, and from him the MacNeils of Vatersay were descended. See J. L. Campbell, 'The MacNeils of Barra and the Irish Franciscans', *Innes Review*, v. 33, and *Tales of Barra, Told by the Coddy*, pp. 32–5.

1088. Niall Glùndubh was High King of Ireland from 916, in which year he restored the Assembly of Taillte, to 919, when he was killed leading his army against the Norsemen of Dublin. He is the eponymous head of the O'Neills of Tyrone, and was claimed as an ancestor by the MacNeils of Barra.

Niall Frasach was High King of Ireland from 763 to 770, when he retired to become a monk at Iona, where he died in 778. He was called 'Niall Frasach' 'Neil of the Showers' because of three showers said to have fallen at Inishowen either during his reign, or at his birth. According to the Annals of Clonmacnoise, the showers were said to have been of silver, wheat, and honey, and to have been a response to prayers of the King and his bishops in time of famine. Niall Frasach was the great-grandfather of Niall Glùndubh.

See *passim* the *Annals of Ulster*; *Annals of Clonmacnoise*; *Annals of the Four Masters*; *Iomarbhágh na bhFileadh*; *Eóin Mac Néill, Phases of Irish History*, etc. It is very interesting to find these Irish High Kings of over a thousand years ago still remembered in a Hebridean Gaelic labour song. Miss Annie Johnston told me that Neil MacPhee, Mingulay, a well-known personality in his time, had told her that in consequence of the showers associated with Niall Frasach, the MacNeils were called

Sliochd Nìll Fhrasaich nan crùn,
Fhuair an achanaich dlùth,
Òr air faiche nam fiù,
Airgead geal agus flùr,
An teaghlach macanta, mùirneach, mór.

'The race of Niall Frasach of the crowns, who obtained the earnest request, gold on the plain of worth, white silver and flour, the active, joyful, great family.'

1089. This Gilleonan can hardly be the same one as the Gilleonan of line 1041, who was Ruairi an Tartair's grandson. He is more likely to have been the Gilleonan who was Ruairi an Tartair's father or grandfather, and who was a member of the council of the Isles which was formed in 1545 to treat with King Henry VIII with a view to giving aid to the English against the Scottish Government in return for the restoration of the Lordship or Kingdom of the Isles. See Donald Gregory, *History of the Western Highlands and Islands*, pp. 171–7.

1093. This line is only in the versions of McD. and of Bean Nìll. McD. has *flùr* for *cruithneachd.*

1094. This is only in McD.

1095. In O. this line comes before 1092, which is there the last in this section: but it is obviously best placed as here.

1096–1104. There are slight variations in the order of the lines of this section in the different versions, but they are not important.

1097–8. These lines are not in the O. version.

1097. Annie Johnston has *Cuiridh mi ort an dubh-chapull,* see line 1107; K. C. C., *Fàgaidh mi ort an dubh chapull*; Canon MacLean, from same source as K. C. C., has *'S fàgaidh mi ort an dubh chapuill,* with *thu* written above *an*; but perhaps this is taken from McD., which has *Fàgamaidh* (*sic*) *mi ort 's tu 'n dubh chapull,* followed by the half-line *'S tu 'n dubh chaile,* which is perhaps a conjecture by the first transcriber which has become incorporated in the text (K. has the same readings).

The *dubh-chapull* (= 'black mare') is explained by D. C. MacPherson in his *Duanaire*, p. 92, in a note which translated reads 'At wedding feasts, the man to whom the *dronn* came had to make a rhyme on it, or the "black mare" (*an dubh-chapuill*) would be on him'. *Dronn* is not explained. The expression is obscure, but defeat in a bardic contest is obviously implied.

1100. O., *Oighreachd*; McD., K., *Deirc*; others *Gibht*, *Git.* The line refers to the fact that the MacNeils of Barra received a charter of Barra from their feudal superiors the (MacDonald) Lords of the Isles, in 1427, see Gregory, *History of the Western Highlands*, p. 79. In later years the superiors of Barra were the MacDonalds of Sleat.

1101. This line is reminiscent of the anecdote of which I recorded a version from the late Duncan MacDonald, Peninerine, on 15/2/50, which tells how MacNeil of Barra once invited Clanranald to dinner at Castle Kismul, and in order to impress his guests with this wealth, told the menservants who were to wait at table to fill their pockets with limpet shells which would clink and sound like coins, and when the wine ran low, to serve wine to Clanranald's party only and water to MacNeil's. These devices did not work. Clanranald perceived that there was great scarcity in Barra, and got up and prepared to leave, remarking in a verse as he did so:

'S mithich dhuinn a bhith triall
A Barraidh chrìon nach eil pailt,
'S na sligean ag innse sgial
Gu bheil Clann nan Niall 'nan airc;
Theirear iasg ri iasg mór,
Theirear iasg ri iasg beag,
Theirear niod ri niod a' gheòidh,
'S ri niod an fhionnan-fheòir, mas beag!

'It is time for us to leave
Withered Barra of distress,
When the shells do tell the tale
That the MacNeils are in want;
A big fish is called a fish,
A little one's a fish too,
A goose's nest is called a nest,
So is a grasshopper's, though small!'

1104. Cf. line 1004.

1106. This was taken by Miss Annie Johnston to refer to the Muilgheartach, the monster sea-hag from Norway who came from Lochlann to Ireland to challenge the Fiantaichean, the subject of a popular ballad which may still survive in South Uist (it was extant 20 years ago there). See Reidar Christiansen, *The Vikings and the Viking Wars . . . in Gaelic Tradition*, pp. 215 and 359. It is, however, an odd coincidence that the name of Niall Glùndubh's most famous son was *Muircheartach na gCochull gCraiceann*, 'M. of the Leather Cloaks', who made a circuit of Ireland with only a thousand men, and fell fighting against the Norsemen in 943 (see the *Annals of the Four Masters*).

1108. *Ruairi an Tartair*. See note on line 1087.

1109. *Niall a' Chaisteil*. See note on line 1054.

1110. *Niall Glùndubh*; *Niall Frasach*. See notes on line 1088.

1114. Kenneth MacLeod translated this 'He would put flowers/ On the dew for them' (*Songs of the Hebrides*, I, 4); but line 1093 shows that it was 'flour'. The expression is an odd one.

1122. A. J. (2) and Songs of the Hebrides have *gachan*, which Kenneth MacLeod translated 'gulping'; but the word is clearly *gachdan* (or *gacan*) on the tape. Dwelly has *gachunnach*, 'harsh; applied in Eigg to a drink strong enough to make one gasp'. Perhaps *gachan*(*n*) = 'strong drink'.

NOTES ON THE TEXT

LXIX

Tàladh Dhòmhnaill Ghuirm

('Donald Gorm's Lullaby')

Recorded by Mrs. Neil Campbell ('Bean Nìll') on tape in November 1957.

Other versions: text alone, Canon MacLean, looseleaf 2 (25 half-lines).

Printed: Text alone, Alexander Carmichael, *An Gàidheal*, V, 68 (1876), a conflated version, as is the one printed in *Bàrdachd Ghàidhlig*, p. 246 (1959 edition); see remarks in letters from Carmichael to Fr. Allan McDonald, in letter dated 28 April 1904, where Carmichael said he had ten or twelve versions of the song (*Éigse*, viii. 262). K.C.C. 11 (28 lines); McD. 35 (164 half-lines, not counting refrain), stated to have been 'composed about 1610. This version was obtained from Miss Frances Tolmie, Edinburgh, who took it down in Skye' (McD., p. xii).

The tune of the version taken down by Miss Tolmie, with a translation of part of the text and some notes, is printed in F. T., no. 78, p. 238.

A version of the tune was printed by Donald MacDonald in his *Collection of Ancient Martial Music of Caledonia*, p. 116, along with ten other 'Airs Composed in the Islands of Uist and Skye'. It is there headed *Mac mo Righ s' dol na eideadh*, and stated to have been 'Sung in the times of the Druids'.

Art version: Mrs. Kennedy-Fraser, *Songs of the Hebrides*, ii. 28, where the song is titled 'To the Lord of the Isles. Buachaille nan Eilean. Air and words from the Traditional singing of Kenneth MacLeod.' Dòmhnall Gorm was not Lord of the Isles, of course.

Gaelic text and art version of tune: *Gairm* 2, p. 239, obtained from Bean Eairdsidh Raghnaill (a daughter of Mrs. Neil Campbell) by Rena Nic 'Illeathain; tune arranged with piano accompaniment by Ian Whyte. Text the same as that of Mrs. Neil Campbell (1954).

The song is of a type which lends itself to confusion with other similar songs, and lines associated with this song appear in *Pòsadh Mhic Leòid*, attributed to Mary MacLeod (J. C. Watson, *Gaelic Songs of Mary MacLeod*, p. 2, and taken from D. C. MacPherson's *Duanaire*, p. 140; examination of D. C. MacPherson's notebook has proved that this is a conflation of three different songs, see *S.G.S.* xi. 174).

Frances Tolmie wrote that the song was 'now only remembered by a small number of elderly persons'. This was in 1911, and the version of the tune which she printed was taken down from Harriet McVicar in North Uist in 1870. It is therefore scarcely surprising that the version recorded by Bean Nìll in 1957 is defective; some half-lines from other versions have been used to make her version complete as far as it goes.

There were several chiefs of the MacDonalds of Sleat known as Dòmhnall Gorm; Professor W. J. Watson considers the song was addressed to the Dòmhnall Gorm who died in 1617; but his successor, Sir Dòmhnall Gorm Òg, who died in 1643, could have been the subject.

1135. Masts are most unlikely to be made of willow, though this is also the term used in the *An Gàidheal*, McD., and *B.Gh.* versions. K. C. C. has *'s dà chrann eile dheth.* The *trì chrainn airgid* of vol. i, l. 1136 would be more appropriate.

LXX

Chuala mi 'n dé sgeul nach b'ait liom

('Yesterday I heard a tale unjoyful')

Recorded from Mrs. Mary Johnston ('Màiri Iain Choinnich') by the Barra Folklore Committee on 9/3/50, wire no. 301.

Other versions: text only, O. 54; D. McI. 43. Printed, K. C. C. 32 (29 lines).

This spirited song does not seem to be well known. As Mrs. Johnston only sung eleven lines, the version in D. McI. is printed here.

1139. O. *gun àth'r fasgath*; D. McI. *gun àr fhasgaidh*; K. C. C. *gun adhar fhasgaidh* (unmetrical). Cf. Fr. Allan, *àrag*, a breath of wind.

1140. This line from the O.; also in K. C. C.

1143. O. *air a h-arcain.*

1147. D. McI. and K. C. C. have *leag i còrsa*; O. has *leag e chòrsa.*

1160. D. McI., *miastadh*; O. and K. C. C., *miannas*. Cf. *Orain Ghàidhlig le Seonaidh Caimbeul*, p. 30:

Gun (d') rinn mi miasdadh a dhol g'a iarraidh

'I made a mistake going to look for it'

Dwelly 'mischief done by cows or horses that have broken loose in corn, etc.' English 'mistake'?

1168. O., in corresponding line, has

Roghainn deth sin 's a bhi reidh riut

K. C. C. has *Roghainn sin dhith 's i bhith réidh rium*

LXXI

Alasdair mhic Cholla ghasda

('Alasdair, son of splendid Colla')

Recorded from Miss Mary Gillies, Garrygall, Barra, at Castlebay, with chorus, by the Barra Folklore Committee on 9/3/50, wire recording no. 303.

Also recorded on disc XIII from Roderick MacKinnon (Ruairi Iain Bhàin) in 1938, and from Calum Johnston on disc LXXIX in 1948. Ruairi

Iain Bhàin's version was published in *Gaelic Folksongs from the Isle of Barra* in 1950, on 12-inch disc and in accompanying booklet, p. 22. Both he and Calum Johnston sung this song very pleasingly in solo style; the version sung by Miss Mary Gillies and chorus was sung in waulking style, is longer, and shows how the complex refrain is divided between the soloist and the chorus, so it is used here.

Other versions: Text alone, MS., A. J. (2) 56; printed, MacD. 40, a collated version based on two, the longer taken down by Frances Tolmie (the song is not in K.).

Text, translation, and tune, F. T. 257 (no. 94) (7 lines only); *G.S.N.S.* 180 (12 lines, from the MS. of the late Jim Hughie MacNeil, Sydney, Cape Breton).

Text, translation, and recording, *G.F.B.* 22, 6 lines only (12 half-lines).

Art version: Mrs. Kennedy-Fraser, *Songs of the Hebrides*, i. 162, 'As phonographed from the singing of Annie Macneill, Barra. An Old Barra Waulking Song.' Ten lines (20 half-lines) of the text are given in the introduction to the song by Kenneth MacLeod.

The song is in praise of Alasdair MacDonald, 'Alasdair mac Colla Chiotaich', who was the Marquis of Montrose's second-in-command in the Civil War in 1644–5. Alasdair was a man of tremendous courage and endurance, and a perfect second-in-command to Montrose; together their force of Highlanders and Irishmen won a series of spectacular victories against odds over the Covenanters. Alasdair was by no means so successful when he fought on his own, and was eventually killed at the battle of Cnoc na nDos in Ireland, near Cork, in 1647; see vol. i, 55. For the Montrose wars, see John Buchan, *Montrose*, London, 1928; and the Book of Clanranald, *Reliquiae Celticae*, ii. 175–201. See also *S.G.S.* ii. 75.

1170. A. J. (2) *As do lann-sgian.*

1171. This was Sir Duncan Campbell of Auchinbreck, who commanded the Covenanting forces, mostly Campbells, at the battle of Inverlochy against Montrose and Alasdair on 2 February 1645, his own chief, the Marquis of Argyll, having little military capacity. Although the Royalists were freshly arrived from an exhausting march across the central Highlands, they routed the Covenanters easily.

1172–3. McD.: *Thiodhlaiceadh e luib a' bhreacain*
Ged is beag mi bhuail mi clach air.

1174. 'Neil of the Castle' was the contemporary MacNeil of Barra. The reason that the killing of Campbell of Auchinbreck cast gloom on Neil must be that Auchinbreck was the grandson of Neil's mother Mary MacLeod by her original marriage to Duncan Campbell of Castleswene. See note to line 1087.

1176. Ni Lachlainn. Cf. line 1318 of vol. i, where she is mentioned as the wife of 'Murchadh Beag', possibly a younger son of MacNeil of Barra.

A. J. (2) *fhéin ga bhasghuil*; McD. *fhéin ga bhasail*. So in Mrs. Kennedy-Fraser, op. cit. i. 162, where Kenneth MacLeod explains it as 'in some districts means to dress a corpse; in others, to wring one's hands in sorrow'.

1177. Nic Dhòmhnaill: not identified.

1182. *Portaibh* here, perhaps, 'forts', see Dinneen. Lines 1178–82 are not in the version sung by Annie and Calum Johnston.

1184. The Royalists did not burn Glasgow; Montrose was welcomed there after his victory at Kilsyth in August 1645.

1185. Aberdeen was sacked by Montrose's men after their victory outside the town on 13 September 1644. It was not a worthy episode in Montrose's campaigns, but it was provoked, at least in part, by the cold-blooded shooting by a Covenanting fanatic of a drummer boy who accompanied Monstrose's messenger under a flag of truce to the Aberdeen magistrates summoning the city to surrender.

LXXII

A phiuthrag 's a phiuthar, ghaoil a phiuthar

('Little sister, beloved sister')

Recorded from Mrs. MacDougall ('Anna Raghnaill Eachainn') at Castlebay in March 1938, disc XXII, and from Calum Johnston in Edinburgh in 1948, disc LXXIX. The first sang it in the waulking style, the second in the solo style.

The Barra text printed here was communicated by Miss Annie Johnston. The singers only recorded a part of the song.

Other versions: text alone, O. 41, a South Uist version, printed here; Fr. Allan MS., fol. 124 (first line only); D. McI. 25, twelve half-lines only, headed 'Fragment', corresponding to the concluding section of the O. version.

Art version: Mrs. Kennedy-Fraser, *Songs of the Hebrides*, i. 38, 'A Fairy plaint' 'Notes from the singing of Mrs. Macdonald, Skallary, Barra', has text of 8 lines corresponding to the opening section of the song here, but the tune is different.

This song must be distinguished from that beginning *Phiuthrag nam piuthar, bheil thu 'd chadal?*, F. T. 177, no. 21, of which there is a version in Fr. Allan MS., see also *T.G.S.I.* xvi. 105.

In Barra the song is said to have been made by a woman imprisoned in a fairy mound appealing to her sister for help; the South Uist version does not necessarily carry this interpretation. That this kind of thing was taken seriously is shown by the trial for witchcraft of Isabel Haldane at Perth in 1623, who 'being askit if she hed onye conversatione with the farye folk, answerit that ten yeiris syne, lying in hir bed, scho was taikin furth quhidder be God or the devill scho knawis not, wes caryit to ane hill syde; the hill oppynnit and scho enterit in, thair scho stayit thrie dayis' (*Register of the Privy Council of Scotland*, 2nd series, viii. 352–3).

1197. Laigheabhal (Laiaval) is a low hill in the north part of North Uist.

1198–1202. Cf. lines 1613–1615.

1207, 1210, 1211. Very similar lines occur in an entirely different waulking song, K. C. C. 83.

1236. Eubhal is the largest hill in North Uist.

LXXIII

'S muladach mi o chionn seachdain

('I am sorrowful since a week')

Recorded from Miss Annie Johnston in March 1938, disc XIII. Recording, text, and translation published in *Gaelic Folksongs from the Isle of Barra* in 1950. No other version either in MS. or in print is known to us. The song must be distinguished from that beginning with the same line of which versions are printed in D. C. MacPherson's *Duanaire*, p. 134; Gaelic Songs of Mary MacLeod, p. 32; K. C. C. 32; *S.G.S.* xi. 185.

The song here contains allusions to the successful hunter, and to players of backgammon, dice, and cards, which are frequent in older waulking songs.

LXXIV

Coisich a rùin, lùb nan geal-làmh

('Walk, my beloved white-armed youth')

This song is (or was) widespread and popular, and many versions have been recorded. From Barra, Janet MacKinnon on tape in 1964 (3 lines); from South Uist, Catriana Campbell, Loch Carnan, on 10/4/51 (wire no. 824; 41 lines); from Mrs. D. J. MacLellan, at a genuine waulking at Iochdar on 29/3/51 (16 lines, wire 649); from Mrs. Archie Munro, on tape, at Lochboisdale on 5/12/63 (4 lines); on Benbecula, recorded from Mrs. Kate MacCormick by the Revd. Fr. John MacCormick for me on wire in 1954 (4 lines).

In Cape Breton I recorded the song from Mrs. Patterson at Benacadie on ediphone on 4/10/37 (24 lines), and in conversation Mrs. Neil McInnis, Glace Bay, later added 10 more lines, and in Antigonish County I recorded a version of 19 lines from Angus 'Ridge' MacDonald later the same month.

Other versions: text alone, O. 7 (48 lines); D. McI. 86; Canon MacLean, III, 16 (from Mrs. Donald Steele, 41 lines); A. J. (2), p. 1; K. 200 (from Marion MacLennan, 22 lines).

Printed, text only, McD. 258 (same as K. 200); K. C. C. 36 (42 lines).

Text, translation, and tune: F. T., no. 53, p. 211, from Margaret M'Leod, Portree, Skye, taken down in 1870 (27 lines).

Art version: Mrs. Kennedy-Fraser, *From the Hebrides*, p. 84, where it is called 'Shoreless Seas. Long air Snamh. Air from Mrs. McKinnon, North Bay, Barra' (i.e. from Bean Shomhairle Bhig) 'Words from an ancient sailing Rune (*sic*!) recovered and collated by Kenneth MacLeod'. The words in fact are 8 lines corresponding to the opening section of Miss Annie Johnston's version.

This, taken down from Ealasaid Eachainn (MacKinnon) around 1930, is printed here, along with the Uist version from D. MacI., these being the best texts of the song which we have seen.

It will be seen that the longer versions of this song embody a number of the stock themes or motifs of the older waulking songs: the 'secret lover', lines 1266–77, 1350–5; the 'successful steersman', 1278–92, 1322–33; the 'wedding feast turned into a wake', 1293–1311; the 'jealous mistress', 1293–1317, 1344–5; the 'successful hunter', 1336–9; and the 'lover drowned', 1340–3.

1261. Some versions have *Coisich a rùin, cum do ghealladh*, 'Walk, beloved, keep thy promise'. O. glosses *lùb nan geal-làmh* as 'poetic for a child'. Bartók and Lord comment on the frequent use of 'white' as a formulaic epithet in Yugoslav traditional poetry (*Serbo-Croatian Folksongs*, p. 293 n.); it is equally common in Scottish Gaelic traditional poetry.

1264–5. Cf. lines 428, 462, 602, 847. Some singers might have proceeded to bring the whole of this passage in; but these lines are not in the other versions of the song I have read or heard.

1278–87, 1322–33; cf. lines 367–73 of vol. i, and lines 950–62 here.

1282. *Ulagan* is glossed 'blocks and tackle' in O.

1294. *Bho'n chiad Mhàrt*. Compare the saying *An Inid, an ceud Mhàrt de'n t-solus Earraich*, 'Shrove Tuesday, the first Tuesday of the Spring moon' (Nicolson's *Gaelic Proverbs*, p. 29). The old style calendar being then in use, this would have been about the middle of our present March. In Gaelic calendar lore, winter was supposed to end on St. Patrick's Day, 17 March. *Geamhradh gu là 'll Phàdraig*.

1312. O. *'S a' bhail' uaibhreach*; Canon MacLean, *'san bàile fhuarach* (*sic*). Miss Annie Johnston has *'sa bhail' uachdrach*, line 1348 here.

1314. *Sùilean ghobhar* 'goats' eyes', presumably amorous or lascivious glances, cf. Irish *cat-shùil*.

1315. *Luadhaim* in Irish can mean 'betroth', *luaidhte* 'engaged to marry' (Dinneen); but it is reasonable to assume from the context that the jealousy of the poetess would be aroused by hearing other girls merely speak of her lover.

1317. Some of the versions have *anail* 'breath' for *feòil*.

1318–21. In O. the equivalent passage comes in the middle of the song, and is as follows:

Mo cheòl, mo cheòl, *mo cheòl fhìn thu,*
Mo cheòl clàrsaich *'n àird 's an ìseal,*
Mo mhil bhìochain, *mo mhil bheachain,*
Mo chrodh-laoigh thu *as na glacaibh,*
Mo dhìtheinean *eadar gartaibh.*

'My music, my music, you're my own music,
My harp music high and low,
My wild honey, my hive honey,
My breeding cattle in the valleys,
My marigolds in the cornfields.'

O. glosses *mil-bhìochain* as 'wild honey', and *mil-bheachain* as 'hive honey'. K. C. C. has *Mo mhil mhìochain*. The term is not in the dictionaries.

1345. The line means literally 'My nose would gush the height of a wave-crest', presumably meaning that she would lose her temper completely, cf. the expressions *leum no nàdar orm*, 'I lost my temper', and *tha sròn air*, 'he is offended'.

LXXV

A Mhic a' Mhaoir, 's daor do shùgradh

('Son of the Steward, costly is your wooing')

First recorded on ediphone from Roderick MacKinnon ('Ruairi Iain Bhàin') at Northbay, Barra, on 26/5/37. Versions recorded in Cape Breton on ediphone from A. J. MacKenzie, retired schoolmaster, Grand Narrows, on 6/10/37, and from Mrs. Neil McInnis, Glace Bay, on 8/10/37, both persons of Barra descent.

Recorded again on Presto from Roderick MacKinnon at Northbay in March 1938, disc no. XIX. His version consisted of lines 1361–3, 1366–7, 1370, the first half of line 1371, and 1372 here. In June 1949 I took down from Miss Elizabeth Sinclair ('Ealasaid Iain Dhunnchaidh') on Vatersay the following additional lines: 1374–5, 1377–8, 1380–3, and 1387–92.

A. J. MacKenzie's version had lines 1361, 1363–9, 1391, and 1390 in that order; and Mrs. Neil McInnis had 1361, 1363–4, 1366–72, 1376–8, 1380–8, and 1390–2.

This song is not widely known, and only an art version had been printed in Finlay Dun's *Orain na'h Albain* (*c.* 1860), p. 74, before its publication in *Gaelic Folksongs from the Isle of Barra* in 1950. Here Ruairi Iain Bhàin's 1937 recording was reproduced on one side of one of the discs, and a text, containing his lines, and lines from Ealasaid Iain Dhunnchaidh and Mrs. Neil McInnis was printed, with translation, in the accompanying booklet, p. 30. The air sung by Ruairi Iain Bhàin was set to words from *C.G.* in *More Songs of the Hebrides* (1929), by Mrs. Kennedy-Fraser, p. 26: 'Like Seagull on Heaving Waters', though Ruairi Iain Bhàin told me she had found it too difficult to write down from him. The phonograph may have been used.

Later a version taken down by Canon MacLean, possibly from Bean Shomhairle Bhig on Barra, became available (ii. 33). This cleared up some earlier difficulties. As this song has strong unity and individuality, I have prepared a collated version of the text based on the version taken down by Canon MacLean, but adding lines from the other singers. Otherwise only minor variations between the different versions occur.

The Canon MacLean version contains the following lines: 1361, 1363, 1366–7, 1373–5, 1377–83, and 1387–90.

1361. This is the usual first line; but Canon MacLean has *Iù na hao ri / Mhic a mhaoir / Iù na hao ri / Mhic 's a ghaoil / Ghaoil 's a rùin / Oh hoirinn ó / Ro ho ro éile / Daor do shùgradh*, etc.

1362. This line is only in Ruairi Iain Bhàin's version.

1363. Canon MacLean has *Leòn* 'wounded' written as an alternative to *Mharbh* 'killed'.

Ruairi Iain Bhàin has *dhùbhghorm* for *dhùbhdhonn.*

1364. This line from A. J. MacKenzie and Mrs. Neil McInnis.

1365. This line from A. J. MacKenzie only.

1366. Mrs. Neil McInnis *'Se t'fhùdar gorm las mo shùilean.* A. J. MacKenzie likewise, with *grad* for *gorm.*

1367. The Cape Breton reciters have *'nam ghlùinean*, 'in my knees', and 'my' for her in similar contexts.

1368–9. These lines from the Cape Breton reciters only.

1371. The second half of this line from Mrs. Neil McInnis.

1374–5. The names mentioned are the names of cows, whose value (great in the Highlands in olden times) would not suffice to pay the fine the Son of the Steward would have to meet for accidentally killing his sweetheart.

This passage was misunderstood when similar lines were taken down from Ealasaid Iain Dhunnchaidh.

1378. Ealasaid Iain Dhunnchaidh had *Na taobh cala nan long siùbhlach*, 'Visit not the harbour of the swift galleys.'

1384–6. These lines from Mrs. Neil McInnis only.

1388. The order of the half-lines is reversed in Canon MacLean but the rhyme shows this is the right order as printed here.

1392. This line is from Mrs. Neil McInnis's version alone, but seems the most suitable concluding line. Ealasaid Iain Dhunnchaidh here had:

Gur math thig sin *air an lasgair*
Deise 'n aodaich *'s daoir a Sasunn,*
Boineid dhubhghorm *air chùl bachlach.*

'Well becomes the youth a suit of the most expensive clothing from England, [and] a dark blue bonnet on his curling hair.'

This, however, is a formulaic passage (cf. vol. i, l. 1321), and is a weak ending to the poem.

As Finlay Dun's *Orain na'h Albain* is now a rare book, it is worth giving his version of this song, which is done in normalized spelling. Dun says that the song, which he calls 'Brave M'Intyre', is 'Supposed to have been sung by a young lady who was accidentally, but mortally, wounded by her lover' (Appendix, p. 3). His text is as follows:

Hi ri libhin ò
Dheagh Mhic an t-Saoir . . . .
Mharbh thu 'n cailin, *'s b'fheàrr a pùsadh;*
Mhuinntir mo ghaoil *na cuiribh cùis air,*
Cha do lùb e *meur no glùn ris,*
'S cha mhoth' chaog e *riamh a shùil ris;*
Leum an aodainn, *'s las am fùdar.*
Buin bàta, *fàg an dùthaich,*
Seachainn Muile, *'s na taobh Diùraidh.*

'Good MacIntyre . . . you have killed the girl, it would have been better to marry her; my beloved folk, do not accuse him; he did not bend finger nor knee to it, neither did he ever take aim with it; the barrel jumped, the powder lit. Get a boat, leave the district, avoid Mull, don't go near Jura.'

Aodainn, cf. Irish *éadan*, 'the end of a barrel, esp. the end opening out', here clearly the barrel of a pistol or gun.

The song must be connected with Argyllshire. It has the appearance of a ballad, but can hardly be referred to the ballad of the 'White Hart', cf. the *Journal of the Folksong Society*, vii. 17, or the Lowland ballad of *Leesome Brand* (Child 15), as there is no question of the heroine's having been shot in the form of an animal here.

After these notes were written, a recording of *A Mhic a' Mhaoir* made by John MacLean, M.A. (Castlebay), from Mrs. Murdo MacDonald ('Bean Mhurchaidh a' Bhealaich') around 1952, came to light. This contains, with slight variations, lines 1361, 1362, 1364, 1363, 1366, 1367, 1370–3, 1377–9, 1381, 1380, 1382, 1387–9 of the version printed here, in that order.

LXXVI

Mo rùn Ailein

('My love Allan')

Recorded from Miss Mary Morrison ('Màiri Eóghainn Mhóir'), Earsary, Barra, at Castlebay on wire on 29/12/49 with chorus (no. 111).

Other versions: Fr. Allan MS., fol. 75 (27 half-lines); Barra MS. (18 half-lines).

Printed: text alone, K. C. C. 39 (32 half-lines); text, translation, and tune, *F.F.S.U.* 240 (27 half-lines); text, translation, tune, and recording made by Miss Mary Morrison (apparently in 1965), *W.S.B.* 4 (41 half-lines). This song is one of the few with a change in the refrain syllables, compare No. LXIV.

1393. A conventional opening, cf. lines 1020–9 of vol. i.

1397. Fr. Allan McDonald has *Chunna mi long chaol 'ga fannadh*, 'I saw a slender galley being gently rowed'. In K. C. C. it is *Chunnaig mi long 'sa chuan Chanach*, 'I saw a galley in the sea off Canna'.

1398. The next line in Fr. Allan McDonald's version is *'S mi gun earbadh riut an leistir'*, 'I would entrust the vessel to you'.

1412. Compare the proverb *Aontachadh brionnaig le breunaig*, quoted by Dwelly under *breunag*. This might be translated 'the flatterer's confirmation of the liar' (female in this case).

1413. Possibly *Sgoilear donn na Beurla* is Alasdair Sgoilear, a personality well known in the tradition of Wester Ross, see *T.G.S.I.* vii. 56 and xlii. 97–9.

LXXVII

Latha dhomh 's mi 'n Caolas Rònaidh

('One day when I was in the Sound of Rona')

Recorded from Mrs. Neil Campbell ('Bean Nìll') on tape at Frobost, South Uist, on 1/2/64.

Other versions: D. C. 67–70 (88 half-lines); K. C. C. 61 (30 half-lines); MacD. 378 (76 half-lines).

Text and tune, contributed by Miss Frances Tolmie to *Gesto Coll.* (1895), Appendix, p. 53. These had been taken down from Margaret Gillies, Ebost, Bracadale, Skye, in 1863. The tune, and a translation of the text, were published by Miss Tolmie in her collection in the English Folksong Society's Journal in 1911, no. 74, p. 234.

The versions recorded in South Uist are only small parts of a much longer song. That published in the MacDonald Collection in 1911 appears to be a copy of the version printed in *Gesto Coll.* in 1895 with a few minor alterations, and the notes on the song in the section on Contents appear to derive from Miss Tolmie's remarks about it in the Folksong Society's Journal. The song is not in K., on which most of MacD. is based, and nothing is said about its origin in that work.

The version taken down by D. C. MacPherson was probably also taken down in the 1860s, but nothing is said in his notebook about the source or the place. Later he combined it with passages from two other songs and printed the conflation in his *Duanaire* in 1868, pp. 140–5, under the title *Pòsadh Mhic Leòid. Conaltradh eadar Màiri Nion Alastair Ruaidh agus Nic-Dhòmhnuill á Tròtairnis*, i.e. 'MacLeod's Wedding. A conversation between Mary, daughter of Alastair Ruadh, and a MacDonald lady from Troternish.'

Unfortunately, the conflated nature of this poem not being known at the time, it was accepted in 1934 by the late Professor J. C. Watson as having been partly composed by the famous bardess Mary MacLeod, and was included by him in his edition of her poems, *Gaelic Songs of Mary MacLeod*, reprinted by the Scottish Gaelic Texts Society in 1965.

The conflated and artificial nature of the *Duanaire* version of *Pòsadh Mhic Leòid* was revealed when D. C. MacPherson's notebook came to light, see J. L. Campbell, 'Notes on the Poems ascribed to Mary MacLeod in D. C. MacPherson's Duanaire', *S.G.S.* xi. 171–91, where the actual version of the present song collected by MacPherson is printed (1968, pp. 174–6).

Nothing was said by Miss Tolmie, who was in much closer connection with the oral tradition of Skye than D. C. MacPherson, about Mary MacLeod's having composed any part of this song; nor does MacPherson say who had told him she did. The song is obviously a flyting between a MacDonald and a MacLeod woman in Skye, where the clans were at bitter odds for nearly the whole of the sixteenth century; but it also contains passages which are associated with other waulking songs, contradictions occur in the two main versions, and it is uncertain to which bardess some of the passages should be assigned. I have done this here tentatively on the basis of the sense of the poem itself. The *Gesto Coll.* version is reproduced here, with one or two readings from the D. C. M. version.

Miss Tolmie said of the song (F. T., 235):

> 'The Song of Strife, sung when reaping or waulking, is commemorative of the feud between Donald Gorm MacDonald, of Sleat, and Rory Mor MacLeod of Harris and Dunvegan, in 1601. Two women hailed one another from each side of the Snizort river which formed a boundary between the territories of MacLeod and MacDonald, and gave expression to their sentiments in the above manner. On a day in harvest, more than a hundred years ago, when every sort of outdoor work was accompanied by songs of suitable rhythm, a party of reapers assembled at Ebost, in Bracadale, divided themselves into two rival bands representing the poetesses who had originally sung the words of strife, and,

while working with all their might to be first at the other end of the field which they were reaping, sang this song with so much fervour that they unconsciously cut themselves with their sickles and had very sore hands at the close of day.'

1417–31. The fragment of the song remembered by Mrs. Neil Campbell expresses MacDonald sentiment only. The same is true of the piece taken down by K. C. Craig from Màiri nighean Alasdair in South Uist.

1424. This is a stock line, cf. no. 1017.

1431. *treas tarraing*, cf. Martin Martin, 'trestarig, *id est* aqua-vitae, three times distilled, which is strong and hot' (*Description of the Western Islands of Scotland*, 1934 edn., p. 85).

1432. I have preferred the *Nic an Tòisich* reading of the D. C. M. version to the *nighean an Leòdaich* 'Macleod's daughter' of Miss Tolmie's, for it seems to me that the dialogue of the song only makes sense if the opening section is ascribed to the MacLeod poetess and the next one to the MacDonald lady, especially if the battle of Glen Haultin was a MacLeod defeat, as Miss Tolmie says it was. As Professor J. C. Watson pointed out, *Mairghread nic an Tòisich* can be reasonably identified as Marjory, daughter of the chief of Macintosh, who married Dòmhnall Gorm Mór (MacDonald) of Sleat around the year 1614. MacLeod of Dunvegan would hardly have travelled to his own daughter's wedding at her own home (line 1436). This and line 1437 are from D. C. M. version.

1438. D. C. MacPherson has *air Chaolas Rònach*, which could mean 'on a seal-haunted sound'; but it is difficult to see how either interpretation could fit in with the tradition that the song was made by two bardesses facing each other across the Snizort river. Nor could either be facing St. Kilda unless the sound were in the Outer Hebrides; but the song is associated with Skye. In MacD. *Uidhist* has been substituted for *Hiort*.

1443. In D. C. MacPherson's version it is *De b'fhasan do Shiol Leoid ud* here, reversing the sense.

1448. The horse was the totem of the MacLeods of Harris and Lewis.

1452. *pruis-òidhidh* (MacPherson *pruis ho ag*) is a call to a horse.

1453. The line in the MacPherson version, *Taoid nam busan 's goid nan srònan*, is better.

1454–5. In Miss Tolmie's version these lines are ascribed to the MacLeod bardess, but this makes no sense if, as she says, Glen Haultin was a MacLeod defeat.

1456. Miss Tolmie translated this line 'Ye stood in the heather like hens', but *cearcan* here is much more likely to mean 'grouse' (*cearc-fhraoich*), and the line would refer to their 'freezing' in the heather to avoid being seen by their enemies. Following this line, D. C. MacPherson has *Eagal deagh Mhac Leoid 'gar faicinn*, 'for fear that good MacLeod would see you'—observe their cowardice, if a MacLeod defeat by the MacDonalds is being described.

1458. Following this line, Miss Tolmie gives in translation a passage ascribed to the Macdonald bardess, of which the original Gaelic is not given in the *Gesto Coll.*, and says it was sung to a different refrain. 'This is intolerable and tedious! Unpleasant is the talk that may not be told in the presence of MacLeod when at dinner!' D. C. MacPherson has a corresponding passage:

Tha seo fuar, *dh'fhàg e sgìth mi,*
'S olc an naidheachd *nach gabh innse,*
Nuair bhios Mac Leòid *ris a dhìnneir*!

1459–64. This is a stock passage, cf. lines 1130–7.

1460. The second half of this line was omitted in *Gesto Coll.* version. In the MacD. Coll. the words *lom-lan eilein* have been inserted here, which make no sense.

1463. *Chuir i bòrd.* The meaning of this expression is uncertain, perhaps 'she beat on the tack', cf. Professor J. C. Watson's note.

1470. Presumably this is Ruairi Mór Mac Leòid of Harris and Dunvegan, who died at Fortrose in 1626. Like other Hebridean chiefs of the time, he had been involved in expeditions to the wars in Ireland.

LXXVIII

Gu dé ni mi nochd ri 'm nàire?

('What shall I do tonight to my darling')

Recorded from Mrs. MacDougall ('Anna Raghnaill Eachainn') Castlebay, Barra, on disc XXVI in March 1938. Words transcribed from recording.

Art version: Mrs. Kennedy-Fraser, *More Songs from the Hebrides*, p. 14, 'An Island Cattle Call. Fire, Faire. From Joseph Campbell, Barra'. This was probably the Revd. Joseph Campbell, later parish priest of Benbecula.

1473. *Nàire*, 'shame' is used as a term of endearment in these old songs. Compare *F.F.S.U.* 259, *Ailein duinn a chiall 's a nàire*. Perhaps connected with *nàr* adjective used in the sense of 'noble' in Irish?

1477–80. Though the rhyme is the same, these lines are on a different subject from the rest of the song. Wednesday was considered a lucky day in Gaelic folklore, and the first day of any quarter of the year was important. A quotation in *C.G.* ii. 272 may be compared:

Thuirt a Mhuime ri mo Shlàn'ear,
Nach e 'n Aona bha 'g an àireamh,
Ach an Luan an tùs an (sic) *ràithe.*

'His Foster-mother said to my Redeemer,
That it was not the Friday they were counted,
But the Monday at the beginning of the quarter.'

John MacKenzie, in a footnote to the Blind Harper's song that begins *A' chiad Di-luain de'n ràithe*, says that it was an old Highland custom 'to meet at an appointed house, on the first Monday of every quarter, to drink a bumper to the beverage of the succeeding, and wish it better or no worse than the present' (*Sàr Obair*, p. 87). See also the Revd. William Matheson's note on this line, on p. 116 of his edition of the poems of the Blind Harper.

LXXIX

'N robh thu 'sa bheinn?

('Were you on the hill')

Recorded from Mrs. MacDougall ('Anna Raghnaill Eachainn') on disc XXVI in March 1938, and from Miss Mary Morrison, Earsary, at Castlebay on 2/3/50, the latter by the Barra Folklore Committee, wire no. 273.

Other versions: MS.: A. J. (2) 103, identical with that of Mrs. MacDougall, which is printed here. Miss Mary Morrison's version was published in *W.S.B.* 3, text, translation, tune, and recording on long-playing disc.

1481. *féidh*, 'deer', poetically used for 'milk cows'.

LXXX

Gura h-e mo ghaol an t-Iain

('My beloved is the Ian')

Recorded from Mrs. Mary MacNeil ('Màiri Ruarachain') at Castlebay on 3/1/50, wire no. 163.

Said to be old, and believed to be unpublished.

1485. The rhyme shows that *Iain* must originally have been *Seathan*, cf. line 488.

LXXXI

'S mise bhean bhochd, chianail, dhuilich

('I am a poor woman, sad and sorrowful')

Recorded from Miss Annie Johnston in March 1938, disc XXXIV. Text transcribed from recording.

Other versions: Barra MS. 7, printed here.

Art versions: Mrs. Kennedy-Fraser, *Songs of the Hebrides*, vol. i, p. xxvii, tune only, from a Mingulay singer; ii. 63, the tune is used as one of the airs in the composite song called 'The Sea Tangle or the Sisters', in iii. 99 the tune was used again in the composite song 'A Barra Love Lilt', the Gaelic words being a version of no. XXIX of *Hebridean Folksongs*.

1500, 1504. 'Murdo' may have been a younger son of one of the MacNeils of Barra. There was such a Murdo in 1587.

1501–3 and 1512–18. Cf. lines 243–6.

LXXXII

'S muladach truagh, 's cianail thà mi

('Sorrowful, sad, miserable am I')

Recorded from Miss Annie Johnston in March 1938, disc XXXVI.

Art version: Mrs. Kennedy-Fraser, *Songs of the Hebrides*, ii. 115, 'A Waulking Song of the Glen. Gone the Boat and Gone my Lover. Dh'fhalbh am bàta, dh'fhalbh thu leannain. Air and words collected by Mrs. Kennedy-Fraser and Annie Johnson (*sic*) at the Glen, Barra.'

In fact the words, and presumably the translation, were provided by Miss Johnston. The air is also printed in the Foreword to the same book, with the refrain syllables but no words, p. xxiv, 'Waulking Song (with variants on verse) from Annie Johnston, Barra'.

Miss Johnston is the only person whom I have ever heard sing this song, and I know of no other version of it.

1529–31, cf. lines 1028–30.

1531. The singer appeared to have *leann*, but the word must be *lìon*.

LXXXIII

Chuir iad mise an ceann na cléitheadh

('They set me at the waulking board's head')

Recorded from Mrs. Neil Campbell ('Bean Nìll') on tape on 30/1/64.

Other versions: D. C. M. 73 (opening lines only, different refrain). Printed: the three opening lines here occur in the version of the song *Mo rùn Ailein* in K. C. C. 39. See *S.G.S.* xi. 177. The second section of the song here has a corresponding passage in the preceding song in K. C. C., also p. 39.

LXXXIV

'S tìm dhomh bhith falbh, bhith cur umam

('I must be going, getting ready')

Recorded from Miss Mary Morrison, Earsary, at Castlebay by the Barra Folklore Committee on 2/3/50, wire no. 272. The only other version known to me is the Uist version in O. 21, which is printed here.

1552–61, 1578–81, compare lines 1158–63 of vol. i.

1567–8. Cf. lines 119–20 and 559–60 of vol. i. *Léin' a' churaidh*, 'the hero's shirt', is what one would expect here.

1582–4, cf. lines 466–70 of vol. i.

1585–9. A very common sentiment in old waulking songs, cf. lines 236–41, 1048–51, and 1131–4 of vol. i.

LXXXV

Dhìrich mi suas an Coire Riabhach

('I climbed up the Brindled Corrie')

Recorded from Mrs. Buchanan ('Ceit Ruairi Iain Bhàin') at Castlebay, Barra, on 5/4/51, wire no. 723.

Other versions (all in MS.), C. J. 51 (Barra); Canon MacLean, i. 18 (printed here); D. McI. 25; O. 52 (South Uist); Mrs. Neil McInnis, Cape Breton, recorded on ediphone on 15/10/37.

1596–1603, 1621–2. A stock passage cf. lines 465–75 of vol. i, and 1582–4 of vol. ii.

1623–9. Cf. lines 713–22 of vol. i.

LXXXVI

Turadh am muigh, 's an là glasadh

('It is dry outside, the day is dawning')

Recorded from Miss Mary Morrison, Earsary, at Castlebay, Barra, on 3/1/50.

So far as I know, this song is unpublished. It is sung to the same air and refrain as the preceding, an unusual thing in the case of waulking songs.

1630. *Glasadh* is the last of four stages of dawning, cf. C.G. vi. 45, under *Coill.*

LXXXVII

Fhir a' chinn duibh 's a' chùil dualaich

('O black-haired one of curling locks')

Recorded from Calum Johnston in November 1949, disc LXXIX. The text is from Miss Annie Johnston (A. J. (2), p. 20).

Other versions: Fr. Allan MS., fol. 77 (printed here).

Compare with this song lines 893–902 of vol. i.

1645–6. What this implies is that she has given up her maidenhood for her lover.

LXXXVIII

'S toil liom, 's toil liom

('I like, I like')

Recorded for me from Mrs. Neil Campbell ('Bean Nìll') by the Revd. John MacLean at Frobost, South Uist, on tape in the winter of 1958/9. Also recorded from Mrs. Neil McInnis in Cape Breton on ediphone on 13/10/37 (text printed here).

Other versions: D. McI. 82 (printed here); K. C. C. 90.

1695–9, 1714–18. Cf. lines 1413–16, and the note thereon.

1704. Probably *faoileann* means 'beach' here, but the word meaning 'sea-gull' can also mean 'a fair maiden' 'a graceful woman' in Irish (Dinneen).

1711–12. Cf. lines 583–4 of vol. i, and lines 1150–1 of this book, and K. C. C. 33. In this context here, the musical instruments would be played for, not by, the 'brown-haired girl'.

MUSICOLOGICAL NOTES

IN Volume I of *Hebridean Folksongs*, the notation of the tunes suffered to some extent in its completeness from the fact that the collection of the texts and of the tunes of the songs were two different operations undertaken by two different people, and which were separated from each other by an interval of over forty years. The texts were collected *without their tunes* by Donald MacCormick, a substantial crofter and school attendance officer in South Uist,[1] in 1893; while the collection of the tunes did not begin until 1937, and was mostly done between 1949 and 1951. These were recorded (naturally from a later generation of singers) by my collaborator J. L. Campbell in South Uist, Eriskay, Benbecula, and Barra, and from remembered Mingulay and Eriskay tradition in the last named island.

The texts of the songs as recorded deviated from the written texts of MacCormick in many minor aspects—in the order of lines, often in the actual wording of the lines themselves, and in the omission of lines or half-lines from one or other of the two collections. The recordings, though true and authoritative renderings in their own right, could therefore give no more than an approximate performance of the songs as textually noted by MacCormick. For practical reasons it was not possible to include or note any such variations of the texts of the recordings from that of the MacCormick text. The words set under the music in the second volume, on the other hand, are those of the recordings.

It needs no more than a cursory glance at the musical transcriptions in Volume I to see that the words below the music frequently differ from those in MacCormick's text, both in line sequence and in actual wording. The reason for this is that the recordings were made from a number of different persons often living on different islands, some of whom were passive rather than active tradition bearers,[2] who did not always have a full version of the words of a particular song in conscious memory. In the case of waulking songs, there is very little indeed of the kind of verbal corruption that one sometimes finds in orally transmitted folksongs, for example in English; but when waulking songs are no longer regularly sung, lines tend to be forgotten and passages from different songs are sometimes confused—the formulaic nature of some of these passages assists this tendency. All in all, however, we have found that in the case

[1] See F. G. Rea, *A School in South Uist*, pp. 27–8.

[2] See C. W. von Sydow, *Selected Papers on Folklore*, pp. 13–15. The same person, of course, could be an active tradition bearer in respect of certain songs, and a passive tradition bearer with regard to others.

of good traditional singers such as Miss Annie Johnston and her brother Calum, in Barra, and Mrs. Neil Campbell in South Uist, surprisingly little has been lost between their versions and those taken down by Fr. Allan McDonald, Donald MacLachlan, and Donald MacCormick fifty years earlier.

In the variations from the basic version of the tunes, also set down for their musical interest, it was often not possible to relate the variations to MacCormick's text. In Volume II, on the other hand, the complete text of each song has been transcribed from the recording; consequently it has been possible to set down variants of the tune with in every case the exact words to which these were sung. One can therefore examine minutely such variants not only in their musical aspect, but in their interrelation to the metric and other deviations of the text. It becomes possible to classify the variants to the basic form of the tune according to type. These may be summarized under the following heads:

METRIC VARIANTS

These occur when the metre of a line of text deviates from the norm of the song in having a greater or lesser number of syllables to the line or half-line. Such deviation requires modification of the tune, if only sometimes slight, to accommodate it. Examples may be seen in XLIII, XLIV (Calum Johnston), XLV, XLVI, and many others.

RHYTHMIC VARIANTS

These may occur when for any reason the normal rhythm of the melody is altered. This may be for instance to accommodate changes of word stress or of vowel duration. One frequent reason for the last is in the reversal of short–long relationship of syllables to long–short or vice versa, cf. XLIV (Miss Janet MacKinnon), LVI, LXXVII, LXXXVI. Such deviations from the normal line almost invariably require an alteration in the rhythm of the musical phrase. See also XLVII, L, LII, LIII, LV, and others. Rhythmic variants are often slight and sometimes seemingly capricious.

MELODIC VARIANTS

This is the commonest form of variation. It seldom arises from any necessity of the text, but generally speaking, simply from the artistic and creative instincts of the singer: to avoid repetitive monotony, and to introduce a note of variety when the singer feels the need of it. Melodic variants most often occur in the verse of the song, this being in the control of the soloist. They are also, however, to be found in the refrain, though this occurs mostly when the refrain is being sung by a solo singer, that is, for the purposes of a recording, than when sung by a group, however informal may be the performance. Melodic variation of the refrain is very seldom heard in an actual waulking, for of course it has to compete with the consensus of the rest of the chorus in the refrain melody already established. Nevertheless, it is not unknown even in those circumstances. Examples of melodic decoration in the songs here are too numerous to quote. They are, however, all marked as such.

DECORATIVE OR ORNAMENTAL VARIANT

This is a term applied in this volume, though not perhaps of general use, to describe a form of variation in which, though conforming to the main established melodic outline, the notes are submitted to decorative treatment, whether by single or double grace-notes, roulades, or other ornamentation. Examples may be seen in Nos. XLIV (Calum Johnston), LX, LXII, LXXI (there styled 'ornamental variant'), LXXIX (Miss Mary Morrison), LXXX (styled 'grace-note variant'), LXXXV.

THE SVARABHAKTI VOWEL

The variation of rhythm or melody arising from the presence of a svarabhakti vowel is of constant occurrence in most of the songs.[1] See the authorities mentioned below. This vowel gives rise, practically, though not metrically, to an extra syllable which has to be accommodated in the melody by one means or another. Paradoxically, it is not counted in the number of syllables to the line for the purposes of metrical scansion.

There are a number of ways in which the svarabhakti vowel may be fitted into the melody; these will be found to recur in different songs, and may be reduced to characteristic formulas. Such are worth studying in some detail, for the general problem of accommodating an extra syllable (or more) to a basic melody is one which constantly occurs throughout the whole art of folksong in almost any national culture.

By far the most common way of dealing with the svarabhakti vowel is to set it to a repetition of the previous note, robbing that note of a little of its time value in order to fit it in. Examples of the process may be found all through the tunes in this book. It will be sufficient to give three examples showing first the basic form of the melody and secondly the alteration to it to accommodate the svarabhakti vowel:

[1] The svarabhakti vowel is enclosed within brackets.

[1] See J. Fraser, 'Accent and Svarabhakti in a Dialect of Scottish Gaelic', *Revue Celtique*, xxxv. 401; Carl Hj. Borgstrøm, 'The Svarabhakti Vowel' in 'Scottish Gaelic as a Source of Information about the Early History of Irish', *S.G.S.* v. 36; Magne Oftedal, 'The Gaelic of Leurbost', *Norsk Tidsskrift for Sprogvidenskap*, Suppl. Bind iv, p. 27.

The svarabhakti vowel, which arises between certain consonants following a short vowel under certain conditions, forms a group with the preceding vowel and consonant which falls under one stress and which Gaelic speakers feel to be the equivalent of a long vowel, with which in fact a svarabhakti group can rhyme in Scottish Gaelic verse.

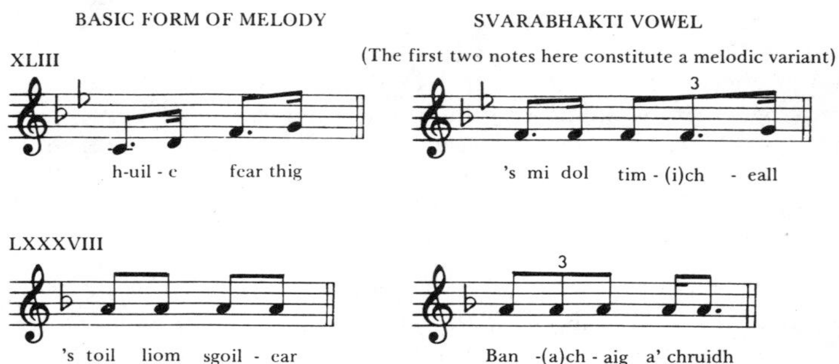

Much less frequently the svarabhakti vowel, robbing the previous syllable of its full time value in the same way, falls one note below the previous syllable:

XLIX. In bar 6, a grace-note in the basic melody becomes a substantive note in order to accommodate the svarabhakti vowel in a triplet rhythm:

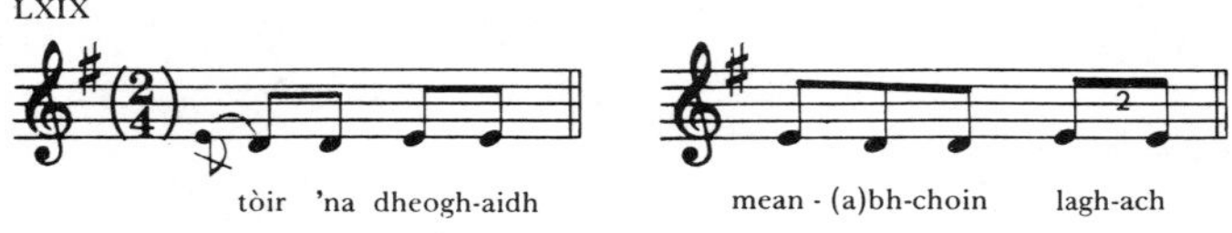

LXI. For a slightly different process, see 7th bar of the tune, and 2nd and 3rd variants.

2nd variant: an extra note is inserted for the syllable previous to the svarabhakti vowel. This extra note forms an ornamentation of the melody. The svarabhakti vowel occupies the basic melody note:

The 3rd variant above shows svarabhakti vowels in two successive bars. The svarabhakti vowel in the word *Mur-(u)ch-adh* is placed on a repetition of the previous syllable as in previous examples; it is also placed so in the next bar of the variation on the word *gor-(o)m*.

In the following example, as in the 2nd variant to LXI above, the previous syllable to the svarabhakti vowel is an ornamental added note to the melody and the svarabhakti vowel itself occupies the basic melody note:

In the next example the svarabhakti vowel is sung to the basic melody note and an extra note inserted for the syllable following:

In the example below, as in LXXVIII, the svarabhakti vowel falls on the note *below* the previous syllable—a rarer case, as has been observed. The previous syllable forms a kind of appogiatura or acciacatura to the svarabhakti vowel-note:

Very occasionally the svarabhakti vowel can be accommodated without any material alteration of the melody or rhythm:

LXXV shows another example of the same. Here there is melodic variation of the melody note before the svarabhakti vowel, but this is immaterial to the point demonstrated, and the rhythm is substantially similar:

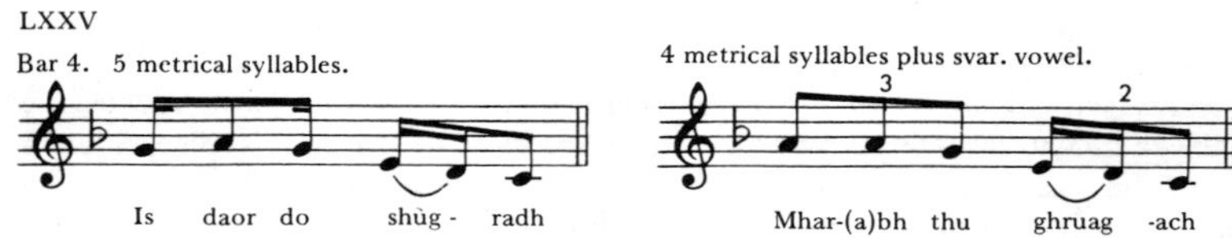

THE UNELIDED VOWEL

A vowel which is normally elided may sometimes be pronounced by a singer for emphasis. This results in an extra syllable, which, like the svarabhakti vowel, is not counted metrically in the number of syllables to the line, but which nevertheless has similarly to be accommodated in the melody. No. XLIX provides an example:

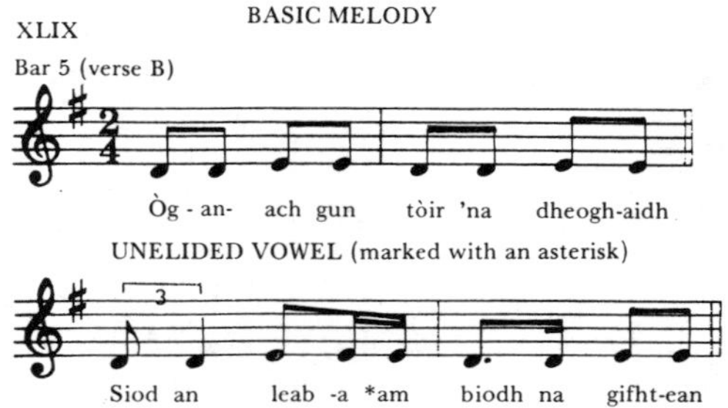

THE SCALES

The scales on which the songs are constructed are assessed and classified by taking the last note of the tune as the lowest or fundamental note of the scale, and reckoning the rest of the scale upwards accordingly. It is the system used in its essence by Bartók and by many other musicologists both preceding and following him. In the transcriptions of these volumes, the last note is indicated in each case by the word *fine* (which may sometimes be found in unexpected places). The point of ending of a waulking song is invariably the end of the refrain, or one of the refrains where there is more than one; this is discussed fully in Volume I (pp. 205 ff. and p. 217).

The songs in both volumes will be found to be constructed upon gapless scales of seven notes (modal), and upon gapped scales of six, five, and four notes. In Volume II there are also four songs constructed on pentachordal scales. The following is a summary of the songs based on the various scales in Volume II, showing the total number of songs based on each scale. It should be added, however, that where more than one singer sings the same song in the same scale, this is reckoned for the purpose of arriving at the total of *different* songs in each scale, as one example of the scale concerned. Where the scale differs in performances of the same song by different singers, each song is reckoned as an independent example of the scale concerned.

THE HEPTATONIC (SEVEN-NOTE) SCALES

These correspond, in their sequence of tones and semitones, to the scales of the so-called church modes; and for convenience are arranged under the titles of the church-modes concerned.[1]

Ionian: XLIX, LXXIII. Total 2.

Dorian: XLVII, LII (Calum Johnston), LXIII, LXXIV (Mrs. A. Munro). Total 4.

Phrygian: none.

Lydian: none.

Mixolydian: XLI (ballad version). Total 1.

Aeolian: XLII, LI (Annie and Calum Johnston), LV, LXXV. Total 4.

Locrian: none.

Indeterminate: XLVII (Mrs. Mary Morrison) (Dorian or Aeolian, according to interpretation of the singer's recorded performance). Total 1.

Total number of heptatonic scales: 12.

HEXATONIC SCALES (SIX-NOTE, GAPPED)

The six notes in many of these scales will be found to be common to two of the heptatonic modal scales, one lying a fourth below the other. Thus the notes of the six-note scale CDEFGA will be found to be common to the scale of the Ionian mode commencing on C and the Mixolydian scale normally reckoned as commencing on G, but transposed for comparison a 4th upwards so as also to commence on C. Another way of expressing this is to say that if the gap in a six-note scale is filled by the step of a semitone or of a tone, the two resulting scales will be found to

[1] For a purist objection (with which this writer does not agree) to the use of the church-mode titles in folksong, cf. Norman Cazden, *A simplified mode classification for traditional Anglo-American song tunes*, Year Book of the International Folk Music Council, vol. 3, 1971, p. 45.

coincide with those of two church modes normally pitched a fourth apart. This is discussed in detail in volume one, pp. 210–11. The following are the hexatonic scales as described above, in Volume II:

Ionian/Mixolydian with 7th note gapped: LIV. Total 1.

Dorian/Aeolian with 6th note gapped: LIX, LXXI, LXXII, LXXIX, LXXXII, LXXXV. Total 6.

Phrygian/Locrian with 5th note gapped: LXIV (Mrs. Neil Campbell), LXXXVIII. Total 2.

Lydian/Ionian with 4th note gapped: LXI. Total 1.

Mixolydian/Dorian with 3rd note gapped: LVI. Total 1.

Aeolian/Phrygian with 2nd note gapped: L, LI, LXIX, LXXXVIII. Total 4.

Locrian/Lydian: none.

Total number of hexatonic scales with their notes common to two church-modes: 15.

A number of the hexatonic scales in this volume will be found not to be common to two modes; if the gap in the scale is filled in by the step of a semitone or a tone, one of the resulting scales will be found to be outwith any of the church modes. The following tunes are in this category:

Like Ionian but with gap: none.

Like Dorian but with 5th note gapped: XLI (waulking song version).

Like Dorian but with 3rd note gapped: XLVIII.

Like Dorian but with 2nd note gapped: LXXIV (Janet MacKinnon).

Total like Dorian: 3.

Like Phrygian but with 5th note gapped. Total none.

Like Lydian but with 7th note gapped: XLVI. Total 1.

Like Mixolydian but with 6th note gapped: XLVII (Miss Annie MacDonald), LXXVIII. Total 2.

Like Aeolian but with 3rd note gapped: LXV. Total 1.

Like Locrian but with gap: none.

Total in this category: 7.

Total number of tunes in hexatonic scales: 22.

PENTATONIC SCALES

The basic (1st) position of the pentatonic scale is here reckoned as CDE—GA; and the 2nd, 3rd, 4th, and 5th positions are the successive inversions of the scale. Thus the 2nd position is DE—GA—C, etc. Two of the tunes in this second volume are constructed on five-note gapped scales which do not fall into the accepted pattern; these are classified here as *pentatonic irregular*.

The following are the songs in Volume II which are constructed upon the pentatonic scale:

First position (CDEGA): XLV, LVII, LXIV, LXVI, LXVIII (Calum and Annie Johnston), LXXIV, LXXXIII. Total 7.

2nd position (DE—GA—C): LXX. Total 1.

3rd position (E—GA—CD): LXI, LXVII. Total 2.

4th position (GA—CDE): XLIV (first tune), LVIII, LXII, LXIV, LXVIII (Mrs. Neil Campbell). Total 5.

5th position (ACDE—G): LXXII (Calum Johnston), LXXIV (Mrs. Kate MacCormick). Total 2.

Total of regular pentatonic tunes: 17.

Pentatonic irregular: LXVII (Annie and Calum Johnston) (2nd tune), LXXXI. Total 2.

Total of all tunes in pentatonic gapped scales: 19.

PENTACHORDAL SCALES

A pentachordal scale may be defined as a scale upon five successively named notes, as CDEFG, DEFGA, EFGAB, etc. There are four songs in this volume constructed upon such scales. One of these, No. LXXVI, commences as a tune in a four-note scale, but becomes pentachordal as it proceeds, by reason of an additional note to the scale in a regularly recurring variant; the scale is then in the basic pentachordal position F, G, A, B flat, C. The others are in inverted position. One, No. LXXIX (Miss Mary Morrison), is on the first inverted position, ABCD—G (basic position GABCD). The other two, LXXVII and LXXXIV are both in the third inversion, ABC—FG (basic position FGABC). It seems rather an astonishing coincidence that two different tunes in the volume should be based on this same quite unusual scale.

These four tunes pose the question, was there ever a series of pentachordal scales in Hebridean music constructed in all five possible inversions of the scale? Such a series envisages something not previously encountered in Scottish music to the writer's knowledge.

To summarize in the same style as above, the tunes in pentachordal scales may be set out as under:

Pentachordal, 1st (basic) position: LXXVI. Total 1.

Ditto, 2nd position (i.e. 1st inversion): LXXIX (Miss Mary Morrison). Total 1.

Ditto, 4th position (i.e. 3rd inversion): LXXVII, LXXXIV. Total 2.

Total number of pentachordal tunes: 4.

SCALES OF FOUR NOTES

Four-note scales may sometimes, though not always, be explained as pentatonic scales of which one of the notes is omitted in performance, perhaps through the song being ill remembered by the singer. This may sometimes be confirmed, or at least made to appear more probable, in a performance of the same song by a different singer, in which the five notes of the pentatonic scale do appear. There are three tunes constructed on four-note scales in this volume, namely Nos. LIII, LXXVI (becoming pentachordal in the course of the song), and LXXX. The first and last of the three could possibly be explained as incomplete pentatonic scales as above, and in fact, in No. LXXX, the fifth note of the pentatonic scale does appear in a variant. To summarize—

Four-note scales, gapped: LIII, LXXX.

Four-note scale becoming pentachordal: LXXVI.

Total number of four-note scales: 3.

MUSICOLOGICAL NOTES

THE SCALES OF THE SONGS IN VOLUME I

It was not found possible in the first volume to list the scales of the songs contained in it, mainly owing to the particular circumstances of production. These are therefore added here, in order that the reader may be enabled to compare the number of the various types of scales found in the songs in both volumes.

It is to be noted that in this list also, a song sung in the same scale by different singers is counted as a single example of the scale concerned. This is even more necessary than in the second volume if a true picture of the relative numbers of the scales is to be presented, as the first volume contains a greater number of versions of the same song (amounting in one case to as many as seven) as recorded from different singers.

Volume I, Heptatonic scales
Ionian: xxxv(a), xl, xxxvi(b). Total 3.
Dorian: i(d), xiii(c), xxv(a) (b). Total 3.
Phrygian: xvi(b). Total 1.
Mixolydian: none.
Aeolian: xvii(a) (c). Total 1.
Locrian: none.
Indeterminate, depending on assessment of place of ending: xvi. Total 1.
Total number of songs in heptatonic scales: 9.

Hexatonic scales with the notes common to two modes
Ionian/Mixolydian with gap at 7: iii(b) (d), xxxi(a) (b), xl(a). Total 3.
Dorian/Aeolian with gap at 6: xxiii(c), xxv(b), xxix(a). Total 3.
Phrygian/Locrian with gap at 5: none.
Lydian/Ionian with gap at 4: ix, xxiv(a) (b), xxvi(a) (b) (c), xxxv(b) (c). Total 4.
Mixolydian/Dorian with gap at 3: xxxii(a) (b). Total 1.
Aeolian/Phrygian with gap at 2: xiii(b), xvii(b). Total 2.
Locrian/Lydian: none.
Total of hexatonic scales common to two modes: 13.

Hexatonic with scale not common to two modes
Like Ionian but with gap at 6: xxxiv. Total 1.
Like Dorian but with gap at 2: xiii(d), xiv(b), xxix. Total 3.
Like Phrygian but with gap: none.
Like Lydian but with gap: none.
Like Mixolydian but with gap at 6: x, xii, xxxviii. Total 3.
Like Aeolian but with gap at 5: viii(e). Total 1.
Like Locrian but with gap: none.
Total number of songs constructed on hexatonic scales: 21.

PENTATONIC SCALES

1st position: ii, iii(c), v, vi(a) (b) (c), vii(a) (b) (c) (d), xviii(a), xix, xxiii(a) (b), xxx(a) (b) (c) (d), xxxvi(a), xxxvii(a) (b), xl(b). Total 12.
2nd position: xxii(a) (b). Total 1.

3rd position: VIII(b) (d), XI, XV(a) (b) (c), XXXIX(a). Total 4.
4th position: IV(a) (b) (c) (d), XX, XXL(b). Total 3.
5th position: XIII(a), XIV(a), XVIII(b) (c), XXI(a). Total 4.
Total number of songs on pentatonic scales: 24.

FOUR-NOTE SCALES

III(a), VIII(a) (c), XXXIII. Total 3.

COMPASS

The compass of the songs ranges from a fifth to an eleventh.

As there may be thought to be a special interest in songs of such small compass as that of a fifth and a sixth, these are listed as follows:

Songs of the compass of a fifth (Volume II): LIII, LXXVI (Miss Mary Morrison), LXXIX (ditto), LXXXIV (ditto).

Songs of the compass of a sixth: XLIX (Calum Johnston), XLV, XLVII, XLVIII, LXII, LXX, LXXXI, LXXXIII, LXXIV.

Songs of the compass of a fifth and sixth in Volume I:

The compass of a fifth: III(a), VIII(a) (c), XVIII, XXIII.

The compass of a sixth: III(b) (e), IV(a), VI(a) (b) (c), X, XII, XV(b), XX, XXVI(a) (b), XXX(a) (b) (c), XXXI(a) (b), XXXIV, XXXVIII(b).

NOTES ON THE TRANSCRIPTIONS

At the head of each transcription the actual pitch of the first note as performed by the singer is set down in a diamond-shaped black note. The metronome mark is also given. The transcription itself is transposed into a pitch convenient for key signature and for the confines of the stave.

The transcription of the long-short and the short-long rhythms of the Gaelic singer presents the same problems as in Volume I. There is often a continuous fluctuation between the dotted rhythm ♫. ♫. and the smoother long-short, short-long of six-eight time, viz. |♩ ♪ ♩ ♪.|♪ ♩ ♪ ♩.| ; and the interpretation of borderline rhythms lying somewhere between the two becomes very much a subjective decision on the part of the transcriber. When much fluctuation occurs within the same song, the time is expressed as $\frac{2}{4}(\frac{6}{8})$ or $\frac{6}{8}(\frac{2}{4})$ according to which appears to be the basic rhythm of the melody.

Only two songs in this volume were recorded at an actual waulking, viz. LI (Miss Penny Morrison's version) and LXXIV (Mrs. D. J. MacLellan), but sixteen others were recorded from a band of experienced traditional singers gathered together by the Barra Folklore Committee for recording, and were sung, often with great spirit, in the genuine waulking style. These are XLV, XLVIII, L (where however the chorus could not reach the soloist's pitch), LIII, LV, LIX, LXI, LXIII, LXX, LXXI, LXXVI, LXXIX (Miss Mary Morrison's version), LXXX, LXXXIV, LXXXV, and LXXXVI. In J. L. Campbell's transcriptions of the texts of these songs, the ways in which the refrains were divided between the soloist and the chorus, and the way in which the songs began and ended, is indicated.

The other songs in this volume are 'fireside recordings', informal performances sung for the specific purpose of recording the song by a single singer of either sex, sometimes with another singer joining in, or taking over the burden of the refrain; when this is done by Miss Annie Johnston, for example, we can depend on a particularly authentic rendering. One of the songs was noted direct from the singer by means of pencil and paper; this is No. LI, from the singing of Annie Johnston. A single vocalist singing a waulking song unaided will sometimes lighten her task by shortening the refrain to a single phrase, presumably the solo phrase, e.g. LVII (Miss Kate MacDonald); this habit has sometimes misled collectors who were ignorant of the true structure of the songs or of the Gaelic language. But some traditional singers, like Annie and Calum Johnston, and Mrs. Neil Campbell, were usually very conscientious about singing the refrains in full even when unaided.

It may be added that some of the songs in the present volume are (now at least) very rare, e.g. XLII, XLV, LII, LVI, LVII, LIX, LX, LXI, LXXV, LXXX, LXXXI, LXXXII, LXXXIII, LXXXVI; some of these, particularly XLII, have been rescued from the verge of oblivion.

In an actual waulking, or a closely simulated one, the rhythm is strongly marked, and driven along by the singers' thumping of the cloth on the table; the beat thus established is described in these volumes as 'the waulking pulse'. This is generally felt to be in duple time with a slightly stronger accent on the first beat than on the second (though this may be partly imaginary and an illusion in the mind of the listener). However it may be, it marks the down and up beats in a two-four or six-eight rhythm that persists inexorably from beginning to end of the song. Some waulking song melodies have an occasional bar of three beats instead of two. This will reverse the accent, real or imagined, in the waulking pulse in each succeeding repetition of the tune. Volume II does not contain any examples of this, but examples are frequent in Volume I, namely I, VII, XV, XXII, XXIII, and XXXIV. Some of these, however, contain an even number of such bars of three beats, which of course restores the accent to its normal position of the first beat in the bar. No LI (Miss Penny Morrison's version) in Volume II shows a waulking pulse which deviates from the normal in its accentuation. For similar deviations in Volume I, cf. p. 222, and example XV(a) thereon.

Frequently the singer does not succeed in striking the basic melody correctly at the start, and has to 'sing herself into it' before it becomes assured and constant and can be accepted as the basic tune. As a matter of interest, this deviation has been set down in many of the transcriptions, either as an introductory refrain, or as a variant. These often throw an interesting light on the methods and mental processes of the traditional Gaelic folk singer.

In selecting the words for setting below the music, it is obviously desirable to choose a line which has the normal, basic number of syllables; which does not contain any svarabhakti vowels; and in which the singer's performance is distinct and unambiguous enough to transcribe it with certainty. Where the poetic line is divided into half-lines separated by a refrain, it is important to choose a cycle of the tune in which the proper sequence of the two half-lines, as well as the correct rhyme-scheme, are both preserved. Through the lack of one or other of these requirements in the opening and following lines, it is often necessary to go some little way through the song to arrive at a suitable line to go under the music. Occasionally one feels compelled by the exigencies of text or performance to set a textual variant under the music, as in XLII, LXXIV (Miss Janet MacKinnon's version), and LXXIV (Mrs. Kate MacCormick).

The singers of the recordings transcribed in the present volume began and ended their songs in a number of ways, some seemingly at haphazard, i.e. some beginning with the verse and some with the refrain, and ending the song with equal capriciousness. It is as well to state therefore that the accepted points of commencement and of the ending of a waulking song have been carefully studied and discussed in detail in Volume I (p. 214 *passim*). It is sufficient to reiterate here simply that the waulking song begins and ends with the chorus refrain; where there are two refrains, it will customarily end with the shorter refrain of the two. There are, however, exceptions to this, of which one may be seen in both versions of No. LXVIII, where the tune ends with the longer refrain.

Many of the above points are treated in greater detail in Volume I, and the study of them there is recommended to the reader.

THE MEANINGLESS REFRAIN SYLLABLES. Further experience of transcribing the songs of Volume II tends to confirm the editors' theories concerning the possible origin and the function of these curious syllables. These theories are both that such syllables possess an underlying rhythmic system, and that they have a mnemonic function in recalling the tune of a song to the singer. This last arises from the apparent fact, as stated in Volume I, that a whole phrase of these refrain syllables never seems to be repeated in the refrain of any other song, so that a line of them comes to be associated with one particular song alone.[1] This is, however, a point which can only be confirmed by further research. The subject, which is an intensely interesting and important one, is discussed fully in Volume I, p. 227 *passim*.

The free use of meaningless syllables in the refrains of Scottish Gaelic waulking songs and other traditional songs may well be extremely archaic. In his book *Primitive Song* (London, 1962), Sir Maurice Bowra suggests that it is characteristic of primitive singing that the use of meaningless syllables for whole songs preceded the use of meaningful words. He remarks of such singing that 'each set of such sounds is constant and tied not only to its own occasion or ceremony but to a fixed tune. There is no question of transferring them from one tune or occasion

[1] It may be noted, however, that in Volume I, versions of No. XXXVIII from Barra and Eriskay, both having the same refrain syllables, are sung to quite different airs, while in Volume II two quite different songs, LXXXV and LXXXVI, are sung to very similar versions of the same air.

to another. They are established by custom and regarded as obligatory' (p. 58).

This is true of the refrains of Scottish Gaelic waulking songs. Sir Maurice Bowra does not suggest that the meaningless syllables were mnemonic devices for calling the tunes to mind; but if the tunes reminded the singers of the syllables, the syllables could hardly fail to remind the singers of the tunes. It is certainly remarkable that while the examples that he gives of this feature of primitive traditional singing are taken from the remotest parts of South America, Australia, and the Arctic, the use of meaningless syllables to express the refrains of waulking songs and their melodies was still in full vigour in the Outer Hebrides.

So much of what J. L. Campbell says of the refrain-forms *aba*, *ab bc*, *abc*, etc. in his remarks on the different metrical types of these waulking songs applies also to the phrase formation of the music of the refrains, that it seems unnecessary to add anything further on the purely musicological side; the phrase structure of each song is analysed in the musical transcriptions. It may be sufficient to add that phrases similar but not identical with each other are marked A^1, A^2; B^1, B^2, etc. Sometimes the similarity in two such phrases may lie in the first part of the phrase and sometimes in the second. The decision to include such phrases under the same symbol, A or B, etc., is often a purely subjective one.

MUSICAL TRANSCRIPTIONS

FRANCIS COLLINSON

XLI (a)

Am Bròn Binn

(as a Ballad)

(*a*) Sung by Mrs. Kate MacCormick (Catriana nighean 'Ill' Easbuig), Benbecula

♩ = about 63, but with tenutos and pauses at end of lines
(b)
ten.
Labh- air Fionn Fal- aich ri fian*
(c)
ten.
(d)
3
"Théid mis- e dh'a h-iarr-aidh dhut, Mi fhìn, mo ghill- e, 's mo chù,
(a)
Fine
'Nar triùir a dh'iarr-aidh na mnà."
*Sic.
7 syllables + svar. vowel, also melodic variant
(b)
ten.
Variants
Chunn- aig Rìgh Al- (a)b- a 'na shuain, An
(c) 7 syllables + svar. vowel
ten. (a)
8 syllables and melodic variant
aon-(a) bhean bu ghil-e snuadh fo'n ghréin Na còmh- rag fir mar bha e fhéin
(b) melodic variant
ten.
(c) 8 syllables
'S gum b'fheàrr leis tuit- eam 'na cion Na còmh- rag fir mar bha e fhéin
(d) melodic variant
(a) melodic variant
Labh- air Fionn Fal- aich ri fian, Théid mis- e dh'a h-iarr -aidh dhut

(d) melodic variant
(d) melodic variant
Seachd seachd- ain - ean is trì mios Mu fac- as ann no fonn
(a) two svar. vowels
(c) two svar. vowels
ten.
Chunn-(a)- cas chaist-eal min - gheal gor- (o)m, As guir-(i)m- e sùil 's as gil-e deud,
(a) 8 syllables and svar. vowel
An déis bhith cuart- ach- adh chuain ghair-(i)bh

Mixolydian, 6th weak
Scale

Eight degrees, nine in variants
Compass

Form: four phrases, ABCD, A and B bear some similarity at the second and fourth crotchets of each.

Structure: a four-bar melody without refrain.

The basic metre is quatrains, ABCD, CDEF, etc., 7[1]. The first and second quatrains contain lines with svarabhakti vowels and extra syllables, and the third quatrain is therefore set under the music.

XLI (b)

Am Bròn Binn

(as a waulking song)

(*b*) Sung by Mrs. MacDougall (Anna Raghnaill Eachainn), Barra, with Annie Johnston joining in the refrain

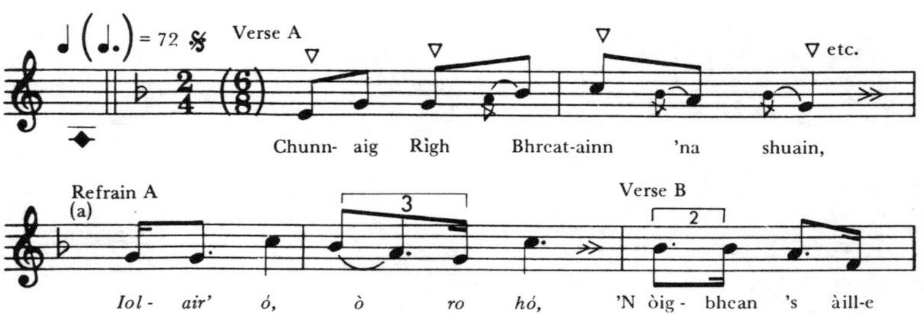
= 72
Verse A
etc.
Chunn- aig Rìgh Bhreat-ainn 'na shuain,
Refrain A
(a)
Verse B
Iol - air' ó, ò ro hó, 'N òig - bhean 's àill-e

The singer commenced the song with the verse as transcribed above.
The metre is 7^1. The song is sung in couplets in the above form, the second line of each couplet being repeated as the first line of the following one.

Variants

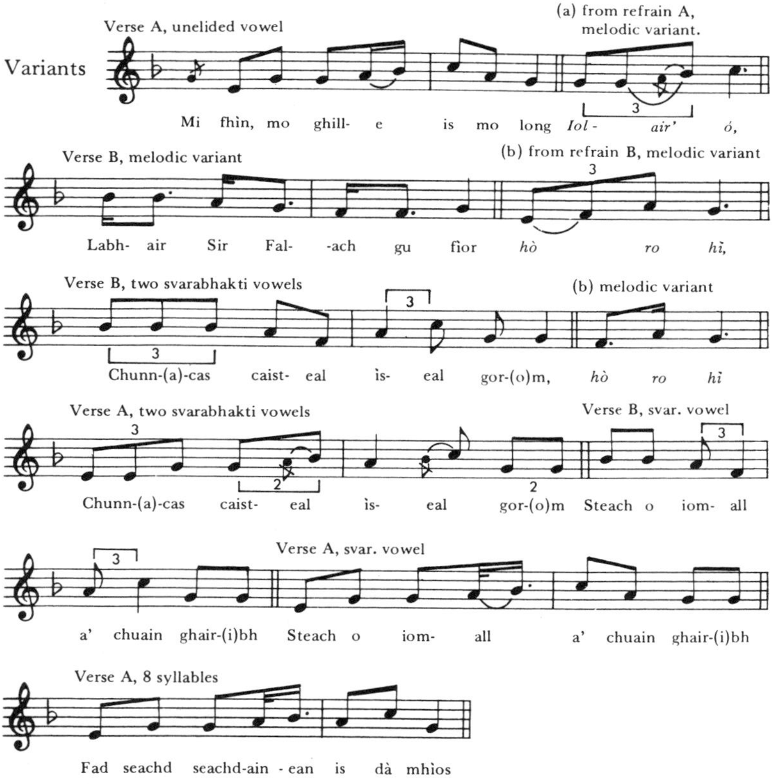

Verse A, unelided vowel — (a) from refrain A, melodic variant.

Mi fhìn, mo ghill- e is mo long *Iol - air' ó,*

Verse B, melodic variant — (b) from refrain B, melodic variant

Labh- air Sir Fal- -ach gu fior *hò ro hĩ,*

Verse B, two svarabhakti vowels — (b) melodic variant

Chunn-(a)-cas caist- eal ìs- eal gor-(o)m, *hò ro hĩ*

Verse A, two svarabhakti vowels — Verse B, svar. vowel

Chunn-(a)-cas caist- eal ìs- eal gor-(o)m Steach o iom- all

a' chuain ghair-(i)bh — Verse A, svar. vowel — Steach o iom- all a' chuain ghair-(i)bh

Verse A, 8 syllables

Fad seachd seachd-ain - ean is dà mhìos

Scale — Hexatonic — Dorian with gap at 5

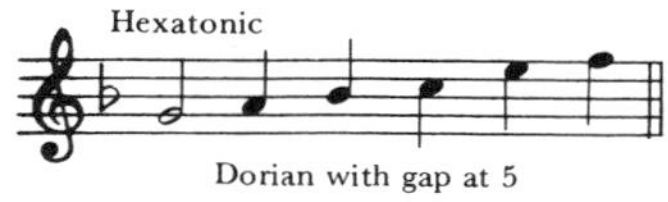

Compass — eight degrees

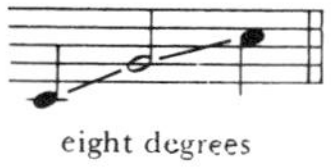

Form: four phrases, A B C D
Structure: an eight-bar melody:
Verse A, 2; Refrain A, 2;
Verse B, 2; Refrain B, 2.

XLII

Ach, a Mhurchaidh òig ghaolaich

Sung by Mrs. Archie MacPhee (Maighread Shomhairle Bhig), Barra

(*Without chorus*)

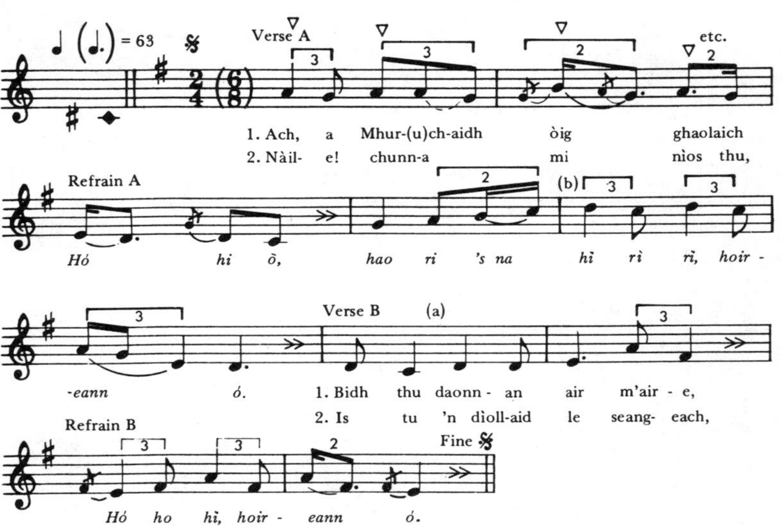

= 63
Verse A
etc.
1. Ach, a Mhur-(u)ch-aidh òig ghaolaich
2. Nàil- e! chunn-a mi nìos thu,
Refrain A
Hó hi õ, hao ri 's na hì rì rì, hoir -
(b)
-eann ó.
Verse B (a)
1. Bidh thu daonn - an air m'air - e,
2. Is tu 'n dìoll-aid le seang- each,
Refrain B
Fine
Hó ho hì, hoir - eann ó.

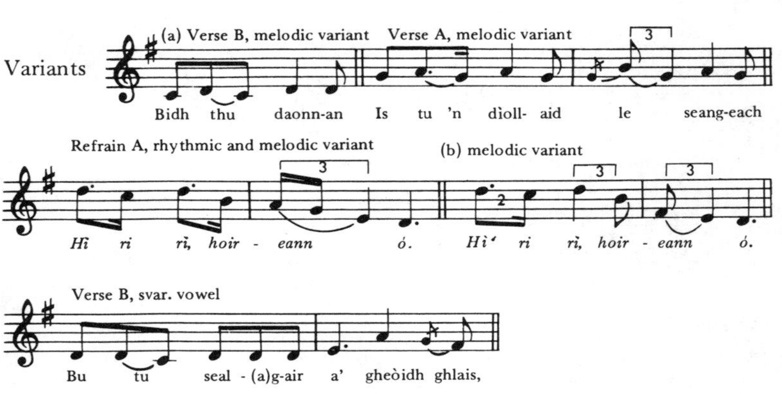

Variants
(a) Verse B, melodic variant
Verse A, melodic variant
Bidh thu daonn-an Is tu 'n dìoll- aid le seang-each
Refrain A, rhythmic and melodic variant
(b) melodic variant
Hì ri rì, hoir - eann ó. Hì' ri rì, hoir - eann ó.
Verse B, svar. vowel
Bu tu seal - (a)g-air a' gheòidh ghlais,

Form: four phrases, A B C D.

Structure: a ten bar melody; Verse A, 2; Refrain A, 4; Verse B, 2; Refrain B, 2.

The singer commenced with Verse A. She only remembered a few lines of the song, which we have not heard from anyone else, except a fragment from her sister.

The song was probably not originally a waulking song. The metre is 7^2, with internal rhyme, and penultimate rhyme in even lines.

XLIII

'S mi dol timcheall na dòirlinn

Sung by Mrs. Neil Campbell (Bean Nìll), South Uist

(*Without chorus*)

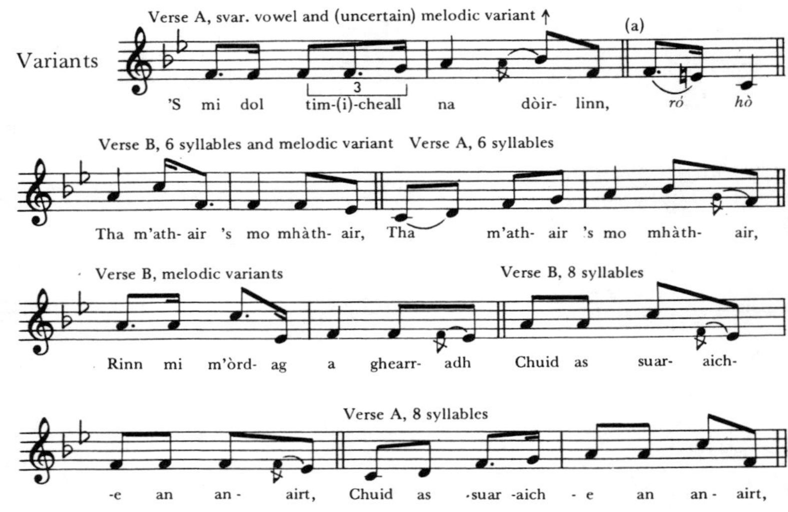
Variants
Verse A, svar. vowel and (uncertain) melodic variant ↑
(a)
3
'S mi dol tim-(i)-cheall na dòir- linn, *ró hò*
Verse B, 6 syllables and melodic variant
Verse A, 6 syllables
Tha m'ath- air 's mo mhàth- air, Tha m'ath- air 's mo mhàth- air,
Verse B, melodic variants
Verse B, 8 syllables
Rinn mi m'òrd- ag a ghearr- adh Chuid as suar- aich-
Verse A, 8 syllables
-e an an- airt, Chuid as suar -aich - e an an- airt,

Scale Dorian Compass eight degrees

Form: five phrases; A B C D E

Structure: a ten-bar melody:
Verse A, 2; refrain A, 2.
Verse B, 2; refrain B, 4.

The metre is 7^2, with internal rhyme, and even lines rhyming on the penultimate. Probably not originally a waulking song. The singer began the song with Verse A. The opening line being a variant, the third and fourth lines are set under the music here. The third note is uncertain, and seems to hover between E flat and F. The second note of the second bar, B flat, is generally somewhat sharp in pitch. In the last variant it is sung as C.

XLIV

Ged is grianach an latha

(*a*) Sung by Calum Johnston (Calum Aonghais Chaluim), Barra

(*Without chorus*)

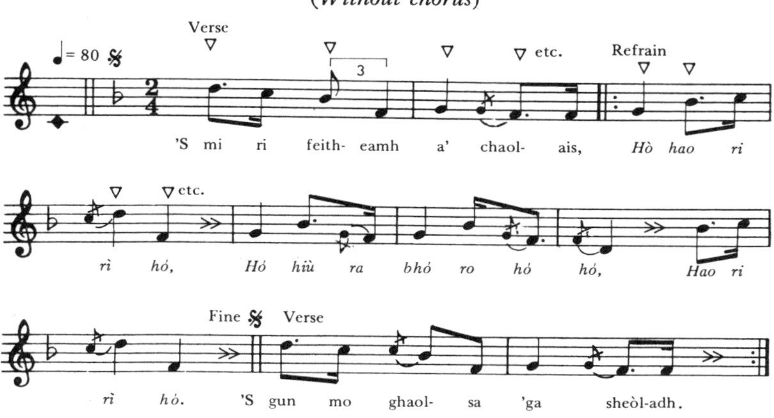

♩= 80
Verse
etc.
Refrain
3
'S mi ri feith- eamh a' chaol- ais,
Hò hao ri
rì hó, Hó hiù ra bhó ro hó hó, Hao ri
rì hó.
Fine
Verse
'S gun mo ghaol- sa 'ga sheòl-adh.

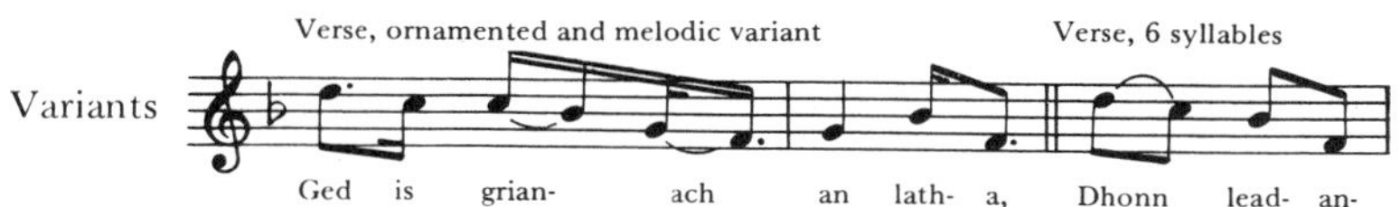

Variants
Verse, ornamented and melodic variant
Verse, 6 syllables
Ged is grian- ach an lath- a, Dhonn lead- an-

-ach bhòidh-each

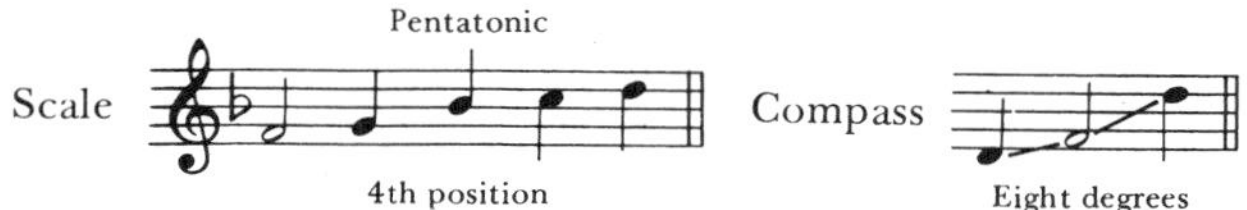

Pentatonic
Scale
4th position
Compass
Eight degrees

Form: four phrases, Verse A || Refrain B[1] C B[2]

Structure: an eight-bar melody: Verse 2, Refrain 6.

The singer commenced with the verse. The first line is sung to a melodic variant, and the third and fourth lines are therefore put under the music. The song is probably a ballad sung as a waulking song. The metre is 7^2, with internal thyme; even lines rhyme on the penultimate syllables, the vowels of most of which are long.

XLIV

Ged is grianach an latha

(*b*) Sung by Miss Janet MacKinnon (Seònaid Shomhairle Bhig), Barra, with Mrs. MacCormick joining in the refrain

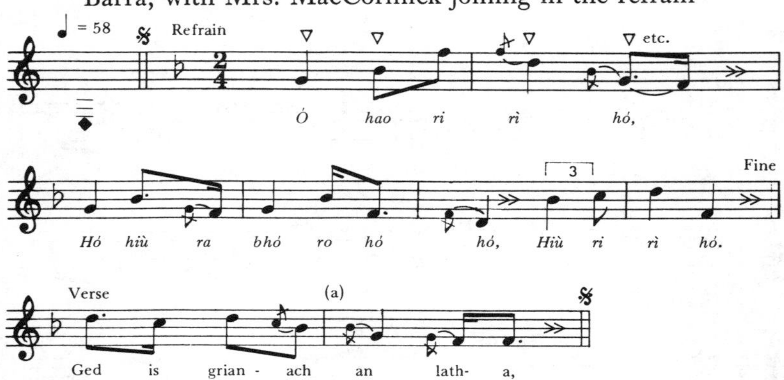

= 58
Refrain
etc.
Ó hao ri rì hó,
Fine
Hó hiù ra bhó ro hó hó, Hiù ri rì hó.
Verse
(a)
Ged is grian - ach an lath- a,

Variants
Verse, rhythmic variant for long-short ending.
Verse, melodic variant.
Air an tul - aich lìon bròn mi, 'S mi gu rach - adh

'nad choinn - eamh,

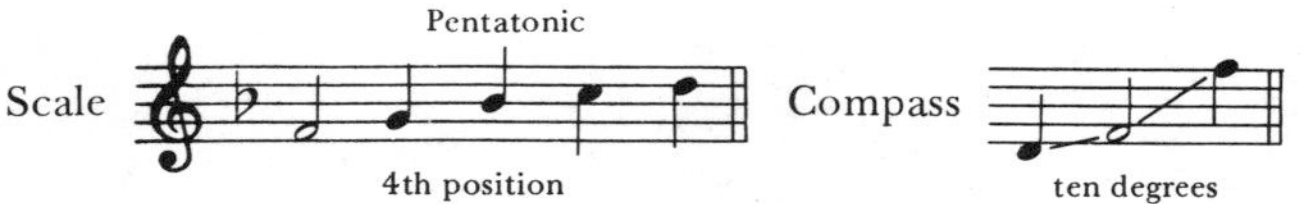

Scale
Pentatonic
4th position
Compass
ten degrees

	Verse	Refrain
Form: four phrases,	A	B C D

Structure: an eight-bar melody: Verse 2, Refrain 6

The singer commenced the song with the verse.

The metre is 7^2. The lines end with long and short vowels alternately, changing the rhythm of the last two syllables from short-long e.g. (lath- a) to long-short: (bròn mi).

The singer only recorded four verses.

XLV

Tha an oidhche nochd fuar

Sung by Mrs. Mary MacNeil (Mairi Ruarachain), Barra

(*With chorus*)

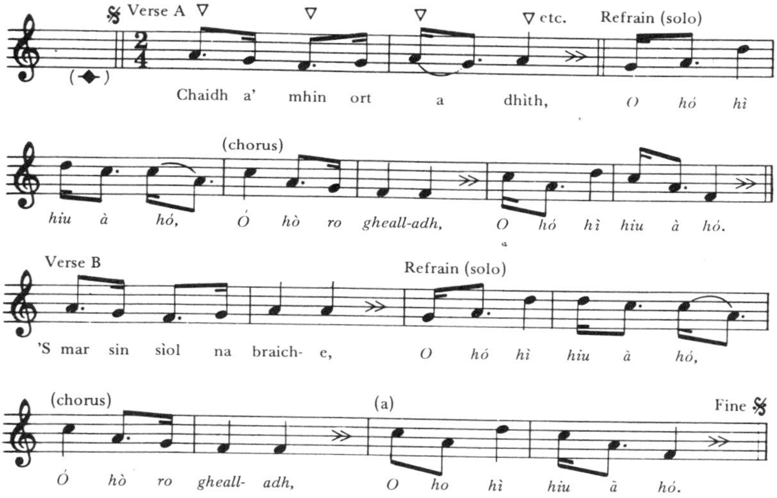

Verse A
etc.
Refrain (solo)
Chaidh a' mhin ort a dhìth, *O hó hì*
(chorus)
hiu à hó, Ó hò ro gheall-adh, O hó hì hiu à hó.
Verse B
Refrain (solo)
'S mar sin sìol na braich- e, *O hó hì hiu à hó,*
(chorus)
(a)
Fine
Ó hò ro gheall- adh, O ho hì hiu ã hó.

Variants

Line 3, 7 syllables
(a) melodic variant
3
Mhic 'ill' Eógh-an- ain 'ic Nìll *O ho hì hiu ã hó*
Verse A, melodic variant
'S fear a chùnnt-adh dhi ni.

Scale

Pentatonic
1st position

Compass

six degrees

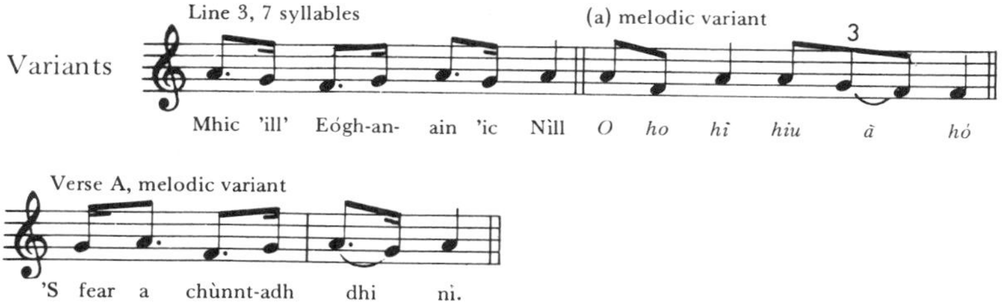

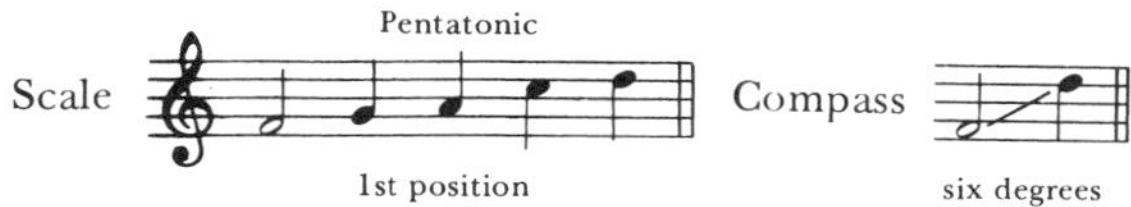

	Verse	Refrain		Verse	Refrain
Form: four phrases	A	B C D	‖	B	B C D

Structure: an eight-bar melody: Verse 2, Refrain 6.

It is fairly clear that this song was not originally a waulking song, as is explained in the notes to the text. The basic metre is $6^1 + 6^2$ (sometimes 5^2), with internal rhyme, but there are irregularities. From the metre it is clear that the singer did not remember all the lines, nor were all sung in the right order. The singer commenced the song with the verse. The first line of six syllables which is sung to the basic melody is line 4 (Line 1 is sung to a variant, and line 2 was erroneously sung to a phrase of the refrain). Lines 11 and 12 are therefore set below the music. The difference between the ways they are sung is very slight, but it is consistent, and accords with the basic metre, therefore the lines are called Verse A and Verse B respectively.

XLVI

Seathan mac Rìgh Éirinn

Sung by Annie and Calum Johnston (Anna agus Calum Aonghais Chaluim), Barra

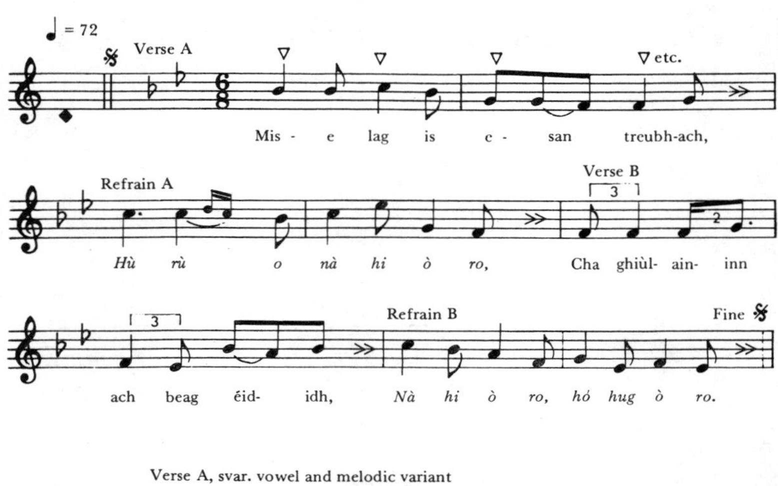

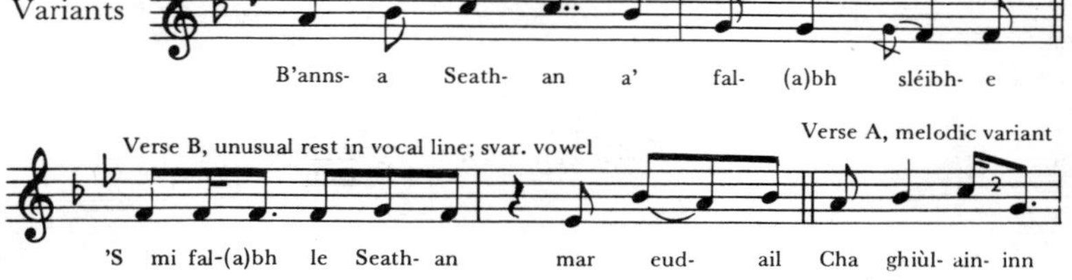

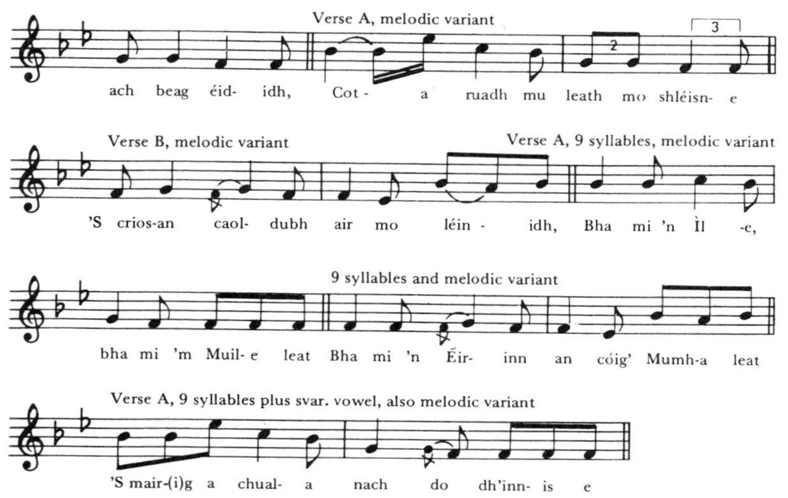
Verse A, melodic variant
ach beag éid- idh, Cot - a ruadh mu leath mo shléisn- e
Verse B, melodic variant
'S crios-an caol- dubh air mo léin - idh,
Verse A, 9 syllables, melodic variant
Bha mi 'n Ìl -e,
bha mi 'm Muil- e leat
9 syllables and melodic variant
Bha mi 'n Éir- inn an cóig' Mumh-a leat
Verse A, 9 syllables plus svar. vowel, also melodic variant
'S mair-(i)g a chual- a nach do dh'inn- is e

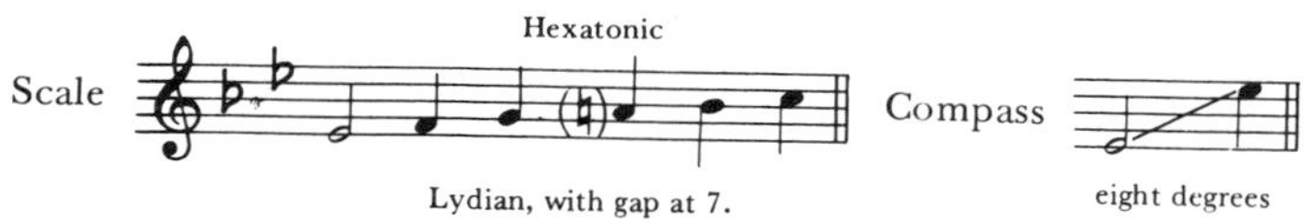
Scale
Hexatonic
Lydian, with gap at 7.
Compass
eight degrees

Form: Four phrases: A B C D
Structure: an eight-bar melody:
Verse A, 2; Refrain A, 2;
Verse B, 2; Refrain B, 2.

The basic metre is 8^2, but there are lines of nine and of ten syllables. Change of subject is marked by the repetition of refrain B, first by the soloist and then by the 'chorus.' This occurs thrice in the course of the song. This singer commenced with Verse A as in 1st variant.

At the end of the second bar of Verse A, the two Fs in the variants become frequent instead of F,G and may possibly be considered as the basic version.

XLVII

(*a*) *Chailin òig as stiùramaiche*

Sung by Mrs. MacDougall (Anna Raghnaill Eachainn), Barra, with Annie Johnston joining in the refrain

♩ = 69
(= g in transcription)
Verse A
etc.
Shuidh sinn air cnoc, 's rinn sinn bàn - ran,
Refrain A
3
2
Chail- in òig a hù ra bhó ho,
Verse B
Shuidh sinn air cnoc,
's rinn sinn bàn- ran,
Refrain B
Fine
Chail -in òig as stiùr - a - maich-e

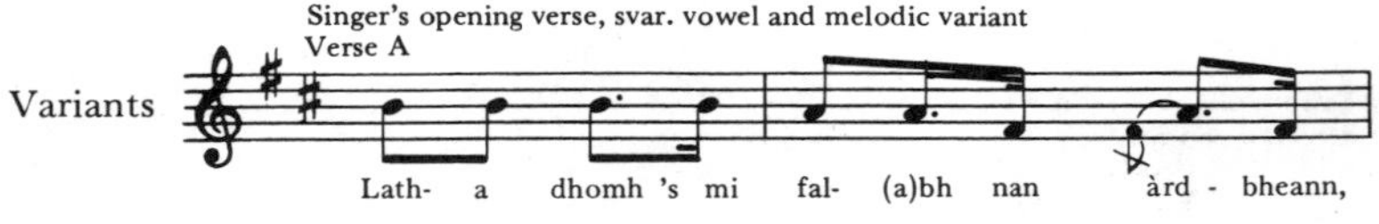

Singer's opening verse, svar. vowel and melodic variant
Verse A
Variants
Lath- a dhomh 's mi fal- (a)bh nan àrd - bheann,

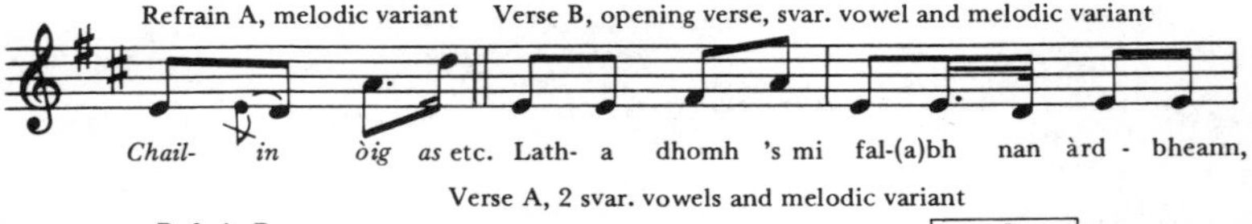

Refrain A, melodic variant
Verse B, opening verse, svar. vowel and melodic variant
Chail- in òig as etc. Lath- a dhomh 's mi fal-(a)bh nan àrd - bheann,

Verse A, 2 svar. vowels and melodic variant
Refrain B
3
Chail- in òig as etc. Thach- air or-(o)ms' an donn -(a)- bhean dhàn- a,

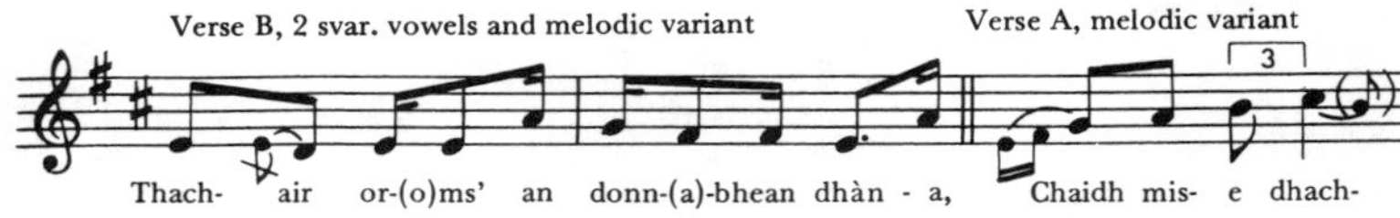

Verse B, 2 svar. vowels and melodic variant
Verse A, melodic variant
3
Thach- air or-(o)ms' an donn-(a)-bhean dhàn - a, Chaidh mis- e dhach-

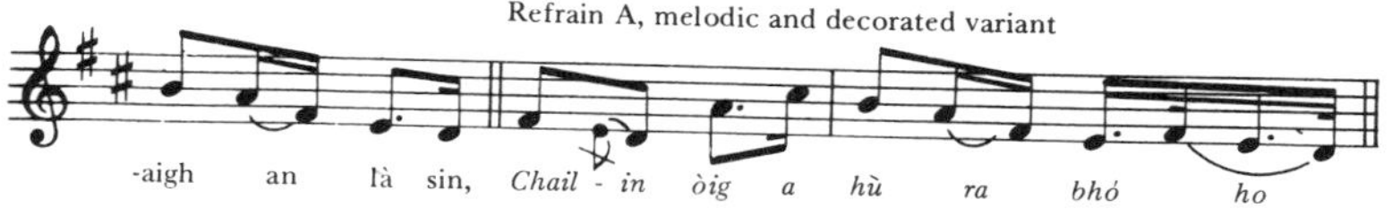
Refrain A, melodic and decorated variant
-aigh an là sin, Chail - in òig a hù ra bhó ho

Scale
Dorian
Compass
eight degrees

Form: four phrases, A B[1] C B[2].
Structure: an eight-bar melody:
Verse A, 2; Refrain A, 2
Verse B, 2; Refrain B, 2.

The singer commenced the song with the verse. The metre is 8². The first two lines (each repeated) have svarabhakti vowels, and are therefore classed as variants. The commencement of the recording is indistinct, but nevertheless presents an interesting example of how a traditional Gaelic singer often 'sings herself into' the melody when she fails to remember the tune to begin with; and the opening verse is included for this reason.

XLVII

Chailin òig as stiùramaiche

(*b*) Sung by Mrs. Mary Morrison (Bean Phluim), Barra

(*Without chorus*)

= 63
Verse
etc.
Chail - in mis- e, buach - aill' thus- a,
Refrain
(a)
Verse
Chail - in òig a hù ra bhó hó, Chail - in mis - e,
Refrain
(b)
Fine
buach - aill' thus - a, Chail - in òig as stiùr - am - aich - e.

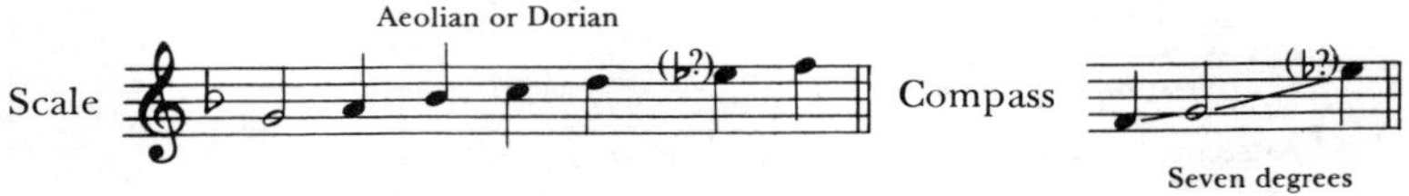

Form: four phrases: A B A B.
Structure: an eight-bar melody of four bars repeated:
Verse 2, Refrain 2, Verse 2, Refrain 2.

This is a transcription of the recording made by Mrs. Morrison in 1937. The singer commenced with the refrain to the words *Chailin òig as stiùramaiche.* The descending cadence at the variants of (*a*) and (*b*), though occurring irregularly throughout the song, tends more often to be used at the line ending *hù ra bhó hó* than at that ending *stiuramaiche*. It may well be that the descending cadence is proper to the first refrain line, and the non-descending to the second. This would regularize the two refrains as Refrain A and Refrain B. They are distinguished in other versions of the air.

The rhythmic form *Chail - in* with the longer note on the second, normally unstressed syllable, is interesting, as it corresponds to the pronunciation of the word in Irish Gaelic.

A striking instance of wrenched accent occurs in line 311 of this song, where the first two words *Mar uan* ('like a lamb') are sung with full stress on the preposition *Mar*, and *uan* is unstressed. Normally the opposite would be the case.

The fourth note of the refrain seems to be intermediate between E flat and E natural and is open to subjective interpretation as to the singer's intention. The note seems to be nearer E natural at the beginning of the song, and gradually to approach E flat as the song proceeds. As far as the mode is concerned, E flat gives the Aeolian mode and E natural the Dorian.

XLVII

Chailin òig as stiùramaiche

(*c*) Sung by Miss Annie MacDonald (Anna Raghnaill), South Uist

(*Without chorus*)

(a) melodic variant
3
(b) at ending
'n deagh-aidh a mhàth- ar, stiùir thu mis- e

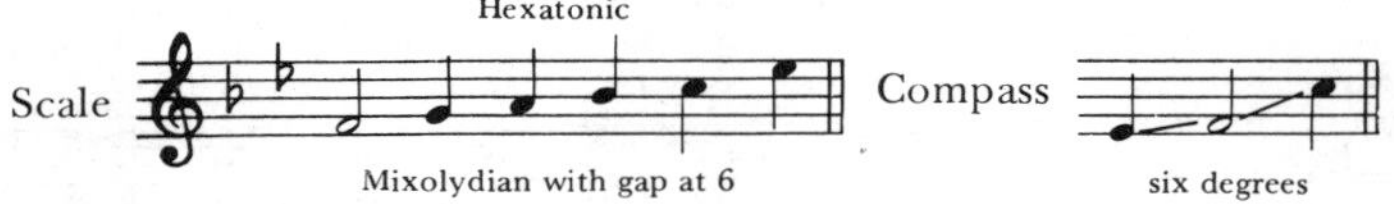
Hexatonic
Scale
Compass
Mixolydian with gap at 6
six degrees

Form: four phrases: A B[1] A B[2].
Structure: an eight-bar melody:
Verse A, 2; Refrain A, 2.
Verse B, 2; Refrain B, 2.

The singer ended the song with Refrain A sung twice. The basic metre is 8^2. The first line has a svarabhakti vowel and is therefore set down as a variant (in addition to which the singer did not there strike the regular melody). The third line, which is followed by Refrain A, is therefore set under the music.

XLVII

Chailin òig as stiùramaiche

(*d*) Sung by Mrs. Kate MacCormick (Catriana nighean 'Ill' Easbuig Ghriomasaidh), Benbecula

(*Without chorus*)

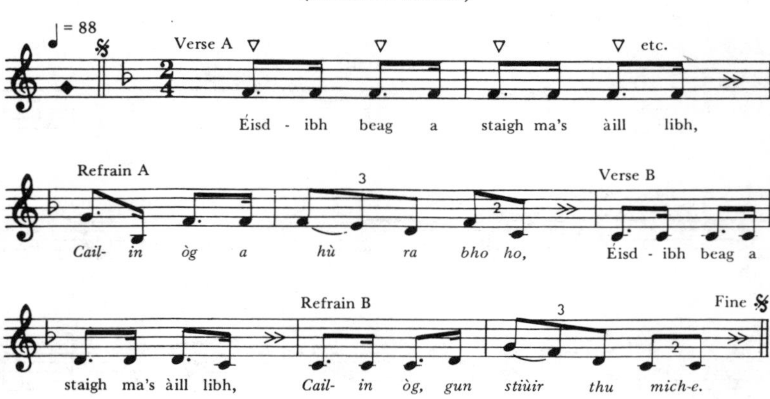
♩ = 88
Verse A
etc.
Éisd - ibh beag a staigh ma's àill libh,
Refrain A
3
2
Verse B
Cail- in òg a hù ra bho ho,
Éisd - ibh beag a
Refrain B
3
Fine
2
staigh ma's àill libh,
Cail- in òg, gun stiùir thu mich-e.

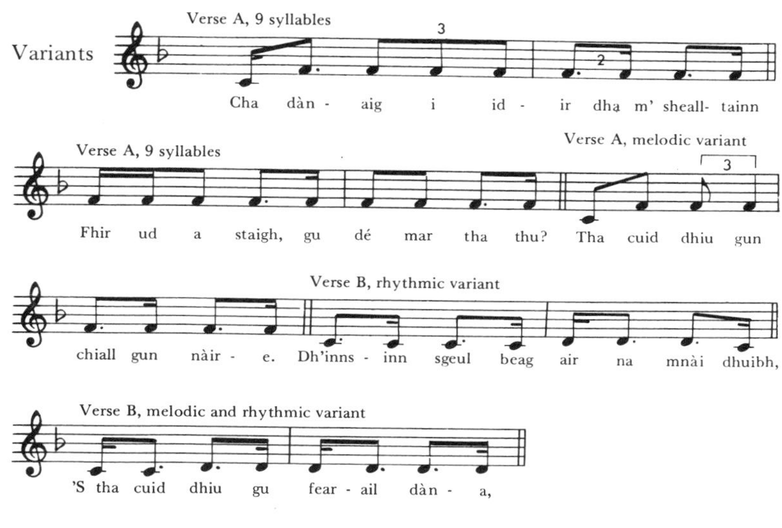
Variants
Verse A, 9 syllables
3
2
Cha dàn - aig i id - ir dha m' sheall- tainn
Verse A, 9 syllables
Fhir ud a staigh, gu dé mar tha thu?
Verse A, melodic variant
3
Tha cuid dhiu gun chiall gun nàir - e.
Verse B, rhythmic variant
Dh'inns - inn sgeul beag air na mnài dhuibh,
Verse B, melodic and rhythmic variant
'S tha cuid dhiu gu fear - ail dàn - a,

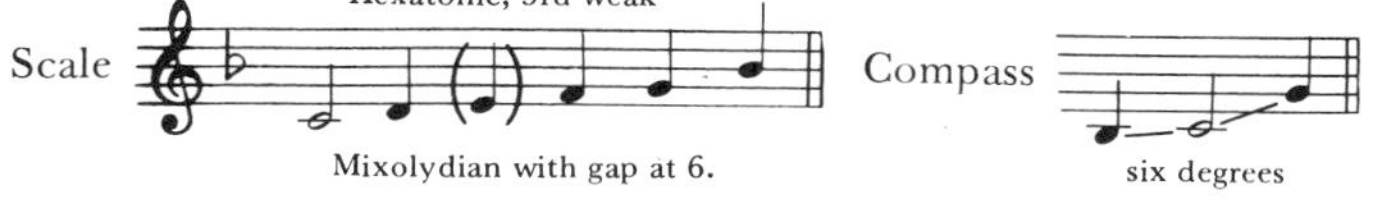
Scale
Hexatonic, 3rd weak
Mixolydian with gap at 6.
Compass
six degrees

Form: four phrases: A B C D
Structure: an eight-bar melody:
Verse A, 2; Refrain A, 2.
Verse B, 2; Refrain B, 2.

The singer commenced and ended the song with Refrain B. The singer has *gun stiuir thu miche* in Refrain B throughout. She rose a tone and a half in pitch towards the end of the song.

Calen o Custure Me

The FitzWilliam Book Version
The Ballet MS. Version – Callino Casturme
T.C.D.Lib. MS. 408, p. 83
John Cameron's Version (*An Deo-Ghreine*, *November 1905*)*
'S cail-in thu- sa, 's bhuach- aill' mi- se, *Chail- in òg, nach*
stiùir thu mi? 'S cail- in thu- sa, 's bhuach-aill' mi- se,
Chail- in òg, i hiù- ribh ò, Chail- in òg, nach stiùir thu mi?
Harris Version (Marjory Kennedy-Fraser, photostat folio 117).
Chail-in òg, an stiùir thu mis- e

*See also *Transactions of the Gaelic Society of Inverness*, xxvii. 61, where the same tune is printed in a lecture given by Malcolm MacFarlane on 3 December 1908, and the tune is stated to be from Ballachulish.

XLVIII

Bha mis' a raoir air an àirigh

Sung by Mrs. Mary Morrison (Bean Phluim), Barra

(*With chorus*)

♩ = 72
Verse A
etc.
Bha mis' a raoir air an àir- igh,
Refrain A
Verse B
Hi ho éil- eadh, ho hoir - eann ó,
Bha mis' a raoir
Refrain B
Fine
air an àir- igh,
Hu hoir- eann ó, hu hoir - eann ó.

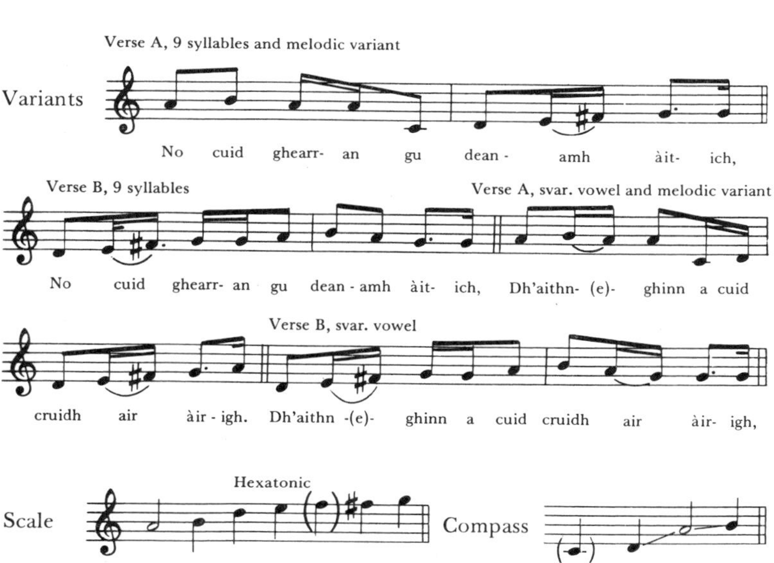
Verse A, 9 syllables and melodic variant
Variants
No cuid ghearr- an gu dean - amh àit- ich,
Verse B, 9 syllables
Verse A, svar. vowel and melodic variant
No cuid ghearr- an gu dean - amh àit- ich, Dh'aithn- (e)- ghinn a cuid
Verse B, svar. vowel
cruidh air àir - igh. Dh'aithn -(e)- ghinn a cuid cruidh air àir- igh,
Hexatonic
Scale
Compass
Dorian, with gap at 3. and Variable 6.
six degrees (seven in Variant)

Form: four phrases: A B C D

Structure: an eight-bar melody: Verse A,2; Refrain A, 2.
Verse B 2; Refrain B, 2.

The singer commenced the song with Refrain B, repeated by the chorus. The song ended with the singing of this refrain three times (chorus, solo, chorus)'

The note F in the melody is remarkably indeterminate as between F♮ and F♯. Thus in bar 2 it tends towards a slightly flattened F#; in bars 3 and 5 it is more often a nearly true F#, while in the last bar it is nearer to F♮ than to F#. The mode is therefore an indeterminate mixture of Dorian and Aeolian.

XLIX

Chaidh mi 'na ghleannain a's t-fhoghar

Sung by Mrs. Neil Campbell (Bean Nìll), South Uist, with Mrs. Patrick MacPhee joining in the refrain

Verse A, 2 svar. vowels, and melodic variant
am bi 'n fhagh-aid Le do ghearr(a)- choin mean-(a)bh-choin lagh- ach,
Verse B, 2 svar. vowels
Le do ghearr-(a)-choin mean-(a)bh -choin lagh-ach,
Verse A, svar. vowel
Cha b'e lur- (a)- ga
bhreac o'n luath i,
Verse A, svar. vowel
Geal o'n tein- e, dear- (a)g o'n fhuachd thu,
Verse B, svar. vowel
Geal o'n tein- e, dear-(a)g o'n fhuachd thu,
Refrain, melodic variant
Hoir- eann ó hi
rì ho ro ho,
Verse A, unelided vowel
Siod an leab- a am biodh na gifht- ean,
Verse B, unelided vowel
Siod an leab- a am biodh na gifht-ean,
Verse A, 10 syllables
Fuaim do ghunn -a, do
ghad -a, do ghoid- ein,
Verse B, 10 syllables
Fuaim do ghunn-a, do ghad- a, do ghoid-ein,
Scale
Ionian
Compass
Eight degrees

Form: Four phrases: A B[1] C B[2]
Structure: An eight-bar melody: Verse A 2, Refrain A 2; Verse B 2, Refrain B 2.

The singer commenced and ended the song with Refrain B., sung twice. The basic metre is 8^2. The first line is a melodic variant, and the second has a svarabhakti vowel. The words of lines three and four are therefore set under the music.

L

Tha caolas eadar mi 's Iain

Sung by Mrs. Buchanan (Ceit Ruairi Iain Bhàin), Barra

(*With chorus*)

♩. = 60
Verse
etc.
Cha chaol a th'ann, ach cuan domh - ain,
Refrain A
Hao ri hiu ò, hao ri e hó,
Verse
Cha chaol a th'ann,
ach cuan domh - ain,
Refrain B
O hao ri rì hì ho ró na,
Hì hoir- eann ó, hao ri e hó.
Fine

Variants
Verse, line 1, 7 syllables
Tha caol - as ead - ar mi 's Iain,
Verse, rhythmic variant
Truagh nach tragh - adh
e fo lath - a,

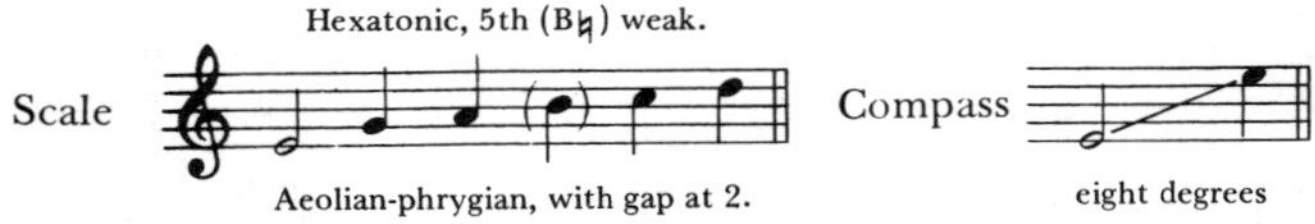

Hexatonic, 5th (B♮) weak.
Scale
Aeolian-phrygian, with gap at 2.
Compass
eight degrees

Form: five phrases: A^1 A^2 A^2 B C.
Structure: a ten-bar melody:

Verse, 2; Refrain A, 2.
Verse, 2; Refrain B, 4.

The metre is 8^2. In the first line the vernacular word for 'John', *Iain*, has probably been substituted for an original *Seathan*, with the result that the line has now only seven syllables. The second line, being normal, is set under the music. The air of the verse is the same in both sections, and is therefore not marked as Verse A and Verse B. The singer commenced with the verse as above.

The chorus tried to join in the refrain, but the singer set too high a pitch for them!

LI

Dh'éirich mi moch madainn Chéitein

(*a*) Sung by Miss Annie Johnston (Anna Aonghais Chaluim), Barra

(*Without chorus*)

Verse A, 9 syllables
(b)
A rinn mo leab- a 'n cois an dor- uis, Hill ir inn is,
(c)
3
lebh ó hi ó ri ri a o

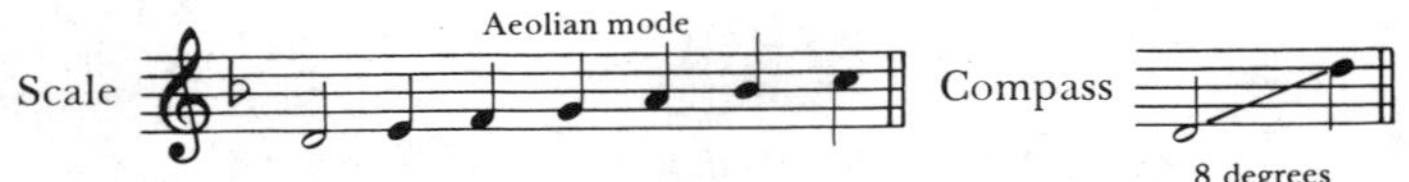
Aeolian mode
Scale
Compass
8 degrees

From: five phrases: A B C D E.
Structure: an eleven-bar melody:
Verse A, 2, Refrain A 2;
Verse B, 2, Refrain B, 3.

Noted direct from Miss Annie Johnston about 1951 by F. Collinson. Variants from recording made from Annie and Calum Johnston for J.L. Campbell by Barra Folklore Committee on 3/8/50.
The opening bar, to the words *Dh'eirich mi moch*, as noted direct, is shown in the recording to be a melodic variant of the basic melody, and is therefore placed among the variants.
The third and fourth lines of the text, as sung in the recording to the basic tune, are placed under the melody. The singer commenced with Verse A.

LI

Dh'éirich mi moch madainn Chéitein

(*b*) Sung by Miss Penny Morrison, Iochdar, South Uist, at a genuine waulking

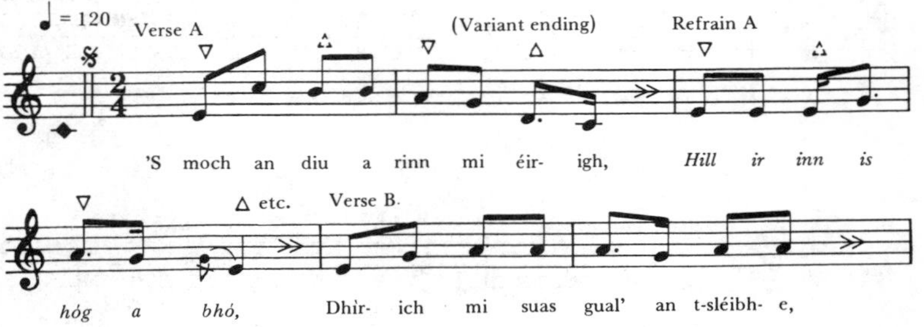
♩ = 120
Verse A
(Variant ending)
Refrain A
'S moch an diu a rinn mi éir- igh, Hill ir inn is
Δ etc.
Verse B
hóg a bhó, Dhìr- ich mi suas gual' an t-sléibh- e,

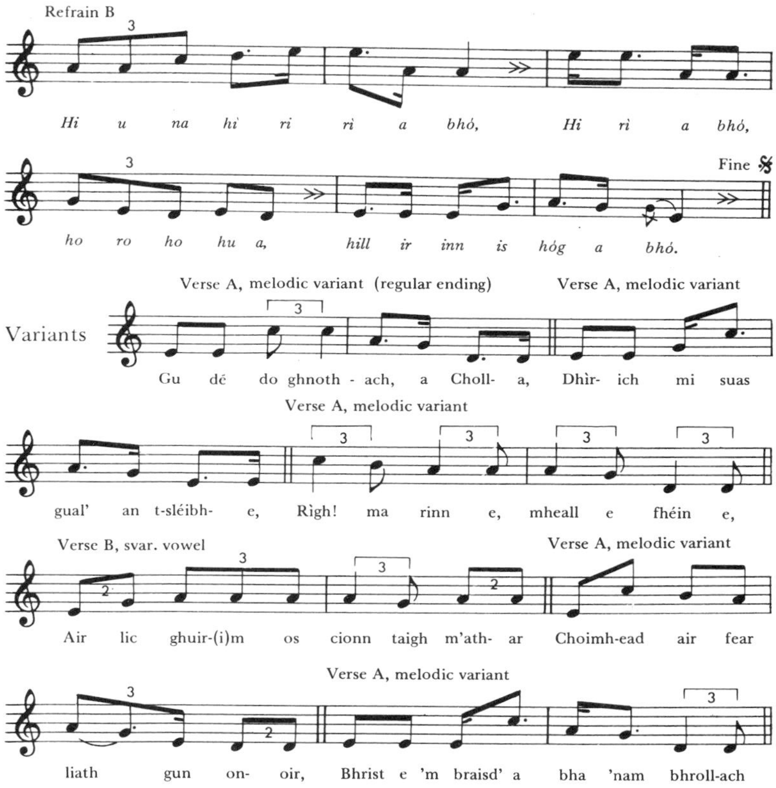

Refrain B

Hi u na hì ri rì a bhó, Hi rì a bhó,

ho ro ho hu a, hill ir inn is hóg a bhó.

Fine 𝄋

Variants

Verse A, melodic variant (regular ending)

Gu dé do ghnoth - ach, a Choll- a,

Verse A, melodic variant

Dhìr- ich mi suas gual' an t-sléibh- e,

Verse A, melodic variant

Rìgh! ma rinn e, mheall e fhéin e,

Verse B, svar. vowel

Air lic ghuir-(i)m os cionn taigh m'ath- ar

Verse A, melodic variant

Choimh-ead air fear liath gun on- oir,

Verse A, melodic variant

Bhrist e 'm braisd' a bha 'nam bhroll-ach

The waulking pulse maintains a fairly consistent pattern in two-bar rhythm, commencing with a strong *sfz* thump on the first beat of the first bar, followed by an almost inaudible thump on the second beat, followed by two *mf.* thumps in the second bar, thus:

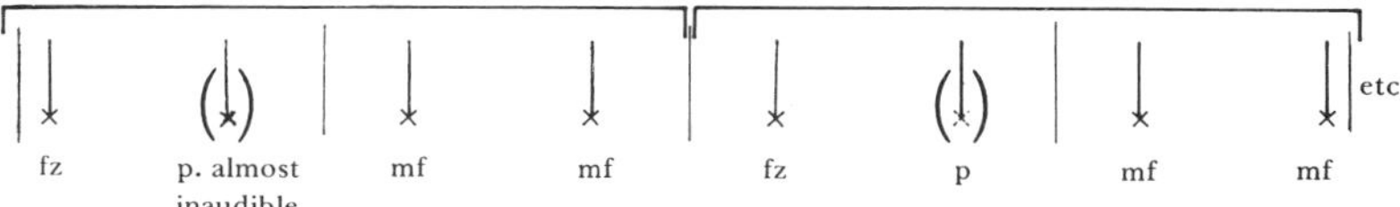

The song begins with the soloist singing Refrain A, repeated by the chorus. It them proceeds from 𝄋 to 𝄋. It ends with the last line sung once followed by the long refrain.

Form: Six phrases: A B C D E B.

Structure: A twelve-bar melody: Verse A 2; Refrain A 2; Verse B 2; Refrain B 6

LII

Tha 'n t-uisg', tha 'n ceò air na beannan

(*a*) Sung by Calum Johnston (Calum Aonghais Chaluim), Barra

(*Without chorus*)

♩. = 88
Verse A
etc.
Tha 'n t-uisg', tha 'n ceò air na beann- an,
Refrain A
Hao ri 's na hao ri ho ró,
Verse B
Tha sneachd - a mór ann le gaill- inn,
Refrain B
Ho lebh o hao ri iù ò,
Ró ho hao ri ri u bhi, Hò na
(a)
hì ho ró bha hao, ri ho ro o.
Fine

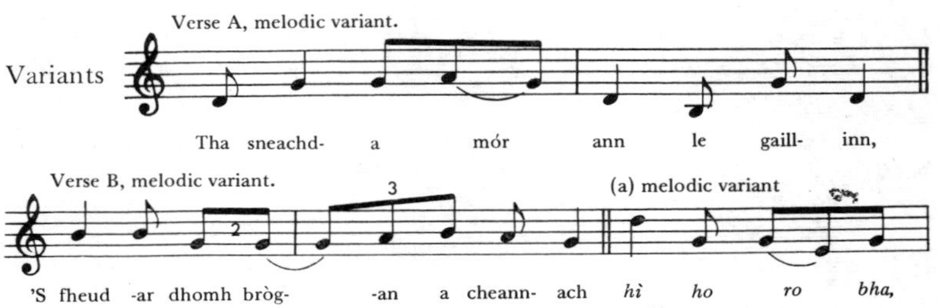

Variants
Verse A, melodic variant.
Tha sneachd- a mór ann le gaill- inn,
Verse B, melodic variant.
(a) melodic variant
'S fheud -ar dhomh bròg- -an a cheann- ach hì ho ro bha,

Form: six phrases: A B C D E F.
Structure: a twelve-bar melody:

Verse A, 2; Refrain A, 2.
Verse B, 2, Refrain B, 6.

The singer ended the song with the long refrain at *fine* as marked, but this cannot be accepted as conclusive (cf. note to the text). He commenced the song with verse A.

In the second variant (Verse B) the prolongation of *bròg* into the following bar by syncopation is exceptional and is not normal practice in Gaelic song.

LII

Tha 'n t-uisg', tha 'n ceò air na beannan

(*b*) Sung by Miss Janet MacKinnon (Seònaid Shomhairle Bhig), Barra, with Mrs. MacCormick joining in the refrain

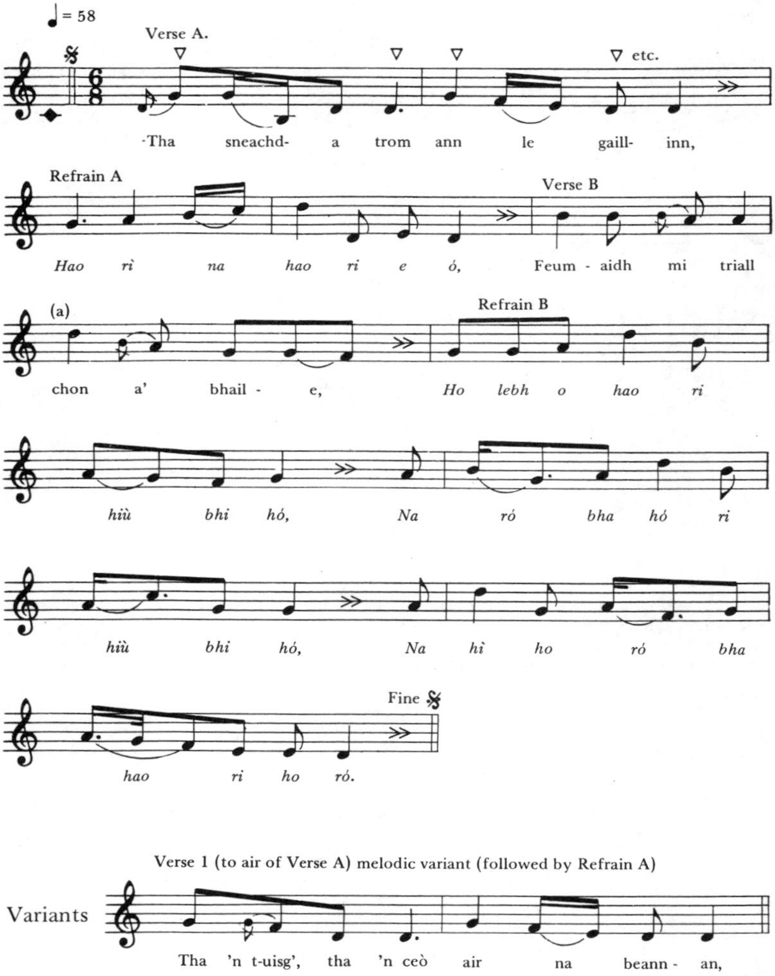

♩ = 58

Verse A. ▽ ▽ ▽ ▽ etc.

Tha sneachd- a trom ann le gaill- inn,

Refrain A

Hao rì na hao ri e ó,

Verse B

Feum - aidh mi triall

(a)

chon a' bhail - e,

Refrain B

Ho lebh o hao ri

hiù bhi hó, Na ró bha hó ri

hiù bhi hó, Na hì ho ró bha

hao ri ho ró.

Fine

Verse 1 (to air of Verse A) melodic variant (followed by Refrain A)

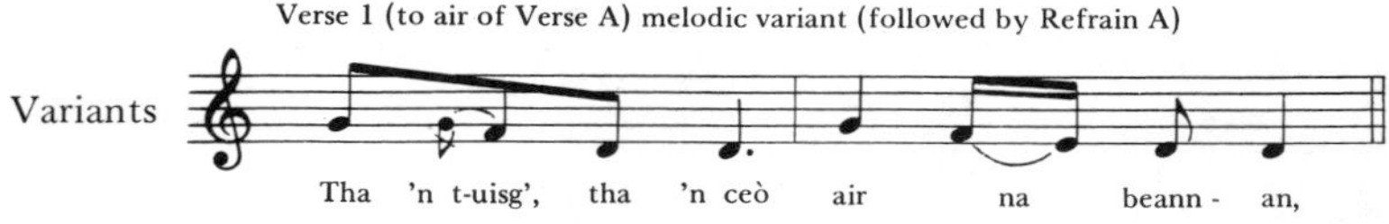

Variants
Tha 'n t-uisg', tha 'n ceò air na beann - an,

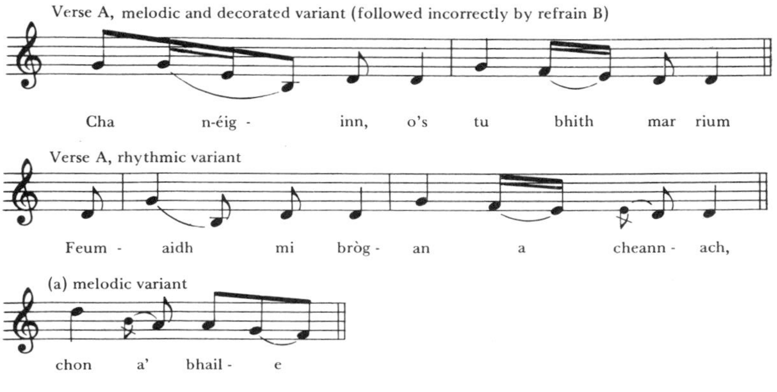
Verse A, melodic and decorated variant (followed incorrectly by refrain B)
Cha n-éig - inn, o's tu bhith mar rium
Verse A, rhythmic variant
Feum - aidh mi bròg - an a cheann - ach,
(a) melodic variant
chon a' bhail - e

Scale
Dorian
Compass
Ten degrees

Form: six phrases: A B C D E F.
Structure: a twelve-bar melody:
Verse A, 2; Refrain A, 2.
Verse B 2; Refrain B, 6.

The metre is 8^2. The singer used incorrectly the melody of Verse A for both the first and second lines, and the second verse is therefore set under the music in order to show the form of the melody more clearly. The singer commenced with verse A.

LIII

Craobhan ó, hòireann o ho

Sung by Mrs. James MacNeil (Anna Mhìcheil Nìll), Barra

(*With chorus*)

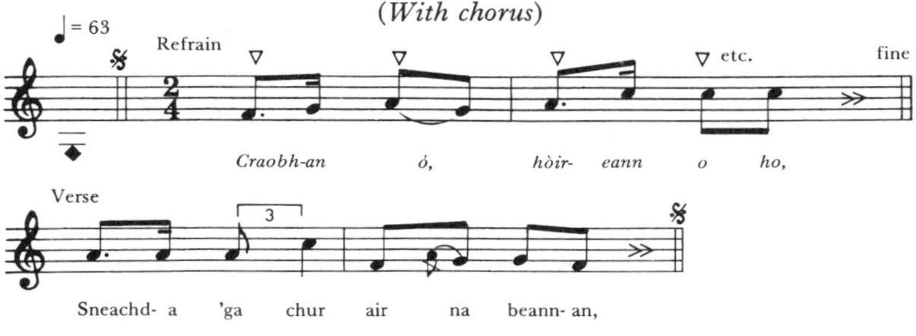
♩ = 63
Refrain
etc.
fine
Craobh-an ó, hòir- eann o ho,
Verse
3
Sneachd- a 'ga chur air na beann- an,

Refrain by soloist at commencement (melodic variant)
Verse, melodic variant
Variants
Craobh-an ó, hòir-eann o ho, Gaoth 'ga reoth- adh
Verse, melodic variant
ris na crann- an Mór mo dhùil gun dig dha'm iarr- aidh,
Refrain, melodic variant
Verse, melodic and rhythmic variant
Craobh - an ó, hòir - eann o ho. Ri fear odh - ar
Refrain, melodic and rhythmic variant.
bodh - ar breòit-each Craobh- an ó, hòir- eann o ho.
Verse, rhythmic and melodic variant
Chuir- inn geall gu faigh- inn cad - al
Scale
A four-note scale
Compass
Five degrees

Form: two phrases: verse A ‖ Refrain B
Structure: a four-bar melody: Verse 2, Refrain 2.

The singer commences the song with the refrain, which is repeated by the chorus. The same formula is used at 'change of subject.' The song quickens slightly at the end.

LIV

Dh'éirich mi 's cha robh mi sunndach

Sung by Annie and Calum Johnston (Anna agus Calum Aonghais Chaluim), Barra

Form: four phrases: Verse A || Refrain B C D
Structure: an eight-bar melody: Verse 2, Refrain 6.

The song ended with the last four bars of refrain repeated, which implies that the first two bars of the refrain are solo refrain and the second and third chorus refrain. The singer commenced with the verse.

LV

Hùgan nan gù, théid mi dhachaigh

Sung by Miss Mary Gillies (Màiri Mhìcheil Nìll), Barra

(*With chorus*)

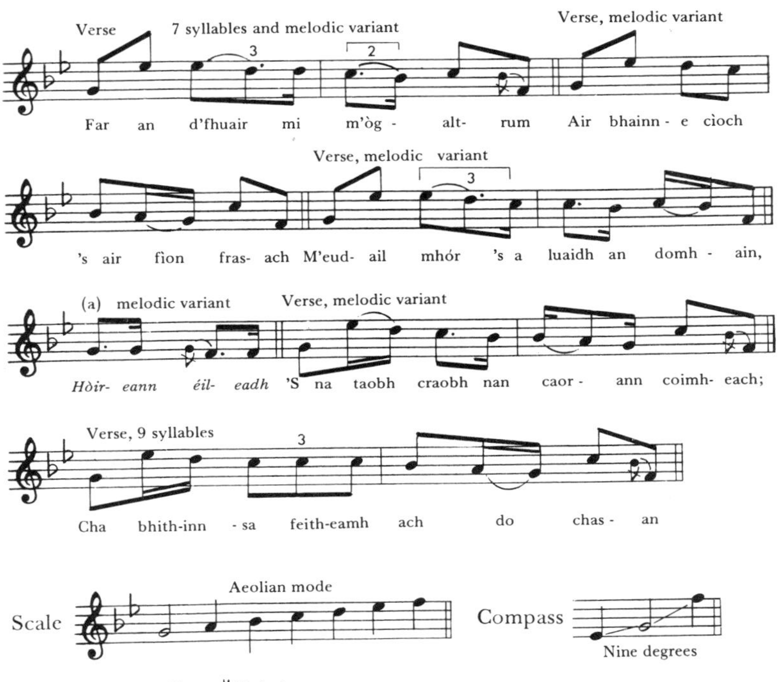

Form: four phrases: Verse A || Refrain B C D
Structure: an eight-bar melody: Verse, 2; refrain, 6.

LVI

Cha n-e uiseag a dhùisg mise

Sung by Mrs. Neil Campbell (Bean Nìll), South Uist

(*Without chorus*)

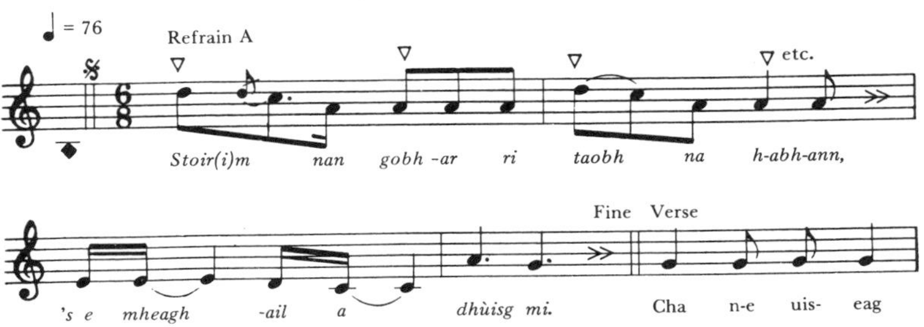

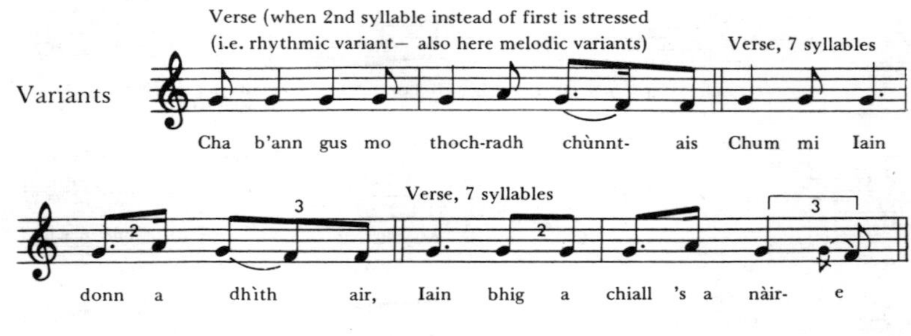

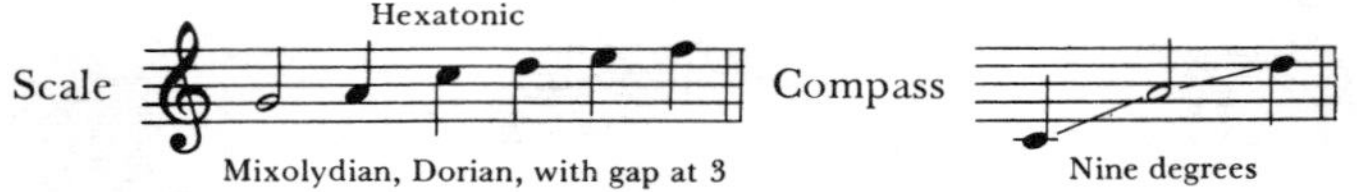

Form: Four phrases: A B[1] C B[2].
Structure: an eight-bar melody:
Refrain A, 4 bars; Verse 2; Refrain B, 2.

In the second and third variants, 'Iain' is probably a late substitution for 'Seathan', as elsewhere.

The singer sang the melody consistently in the above sequence, *i.e.* beginning the stanza with the long refrain A, followed by the verse, followed by the short refrain B. She made a substantial breath pause each time after the short refrain, and obviously regarded the tune as finishing there, commencing afresh with the long refrain A, as written here. This is unusual.

LVII

Tha 'n crodh an diu dol air imprig

Sung by Mrs. Angus John MacLellan (Penny Aonghais, 'ic Raghnaill), Benbecula

(*Without chorus*)

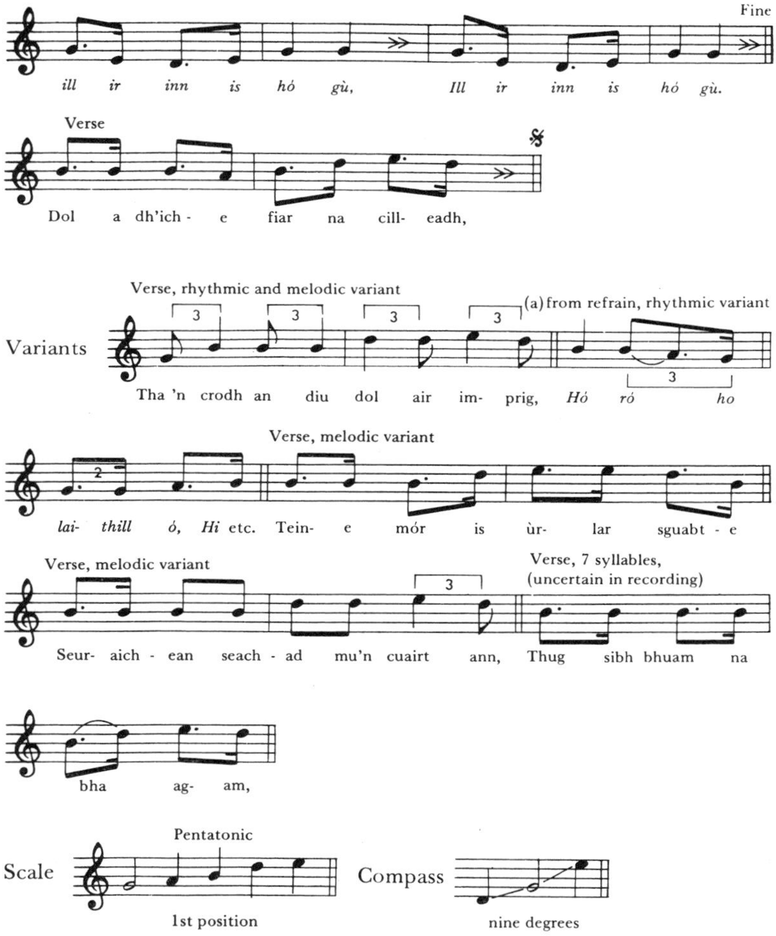

Fine

ill ir inn is hó gù, Ill ir inn is hó gù.

Verse

Dol a dh'ich - e fiar na cill- eadh,

Variants

Verse, rhythmic and melodic variant

Tha 'n crodh an diu dol air im- prig,

(a) from refrain, rhythmic variant

Hó ró ho lai- thill ó, Hi etc.

Verse, melodic variant

Tein- e mór is ùr- lar sguabt - e

Verse, melodic variant

Seur- aich - ean seach - ad mu'n cuairt ann,

Verse, 7 syllables, (uncertain in recording)

Thug sibh bhuam na bha ag- am,

Form: five phrases: Verse A || Refrain B C D D
Structure: a nine-bar melody: Verse 2; Refrain 7.

The singer commenced the song with the full refrain, of which the first prase would probably be a solo refrain at an actual waulking, or in performance with a chorus. The opening line is sung to what is probably a melodic variant. As nearly every line differs from the others melodically however, it is difficult to say what the *basic* version of the melody should be. The singer, who was the only person we found to know the air of this song at all, only knew a few lines of the words.

LVIII

Mo shùil silteach, mo chridhe trom

(*a*) Sung by Miss Kate MacDonald (Ceit Dhunnchaidh), South Uist

(*Without chorus*)

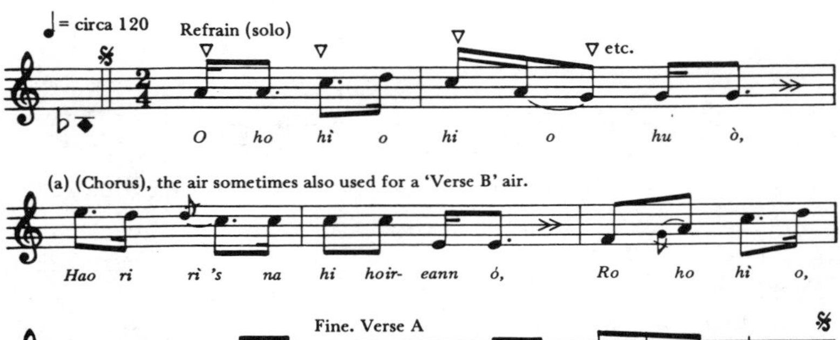
♩ = circa 120
Refrain (solo)
etc.
O ho hì o hi o hu ò,
(a) (Chorus), the air sometimes also used for a 'Verse B' air.
Hao ri rì 's na hi hoir- eann ó, Ro ho hì o,

Fine. Verse A
3
hi o hu o. Mo shùil silt - each, mo chridh- e trom.

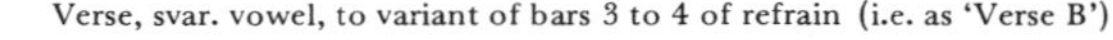
Verse, svar. vowel, to variant of bars 3 to 4 of refrain (i.e. as 'Verse B')

Variants
Mu'n òg bhuidh-e cham-(a) -lag - ach dhonn,

Verse A, svar. vowel
Verse B, melodic variant
Dh'fhal-(a)bh an dé air bharr-aibh nan tonn. Cha b'e 'n coit - e

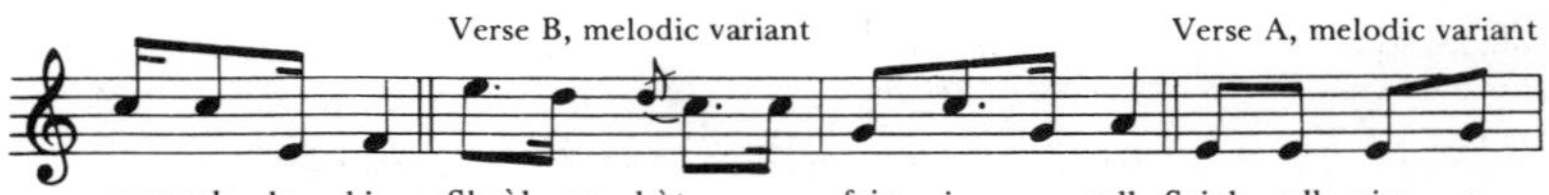
Verse B, melodic variant
Verse A, melodic variant
corr-ach do mhiann Sheòl am bàt - a fair - is a null, Sgiob - adh oirr- e

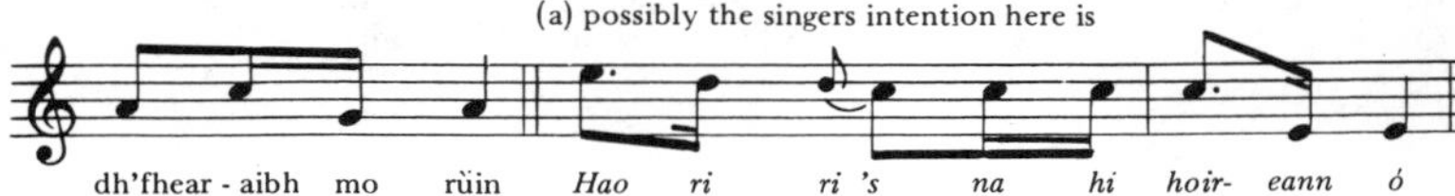
(a) possibly the singers intention here is
dh'fhear - aibh mo rùin *Hao ri ri 's na hi hoir- eann ó*

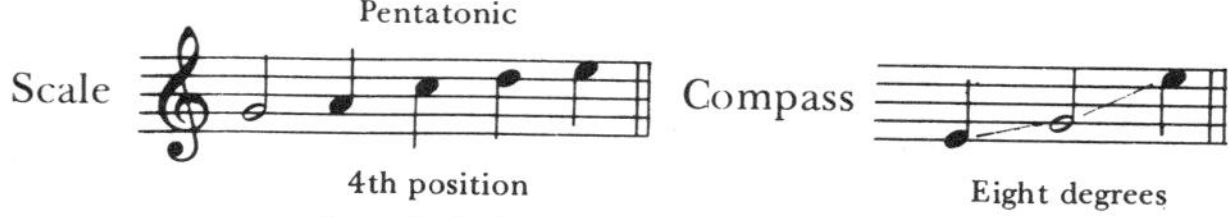

Form; four phrases, Verse A || Refrain B C B
Structure; an eight-bar melody: Verse, 2; Refrain, 6.

The singer commenced the song with the chorus refrain. She thereafter lightened her task by singing the first phrase of the refrain only, i.e. bars 1 and 2. Thereafter, she used a variant of the tune of bars 3 and 4 for the verse line, turning it therefore into a Verse B, and the whole tune into a Verse and refrain A, Verse and refrain B structure.

The metre of this song, 8[1], is a very unusual one and gives rise to much variation in the positions of stressed syllables within the lines, producing melodic variations.

LVIII

Mo shùil silteach, mo chridhe trom

(*b*) Sung by Miss Kate MacMillan (Ceit Ruairi), Benbecula

(*Without chorus*)

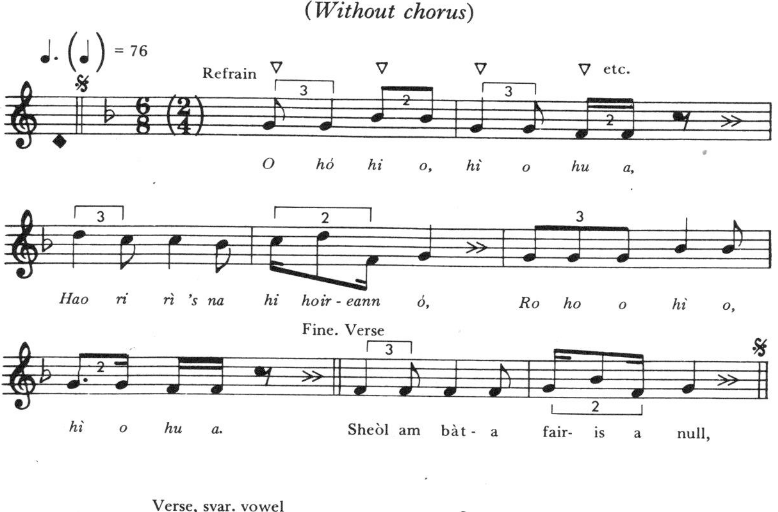

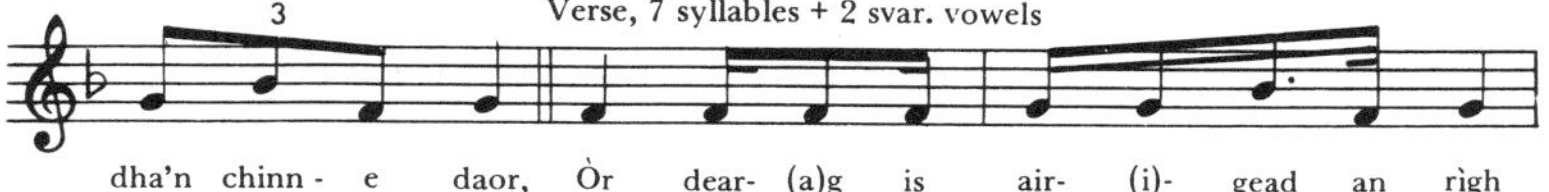

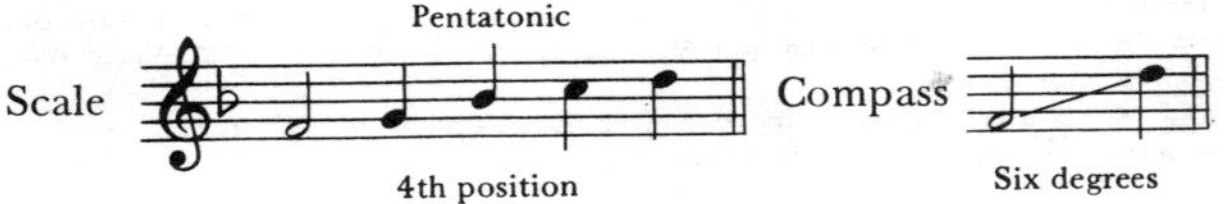

Form; four phrases, Verse A ‖ Refrain B C B
Structure; an eight-bar melody; Verse 2; Refrain 6.

The singer commenced the song with the verse. In an actual waulking the song would begin with the refrain. The quaver rest in the vocal line at the end of the refrain is unusual, but is quite distinct, and recurrent in the recording. This is probably the regular version, without any 'Verse B'; the singer, a very good one, belonged to an older generation.

LIX

Chì mi ghrian 's i falbh gu siùbhlach

Sung by Mrs. Mary Johnston (Màiri Iain Choinnich), Barra

(*With chorus*)

Variants
melodic variant
É ho hi o ho, hi iù ra bhó,
Ho ró ho hì o hó hì, Na
hao ri ri ó ho, hi iù ra bhó. Ho ró ho hì,
(a) melodic variant
(b) rhythmic variant
(a) melodic variant
Hi iù ra bhó. Ho ro ho hì ó ho hì, Na etc.
Verse, svar. vowel
Chì mi ghrian 's i fal- (a)bh gu siùbh- lach
Verse, svar. vowel
O, 's i dol tim- (i) - cheall Rubh' an Dùin - e

Hexatonic

Scale — Dorian-Aeolian, with gap at 6; Compass — Eleven degrees

Form; four phrases, Verse A || Refrain B C D
Structure; an eight-bar melody; Verse 2; Refrain (solo) 2, (chorus) 4.

The singer commenced the song with the refrain, in a melodic variant as set down below. The basic metre is 8^2. The first two lines sung contain svarabhakti vowels, and are therefore shown below as variants. The third line is set below the music.

LX

'S trom an dìreadh

Sung by Mrs. Effie Monk, Benbecula

(*Without chorus*)

= 58
Refrain
(d)
etc.
E ho a hó 'S trom an dìr -eadh.
(c)
Hì hoir-eann ó, 'S trom an dìr - eadh, É ho a hó
(e)
Fine. Verse (b)
(a)
'S trom an dìr - eadh, Chì mi Rum is Eig' is Ìl - e,
Refrain
É ho a hó.'

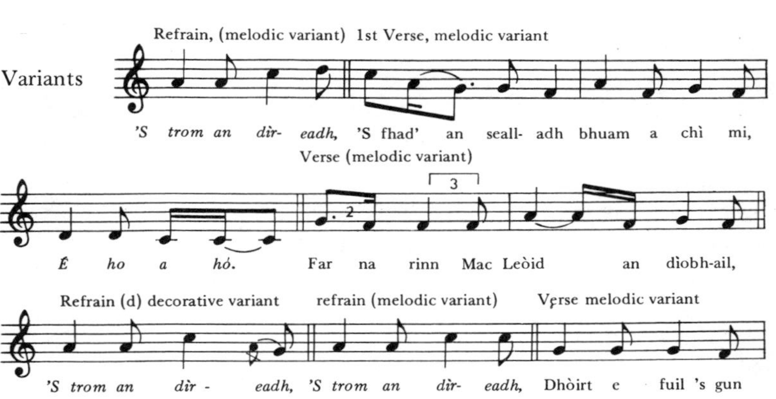

Variants
Refrain, (melodic variant) 1st Verse, melodic variant
'S trom an dìr- eadh, 'S fhad' an seall- adh bhuam a chì mi,
Verse (melodic variant)
3
É ho a hó. Far na rinn Mac Leòid an dìobh-ail,
Refrain (d) decorative variant refrain (melodic variant) Verse melodic variant
'S trom an dìr - eadh, 'S trom an dìr- eadh, Dhòirt e fuil 's gun

Verse
chaisg e ìot- adh, Chì mi Barr- aidh, an tìr ìs- eal
Verse (a)
Verse (b)
Refrain (c) with verse words
Nam fear fial - aidh Far an dian- ar Có nì sùg - radh
Refrain (e) with verse words.
É ho a hó Có nì sùg- radh? Có nì 'n gunn - a
Refrain (d) decorative variant
caol a ghiùlain? *'S trom an dìr - eadh,*
Pentatonic
Scale
3rd position
Compass
Eight degrees

Form; four phrases; A¹, A² = A¹ transposed, A³, A² = A¹ transposed.
Structure: an eight-bar melody; Verse 2, Refrain 6.

The singer commenced as in the transcription.
The overlapping of verse and refrain across the musical phrase is unusual. The metre is, as usual, 8^2.

LXI

Cha déid mi a Chille Moire

Sung by Mrs. John Galbraith (Mór Iain Dhòmhnaill Phàdruig), Barra

(*With chorus*)

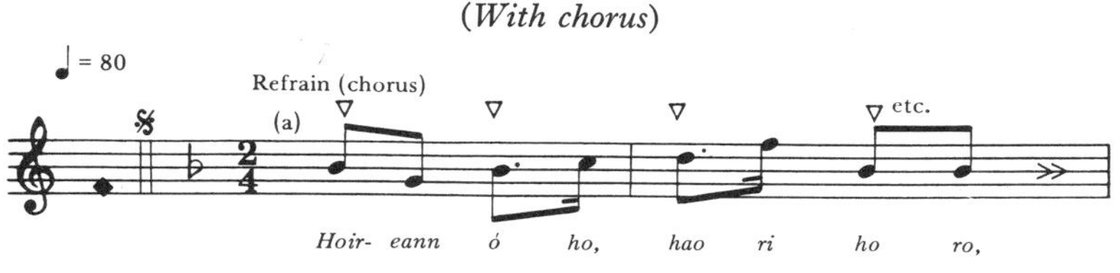
♩ = 80
Refrain (chorus)
(a)
etc.
Hoir- eann ó ho, hao ri ho ro,

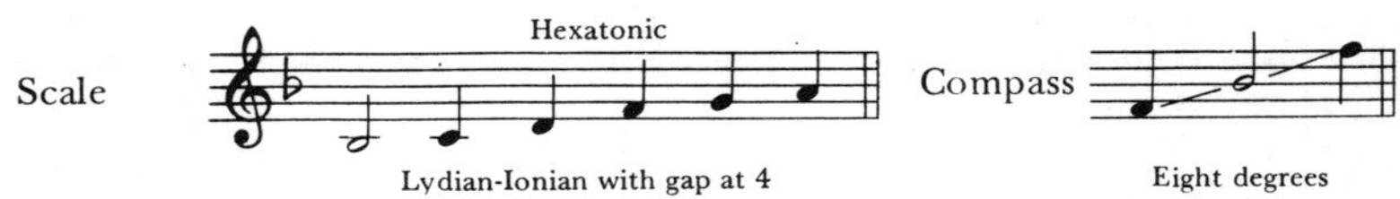

Lydian-Ionian with gap at 4 Eight degrees

Form; four phrases: Verse A ‖ Refrain B A B
Structure; an eight-bar melody: Verse, 2; Refrain (chorus) 2; (solo) 2; (chorus) 2.

The singer commenced the song with the chorus refrain, which is repeated by the chorus. The song ends with the chorus refrain, repeated by the soloist and repeated again by the chorus. The metre is 8^2. Each line except the first was sung twice; but the three-line refrain which presumably would alternate with the one-line refrain, was only sung once, i.e. after the first line. Throughout the rest of the song, only the first phrase of the refrain was sung (by the chorus) and the solo refrain, to the syllables *Hùg is hùg is hùg is hoireann* was omitted.

LXII

Chaidh mis' a dh'Eubhal imprig

Sung by Mrs. Fanny McIsaac (Fanny nic Dhunnchaidh Ruaidh), Benbecula

(*Without chorus*)

♩ = 88
Refrain
etc.
(a)
Hem bó, ho luì leó, Ro chall- a leó
Fine
éil- eadh, Hem bó, ho luì leó.
Verse
'S thog mi gàrr - adh, lìon mi ioth- lann,

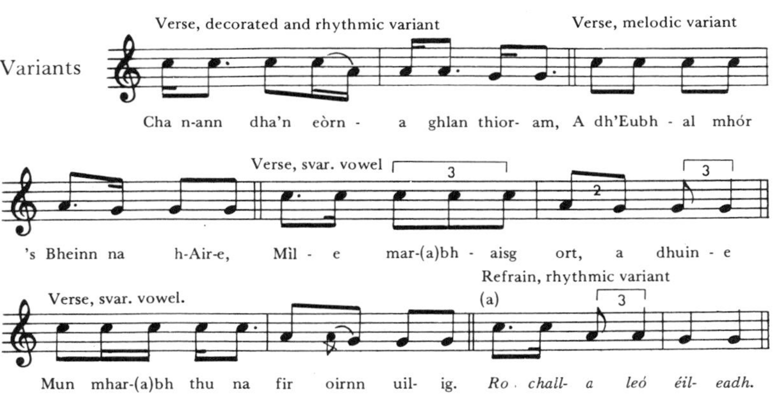

Variants
Verse, decorated and rhythmic variant
Verse, melodic variant
Cha n-ann dha'n eòrn - a ghlan thior- am, A dh'Eubh - al mhór
Verse, svar. vowel
3
2
3
's Bheinn na h-Air-e, Mìl - e mar-(a)bh - aisg ort, a dhuin - e
Verse, svar. vowel.
Refrain, rhythmic variant
(a)
3
Mun mhar-(a)bh thu na fir oirnn uil- ig. *Ro chall- a leó éil- eadh.*

Scale
Pentatonic
4th position
Compass
Six degrees

Form: four phrases: Verse A¹ ‖ Refrain B A² B
Structure: an eight-bar melody: Verse 2; Refrain 6.

The singer commenced the song with the verse. She did not strike the air correctly until the second verse, which is therefore set under the music.

LXIII

Chatriana a dh'fhalbhas gu banail

Sung by Mrs. Mary Johnston (Màiri Iain Choinnich), Barra

(*With chorus*)

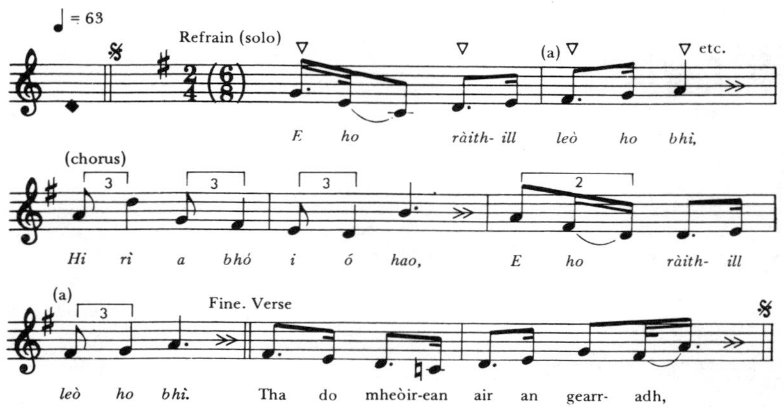

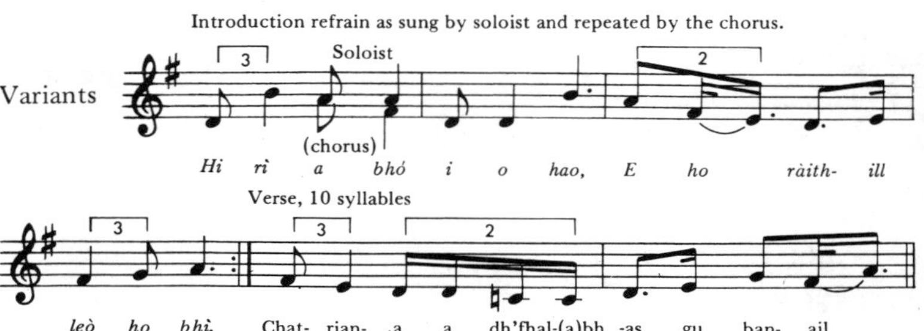

The second bar of the refrain and the corresponding sixth bar fluctuated between the following rhythms;

'Change of rhyme' (*atharraich*) is indicated by the following refrain sequence:

(Solo) *E ho ràithill leò ho bhì,*
(Chorus) *Hi rì a bhò i o hao,*
E ho ràithill leò ho bhì,
(Solo) *Hi rì a bhò i o hao,*
(Chorus) *E ho ràithill, leò ho bhì,*
Hi rì a bhò i o hao,
E ho raìthill, leò ho bhì.

Form: four phrases: Verse A || Refrain B^1 C B^2
Structure: an eight-bar melody: Verse 2, Refrain 6.

The singer commenced the song with the chorus refrain as usual, and this is repeated by the chorus in a variant of the tune, as shown in the variants above. The opening line however has nine syllables and a svarabhakti vowel, and is therefore shown as a variant below; and the second line of the poem, being regular, is here set below the music.

LXIV

O, 's e mo ghaol an Anna

(*a*) Sung by Miss Elizabeth Sinclair (Ealasaid Iain Dhunnchaidh), Vatersay

(*Without chorus*)

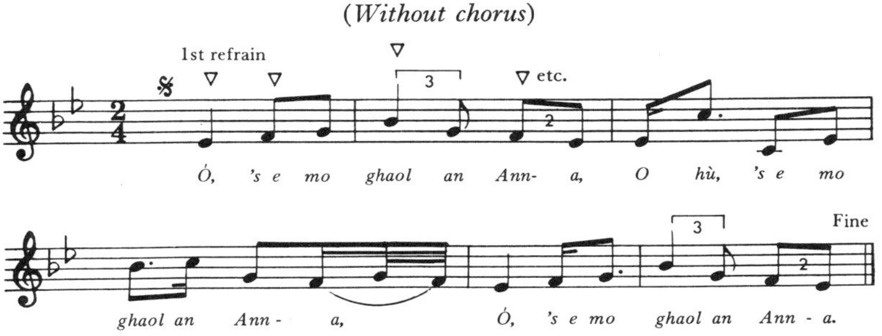

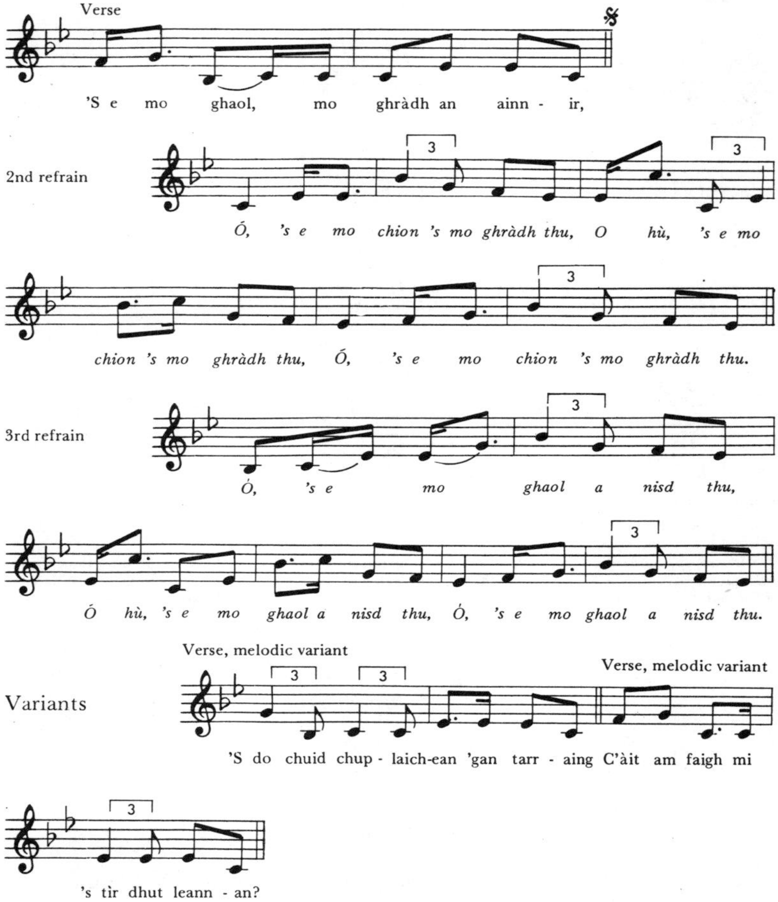

Verse

'S e mo ghaol, mo ghràdh an ainn - ir,

2nd refrain

Ó, 's e mo chion 's mo ghràdh thu, O hù, 's e mo chion 's mo ghràdh thu, Ó, 's e mo chion 's mo ghràdh thu.

3rd refrain

Ó, 's e mo ghaol a nisd thu, Ó hù, 's e mo ghaol a nisd thu, Ó, 's e mo ghaol a nisd thu.

Variants

Verse, melodic variant

'S do chuid chup - laich-ean 'gan tarr - aing

Verse, melodic variant

C'àit am faigh mi 's tìr dhut leann - an?

Form; 4 phrases: Verse A || Refrain B C B
Structure; an eight-bar melody: Verse 2, Refrain 6.

There are three different sets of refrain words, all written out above.

The recording, made on an Ediphone phonograph cylinder in 1949, and transcribed in 1951, is not now available for checking. Except in the first verse and refrain, the fitting of the text to the tune is consequently here tentative. The pitch and metronome speed were not noted.

LXIV

O, 'S e mo ghaol an Anna

(*b*) Sung by Mrs. Neil Campbell (Bean Nìll), South Uist, with Mrs. MacPhee and one or two others joining in the refrain

♩ (♩.) = 70

Refrain I. (Three lines)

(a)

Hó 's e mo ghaol an Ann- a,

(b) (c)

Ho hì, 's e mo ghaol an Ann - a, Hó, 's e mo

(d)

ghaol an Ann - a.

Verse

Bean a' chuail - ein chuach-aich chlann - aich,

Refrain II (four lines)

Ho hì, 's e mo ghaol a nisd thu,

(b)

Hó 's e mo ghaol a nisd thu, Ho hì 's e mo

ghaol a nisd thu, Hó 's e mo ghaol a nisd thu.

The first occurrence of Refrain II is of 4 lines (8 bars) as above.

Subsequent repetitions of this refrain are of the three lines only, commencing at ⊕ (i.e. 6 bars).

The first occurrence of Refrain III is of the two lines only, from the beginning to ⧖ (i.e. 4 bars). Subsequent repetitions of this refrain are of three lines, commencing at ⧖ to end (i.e. 6 bars) of refrain. The mark ↓ at the fifth bar indicates that the B♮ is slightly flattened (in both refrains I & II).

Refrain III

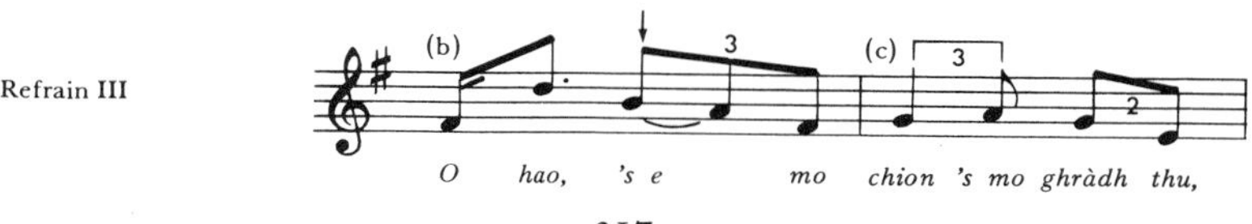

Hó 's e mo chion 's mo ghràdh thu. O hì, 's e mo
chion 's mo ghràdh thu, Hó 's e mo chion 's mo ghràdh thu.
Refrain IV
O hao, 's e mo luaidh 's mo ragh- ainn thu,
(a)
Hó 's e mo luaidh 's mo ragh- ainn thu, O hao 's e mo
(c)
luaidh 's mo ragh- ainn thu, Ó 's e mo luaidh 's mo ragh- ainn thu.

The first occurrence of Refrain IV is of four lines (8 bars) as above. Subsequent repetitions of this refrain are of the last three lines only (i.e. 6 bars).

Variants
(a) melodic variant
(b) melodic variant
ghaol an Ann - a, Ho hì 's e mo
melodic variant
(b)
(c) melodic variant
ghaol an Ann- a, Ho hì, 's e mo ghaol a nisd thu
Verse, svar. vowel
Verse, interesting rhythmic variant
Dh'fhal-(a)bh mo ghaol à dh'Eil- ar- Nis bhuam, Stior- ap - an fo d'
Verse of 9 syllables
bhròg- an àrd- a. Leag- ar fiadh bho thùs na greigh-eadh leat,
(d) melodic variant
Ending as sung
(d) melodic variant
Fine
ghaol an Ann- a. Ó, 's e mo ghaol an Ann- a.

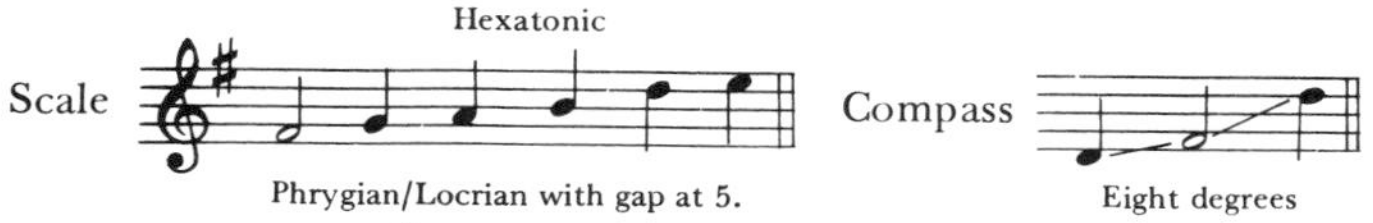

Form: 4 phrases; Verse A || Refrain B C B
Structure: an eight-bar belody; Verse 2, Refrain 6.

The chorus singers are uncertain of the melody, particularly towards the end of the refrain, and occasionally even end the refrain in the wrong key (a tone too low). The proper key is generally restored by the soloist, but she also lowers the key of the song more than once. It is in consequence difficult to establish the basic melody.

SCALE: The melody ends nearly every time on the note G as the last note of the refrain, though the feel of the tune suggests D as the 'keynote.' The actual conclusion of the song however is distinctly on the note F sharp, as shown in the *ending as sung*, above. If this is accepted as the final of the mode, it gives the scale as shown. The singer commenced with the refrain.

LXV

'S moch an diu a rinn mi éirigh

Sung by Mrs. Neil Campbell (Bean Nìll), South Uist

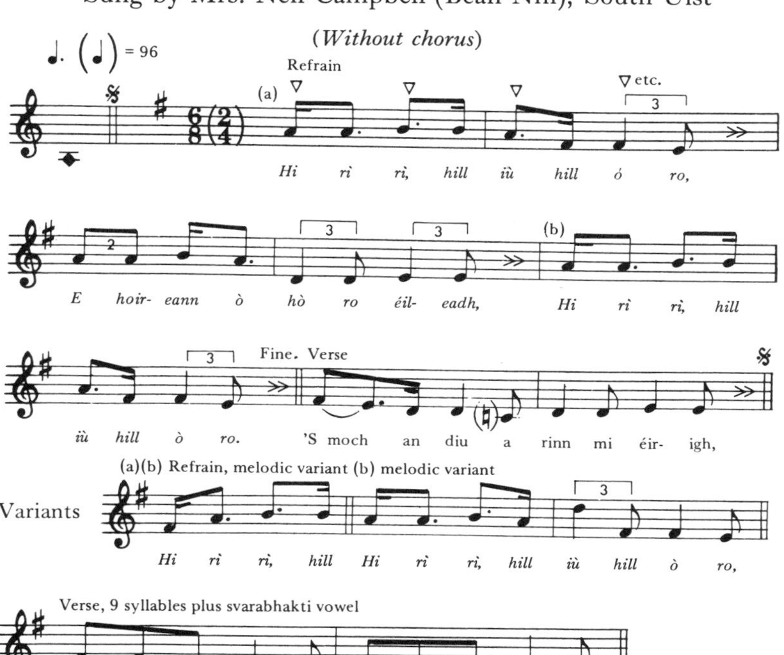

Hexatonic
Scale
Aeolian, gap at 3
Variant
Compass
seven degrees (nine in variant)

Form: four phrases: Verse A || Refrain B, C, B
Structure; an eight bar melody: Verse, 2; Refrain, 6.

The singer commenced the song with the complete refrain.

Before the first change of subject, after the usual three line refrain is sung, the singer repeats the last two lines (i.e. four bars) of the refrain (presumably chorus refrain). At the corresponding second change, the ordinary three-line refrain was sung once only, doubtless to lighten the task of the singer in solo performance.

LXVI

Tha sneachd air na beannan Diùrach

Sung by Mrs. Catriana Campbell (Catriana Seònaid), South Uist

(*Without chorus*)

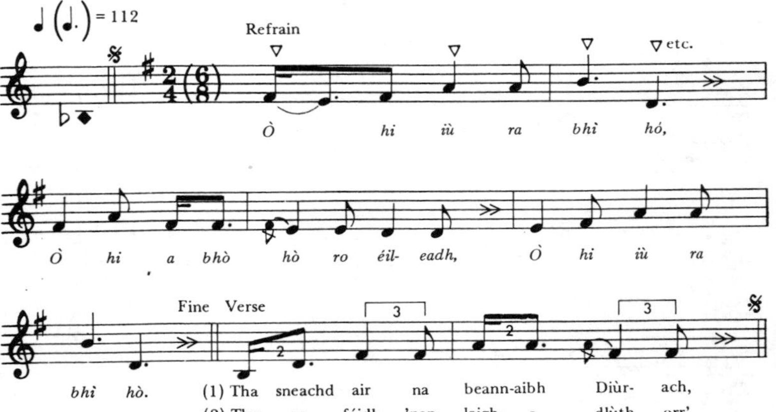
= 112
Refrain
etc.
Ò hi iù ra bhì hó,
Ò hi a bhò hò ro éil- eadh, Ò hi iù ra
Fine Verse
bhì hò.
(1) Tha sneachd air na beann-aibh Diùr- ach,
(2) Tha na féidh 'nan laigh- e dlùth orr'.

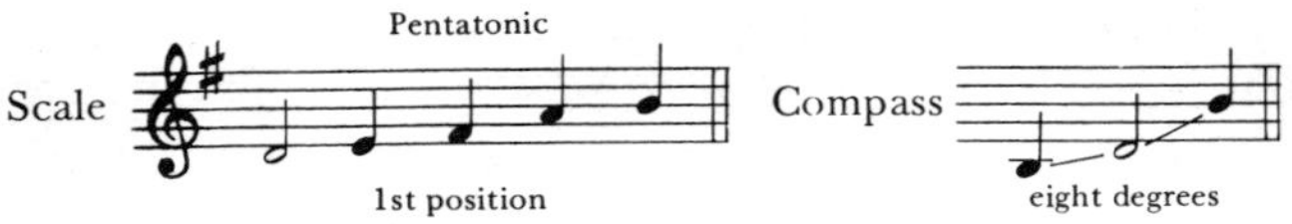
Pentatonic
Scale
1st position
Compass
eight degrees

Form; four phrases; Verse A || Refrain B C B
Structure; an eight-bar melody; Verse, 2; Refrain, 6.

The singer only sang two lines of the song. The metre is 8^2. A full text was recorded in Cape Breton from Mrs Neil MacInnis in 1937. The singer commenced with the verse.

LXVII

Cha déid Mór a Bharraidh bhrònaich

Sung by Annie and Calum Johnston (Anna agus Calum Aonghais Chaluim), Barra

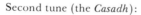

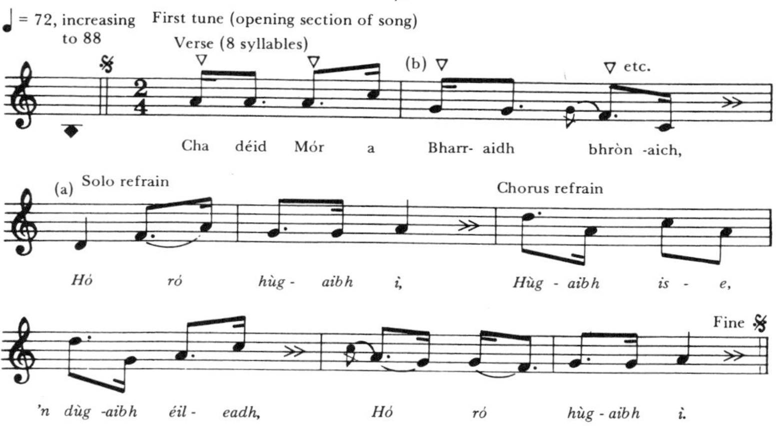

Variants

Second tune (the *Casadh*):

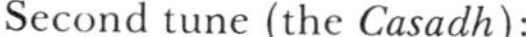

The singer commenced with the verse.

The final section, from the line *'S truagh nach robh thu seal air m' òrdan* returns to the first tune, verse and refrain, commencing with the chorus refrain, and accelerates from 92 to 104.

First tune

Form: four phrases: Verse A || Refrain B^1 C B^2
Structure: an eight-bar melody: Verse 2, Solo Refrain 2, Chorus Refrain 4.

The second tune (i.e. the 'Casadh' or middle section of the song) consists of one phrase of two bars repeated *ad lib.*, the sequence being Refrain, Verse, the final of the scale thereof falling on C, the last note of the verse. The tempo is quicker, and scale is different from that of the first tune, *i.e.*

Second tune

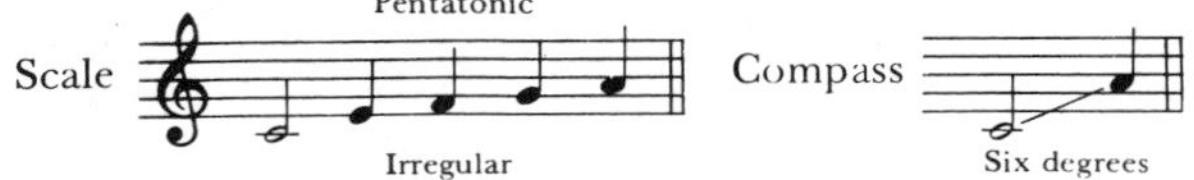

LXVIII

'S a Dhia! 's gaolach liom an gille

(*a*) Sung by Mrs. Neil Campbell (Bean Nìll Catriana), South Uist, with Mrs. Patrick MacPhee taking up the refrain

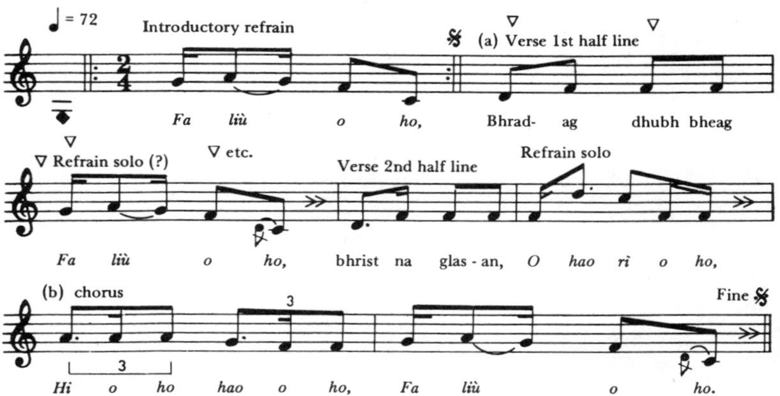

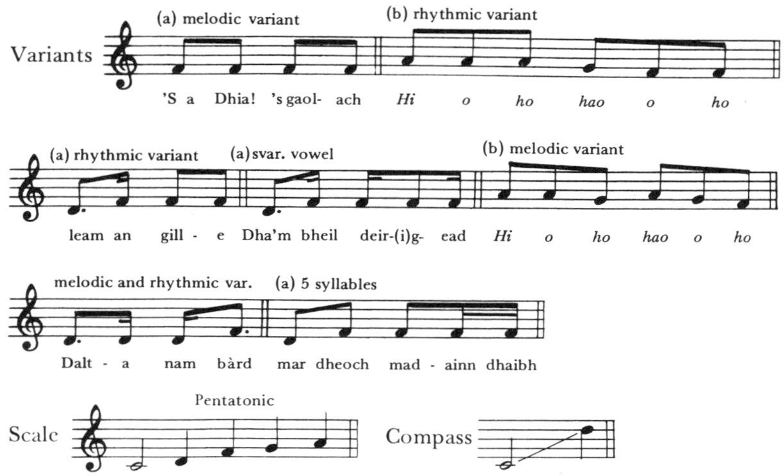

The note D in the scale only occurs a few times in either octave, and much of the tune is in the Pentachordal scale F G A B♭ C (1st inversion, i.e. commencing on G).

Form: three phrases: A B C.
Structure: a six-bar melody: Verse 1, Refrain 1
Verse 1, Refrain 3

The first complete line of text which is musically in regular and basic form, melodically, metrically and rhythmically is the one here set under the music.

The ending of the song with the longer of the two refrains forms an exception to the more usual ending with the shorter refrain (cp. Vol.1. p. 217). For a similar version of the text set out in full in detail, cp. the MacDonald Collection of Gaelic Poetry p. 230. This confirms the ending with the long refrain.

At an actual waulking the song would end with the soloist repeating the chorus refrain (i.e. the last two bars of the tune here) which would then be repeated in turn by the chorus

LXVIII

A bhradag dhubh a bhrist na glasan

(*b*) Sung by Annie and Calum Johnston (Anna agus Calum Aonghais Chaluim), Barra

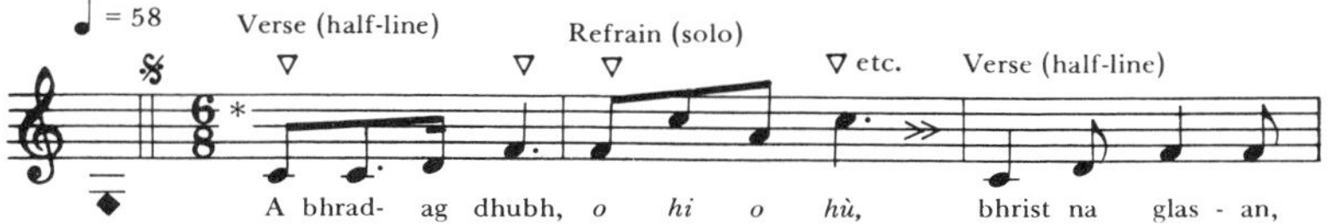

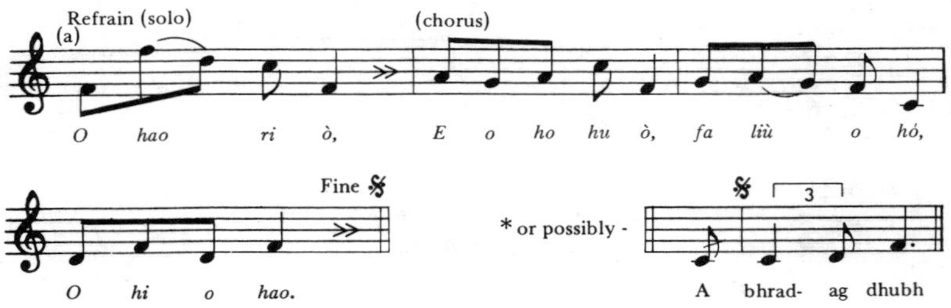

(1) This variant occurs frequently, but one gets the impression from the recording that high F is the note intended, not Eb.

(2) The syllable *Nan* falls into the time of the previous bar, as indicated. The rhythem of the verse air varies according as the stresses fall. Stress on the first and the third syllable is normal, but it can fall on the second and fourth. For example, (syllables 1 and 3) bhríst na glàsan; (2 and 4) A bhràdag dhúbh; (1 and 4) Bhéireadh am fónn.'

E♭ occurs in the scale in a variant, but it is doubtful if the note is intentional. It would make the scale hexatonic (Mixolydian with gap at 4).

Form: three phrases: A B C. (B commences similarly to A).
Structure: a seven-bar melody: Verse, 1; Refrain (solo) 1: Verse, 1; Refrain (solo) 1, Chorus 3.

The metre is 8^2 divided into half-lines, each half line being followed by a bar of solo refrain. At the third line from the end of the song, i.e. from 'Sùrd air dannsa', the tempo accelerates to ♩ = 98.

The song commenced as above, with the verse sung solo by Annie Johnston, with no chorus.

LXIX

Tàladh Dhòmhnaill Ghuirm

Sung by Mrs. Neil Campbell (Bean Nìll), South Uist

(*Without chorus*)

♩= 96
Verse A (half-line)
etc.
Refrain A
[Ar liom gur h-i] *Ho nàil ì bhó ho,*
Verse B (half-line)
Refrain B
Fine
Ghrian 's i 'g éir - igh, *Ho nàil ì, ro ho ì.*

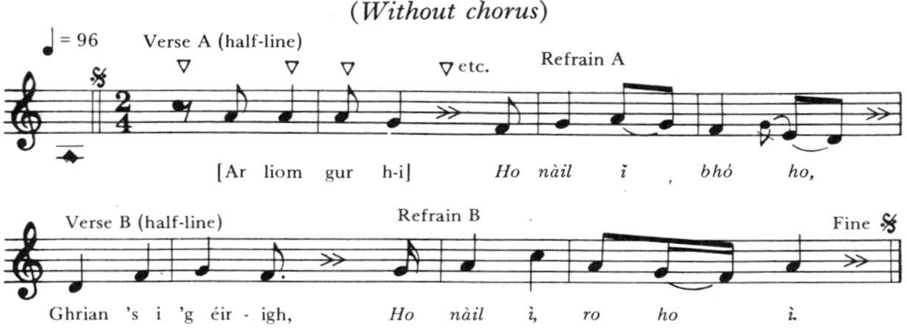

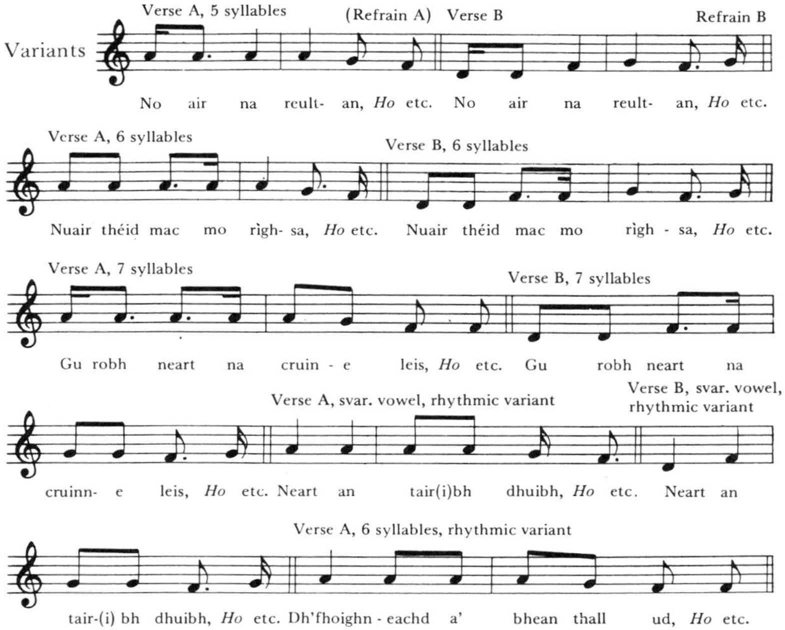

Variants
Verse A, 5 syllables
(Refrain A)
Verse B
Refrain B
No air na reult- an, *Ho* etc. No air na reult- an, *Ho* etc.
Verse A, 6 syllables
Verse B, 6 syllables
Nuair théid mac mo rìgh- sa, *Ho* etc. Nuair théid mac mo rìgh - sa, *Ho* etc.
Verse A, 7 syllables
Verse B, 7 syllables
Gu robh neart na cruin - e leis, *Ho* etc. Gu robh neart na
Verse A, svar. vowel, rhythmic variant
Verse B, svar. vowel, rhythmic variant
cruinn- e leis, *Ho* etc. Neart an tair(i)bh dhuibh, *Ho* etc. Neart an
Verse A, 6 syllables, rhythmic variant
tair-(i) bh dhuibh, *Ho* etc. Dh'fhoighn - eachd a' bhean thall ud, *Ho* etc.

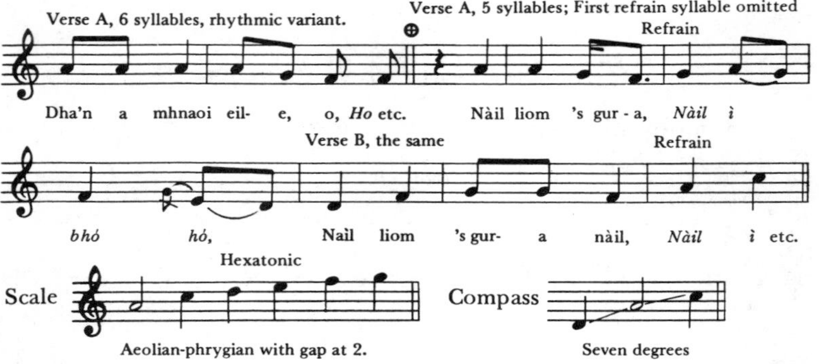

Form: four phrases: A B C D.
Structure: an eight-bar melody:
Verse A, 2; Refrain A, 2;
Verse B, 2; Refrain B, 2.

The singer commenced the song with Refrain A.

The metre varies frequently; the first five half-lines (ignoring repetitions) have four, five, six, and seven syllables. The first line of the text, *Ar liom gur h-i* is actually omitted in the recording. It is nevertheless set below the melody in the transcription, as the next regular pair of four syllable half-lines does not occur again until the seventh line of the song, and the melody is obvious from parallel four-syllable lines. The crotchet rest at ⊕ is most unusual, but the singer sings it thus both in the song and in a reprise of it at the end. The repetition of the line in Verse B contains more syllables, and the crotchet rest does not occur.

LXX

Chuala mi 'n dé sgeul nach b'ait liom

Sung by Mrs. Mary Johnston (Màiri Iain Choinnich), Barra

(*With chorus*)

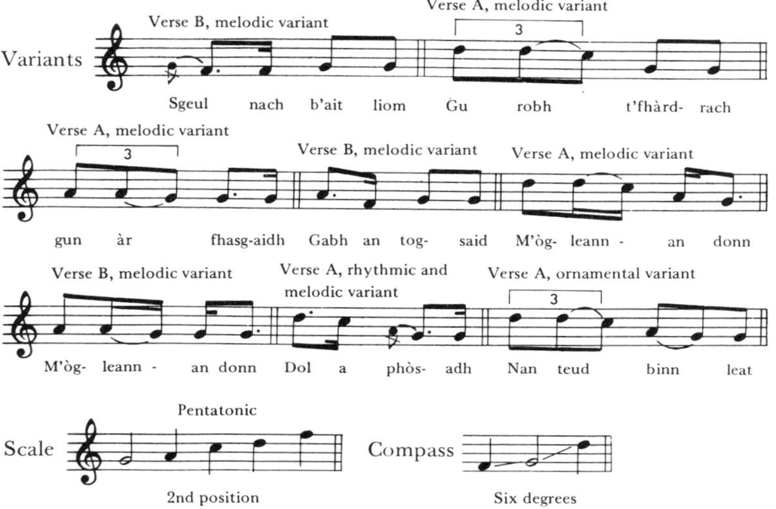

Form: three phrases: A B C.
Structure: a six-bar melody.
Verse A, 1; Refrain A, 3;
Verse B, 1; Refrain B, 1.

At change of subject, and at the end of the song, the soloist repeats refrain B after the chorus who then repeat it in their turn.

LXXI

Alasdair mhic Cholla gasda

Sung by Miss Mary Gillies (Màiri Mhìcheil Nìll), Barra

(*With chorus*)

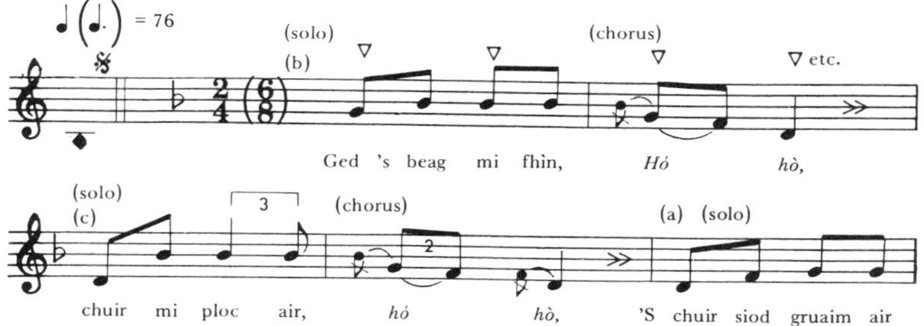

(chorus)
(solo)
(d)
(chorus)
hó hò, Niall a' Chaist- eil, trom éil- e.
Solo refrain
(chorus)
(g) (solo)
Chall éil - eadh i, Chall o ho ró, Chall éil - eadh i,
(chorus)
(solo)
Chall o ho ró, Chall- a na hao ri ri,
(e) (chorus)
(f)
Fine
Chall o ho ro ó, Hagh- aidh o ho ó, trom éil - eadh.
Singer's tentative opening 4 bars.
Variants
Al - as - dair mhic, hó hò, Choll- a gasd - a,
(a) melodic variant
(a) melodic variant
Hó hò, 'S bha Ni Loch- lainn Cha b'iaon- adh sin,
(b) melodic variant
(c) melodic variant
(b) melodic variant
Cha b'iaon- adh sin, b'fhiach a mac e, Dronnc- air, pòit- eir,
(a) melodic variant
(b) ornamental variant
(b) interesting svar. vowel
Sheinn-eadh pìob leat Dh'òl - adh fìon leat Glas - (a)ch -u beag
(d) 5 syllables and ornamented variant
(d) melodic variant
An déidh a chreach- adh. 'n oir an loch- ain

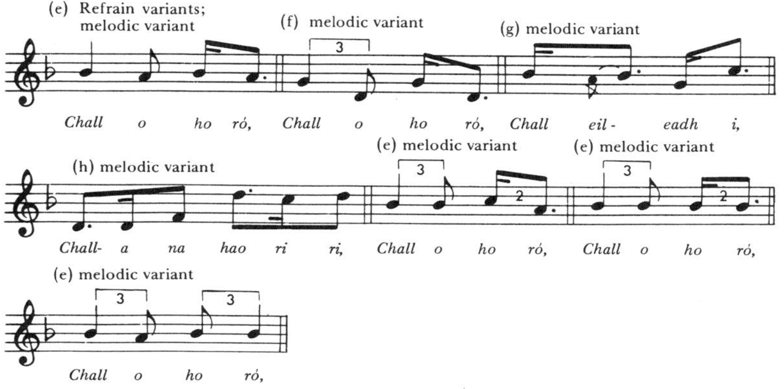

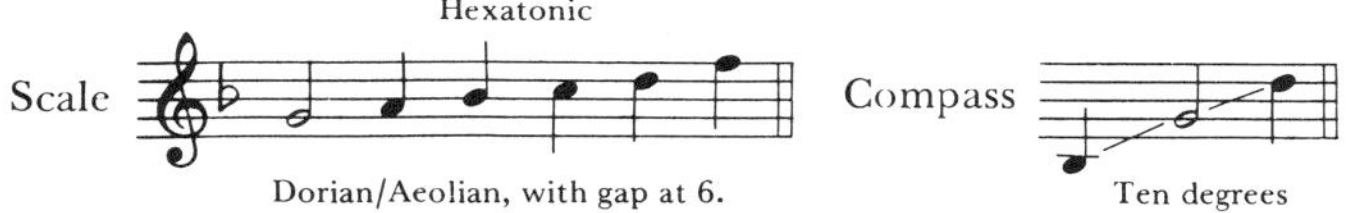

Form: 8 phrases: A^1 A^2 BC, DEFG.
Structure: a sixteen-bar melody:
Verse 1, Refrain 1, Verse 1, Refrain 1; Verse 1, Refrain 1; Verse 1, Refrain 1 (total 8)
followed by a long refrain of 8 bars.

The singer did not strike the correct melody in the first four bars (i.e. the first line of the text) these bars are included in the variants as a matter of interest.

By reason of svarabhakti vowels and of words omitted by the singer, the first complete pair of lines giving the basic melody is not reached until lines 8 (on its repetition) and 9 of the text, beginning *Ged's beag mi fhìn*; and these two lines are therefore set under the music.

The drop of an octave in the second bar of the refrain is not always accurately achieved by the singers, and one hears the interval of a 7th, 9th, and 10th at different times. These are not of course true i.e. intentional, variants.

LXXII

A phiuthrag 's a phiuthar

(*a*) Sung by Mrs. MacDougall (Anna Raghnaill Eachainn), Barra, with Miss Annie Johnston joining in the refrain

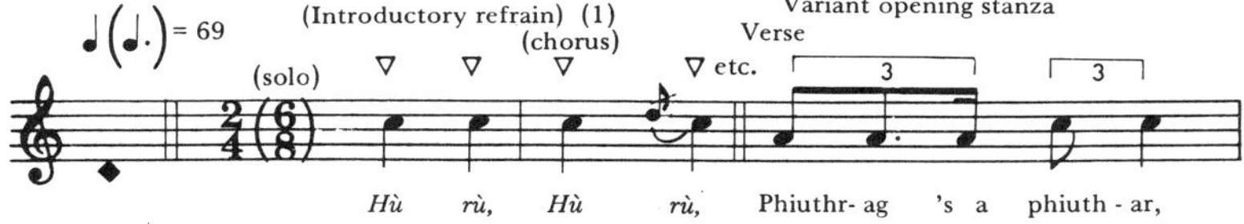

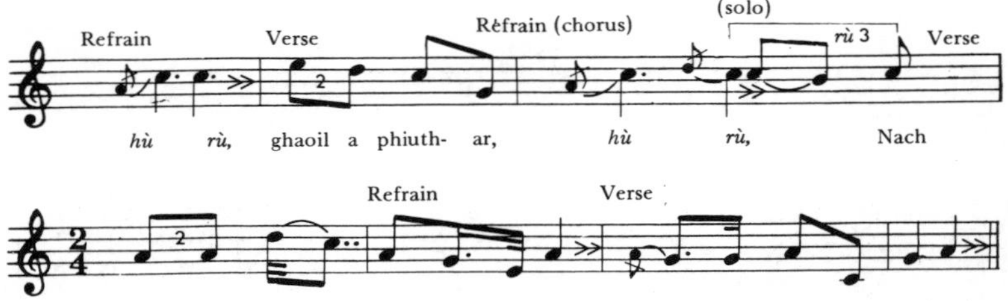
Refrain
Verse
Rẻfrain (chorus)
(solo)
rù 3
Verse
hù rù, ghaoil a phiuth- ar, hù rù, Nach
Refrain
Verse
truagh leat fhéin, ho hol ill eó, mi 'gad chumh - a, hù rù.

(1) These two bars are very faint on the recording, and are partly conjectural. They are in line with the customary formula.

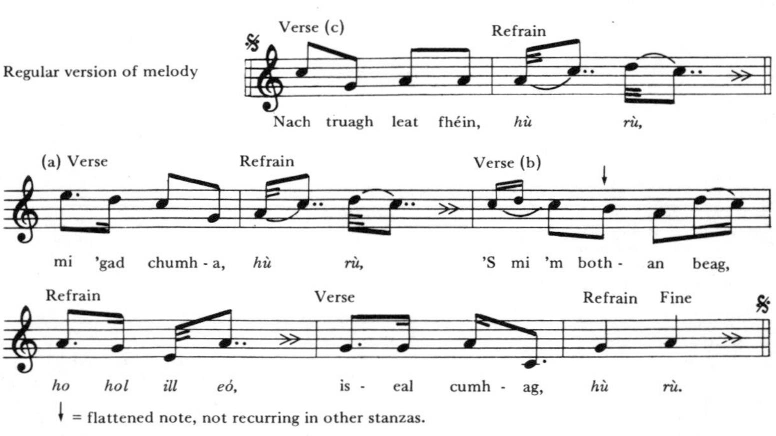
Regular version of melody
Verse (c)
Refrain
Nach truagh leat fhéin, hù rù,
(a) Verse
Refrain
Verse (b)
mi 'gad chumh - a, hù rù, 'S mi 'm both - an beag,
Refrain
Verse
Refrain Fine
ho hol ill eó, is - eal cumh - ag, hù rù.
↓ = flattened note, not recurring in other stanzas.

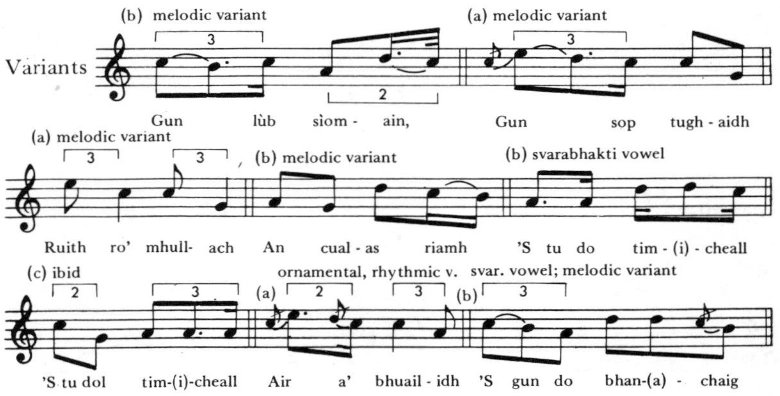
Variants
(b) melodic variant
(a) melodic variant
Gun lùb sìom - ain, Gun sop tugh - aidh
(a) melodic variant
(b) melodic variant
(b) svarabhakti vowel
Ruith ro' mhull- ach An cual - as riamh 'S tu do tim - (i) - cheall
(c) ibid
ornamental, rhythmic v.
svar. vowel; melodic variant
(a)
(b)
'S tu dol tim-(i)-cheall Air a' bhuail - idh 'S gun do bhan-(a) - chaig

Form: four phrases, A¹, A², B, C.
Structure: an eight-bar melody, each pair of bars consisting of a one-bar verse followed by a one-bar refrain.

The opening verse, besides differing melodically from the regular version, is a metrical variant, having five syllables instead of the normal four of the rest of the song.

LXXII

A phiuthrag 's a phiuthar

(*b*) Sung by Calum Johnston (Calum Aonghais Chaluim), Barra

(*Without chorus*)

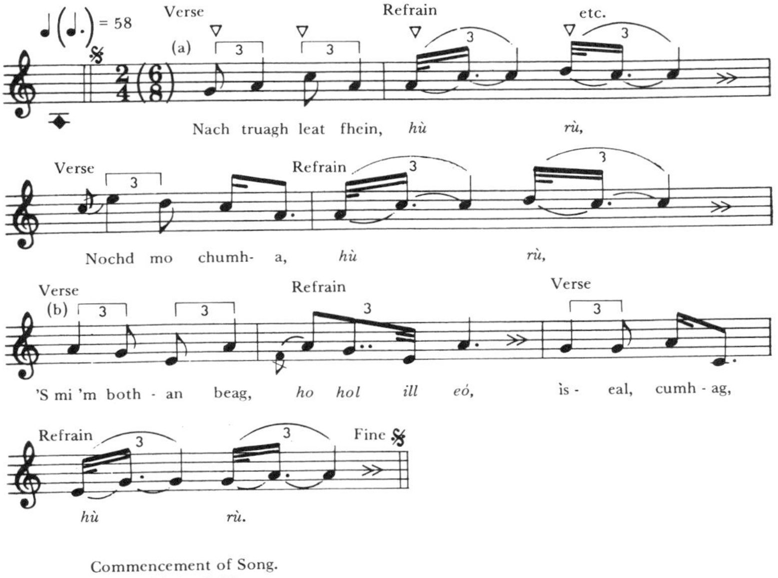

♩(♩.) = 58

Verse (a) — Refrain — etc.

Nach truagh leat fhein, *hù* *rù,*

Verse — Refrain

Nochd mo chumh- a, *hù* *rù,*

Verse (b) — Refrain — Verse

'S mi 'm both - an beag, *ho hol ill eó,* is - eal, cumh - ag,

Refrain — Fine

hù *rù.*

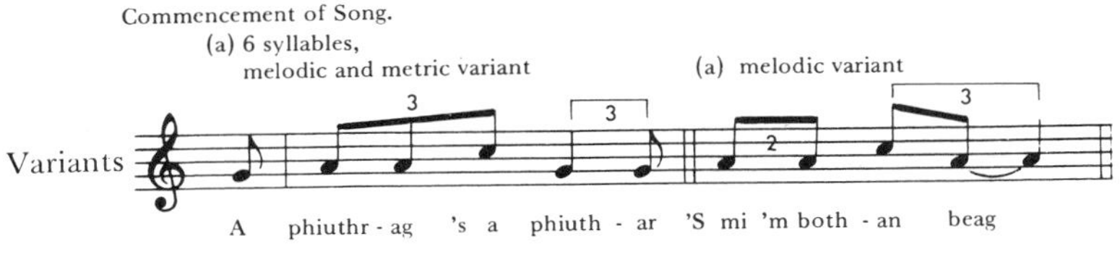

Commencement of Song.
(a) 6 syllables, melodic and metric variant — (a) melodic variant

Variants

A phiuthr - ag 's a phiuth - ar 'S mi 'm both - an beag

Form: four phrases: A[1] A[2] B C.

Structure: an eight-bar melody, each pair of bars consisting of a one-bar verse followed by a one-bar refrain.

The structure is therefore Verse 1, Refrain 1, Verse 1, Refrain 1, Verse 1, Refrain 1, Verse 1, Refrain 1.

The metre is 8[2] divided into half-lines. The opening line being of five syllables instead of four, is therefore a variant, and is included in this category. The second line, being regular, is set below the music. The vocative syllable 'A', commencing the song, which has possibly been added by the singer himself in the process of developing a solo version, makes an extra syllable to the existing five-syllable first verse, thus making six syllables in all.

LXXIII

'S muladach mi o chionn seachdain

Sung by Miss Annie Johnston (Anna Aonghais Chaluim), Barra

(*Without chorus*)

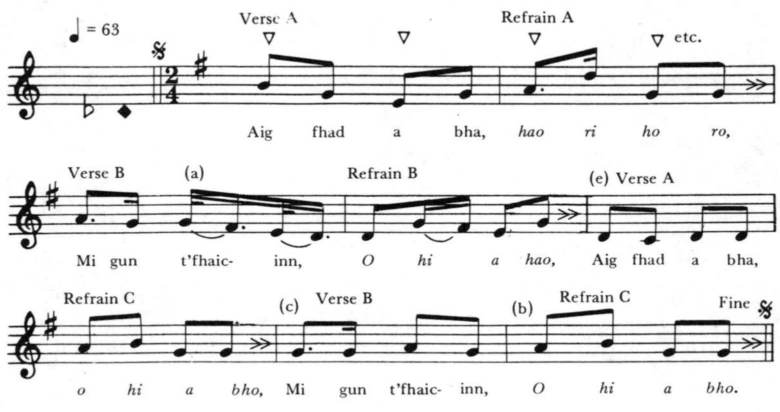

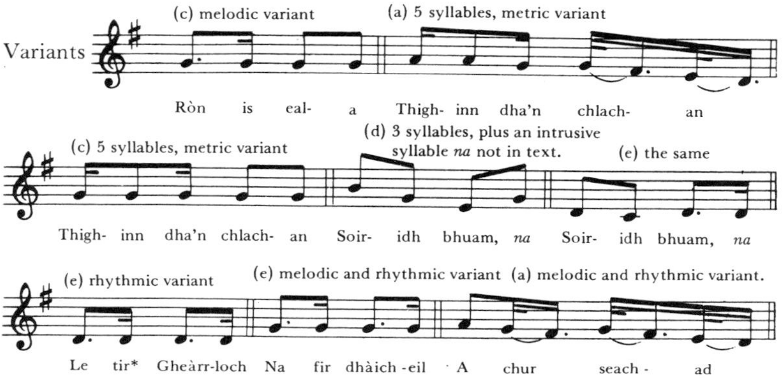

*The rhythm of the tune completely dominates the vowel lengths here, and *Le tìr* is pronounced like 'leitir.'

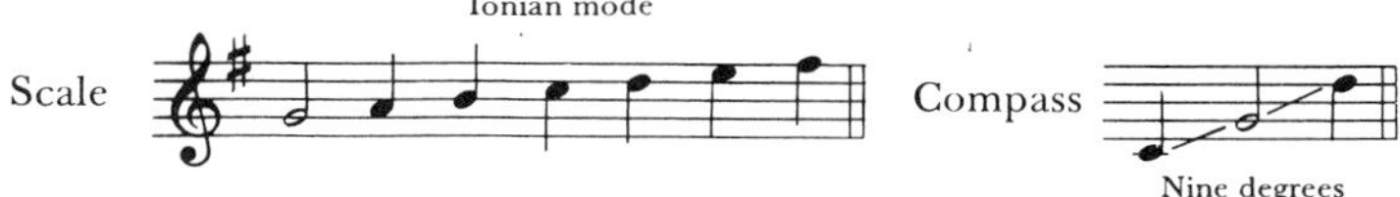

Form: 4 phrases, A B C D. There is similarity of ending between phrases A, C and D.
Structure: an eight-bar melody: Verse 1, Refrain 1, Verse 1, Refrain 1;
Verse 1, Refrain 1, Verse 1, Refrain 1.

The basic metre is of 4 syllables to the half line, but there are 5 and 3 syllable variants which are shown below. At (a) one or both pairs of dotted notes are sometimes sung as even semiquavers. Before the change of subject, the bar (b) is repeated twice by the singer. In an actual waulking the first repetition would be sung by the soloist and the second by the chorus.

LXXIV

Coisich, a rùin

(*a*) Sung by Miss Janet MacKinnon (Seònaid Shomhairle Bhig), Barra, with Mrs. MacCormick joining in the refrain

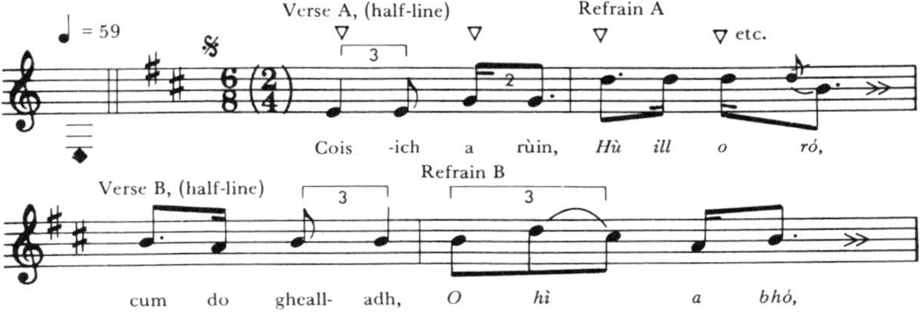

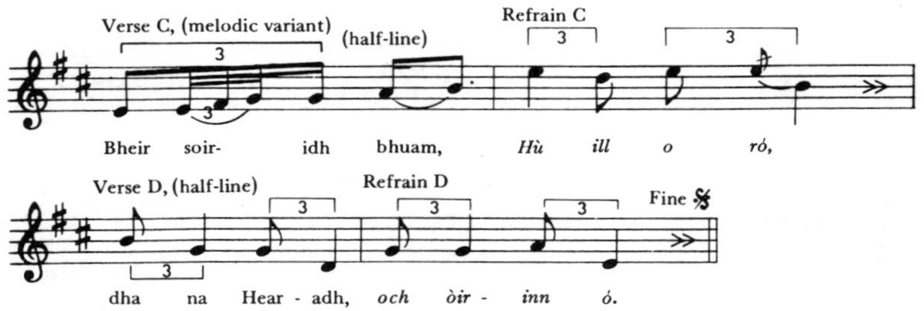

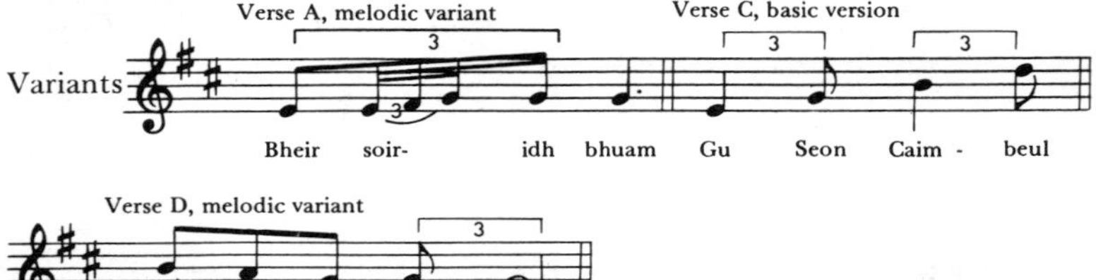

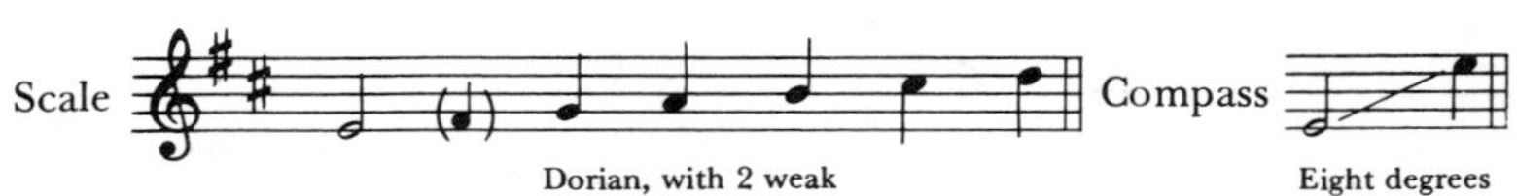

Dorian, with 2 weak

Eight degrees

(The 2nd degree is present in weak form, making the scale complete Dorian).

Form: Four phrases: A^1 B A^2 C.
Each of the four two-bar phrases consists of a half-line verse of one bar followed by a refrain of one bar.

Structure: an eight-bar melody:
Verse A, 1; Refrain A, 1; Verse B, 1; Refrain B, 1;
Verse C, 1; Refrain C, 1; Verse D, 1; Refrain D, 1.

In this song, as in all the others in this section, the metre is 8^2 divided into half-line 'verses'. When this song is sung in full, as at a waulking, each pair of half-lines, except the first and last, is repeated, the repetition coming on the other half of the tune. The formula then is *Aa, Bb, Ca, Dc; Da, Db, Ea, Ec* (counting Refrains A and C above as identical, which they are from the point of view of a traditional Gaelic singer.) When the song is sung as a solo, the repetition of pairs of half-lines is often not done, in which case each pair will come on different halves of the tune alternately.

LXXIV

Coisich, a rùin

(*b*) Sung by Mrs. Archie Munro (Màiri a' Ghobha), South Uist

(*Without chorus*)

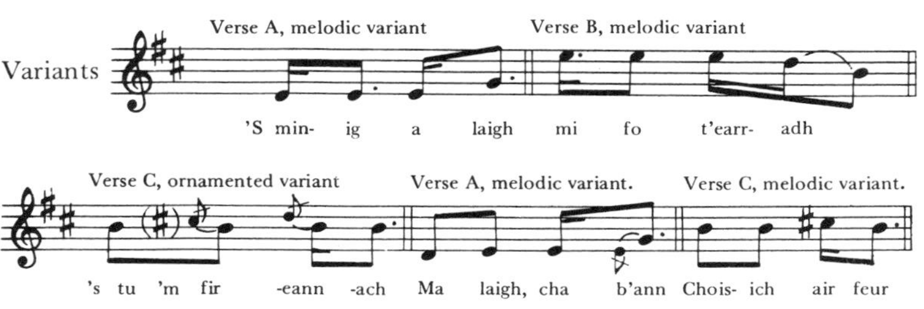

Form: four phrases: A B C D.
Structure: an eight-bar melody; Verse A, 1; Refrain A, 1; Verse B, 1; Refrain B, 1.
Verse C, 1; Refrain C, 1; Verse D, 1; Refrain D, 1.

The singer commenced the song with Verse A as above.

The metre, unvaried throughout, is 8^2 divided into half lines of 4 syllables. Except for the first and last pair of half lines, each pair is repeated, the repetition coming on the other half of the tune. The formula is Aa, Bb, Ca, Dc; Ca, Db, Ea, Fc, etc., counting Refrains A and C here as identical in having the same meaningless syllables and the same rhythm.

LXXIV

Coisich, a rùin

(*c*) Sung by Mrs. D. J. MacLellan (Màiri Mhìcheil), South Uist, at an actual waulking

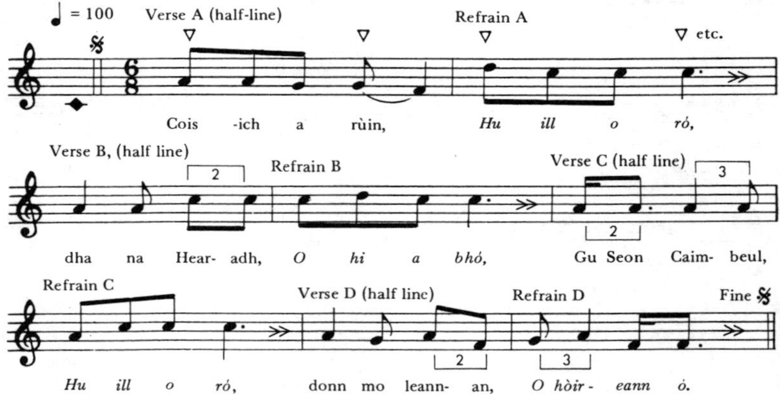

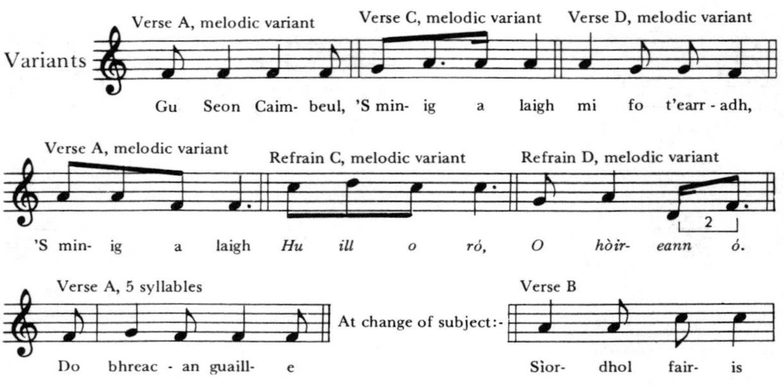

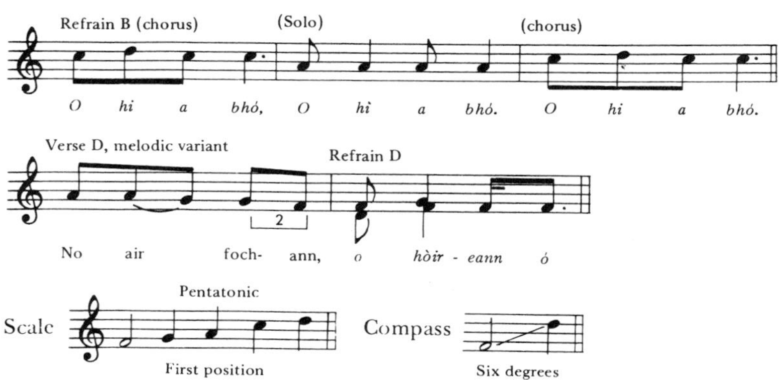

Form: four phrases: A[1] A[2] A[3] B.
Structure: an eight-bar melody:
Verse A, 1; Refrain A, 1; Verse B, 1; Refrain B, 1;
Verse C, 1; Refrain C, 1; Verse D, 1; Refrain D, 1.

The metre is 8^2, divided into half lines of 4 syllables. Each half-line, occupying one bar of music, is followed by a bar of chorus refrain.

LXXIV

Coisich, a rùin

(*d*) Sung by Mrs. Kate MacCormick (Catriana nighean 'Ill' Easbuig), Benbecula

(*Without chorus*)

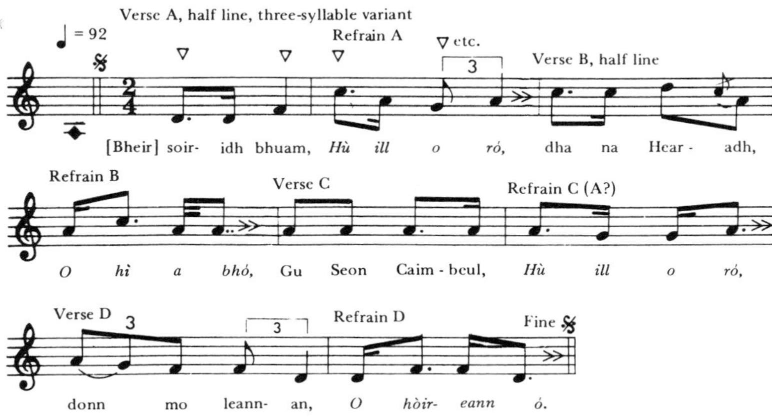

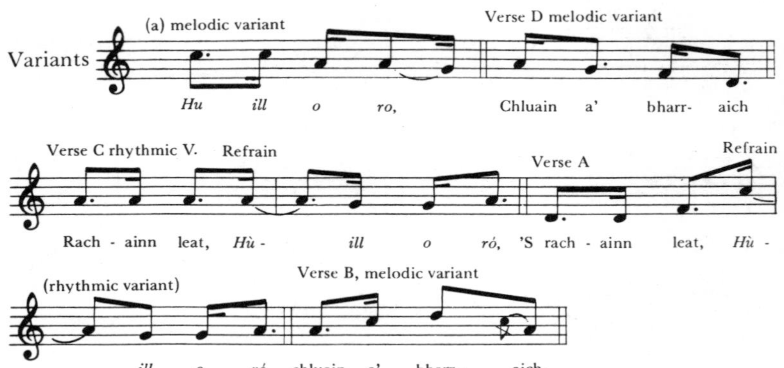

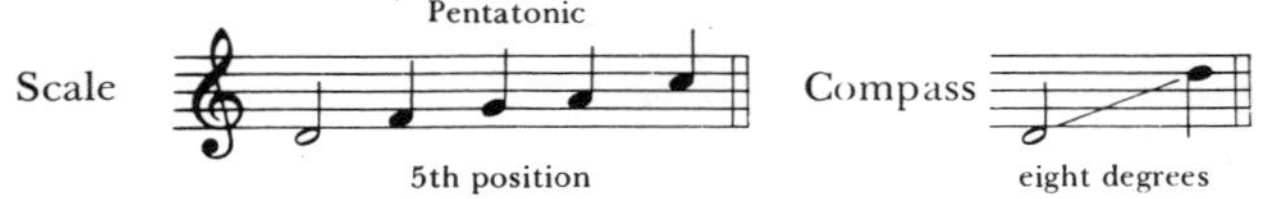

Form: four phrases: A B C D.
Structure: an eight-bar melody:
Verse A, 1: Refrain A, 1; Verse B, 1; Refrain B, 1;
Verse C, 1; Refrain C, 1; Verse D, 1; Refrain D, 1.

The basic metre consists of a couplet of two lines of 8^2 divided by short refrains of one bar in length, into two half lines of four syllables. The recording does not however contain a complete couplet of basic metre. The usual first word of the opening half-line, *Bheir*, is omitted, resulting in a three-syllable half-line. This is set under the music, but is marked as a variant. In performance, Bheir might be sung on D, as the last quaver of (an imaginary) previous bar.

At the three-syllable half-line, 'Rachainn leat', the refrain appears to anticipate the first beat of the second bar. This however is not normal and may not be intentional.

LXXV

A Mhic a' Mhaoir

(*a*) Sung by Roderick MacKinnon (Ruairi Iain Bhàin), Barra

(*Without chorus*)

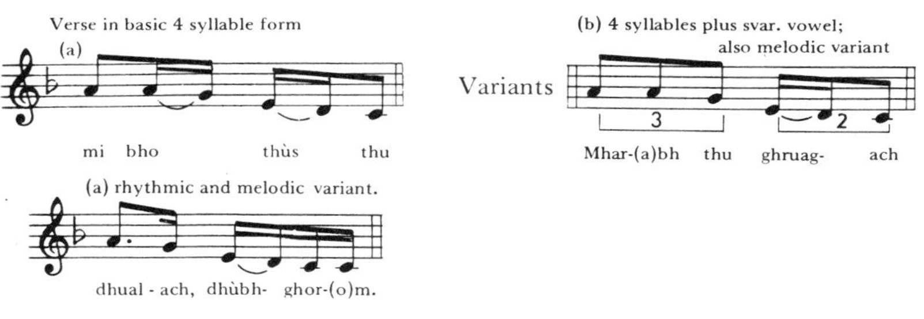

Form: 3 phrases: A[1] A[2] B.
Structure: 6 bars—Refrain 1, Verse 1, Refrain 1, Verse 1, Refrain 2.

The usual practice in this book of tabulating the structural description of the tune by setting down first the verse and then the refrain has to be departed from here, as the opening one-bar refrain obviously forms the first bar of a two-bar phrase, and cannot be detached from it.

The last bar is seemingly an idiosyncratic addition by the singer, to indicate, after pausing for breath, that the last bar should actually link up with the first without a break. The first note of this bar is fleeting and hard to catch and identify; it could be A, B flat, B natural or C. The device is quite exceptional, and the extra bar cannot be considered as part of the basic melody; e.g. it would not be sung at an actual waulking.

The basic metre of the song is 8^2 divided into half-lines, but the opening half line is followed by two half lines of five syllables (each repeated). The first of these, though a variant, is set under the music for convenience, in order to complete the full line of eight syllables. The basic four-syllable form of the verse air at that point is shown below.

The opening refrain syllable, *Hiù*, though really a diphthong, is sung by this singer as a dis-syllable, i.e. *Hi-ù*. It is however set down in its more usual one-syllable diphthong form.

LXXV

A Mhic a' Mhaoir

(*b*) Sung by Mrs. Murdo MacDonald (Bean Mhurchaidh 'a Bhealaich), Barra

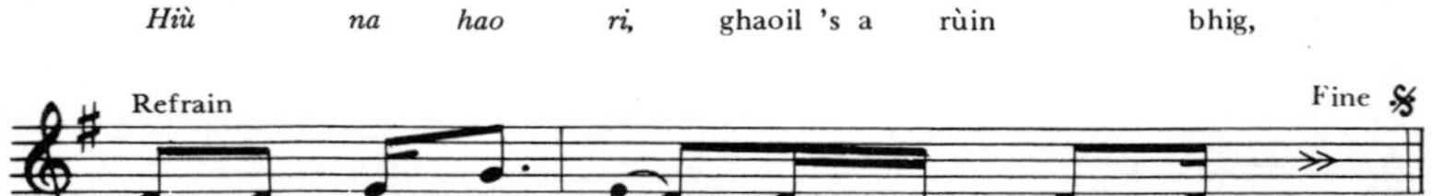

Refrain Fine
O hoir- eann ó, ro ho o éil - e.

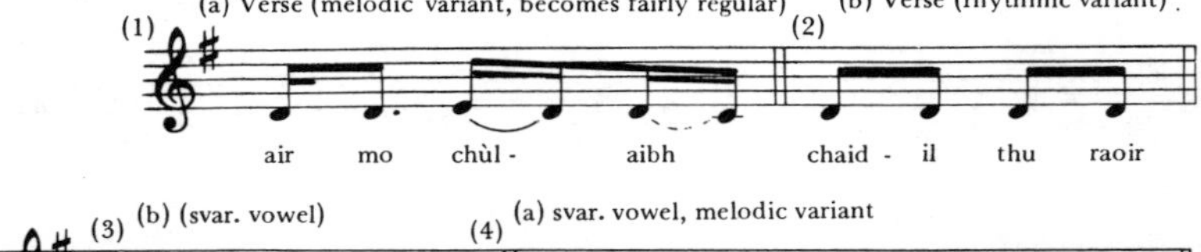

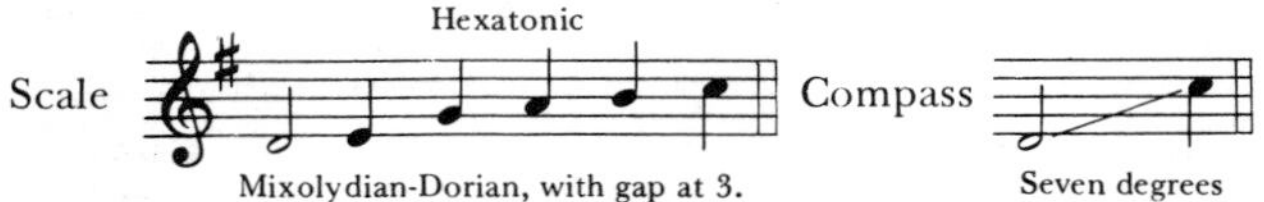

Form: three phrases, A A B.
Structure: a six-bar melody – refrain 1, ½ line verse, 1,
refrain 1, ½ line verse, 1.
refrain 2.

In bar 4 of the tune and in variants 1 and 4 the legato is broken between the last two quavers in the bar, although they are both sung to the same syllable. This is a frequent practice among some of the older traditional singers.

It is remarkable to find in primitive vocal melody such a sophisticated 'modern' melodic progression as two descending fourths as in bars 1 and 2, (repeated in bars 3 and 4). The first of the pair is of course slightly modified by the intervening grace-note. The singer commenced as above.

LXXVI

Mo rùn Ailein, hó hò

Sung by Miss Mary Morrison (Màiri Eóghainn Mhóir), Barra

(*With chorus*)

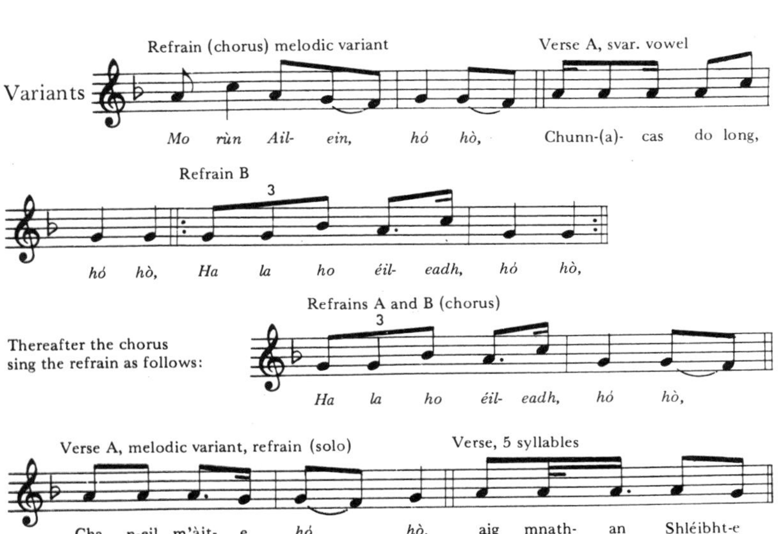

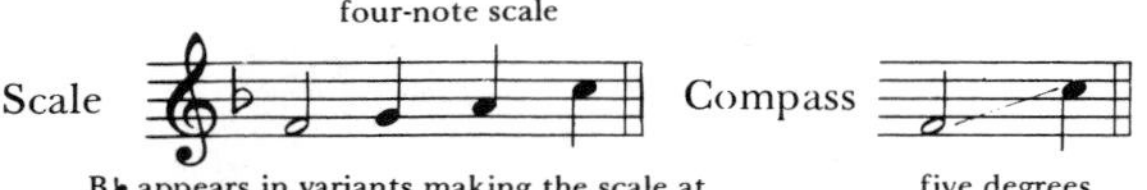

B♭ appears in variants making the scale at that point five-note pentachordal.

five degrees

Form: four phrases: A^1 B A^2 B.

Structure: an eight-bar melody:

Verse A, 1; Refrain A (solo) 1; (chorus) 2.

Verse B, 1; Refrain B (solo) 1; (chorus) 2.

The singer commenced the song with the chorus refrain sung solo, which was repeated by the chorus. The metre is 8^2 divided into half-lines. The tune of Verse A differs by only one note from Verse B; nevertheless the difference is regularly maintained. At the sixteenth line, the refrain words change to *Ha la ho éileadh*, in place of *Mo run Ailein.* The song ends with the refrain *Ha la ho éileadh* sung by the soloist and repeated by the chorus.

LXXVII

Latha dhòmh 's mi, ó hó

Sung by Mrs. Neil Campbell (Bean Nìll), South Uist

(*Without chorus*)

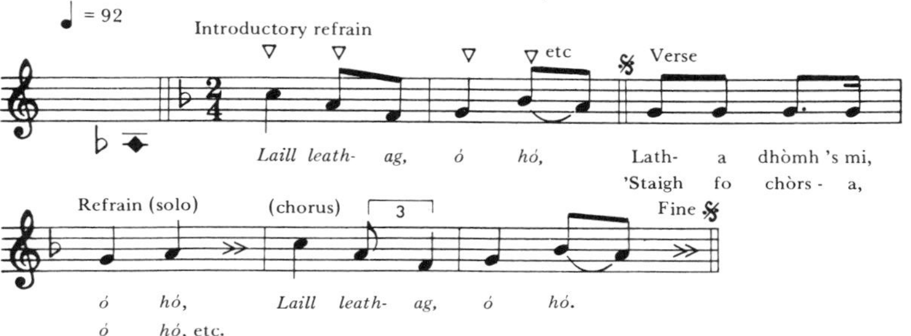

Variants (The melodic variation may have been unintentional on the singer's part.)

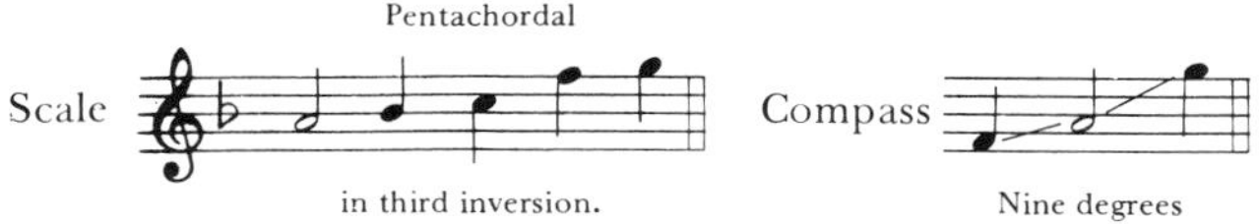

Form: two phrases: A B.
Structure: a four-bar melody; Verse A, 1; Refrain A, 3.

The basic metre of the poem is 8^2, divided into two half-lines of four syllables, each followed by the refrain. The tune embracing the half line (verse and refrain) consists of four bars repeated, with appropriate variation of verse-rhythm to accomodate the second half of the line.

The complete lines end with penultimate rhyming of *long* vowels, a fact obscured by the singer's forgetting some of the second-half lines; the opening half-lines however mostly end with two short syllables, which result in a difference of rhythm between the ending of the two half-lines. This difference is well exemplified in the third line, i.e.

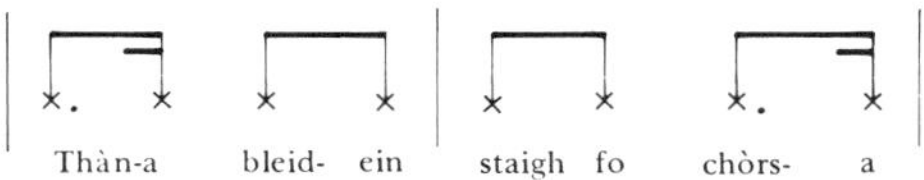

The opening half line, *Latha dhòmh 's mi*, ending exceptionally in a penultimate long vowel must be considered as a metric variant.

LXXVIII

Gu dé nì mi nochd ri m' nàire?

Sung by Mrs. MacDougall (Anna Raghnaill Eachainn), Barra, with Miss Annie Johnston joining in the refrain

Hexatonic

Scale — Mixolydian with gap at 6.

Compass — Eight degrees

Form: Four phrases, A B C D.
Structure: an eight-bar melody;
Verse A 1, Refrain A (solo) 1, (chorus) 2.
Verse B 1, Refrain B (solo) 1, (chorus) 2.

The singer commenced the song with the refrain. She ended the song at *Fine* as marked. The section of the melody preceding *Fine* as here transcribed is therefore marked Verse and Refrain B.

LXXIX

'N robh thu 'sa bheinn?

(*a*) Sung by Mrs. MacDougall (Anna Raghnaill Eachainn), Barra, with Annie Johnston joining in the refrain

Form: four phrases, A[1] B[1] A[2] B[2] All four phrases end similarly.
Structure: an eight-bar melody:

Verse A, 1; Refrain A (solo) 1, (chorus) 2;
Verse B, 1; Refrain B (solo) 1, (chorus) 2.

The song ends with the chorus refrain A. The metre is 8^2, divided into half-lines of four syllables.

The note D in the scale only occurs a few times, and most of the tune is in the pentachordal scale FGAB♭C (1st inversion).

LXXIX

'N robh thu 'sa bheinn?

(*b*) Sung by Miss Mary Morrison (Màiri Eóghainn Mhóir), Barra

(*With chorus*)

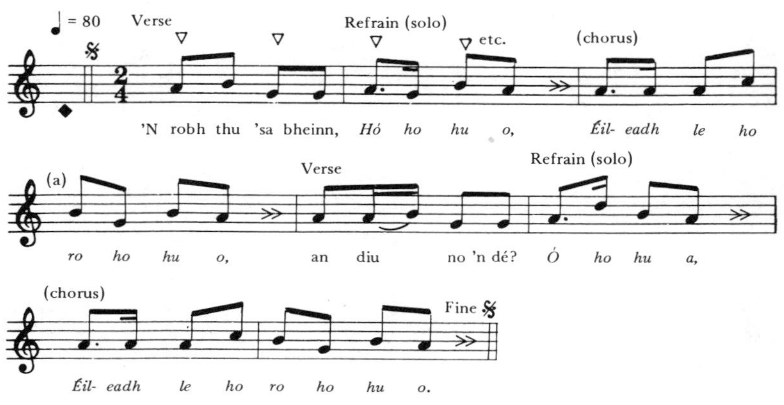

♩ = 80 Verse
Refrain (solo)
etc.
(chorus)
'N robh thu 'sa bheinn, *Hó ho hu o, Éil- eadh le ho*
(a)
Verse
Refrain (solo)
ro ho hu o, an diu no 'n dé? *Ó ho hu a,*
(chorus)
Fine
Éil- eadh le ho ro ho hu o.

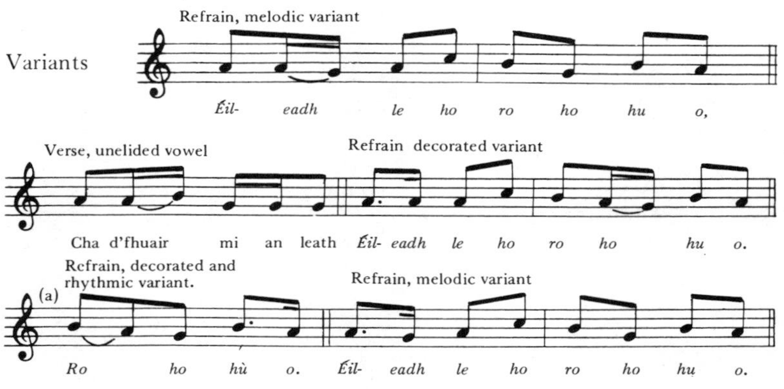

Variants
Refrain, melodic variant
Éil- eadh le ho ro ho hu o,
Verse, unelided vowel
Refrain decorated variant
Cha d'fhuair mi an leath *Éil- eadh le ho ro ho hu o.*
Refrain, decorated and rhythmic variant.
(a)
Refrain, melodic variant
Ro ho hù o. Éil- eadh le ho ro ho hu o.

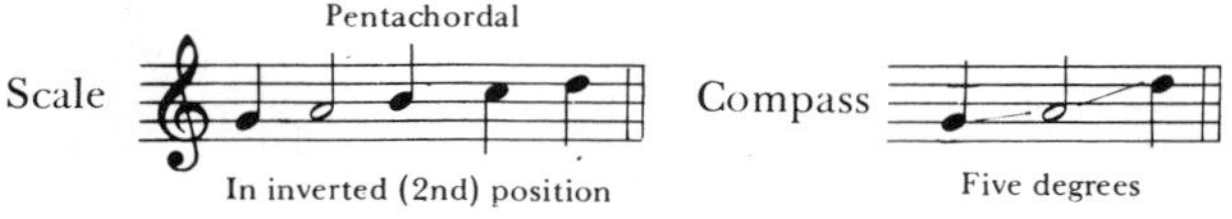

Pentachordal
Scale
In inverted (2nd) position
Compass
Five degrees

Form: Four phrases, A^1 A^2 A^3 A^4.
Structure: an eight-bar melody:
Verse 1; Refrain 3;
Verse, 1; Refrain 3.

The melody of the solo refrain differs in alternate stanzas by only one note, but as this occurs with fair regularity, the melody is set out as of eight bars rather than of four bars repeated. The difference between the first four bars and the second four is however too slight to label them as 'Verse and refrain A and B.'

The song ends as usual with the chorus refrain, sung by the chorus, then repeated by the soloist and repeated again by the chorus.

LXXX

Gura h-e mo ghaol an t-Iain

Sung by Mrs. Mary MacNeil (Màiri Ruarachain), Barra

(*With chorus*)

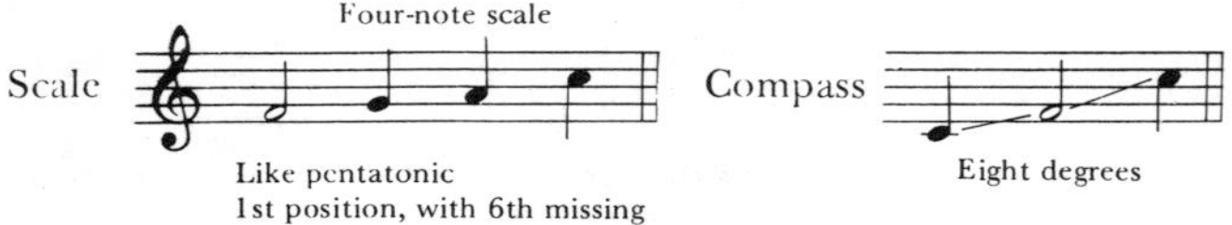

The note D occurs in bar 3, as a variant

Form: Four phrases, A[1] B[1] A[2] B[2] (the second bar of each of the four phrases is identical)
Structure: an eight-bar melody:
Verse 1, Refrain (solo) 1, (chorus) 2;
Verse 1, Refrain (solo) 1, (chorus) 2.

The singer commenced the song with the solo and chorus refrain (both sung solo) the chorus refrain was then repeated by the chorus. The metre is 8^2 divided into half lines; but regularity of metre in both half lines is not met until the last two half lines of the song – *Sìobadh fionn, 's gun gàbhadh mara.* In order to transcribe a complete sequence of first and second half-lines, the opening of the song, although irregular, is transcribed as sung. Each-half line is repeated. The song ends in the usual way of chorus refrain repeated by the soloist and then repeated again by the chorus. The tune is only four bars in length. The transcription commences with the *verse* to avoid splitting the musical phrase.

LXXXI

'S mise bhean bhochd chianail dhuilich

Sung by Miss Annie Johnston (Anna Aonghais Chaluim), Barra

(*Without chorus*)

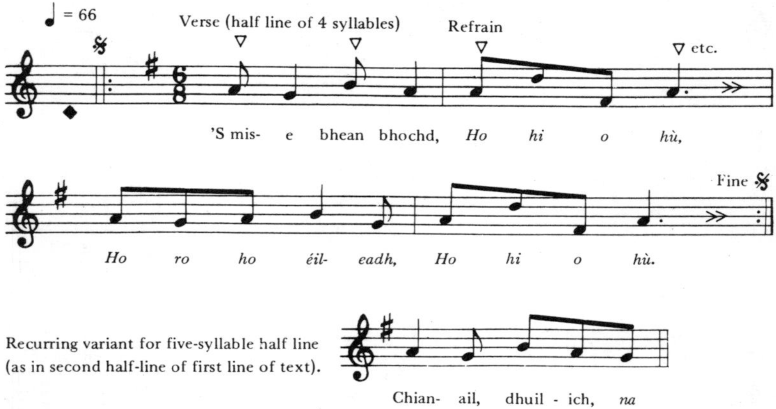

The extra syllable *na* is characteristic of the second (rhyming dis-syllable-ending) part of the line. It does not occur where the last word is a monosyllable.

Form: four phrases, A^1 A^2 A^1 A^2
Structure: an eight-bar melody of four bars repeated:
Verse, 1; Refrain 3; Verse 1, Refrain 3.

The air of the verse fits a half-line of the poem, and the whole melody is therefore repeated to take in the second half-line. The basic metre is 8^2 with four syllables to the half-line; the frequent addition of the meaningless syllable *na* to the second half-line is probably a personal eccentricity of the singer; compare No. XXXVII in Vol. I where the meaningless syllable *a* is frequently added to the lines of a song in 8^2 metre by another singer. The only other irregularities here are from words containing a svarabhakti vowel.

The singer commenced the song with the refrain.

LXXXII

'S muladach truagh, 's cianail thà mi

Sung by Miss Annie Johnston, Barra

(*Without chorus*)

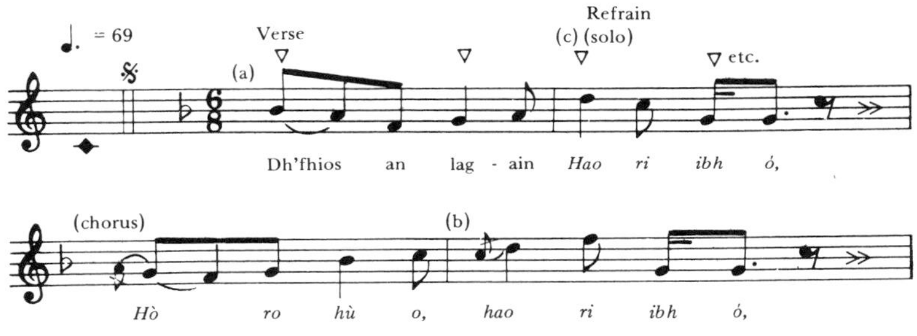

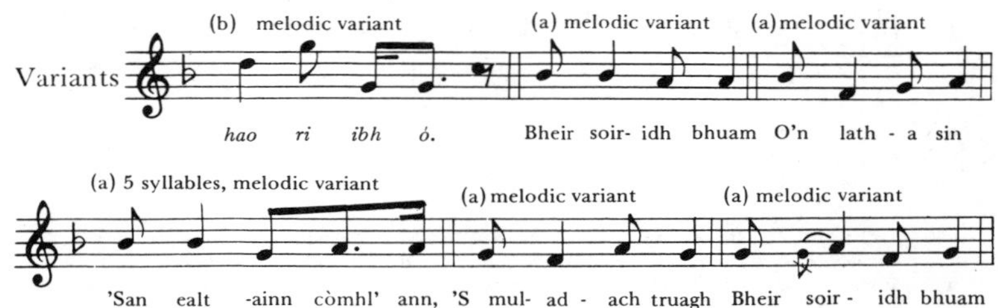

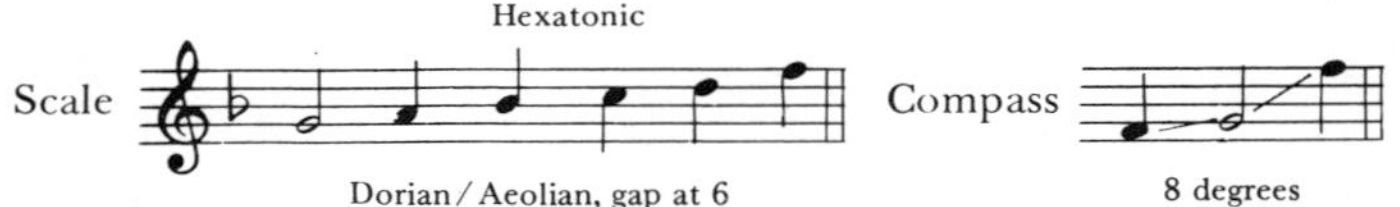

Form: 4 phrases: A¹ A², A¹ A².

Structure: an eight-bar melody: Verse 1, Refrain 3
Verse 1, Refrain 3.

The recording is defective in the opening, but the singer obviously commenced with the chorus refrain as usual, i.e. the last two bars of the tune as above.

The basic metre is 8^2 divided into half lines, and this occurs in the opening, but the singer did not hit the proper melody to begin with. Line 6 is the next line to have four syllables in each half line, and this is therefore set under the music.

She was apt to exchange the melody of bars (b) and (c) indiscriminately.

LXXXIII

Chuir iad mise 'n ceann na cléitheadh

Sung by Mrs. Neil Campbell (Bean Nìll), South Uist, with Mrs. Patrick MacPhee joining in the refrain

Form: four phrases, A, B[1], C, B[2].

Structure: an eight bar melody: Verse A, 1; Refrain (solo) 1; (chorus) 2.
Verse B, 1; Refrain (solo) 1; (chorus) 2.

The melodic differences between refrains A and B are slight; but they are constant after the tune settles down to a regular form, which occurs at the half line *tulgag eutrom*.

The basic metre is 8^2 divided into half-lines.

LXXXIV

'S tìm dhomh bhith falbh, bhith cur umam

Sung by Miss Mary Morrison (Màiri Eóghainn Mhóir), Barra

(*With chorus*)

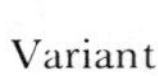

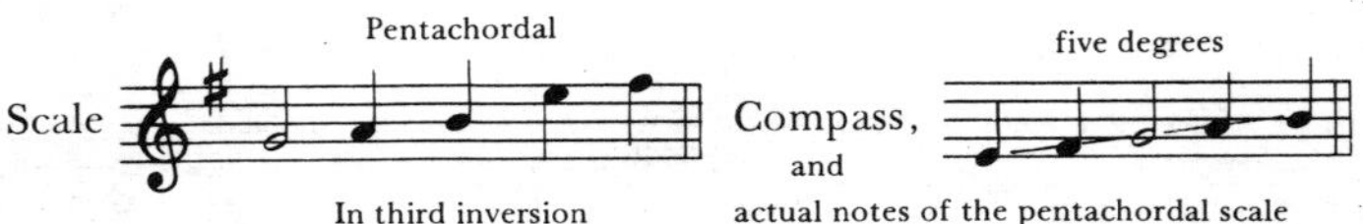

Form: four phrases: A^1 B A^2 B.

Structure: an eight-bar melody:

Verse A, 1; Refrain, (solo) 1, (chorus) 2.

Verse B, 1; Refrain, (solo) 1, (chorus) 2.

The song began with the refrain sung by the soloist and repeated by the chorus. It ended irregularly as follows:

solo: *Ho hì e bhó,* chorus: *hò ro nàilibh, ho hì e bhó,*

solo: *Ho hì e bhó, ho ro nàilibh ho hì e bhó,*

chorus: *Ho ro nàilibh, ho hì e bhó.*

The opening half-line, having a svarabhakti vowel, is a variant. The second half-line, *bhith cur umam*, being of four syllables, is set under the music of Verse B. The verse followed by the solo refrain makes a complete musical phrase. In bars 4 and 8, some of the chorus sang the third note as A and some as E.

LXXXV

Dhìrich mi suas an Coire Riabhach

Sung by Mrs. Buchanan (Ceit Ruairi Iain Bhàin), Barra

(*With chorus*)

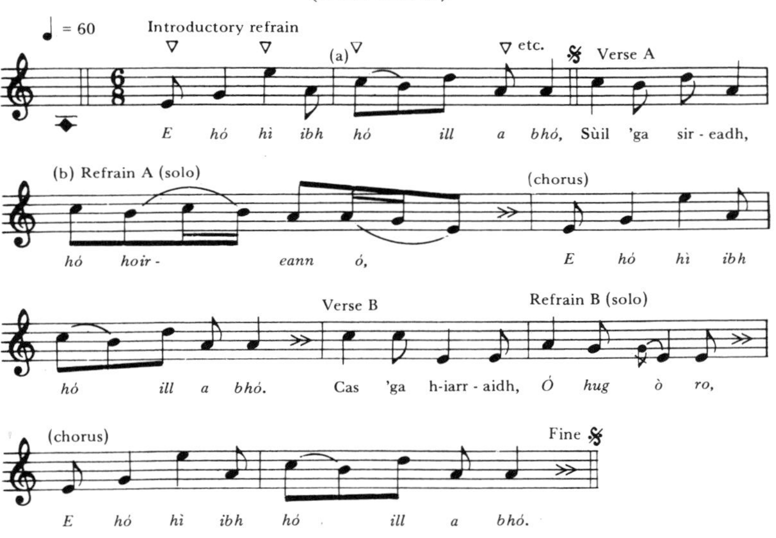

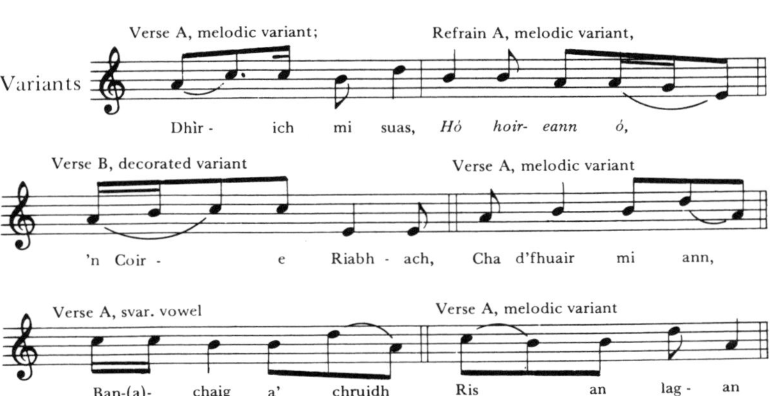

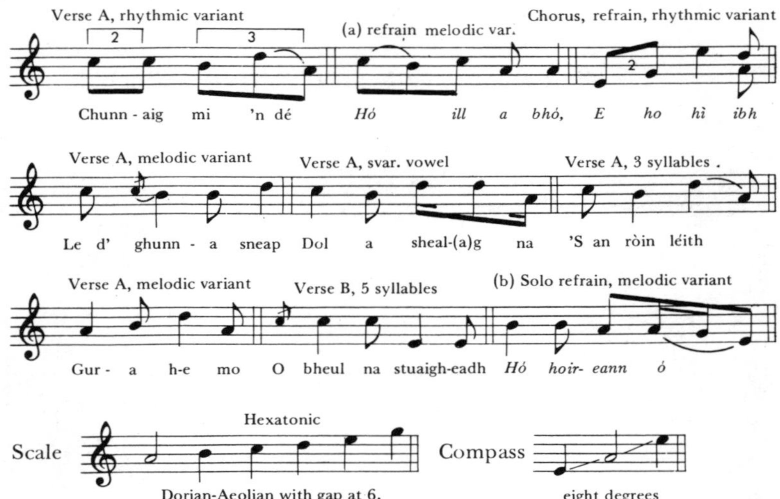

Form: four phrases; A B C B.

Structure: an eight-bar melody: Verse A, 1; Refrain A (solo) 1, (chorus) 2;
Verse B, 1; Refrain B (solo) 1, (chorus) 2.

The song finished with the chorus refrain repeated by the soloist and again by the chorus. The basic metre is 8^2 in half-lines. The first three lines are variants, either melodic or rhythmic, and line four is therefore set under the music.

LXXXVI

Turadh am muigh

Sung by Miss Mary Morrison (Màiri Eóghainn Mhóir), Barra

(With chorus)

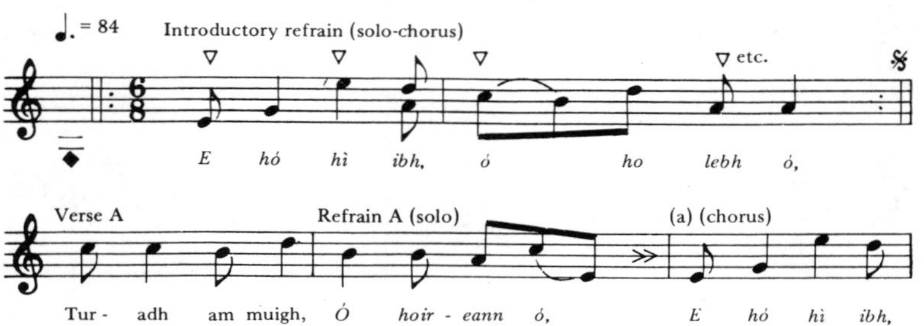

(b)
Verse B
Refrain B (solo)
ó ho lebh ó. Tur- adh am muigh, Hó hug ò ro,
(chorus)
Fine
E hó hì ibh, ó ho lebh ó.

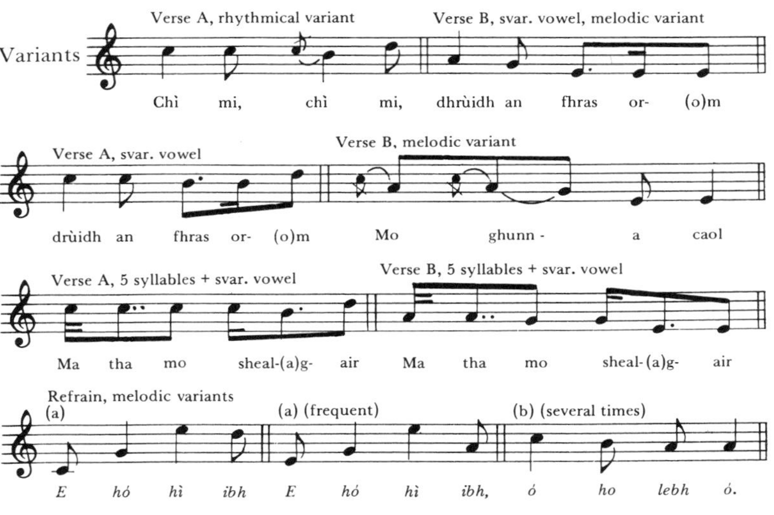
Variants
Verse A, rhythmical variant
Verse B, svar. vowel, melodic variant
Chì mi, chì mi, dhrùidh an fhras or- (o)m
Verse A, svar. vowel
Verse B, melodic variant
drùidh an fhras or- (o)m Mo ghunn - a caol
Verse A, 5 syllables + svar. vowel
Verse B, 5 syllables + svar. vowel
Ma tha mo sheal-(a)g- air Ma tha mo sheal-(a)g- air
Refrain, melodic variants
(a)
(a) (frequent)
(b) (several times)
E hó hì ibh E hó hì ibh, ó ho lebh ó.

Scale
Hexatonic
Compass

Dorian-aeolian with gap at 6.

Nine degrees.

Form: four phrases: A B C B.

Structure: an eight-bar melody:

Verse A, 1; Refrain (solo) 1, (chorus) 2.

Verse B, 1; Refrain (solo) 1, (chorus) 2.

The song ends with the chorus refrain sung three times, by:- chorus, soloist, chorus. The same formula is used at change of subject.

The tune is simply a version of that of the preceding song. It is rare for two different waulking songs to be sung to the same air and refrain. It is of interest to observe that the meaningless refrain syllables are basically the same in both songs.

LXXXVII

Fhir a' chinn duibh

Sung by Calum Johnston (Calum Aonghais Chaluim), Barra

(*Without chorus*)

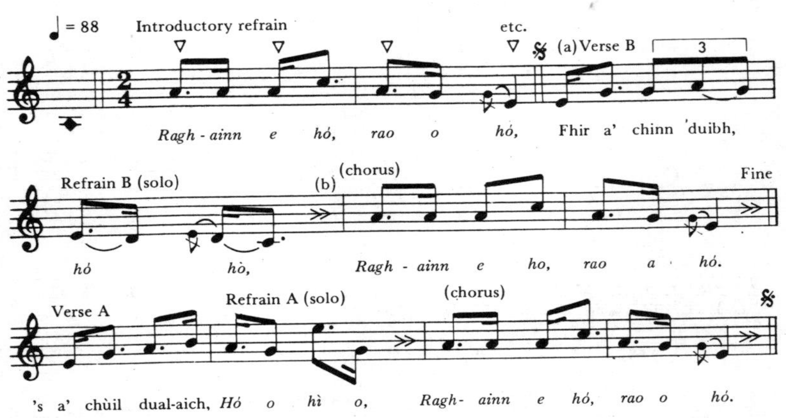

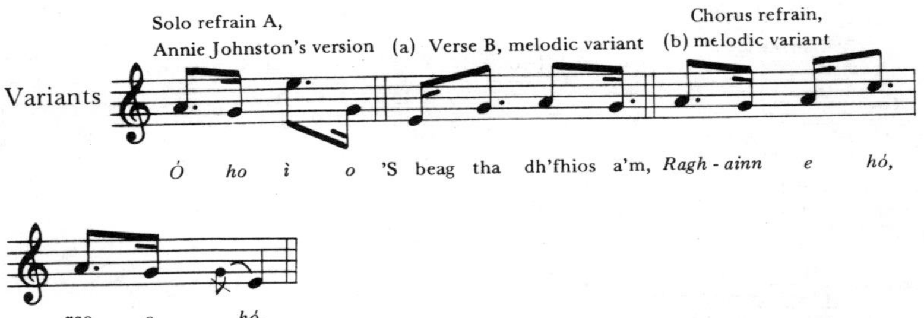

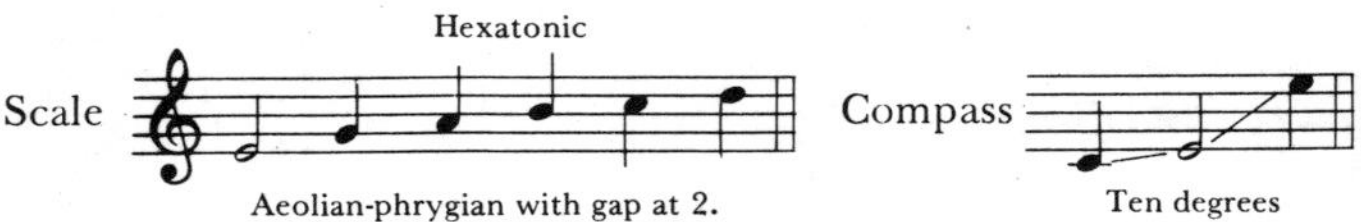

Aeolian-phrygian with gap at 2.

Ten degrees

Form: four phrases, A, B, C, B.

Structure: an eight-bar melody;

Verse A, 1; Refrain A (solo) 1, (chorus) 2.

Verse B, 1; Refrain B (solo) 1, (chorus) 2.

After the introductory refrain, the singer continued the song with the *second half* of the melody, which is therefore marked Verse and Refrain B. He finished the song irregularly with the solo refrain B. In an actual waulking, the song would end with a double repetition of chorus refrain B; and the sign *Fine* is accordingly set down at that point. The chorus refrain is identical in both refrains A and B, and the only difference lies in the single bar of solo refrain. Annie Johnston, sister of Calum, who provided a written text for this song, makes the slight difference in the refrain syllables and rhythm of solo refrain A as shown in the first of the variants above.

LXXXVIII

'S toil liom, 's toil liom, 's toil liom aona-mhac

Sung by Mrs. Neil Campbell (Bean Nill), South Uist

(*Without chorus*)

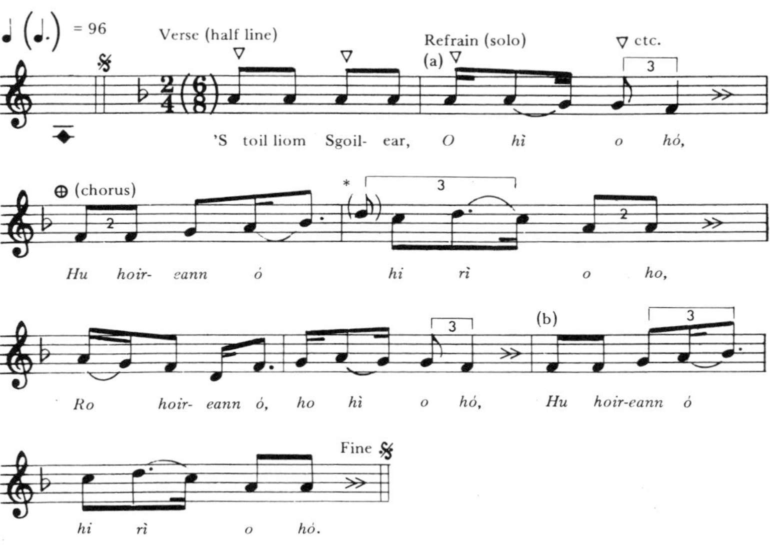

*alternative

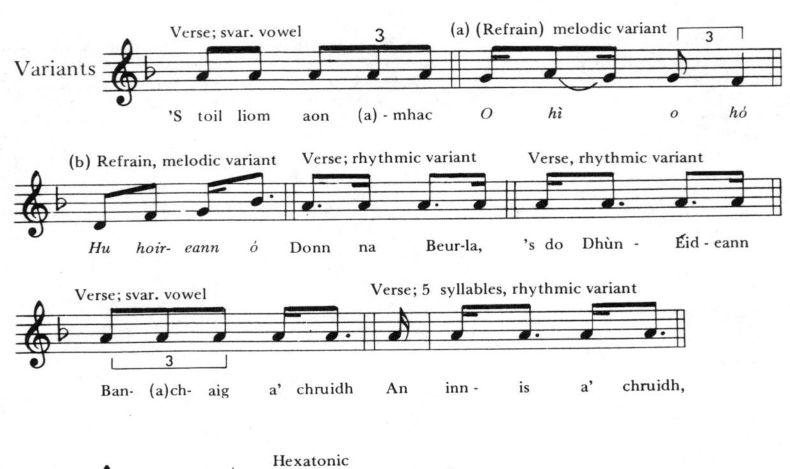

Hexatonic

Scale

Phrygian/Locrian with gap at 5

Compass

8 degrees

Form: Four phrases; Verse A || Refrain B C B

Structure: An eight-bar melody: Verse 1, Refrain, (solo) 1, (chorus) 6.

The singer commenced the song at ⊕.

The verse air takes in a half line of the text. This half line and its refrain is repeated, after which the second half of the line is sung to the verse air, and repeated with the refrain in the same way. The basic metre is 8^2. The opening half of the first complete line, *'s toil liom aona-mhac*, contains a svarabhakti vowel, and is therefore given as a metric variant below.

GLOSSARIAL INDEX

EXCEPT in a few cases, words which are already adequately explained in the Glossarial Index to Volume I of *Hebridean Folksongs* are not included here.

A

achanaidh, *a prayer, supplication*, 673.
aigeal, *gen.* aigeil, *the ocean*, 656.
ainnir, *a maiden*, 869.
àireach, *a ploughman*, 399.
aithnte, *Uist for* aithne, 174.
allail, *renowned*, 140.
alpach, *greedy, voracious, grasping*, LXVII preface; *see* Dinneen.
amhach, *neck*, ge b'oil le t'amhaich, 920, *might be translated 'although it chokes you'*.
annsgair, *uproar*, 1124 (an-sgairt).
àr, gur bean eile dh'àr gu làr i, 391?
àr, *in* àr fasgaidh, 1139, ? = adhar fasgaidh, *a wind of speed* (*cf.* Dinneen, i mbárr na bhfáscaidhthe, *at full speed. Or* àbhar (adhbhar) fasgaidh, *means of sheltering*?
àrainn, air t'à., *in your vicinity*, 684.
àrdrach, *a ship*, 1139.
àsuig, *a boat*, 1423. *See* Fr. Allan.

B

baideal, *a tower*, 632; baidean, 655.
bàin, *see* bàir.
bàir, *a goal at shinty*, chuir mi b. air, *I scored a goal against him*, 333; chuir mi b. leis, *I hit a goal with it*, 356; bàin, chuir mi bàin air, 382. *See* pàm.
bàireach, dh'fhalbh thu, leannain, dh'iomain na bàirich, *you went, my love, to play shinty* (?), 1522.
banchaig (*d. for nom.*), *the woman in charge of a dairy* (*not a mere dairy-maid*), 320, 359, 400, 402, 1240, 1682, etc.
bannadh, *binding, securing*, 1640.
barrach, làn bòsd agus barraich, 134, = barrachd, *superiority*.
barriall, *a latchet*, 1487. (*Stress on first syllable.*)
basadh, 'ga bh., *wringing hands for him*, 1176.
beul, *the muzzle of a gun*, gunna bheòil bhig, *a small bored gun*, 1584.
biatach, *a hospitaller*, 538.
bile, *a rim, edge*, fo bh. na luinge, *below the ship's gunwale*, 1276.
bileach, *lipped*, bròg bh., *a welted shoe*, 891.
blad-chraois, a *broad gluttonous mouth*, 997.
bleidein, *a bletherer*, 1418, 1425, 1440.
bòrd, *a tack when sailing* (?), 1463.
bòrd fuaraidh, *the weather side of a boat*, 1284.
bradag, *a little female thief*, 1020, 1071.
braich, sìol na braiche, *malt grain*, 206.
braighdeanach, *a captive*, 61.
breacag, 679, *cf. C.G.* vi. 19, '*a large thin cake. The* bonnach *is a thick round bannock*'. Breacag arain, *a large flat round scone cooked on a griddle* (Barra). *It is obvious from references in waulking songs that the* breacag *was considered a very inferior item of diet.*
bréinein, *a 'stinker'*, 1412. *See note, also under* brionnag *in C.G.* vi. 21–2.
bruinnein, *a gossip, a deceitful person*, 1412. *See note, and preceding reference in C.G., also C.G.* iii. 142, Far nach bitheadh brionnag no breugag/ A thoir sgeula dh'an t-saoghal, *translated 'Where was no babbler nor*

bruinnein (*cont.*): *gaddler To give twaddle to the world*'.

buarach, *a cow fetter, spancel*, 1228, 1651. *See* lunndrainn.

bùrn, *water*, 1083, 1092.

C

cairt, *a compass*, 744.

cas (*vb.*), *to utter a cry*, 532; *to approach*, 570.

casadh, *the second part of a song*, LXVII; *see* Dinneen.

catach, *cat-like*, LXVII preface.

ceanndard, *Uist for* ceannard, 1180.

ceòl-ghàire, *the sound of laughter*, 1111.

cion, *love*, tha mo ch. air an fhleasgach, *I love the youth*, 189; gum b'fheàrr leis tuiteam dh'a cion, *he preferred to fall* (*die*) *for her love*, 71; O, 's e mo chion 's mo ghràdh thu, *Oh, you are my love and my darling*, LXIV, alternative refrain.

ciùrradh, *hurting*, 1365.

claban, *the brain-pan*, 1069.

cléith-luadhaidh, *a waulking board*, 942; cliath-luadhaidh, LXVII preface.

cliath, *a waulking board*, an ceann na cléitheadh, *at the head of the waulking board*, 1532; an cois na cléitheadh, *at the foot of the waulking board*, 1402.

cluain, *a plain*, chuireadh c. ri muir ghreannaich, *that would calm a rough sea*, 128.

cluichd, *Uist for* cluich, 358, 383.

coitich, *to row a boat*, fhad' 's a choiticheadh dà ràimh i, *as long as two oars would row her*, 443.

còrn, *a drinking-horn*, 84; *pl.* còirn, 24.

corrach, *unsteady*, coite c, *an unsteady boat*, 739, *cf. C.G.* iv. 356, coit chaol chorrach, *translated* '*skiff crank and narrow*'; *steep*, nan corrbheann c., *of the steep pointed hills*, 268; *rolling* (*of eyes*), sùil ch., 1609 (*cf.* Dwelly).

corrbheann, *a round pointed hill*, 267.

còrsa, *a coast*, 1418, 1426, *cf.* A. M. D. 1751, 180, Ach a sgeith air córsa Chana, '*but may she be spewed up on the shore of Canna*'.

corruiche, *rage*, 1157.

cruit, *a harp*, 52, 55, 96, 97, 1124, etc.

cubhais, *conscience*, 39. *See note.*

cuileanach, ? 1567. *See note.*

cuireadach, *tricky*, 546.

currac, *a cap*, 225.

cumhag, *Uist for* cumhang, 1188.

cudaig, *a cuddy, young saithe*, 1076.

cutach, *stumpy*, LXVII preface.

D

dabhach (*f.*), *a vat*, 949, 974.

dallagan, *spotted dogfish*, 1005.

dàimh, *relations, kinsmen*, 338.

dealbh-mhac, *shapely son*, 257 (*other versions have* dearbh-mhac, *true son*).

dìobhail, *harm*, 790.

dìtheannach, ? LXVII conclusion. ? deitheineach, A. M. V. 138, *dainty*; *R.I.A. Contrib.* deithidnech, *careful, attentive, earnest.*

dìthein, *a marigold*, 1199, 1608; *pl.* dìtheinean, 1321

dòirlinn (*f.*), *an isthmus*, 151.

dòltram, *gloom, depression*, 1009. *Cf. Vol. I, l.* 507, chuir siod dòltramachd air m'aire; *and C.G.* ii. 166, chaidh reul an iuil an aird gu much. . . . Dh'fhoillsich doltrom agus struth, translated '*the star of guidance . . . illumed doldrum and current*'.

don-bhuaidh, *ill success*, 1460.

draghadh (*vb.*), *to drag, pull*, 1061; *intrans., to draw, move*; gaoth nan àrdbheann d. fairis, 1270; dhragh i 'n t-acair', 1141. O.N. *draga.*

drùidh, *soak*, 1632; (*v.n.*), drùdhadh, 771.

duathail, *stubborn*, 456.

duatharra, *gloomy*, 94.

dubh-chapull, *some kind of penalty for a defeat in a bardic contest*, 1097, 1108. *See note. R.I.A. Contrib.* capull = tòin?

dùdan, *mill-dust*, 1450. *Also* '*finely powdered seaweed*', Fr. Allan.

dùraig (*vb.*), *dare*, 184.

E

ealaidh, *art, science*, toirt ùmhladh do'n e., 110. Dieckhoff eallaidh, *art, habitual practice.*

ealtainn, *a flock of birds*, 1119, 1526.

eileineach, 995, 1074, *in this context, an inhabitant of one of the small islands south of Barra, such as Mingulay.*

éirig, *a ransom*, 1501, 1512.

eirthire, *a coast*, 1131.

éisgeach (*adj.*), *satirizing*, 1047.

éisginn (*n.*), *satire*, 1014.

éiteag, *a fair maid*, lit. *a jewel*, 29.

eòrlaig, e. arain, 523, *the heel of the loaf? Cf. C.G.* ii. 14, 285, eòrlain, '*floor, bottom, lower part*'.

F

fachach, *a Manx shearwater, puffinus puffinus*, 1102.

fàilidh, *quietly*, LXVII conclusion.

fàireadh, *skyline*, 331; fàire, 380.

falairidh, *a wake*, 269.

faoileann, *a beach*, 1704. *Cf. C.G.* v. 302, 'S mi am shuidh air an fhaoilinn, '*As I sit on the beach*'; *T.G.S.I.* xxxvii. 24, 'faoghlainn, *a ridge above a sandy beach with a marsh on its landward side. Sometimes* faoghlainn *is awash during spring-tides.*' *C.G.* vi. 70, *A 'level raised beach. . . . In some parts a sandy spit, a sandy part of the shore where rocks abound on either side*'.

farbhalach, *a stranger, foreigner*, 47.

farspach, *a black-backed gull*, 1118; *pl.* farspaich, 1458.

fàsach (*f.*), *a pasture, 'wild untilled grassy land', not necessarily unpleasant* (Duanaire Finn, iii. 262), 335, 1230.

fasanta, ? *well-fashioned*, armailt . . . innealt, fhasanta, 1494 (Armailt *fem. in Irish*).

fiadhaire, *see* iadhaire.

fiarach, *grazing*, 843; feurach, 931.

fidir, *to perceive, take notice of*, 36.

filidh, *a poet*, 1080.

fleòdradh, *washing*, 1004, 1104, *cf.* Fr. Allan, '*washing, as of the sea washing the shore*'. *See note. Cf.* A. M. D. 178, Tilg amach iad uil' air fleodradh, '*throw them all out to be washed*'.

fochann, *braird, young oats or barley*, 1290, 1385.

fòghlach, *rank grass such as grows on middens*, 1449.

foinneil, *handsome* (*cf.* Dieckhoff), 799, 804; *but see note.*

foirm, *noise*, 222.

fòtas, *a serious defect*, 1019.

fraochan, *fury*, 835.

freasdal, 1297, *depending on*, cf. Vol. i, l. 301, *and* Fr. Allan; *colloquially, and probably in the present context, 'having only', 'down to'* (e.g. *of clothing*).

G

gachdan, gachan, ? *strong drink*, 1122. *See note.*

gart, *a cornfield*, 1321, 1359.

gearradh, *a tax*, 524.

goidean, g. goidein, *a little withy*, 485, 486.

gòisne, *see* òisneag.

gràinne, *embroidery*, 1550, 1567 (*probably the meaning in Vol. I instances also*).

grìs, *gooseflesh, pimples*, 446.

gulm, g. eòrna, *the awns of barley. Cf. C.G.* iv. 246, *where* Gulm naodh calg *is given as an alternative reading to* Culg naodh culg, *translated 'Awn of nine awns'*. McD. 378, gulam eòrna, *in same context. See note.*

H

haitse, *a hatch*, 1148. *Cf.* A. M. V. 111, a saitse, *the hatches.*

hùgan nan gù, *an expression of delight, cf.* A. M. D. 13, guiliugag.

I

iadhaire, *land long lying fallow, difficult to plough*, 662; *usually* fiadhaire.

ìbhri, *ivory*, 886.

ichinneach, *provisions, eatables*, 1027.

impis, an i. gabhail, *on the point of lighting*, 583.

imprig, *a flitting, removal*, 728, 807.

inich, liom a b'inich do phòsadh, *I think it would be fitting to marry you*, 192. *Cf. C.G.* iv. 221, Triuir innich nam buadh, *translated 'the perfect Three of power'*; *R.I.A.*

inich (*cont.*):
Contrib. inich, *perfect, complete, full.*

inisgeil, *reproachful*, 1047. A. M. D. inisgeach, Go h i. air an t-seòrs' u, *though you are reproachful of that sort*, 177.

iollagach, *giddy*, 1045; A. M. D. 138, gle iollagach is rímheach, *somewhat florid and gay* (?*Latin* nitidus). A chionn gu bheil nigheanan Shioin uallach, agus . . . ag imeachd le ceumaibh iullagach, *Because the daughters of Zion are haughty, and walk . . . mincing as they go*, Isaiah 3: 16.

ionasdach, ? 1046.

iothlann, *a stack-yard*, 808, 1505.

iùbhrach, (*f.*), *a boat*, 774.

L

leacrach, *a stony slope*, 979.

leus, *a light*, 1360.

leòdhadh, g. leòite, *act of cutting*, faobhar leòite, *a cutting edge*; *cf. Irish* leodhaim, *I cut*, Dinneen; *R.I.A. Contrib.* léod, *act of cutting.*

liaghan, *sea tangles*, 314, 1328.

linge, *Uist for* linne, 1083.

lùb, *a young man or woman*, 1261.

lùgach, *crooked*, 1045; *cf. C.G.* i. 52, ceart a mhadaidh ruaidh, lugach, liugach, lamalach, '*like the justice of the fox, crooked, cunning, corrupt*'.

luinn, 1693, ? 'S luaith' thu na 'n luinn, 1693. (*In another version*, 's luaith' thu na'n gunn', 1685.)

lunndair, ? *fasten.* Lunndrainn buarach, 1624. *Cf. Vol. I, l.* 716, gun lunnainn a' bhuarach.

M

mainnir, *an enclosure to separate goats from kids*, 842. *See note.*

mala, *eyebrow*; bun do mhaladh, 926; té gun smùr air a malaidh, 172.

marcrachd, 1179, *Uist for* marcachd.

meaghail (meoghail), *bleating*, LVI refrain. *See note.*

meilbheid, *velvet*, 1419, 1427.

mèilich, *bleating*, 311. ? < meighilich, meaghailich. *Cf. Dàin Iain Ghobha*, i. 218, méighlich.

miannas, *intense desire*, 1575. *Cf. R.I.A. Contrib.* míangus.

minig, 237, 258, *Uist for* mairg.

mìostadh, *mischief*, 1160. *Cf. C.G.* iii. 136, mìostath, *translated* '*scorn*'.

mìothlainn, *displeasure*, 1158. *See* Fr. Allan.

miuchair, *kind*, 211. *Cf.* Dieckhoff, meachar; A. M. D. 18, mechire.

morghan, *shingle*, 656.

muirsgein, *razor-fish*, 1008.

muirtiachd, *jellyfish*, 398.

N

nàire, *a term of endearment*, 1473. *See note.*

nì, *goods, wealth in cattle*, 219, 1249.

niosach (*adj.*), of weasel skin, 897.

O

obag, *a spell*, 1020.

òisneag, *an incantation* (? for gòisneag), 1020. *See note.*

P

paidir, *a rosary*, 555.

pàm, *a goal at shinty*, 304. *See* bàir.

pìoba, *bagpipes*, 1123, 1150, 1389, 1711.

piorraid, *a periwig or wig*, 1569, *English* perruke.

piostol, *a pistol*, 1365.

ploc, *a sod*, 1173.

plod, thuit (i) 'na p., *she fell stone dead*, LXVII conclusion.

port, (1) *a harbour*, 986; (2) *a fort*, 1182; (3) *a tune*, 985, 988.

pruis-òidhidh, *a call to a horse*, 1452.

R

ràithe (*pronounced* ràiche), *a quarter of the year, a season.* Bliadhna mhór is ràithe, *a long year and a quarter*, 293, 369; an ceann a' chóigeamh r., 343, an ceann nan cóig ràithean, 295, 325, 370, *at the end of fifteen months*; Ciadaine tùs na ràithe,

Wednesday beginning of the quarter, 1480.
rocach, *sea tangles*, 1342.
ruaidhe, *erysipelas*, 446.
rùm, *extent*, 1103.

S

sac, *shortness of breath, asthma*, 735.
sad, *a blow such as would raise dust*, 418.
saor (*adj.*), *free* (*here from marriage bond or pregnancy*), 920.
saor (*vb.*, *intransitive*), shaorainn . . fhathast, *I would be free yet* (*i.e. from marriage or pregnancy*), 558, 587.
sarcuinn, ? *sarking*, 1472.
seadhach, *sensible*, 469.
seanail, *a channel*, 1397.
seang, *slender, not pregnant*, 1577.
séisd, *a tune*, 1706; Dieckhoff séist, *the chorus of a song*.
seisein, *a kirk session*, 726.
seisreach, *a team of ploughing horses*, 1358.
seur, (*pl.*), seuraichean, *chairs*, 733.
sgòd, *a piece of cloth*, 216. *Cf.* Fr. Allan.
sic, s. a cinn, *the membrane around her brain, the inside of her skull*, 541. *Cf.* McEachen sichd.
sìoman, *a heather rope*, 1215.
siorram, 'na sh. fann, 58; 'na sh. shuain, *in an enchanted sleep*, 99. *See* Éigse, viii. 248.
sìothladh, *subside, strain* (*of liquids*). Gruaidh as glan s., *of bright complexion*, 1610. *Cf.* Ailean Dall, Poems, p. 121 (1829), Suil ghorm is glan lionadh,/Gruaidh is maisiche sioghladh;/'S a bheil lasadh an fhiona, '*Blue eye of bright fulness, Cheek of most beautiful complexion, in which is the flush of wine*'; *and ibidem*, p. 129, 'S an fhuil mhoralachd, phriseil, / Na d' ghruaidh air sioghladh mar ros, '*and the proud, precious blood, in your cheek flushed like a rose*', *in the lament for* Dòmhnall Mór Òg Cameron. *The allusion presumably is to the circulation of the blood.*
sluasaid, *a shovel*, 838.
smuig, *a snout, face* (*contemptuous*), 1017.
sneap, *a trigger, in the expression* gunna sneap, 779, 1599, 1623.
spìdeadh, g. spìdidh, *strength, vigour*, 1466.
spreillean, *thick lips*, 999.
sprògach, le busa s., *with protruding lips* (?), 1419.
staighìr, *a stair*; staighre, 344.
staoileadh, *style, title*, 1098.
stìom, *a snood, the headband formerly worn by unmarried women in the Highlands*, 1646. *See C.G.* vi. 132.
stòbhadh, *stewing*, 1034.
stoirm, *a storm*, 1354; *a noise*, LVI refrain. *See note to line 1268 in Vol. I.*
stròl, *a banner*, 1360; *a dress*, stròl dha'n t-sìoda, *a silk dress*, 91. *Cf.* Dieckhoff, stròl, *the fine, bright dress of a lady*. 250, a silk sheet.
strùbain, *cockles*, 1007.
struth, *a tidal current*, 1378.
stuagh (*f.*), (1) *a wave*, 1602. *Cf. C.G.* vi. 139, 'stuagh *is the upstanding crest of the wave immediately before breaking*'. (2) *a gable*, leumadh mo shròn àird na stuaighe, *my nose would gush the height of the gable*, 1345.
suanach, gu s., *quietly*, 285.

T

tàileasg, *backgammon*, 1256.
tasgaidh, *a safe place, a hiding place* (*here euphemism for the grave*), 1639.
tàthadh, *joining together*, saor an tàthaidh, 1540.
teasach, *a high fever*, 294, 323, 342.
tiodhlaig (n.), *a gift*, 274.
tiodhlaig (vb.), *to bury* (*term used by Catholics in the Highlands*), 278.
tiùrr, *the top of high tide*, 748. *See* Fr. Allan. *C.G.* v. 278, ann an tiùrr an làin, *translated* '*among the tidal wrack*'.
torghan, *a musical sound*, 941. *Cf. C.G.* v. 126, có chunnaig e ach a' bhean-shìdh cùl creige agus torghan

torghan (*cont.*):
binn 'na beul, *translated 'whom saw he but the fairy woman behind a rock, and a sweet strain of music in her mouth'.*

treas-tarraing, *thrice distilled whisky, 'trestarig'*, 1431, 1446.

tubhailtean, *table-cloths*, 1035. *In Sir John Sinclair's* 'Observations on the Scottish Dialect', *1782, the word 'towel' is given as a Scotticism for English 'napkin'*, p. 162.

tùchan, *a bird-call*, an eala bhàn as binne t., *the white swan of sweetest call*, 984. *Used by* A. M. D. *of the blackcock*, p. 42.

tuilinn, *twilly*, 1550. *See* Fr. Allan (*doubtful here*).

tulgag, *a tossing*, 1534, *cf. R.I.A. Contrib.* tolg, *an attack*.

turadh, *dry weather*, 1630.

U

uarach, *upper*, 1312.

uinneineach, *having thick ankles*, 996, 1075, LXVII preface.

ùirsgeul, *information*, 392.

ulagan, *pulleys*, 1283.

ulpach, *lumpish*, LXVII preface. *R.I.A. Contrib.*, ulpán = alpán, *a little lump*.

ùmhladh, *submission, obedience*, 110; *Irish* umhla.

ùnnlagh, *a fine*, 1374.

ursann, *a door-post*, 298, 372.

NAMES OF COWS

Blàrag, *from* blàr, *having a white forehead*, 1475.

Buidheag, *from* buidhe, *yellow*, 1475, 1483.

Ciar, *'dun'*, 1375.

Donn, *'brown'*, 1374.

Dubhach, *'dark'*, 1224.

Dubhbheag, *'little black one'*, 1373.

Duibhean, *'small black'*, 1223, 1617.

Gruagan, *'small hairy one'*, 1617.

Ruadhan, *'small russet one'*, 1223, 1483.

Siùbhlach, *'restless one'*, 1375.

Subhach, *'happy one'*, 1618.

INDEX OF PERSONS AND PLACES

Moire Mhìn, *the Blessed Virgin Mary*, 277; Moire Mhàthair, 350.
Mór, *Marion, daughter of MacNeil of Barra*, 1001.
'Mór bhàn', 171.
Mórair, *Morar*, 543, 701.
Mùideart, *Moydart*, 858.
Muile, *the Isle of Mull*, 234, 859, 1253.
Muilgheartach, M. nan cochull craicinn, 1106. *See note*.
'Murchadh', 798, 800, 803, 1500.
'Murchadh Òg', 105, 123, 143.

Na Hearadh, *Harris*, 1262, 1334.
Niall a' Chaisteil, *'Neil of the Castle' (a MacNeil of Barra)*, 1054, 1109, 1174. *See note*.
Niall Frasach, *'Neil of the Showers', High King of Ireland*, 1088, 1110. *See note*.
Niall Glùndubh, *'Neil Black-knee', High King of Ireland*, 1088, 1110. *See note*.
Nic a' Mhanaich, *'daughter of the monk'*, LXVII preface.
'Nic Dhòmhnaill', 1177.
Nic Iain Fhinn, *'daughter of fair-haired John'*, LXVII preface *and* conclusion, 995, 1074.
'Ni Lachlainn', 1176.

Obair-eadhain, *Aberdeen*, 1185.
Òlaind, *Holland*, 1146.

'Ràghall', 817.
'Raghnall', 817.
Raghnall mac Ailein, *Ranald MacDonald of Benbecula*, 903.
Ratharsair, *the island of Raasay*, 202.
Rìgh Artair, *King Arthur*, XLI preface, 1, 65.
Rìgh Bhreatainn, *the King of Britain*, 5, 69.
Ròdha, an R., *the Ròdha in South Uist*, 1011.
Ruadal, *Rodel in Harris*, 678.
'Ruairi', 426, 853, 953, 1620.
Ruairi (*Rory Mór MacLeod of Dunvegan*), 1470.
Ruairi an Tartair, *'Noisy Rory', MacNeil of Barra*, 1087, 1111. *See note*.
Rubha Àird an aisig, 708.
Rubh' an Dùine, *in North Uist*, 758.
Rùm, *the island of Rum*, 789.

Sasunn, *England*, 1414, 1510, 1679, 1697, 1715.
'Seathan', 227, 232, 243, 247, 252, 256. *See* 'Iain'.
'Seumas', 1695.
'Sgoilear donn na Beurla', 1413, 1678, 1696, 1714.
Sìol Ailein, *the MacDonalds of Clanranald*, 138.
Sìol nan Leòdach, *the MacLeods*, 1447.
Sir Bhalbha, *Sir Gawain*, XLI preface, 4, 13, 45, 68.
Sir Falach, 73. *Cf. preceding*.
Sléibhte, *the district of Sleat in Skye*, 149, 534, 572, 611, 1406.

'Teàrlach', *Charles*, 816, 1521.
Tùr, an T., *the Tower, i.e. Kishmul Castle in Barra*, 1068; Mac Nìll bho na Tùraibh, 139.

Uibhist, *Uist*, 234, 544, 793, LXVII preface, 1406; Uibhist an eòrna, *Uist of the barley*, 131.
Ùige, *Uig in Skye* (?), 773.
'Uisdean', 816.
Uisdean mac 'ill' Easbuig Chléirich, *Hugh, son of Archibald the Clerk*, 824, 828; Uisdean mac 'ill' Easbuig Chaluim, 839.